Growing out of the plan

Growing out of the plan

Chinese economic reform, 1978–1993

BARRY NAUGHTON
University of California, San Diego

CAMBRIDGE
UNIVERSITY PRESS

Published by the Press Syndicate of the University of Cambridge
The Pitt Building, Trumpington Street, Cambridge CB2 1RP

CAMBRIDGE UNIVERSITY PRESS
The Edinburgh Building, Cambridge CB2 2RU, United Kingdom
40 West 20th Street, New York, NY 10011-4211, USA
10 Stamford Road, Oakleigh, Melbourne 3166, Australia

First published 1995
Reprinted 1996
First paperback edition 1996

Printed in the United States of America

Library of Congress Cataloging-in-Publication Data
Naughton, Barry.
Growing out of the plan : Chinese economic reform, 1978–1993 /
Barry Naughton.
p. cm.
Includes bibliographical references (p.   ) and index.
ISBN 0-521-47055-2
1. China – Economic policy – 1976– 2. China – Economic
conditions – 1976– I. Title.
HC427.92.N38   1995
338.951\009047 – dc20   94–133498
                                                         CIP

A catalog record for this book is available from the British Library.

ISBN 0-521-47055-2 hardback
ISBN 0-521-57462-5 paperback

Contents

Tables and figures

Tables

Preface

I began work on this book in the early 1980s as a graduate student at Yale University. At that time, some of the most basic facts about the Chinese economy and its characteristic institutions were unknown in the West. Inevitably, the early stages of my research were motivated by a simple curiosity to understand how this economy worked, and what were the prospects for its reform and opening to the outside world, then just beginning. I was extraordinarily lucky to have had the guidance of two superb teachers. Nicholas Lardy knew everything about the Chinese economy that was available in the West at that time, and he generously shared his knowledge of the Chinese economy and of the use of Chinese sources. John Michael Montias taught the European command economies, and provided a broad analytic approach to the socialist economy in which macroeconomics and development strategy mattered as well as the incentives, information, and institutions that structured individual behavior. James Tobin provided inspiration from the example of his work and from direct personal encouragement. Later, with the assistance of a Fulbright-Hays Fellowship, and the hospitality of Wuhan University, I spent the year 1982 in China. This allowed me to immerse myself in the Chinese sources at the University Library, and to conduct my first interviews at Chinese factories.

The mid-1980s was a period of great excitement as we struggled to develop an understanding of the Chinese economic system, even as that system was undergoing rapid changes. During this period, I benefited particularly from discussions with William Byrd and Christine Wong. They were also vital members of the lively community of American specialists on the Chinese economy from whom I have learned a great deal, and undoubtedly stolen many good ideas. This group of course includes Robert Dernberger, Gary Jefferson, Albert Keidel, Dwight Perkins, Penny Prime, Thomas Rawski, and Carl Riskin. A brief but very productive visit to China in December 1984, organized by the National Committee on United State-China Relations, and guided by Janet Cady, provided direct insight into Chinese reform policy at a crucial moment in the overall process.

In the late 1980s, it became possible to do direct research in China, and to collaborate with Chinese economists. Visits to China became much more frequent, and structured research began. I am grateful to the Ford Foundation, which provided financial support, beginning in 1988, for research on Chinese state-owned industrial enterprises, carried out in collaboration with the Institute of Economics of the Chinese Academy of Social Sciences. Peter Geithner of the Ford Foundation helped make this collaboration possible, and the enthusiastic support of Dong Furen, the head of the Institute of Economics at that time, made it a reality. The value of the collaborative project was enriched by the participation of Roger Gordon from the University of Michigan and Cyril Lin from Oxford. The data collected, as well as the insights derived from the accompanying interviews in Chinese factories, were crucial in shaping the view of Chinese industry presented in this book.

In this and other respects, the late 1980s was marked by steadily increasing interaction with Chinese economists. The rapid development and originality of Chinese economics in the 1980s was particularly impressive, and I have tried to present a glimpse of that richness in Chapter 5 of this book. On a personal level, it was a privilege to have my own academic knowledge of China enriched by personal contact with many Chinese economists. Moreover, such personal contacts helped sustain sympathy toward the Chinese reform process after the Tiananmen incident. I am indebted to a large number of Chinese economists who have extended kindnesses ranging from simple courtesy to profound influence and direction. A simple list of names is inadequate to express the depth and diversity of my gratitude, but a minimum list of indispensable names would include Cheng Xiaonong, Diao Xinshen, Dong Furen, Hua Sheng, Huo Xiaohu, Liu Guoguang, Lou Jiwei, Song Guoqing, Wu Jinglian, Zhang Fan, Zhang Xiaojie, Zhang Xuejun, Zhang Zhuoyuan, Zhao Renwei, and Zhou Xiaochuan.

I am indebted to members of the broad China community in the United States. David Bachman, Don Clarke, Joseph Esherick, Nina Halpern, and Richard Kraus, in particular, have influenced my thinking about China. A year and a half at the University of Michigan in 1987–88 was an invaluable opportunity to concentrate on research, as well as a chance to enjoy the intellectual fellowship of Mike Oksenberg, Ken Lieberthal, and the rest of the Michigan community. Work with and through the World Bank since 1988 has given me the opportunity to know and be influenced by Peter Dittus, Peter Harrold, Ed Lim, and Shahid Yusuf.

Since 1988, I have taught at the Graduate School of International Relations and Pacific Studies (IR/PS) of the University of California at San Diego. IR/PS has been lively and stimulating place from its earliest days, and I am deeply grateful to my colleagues for their support and inspiration. John McMillan has been a friend and collaborator who also read and commented on an early draft of this book, and deserves credit or blame for some of the ideas advanced. Susan Shirk has long been a colleague in the China field, and has been a constant source of ideas and stimulating conversation since I came to IR/PS. Peter Gourevitch has been unfailingly supportive towards this research, as well as a lively intellectual companion.

I am grateful to Nicholas Lardy and Thomas Rawski, as well as to two anonymous reviewers, who read and commented on an earlier draft of this book. In the final analysis, Thomas Naughton provided much of the world view that shapes this book's analysis, and it would have been interesting to know what he would have thought of it. Coleen Lassegard shares life's daily labors and satisfactions, and it would be impossible to contemplate this – or any other – finished project without thinking of her assistance, forbearance, and support. In a project with such a long gestation period, there are undoubtedly many other debts that should be acknowledged. For these omissions, as well as for other shortcomings and errors, I apologize and accept sole responsibility.

Introductory

Introduction: China's economic reform in comparative perspective

The traditional Soviet-style economic system scarcely exists any longer, but its impact and legacy will be felt well into the next century. Major economic reform programs are now underway in a dozen formerly socialist command economies. These reform programs differ in their speed, coherence, and general approach, but in all these countries an irreversible process of transition away from the Soviet model has begun. Each of the former planned economies is struggling to devise strategies of economic change while coping with the burdensome legacy of past development choices, and it is clear that the process of transition will be protracted. Economic reform of a planned economy is a process that takes decades, and several different paths lead through the borderlands separating planned and market economies.

Among this large and diverse group of nations, China has a particular claim on our attention. The chain of events that led to the collapse of Soviet-style socialism by the end of the 1980s can be traced back to the very beginning of the decade. At that time, profound change of radically different character began in two widely separated socialist countries. In China, beginning in 1979, radical economic reforms marked the first fundamental attempts to change the command economic system since the Yugoslav reforms of the 1960s. In Poland in 1980, the independent labor union Solidarity was formed, marking the first fundamental break with the Communist Party's monopoly of the political system. Both these innovations were one-sided. Polish political revitalization was not accomplished by realistic attempts to grapple with economic problems until a decade later in 1990. Chinese economic progress was accompanied with political relaxation but no democratization, and even relaxation was substantially curtailed after 1989. These two innovations – one political, the other economic – touched off a process of change that was at first resisted, but eventually embraced, in the Soviet Union, and that then echoed and amplified throughout the socialist world,

3

until it finally culminated in the dissolution of the traditional economic system and the collapse of the Soviet Union.

The early successes of Chinese economic reform were important in convincing Soviet economists that reform was not only desirable, but also feasible. Although some argued for emulating the Chinese approach, this was not the dominant strand.[1] Rather, the Soviets found evidence in China as well as in Hungary that there were feasible alternatives to the classical command economy, and that there were different approaches to reform that were compatible with continued or accelerated economic growth. Soviet leaders were encouraged to explore reforms on their own after seeing the success the Chinese had with exploratory reforms. Change in the Soviet Union would not have unfolded as rapidly as it did without the prior example of Chinese economic success.

During the *annus mirabilis* of 1989, China suddenly lost its position as a pioneer of socialist reform. The violent repression of the student movement at Tiananmen Square in June of 1989 put an end to the steady liberalization of the late 1980s. Moreover, China's new hardline leadership, in its drive for political control, seemed determined to reverse many of the hard-worn gains of economic reform. In Eastern Europe, multiple revolutions brought rapid political change and a new determination to change economic systems. Most Eastern European countries made plans to change over to market economies as rapidly as possible. The contrast between China and Eastern Europe was symbolized by the fact that on the very day of the Tiananmen massacre – June 4, 1989 – Poland held the first free elections in a Communist state, marking the successful completion of its first stage of democratization.

Yet it soon became clear that China's economic reform process had not been halted by the post-Tiananmen hardline leadership. Indeed, its fumbling attempts to reassert control over the economy only demonstrated that the economic changes that had already occurred in China were more profound than many had realized, and were virtually irreversible. Moreover, beginning with Poland's economic "big bang" on January 1, 1990, the Eastern Europeans discovered that they were entering a period not only of accelerated systemic change, but also of serious economic recession. Still another contrast was emerging between China and Eastern Europe. While the Eastern Europeans and residents of the former Soviet Union were purchasing significant economic change at the cost of substantial foregone growth, the robust growth that accompanied Chinese reforms was continuing and even showing signs of accelerating. To be sure, China's superior growth performance partially reflects the advantages China enjoyed from having started the reform process a full ten years earlier than the Eastern Europeans. But even this simple truth draws attention to the fact that China has been undergoing a genuine process of economic transition. China was the only socialist country to undertake system transformation without tumbling into profound economic crisis. Indeed, since the early 1980s, China has been the fastest growing large economy in the world, and by a large margin. Contemporaneous with social and political changes that are complex and often disappointing, the Chinese economic reform process has been resilient and profound, and accompanied by accelerated economic growth that has lifted a huge portion of the world's population out of poverty.

The story and problem of economic reform

The aim of this book is to present a comprehensive view of Chinese economic reform. The first task must inescapably be to provide a narrative of the reform process as a whole. Surprisingly, despite the widely acknowledged importance of Chinese reforms, there is no currently available account that covers the main events of the reform process. Yet a narrative approach is strongly indicated by one of the most distinctive characteristics of the Chinese reform process: Reforms have been gradual and evolutionary. Reforms were not clearly foreseen or designed in advance, and so the elements of the reform have inescapably been time dependent. Reforming without a blueprint (Lin 1989), neither the process nor the ultimate objective was clearly envisaged beforehand. The Chinese expression for this process is "groping for stones to cross the river," a metaphor that implies that each step depends on the previous step. Since the reform process has been marked by substantial ex post coherence, and by significant resilience as well, such an approach might be admired as the strategy of not having a strategy, or as we might say, of "muddling through" (Lindblom 1959). But to appreciate such a process, we must look at the "what" or the reform process, the particularity of how one thing led to another. This book is thus concerned not only with the outcome of economic reform, but also with the sequence of reform-induced changes.

At the same time, there is clearly no single story of economic reform. On the contrary, the reform process is woven together from many strands and from the actions of millions of individuals pursuing their own interests. Economic reforms can only be understood as part of a process that includes economic development strategy and macroeconomic policy as well as system reform more narrowly defined. Moreover, the ultimate objective is to analyze the reform process and identify its really distinctive and interesting aspects. This clearly requires an analytical approach that is to some extent in tension with the book's narrative organization. The required analysis, though based on economic reasoning, is never technical and should not present problems to anyone with an interest in the general topic. The book combines an overall narrative organization with stretches of economic analysis – the aim has been to make it about 30% policy narrative and 70% economic discussion.

In order to achieve a broad view of system change while keeping the narrative intact and the material manageable, I have focused on industry and macroeconomic policy. Other areas are brought in occasionally, when they are indispensable to the overall story, but they do not receive comprehensive treatment. The neglect of agriculture and foreign trade is particularly regrettable, since these are very important to the economy, and relatively successful aspects of Chinese reform. The justification is that both agriculture and foreign trade can be at least partially separated from the most difficult problems of system change. Both involve a relationship between the institutions of the traditional command economy and institutions in another sector that operate on different principles. In the case of agriculture, these are peasant households, which operate with hard budget constraints and strong incentives for economically rational behavior; in the case of foreign trade, it is the competitive world marketplace. In these sectors, the incentives and opportunities from outside the planned economy can be used to further institutional change, as long as the links with the planned economy can be significantly loosened. Moreover, these sectors have been relatively well covered in the literature, and the interested reader can refer to a number of excellent works.[2]

By contrast, reform of industry is especially difficult, for industry is the central component of virtually every aspect of the traditional command economy. Industry is the focus of development strategy. It is the sector in which the traditional control techniques of the command economy – such as material balance and quantity output planning – are most developed, and as such it is the exemplar of the traditional command system. Finally – and this is less generally appreciated – industry is also the crux of macroeconomic relations in the command economy. Because of the way price relations are structured in the command economy, state-run industry serves as the government's cash cow and carries out the bulk of national saving, while also being the recipient of the greatest part of national investment. Industry is thus the main element determining both the government's fiscal policy and the overall balance of savings and investment in the economy. When industry is successfully reformed, the old command economy, with its distinctive systemic and macroeconomic characteristics, has ceased to exist. Inevitably, then, industry is the main character in the reform drama.

These perspectives on industry also serve to remind us of the fundamental problem of reform of socialist economies. That problem is that all the elements of the old system were interrelated. Replacing one coordination mechanism with another – switching from plan to market – is only one part of a broader transition process. The output structure of the economy must change – there must be a process of reindustrialization. The macroeconomic mechanisms must make a transition, such that there are alternative sources of saving in order to maintain the investment essential for growth and reindustrialization. A whole set of new institutions must be built to serve the new economic system. There are different ways to approach these problems, and not all approaches have been equally successful.

The distinctiveness of China's economic reform

A distinctive pattern characterizes China's economic reforms. Because of the coherence of Chinese reforms, I will sometimes refer to a Chinese *strategy* of economic reform. However, this term should be used with caution. Strategy implies conscious design of the sequence of reforms, or at least that certain principles about how to respond to contigencies could have been described in advance. This was not true in China. But China's reforms also did not develop purely fortuitously: A limited number of crucial government decisions and commitments were required in order to allow reform to develop. In certain periods, policymakers acted as if they had a commitment to a specific reform strategy. The overall distinctive pattern of reform, though, emerged from the interaction between government policy and the often unforeseen consequences of economic change. Only through this evolving process did the goal of a market economy gradually emerge as the generally agreed upon objective of the transitional process. By the later stages of the transition, there were clearly leaders who saw and embraced it as a strategy, but this should not be taken to mean that it was seen as such at the outset.

There are a number of characteristic features of the Chinese transition process. The discussion begins here with the characteristic feature that is most closely linked to the core institutions of the command economy – with the coordination mechanism in industry. Here the characteristic feature has been the adoption of a dual-track system as a transitional device. From the dual-track system, the discussion of characteristic features is gradually broadened to encompass nine distinctive features that define the Chinese transition process, and concludes with a note on the ex-post coherence of the process. In the subsequent section, these features are contrasted with two other models of the economic reform process.

The dual-track system

The first distinctive element of the Chinese reform process is described by the phrase "dual-track system." This Chinese term (*shuangguizhi*) refers to the coexistence of a traditional plan and a market channel for the allocation of a given good. Rather than dismantling the plan, reformers acquiesced in a continuing role for the plan in order to ensure stability and guarantee the attainment of some key government priorities (in the Chinese case, primarily investment in energy and infrastructure). Having a dual-track implies the existence of a two-tier pricing system for goods under that system: A single commodity will have both a (typically low) state-set planned price and a (typically higher) market price.

It is important to stress that the dual-track refers to the coexistence of two coordination mechanisms (plan and market) and not to coexistence of two ownership systems. By the mid-1980s, most state-owned firms were still being assigned a compulsory plan for some output, but had additional capacity available for production of above-plan, market goods. Thus, the dual-track strategy was one that operated within the state sector – indeed, within each state-run factory – as well as in the industrial economy at large. This was essential, because it meant that virtually all factories, including state-run factories were introduced to the market, and began the process of adaptation to market processes. The dual-track system allowed state firms to transact and cooperate with non-state, marketized firms, allowing valuable flexibility. But the growing importance of collective, private, and foreign-invested firms should be considered apart from the dual-track system strictly defined, since most of these firms were predominantly market-oriented from the beginning.

Growing out of the plan

The mere existence of a dual-track system is not itself sufficient to define a transition strategy. All planned economies have something of a dual-track system, in the sense that none of them ever completely eradicates various kinds of black market trading that inescapably takes place at market-influenced prices. Thus it is a crucial feature of the Chinese transition that economic growth is concentrated on the market track. I coined the phrase "growing out of the plan" in 1984 after Chinese planners in Beijing had described in interviews their intention to keep the size of the overall central government materials allocation plan fixed in absolute terms. Given the obvious fact that the economy was growing rapidly, this implied that the plan would become proportionately less and less important until the economy gradually grew out of the plan. Planners concurred in this description: Chinese policymakers were making a generally credible commitment to freeze the size of the traditional plan. This guaranteed a long-run dynamic process that would gradually increase the share of non-plan, market transactions in the economy and made the dual-track system into an unabashed transitional device. The phrase "growing out of the plan" has already achieved some currency in the English language literature (Byrd 1987: 299; Hartland-Thunberg 1989; Naughton 1986: 605; Shirk 1989: 354–57; Wang Xiaoqiang 1993: 36).

. The commitment to growing out of the plan was of great importance for the individual enterprise as well. With their plans essentially fixed, enterprises faced "market prices on the margin." Even those firms with compulsory plans covering, say, 90% of capacity, were in such a position that future growth and development of profitable opportunities would take place at market prices. The plan served as a kind of lump-sum tax on (or subsidy to) the enterprise. So long as the commitment not to change it was credible, it really had no impact on any of the enterprise's decision-making. Current decisions would be based on market prices. If the enterprise was induced to operate as a profit-maximizing firm, that profit maximization would be carried out on the basis of market prices. In that sense, the plan was irrelevant (Byrd 1989).

Entry

The central government's monopoly over industry was relaxed. In China, the protected industrial sector was effectively opened to new entrants beginning in 1979. Large numbers of start-up firms, especially rural industries, rushed to take advantage of large potential profits in the industrial sector, and their entry sharply increased competition and changed overall market conditions in the industrial sector. Most of these firms were collectively owned, and some were private or foreign-owned. But local governments also sponsored many new start-up firms during the 1980s, and these firms were often "state owned." The crucial factor is that the central government in practice surrendered its ability to maintain high barriers to entry around the lucrative manufacturing sectors. This lowering of entry barriers was greatly facilitated in China by the nation's huge size and diversity, and the relatively large role that local governments play in economic management even before reform. Large size and diversity meant there was scope for competition among firms in the "public sector," even if each of these firms remained tied to government at some level.

Prices that equate supply and demand

Flexible prices that equated supply and demand quickly came to play an important role in the Chinese economy. Beginning in the early 1980s, a significant proportion of transactions began to occur at market prices, and in 1985, market prices were given legal sanction for exchange of producer goods outside the plan. This meant that state firms were legally operating at market prices, since virtually all state firms had some portion of above-plan production. Gradual decontrol of consumer goods prices – initially cautious – steadily brought most consumer goods under market price regimes (see Table A.1). An important benefit of the legitimacy given to market prices was that transactions between the state and non-state sector were permitted, and they developed into a remarkable variety of forms. Simple trade was accompanied by various kinds of joint ventures and cooperative arrangements, as profit-seeking state-run enterprises looked for ways to reduce costs by subcontracting with rural non-state firms with lower labor and land costs.

Incremental managerial reforms in the state sector

This market framework for the state firm facilitated the maintenance and incremental reform of the management system of state enterprises. As state firms faced increasing competitive pressures, government officials experimented with ways to improve incentives and management capabilities within the state sector. This experimental process focused on a steady shift in emphasis away from plan fulfillment and toward profitability as the most important indicator of enterprise performance. Moreover, as discussed in Chapter 6, there is substantial evidence that the combination of increased competition, improved incentives, and more effective monitoring of performance did improve state enterprise performance over the 1980s. It is characteristic of China's reform that the improved – and in some ways intensified – monitoring of state enterprise performance was an alternative to large-scale privatization. Logically, there is no reason why privatization cannot be combined with a dual-track transitional strategy, but practically there are obvious reasons why they would tend to be alternatives. Urgent privatization tends to follow from a belief that state sector performance cannot be improved, and often leads to a short-run "abandonment of the enterprise" as the attention of reformers shifts away from short-run performance and to the difficult task of privatization. Conversely, the sense that privatization is not imminent lends urgency to the attempt to improve monitoring, control, and incentives in the state sector.

Disarticulation

Along with measures to reform the core of the planned economy, Chinese reforms also advanced by identifying economic activities that were the least tightly integrated into the planning mechanism and pushing reform in these limited areas. Chinese reform might thus also be labeled a strategy of "disarticulation," in which successive sections of the economy are separated from the planned core, which persists. This was clearly not an intentional strategy, but rather one that emerged from the nature of the policy process and from the concern of Chinese policymakers not to disrupt the core economy. The early establishment of Special Economic Zones is the most obvious example of such policies – export-oriented enclaves were created that initially had almost no links to the remainder of the economy. This approach is also one of the reasons that reforms succeeded first in the countryside. Policymakers realized that it was not necessary that all the countryside be integrated into the planned economy. Beginning with the poorest areas, some regions were allowed to detach themselves from the planned economy. So long as the state could purchase sufficient grain to keep its storehouses full, it could afford to let the organizational form in the countryside devolve back to household farming. (Poland, of course, ran a command economy along with household farming from the 1950s until 1990.) Cautious policymaking led to a reform strategy of disarticulation.

Initial macroeconomic stabilization achieved through the plan

Macroeconomic stabilization and reorientation of development strategy were initially carried out under the traditional planned economy. Rather than combining stabilization and reform into a single rapid but traumatic episode, the Chinese used the instruments of the planned economy to shift resources toward the household sector and relieve macroeconomic stresses at the very beginning of reform. This dramatic shift in development strategy created favorable conditions for the gradual unfolding of reform. Particularly striking is the fact that reforms began within a strengthening of the government's guarantee of full employment to all permanent urban residents. Indeed, the initial shift toward a more labor-intensive development strategy was motivated in part by the need to provide jobs for a large group of unemployed young people.

Macroeconomic cycles persisted throughout the reform process

After the beginning of reforms, a pattern developed in which bold reform measures tended to be implemented after stabilization had achieved some success. Reform measures then contributed to renewed macroeconomic imbalances, eventually leading to a new period of macroeconomic austerity. As a result, macroeconomic policies have been of fundamental importance in determining the success or failure of reforms during individual periods.

At the same time, the alternation between expansionary and contractionary phases of the macroeconomic cycle has contributed to marketization of the economy over the long run. Periods of macroeconomic austerity led to abundance of goods and the temporary elimination of shortages. Under those conditions, the demand for planning was reduced, and the position of markets strengthened. More generally, the planning apparatus has been buffeted by the rapid change in economic conditions, and its importance receded as a result of its inability to respond quickly to quick changes in the economic environment. The almost intractable task of planning an economy can only be carried out in conditions of artificially imposed stability; without that stability, the inadequacy of attempts to plan the economy became increasingly evident.

Continued high saving and investment

Steady erosion in government revenues – ultimately traceable to the dissolution of the government industrial monopoly – led to a sustained reduction in government saving. At the same time, though, steady increases in household income and the increasing opportunities in the economic environment led to a rapid increase in household saving. These offsetting changes meant that total national saving remained high sustaining high levels of investment and growth. One consequence has been a vastly enhanced role for the banking system, serving as an intermediary channeling household saving to the enterprise sector. While this process has been relatively smooth, it has been difficult for the government both to acquiesce in and to manage the decline in its resources, and macroeconomic policymaking has become more complex and more difficult.

Ex-post coherence

The preceding nine features have been the crucial distinctive elements of China's systemic transition within industry. It can be seen, ex-post, that there is substantial coherence to these different elements. Reduction of the state's monopoly led to rapid entry of new firms. Entry of new firms, combined with adoption of market prices on the margin, led to enhanced competition, and began to get state-sector managers accustomed to responding to the marketplace. Gradual price decontrol was essential. Competition eroded intially high profit margins for state firms, and induced the government, as owner of the firms, to become more concerned with profitability. The government experimented with better incentive and monitoring devices, and this improved state-sector performance. Nonetheless, the state sector grew more slowly than the newly entrant sectors. The economy gradually grew out of the plan, as both the plan itself and the state sector as a whole became less dominant elements in the economy as a whole. Yet this occured with the stability attributable to the maintenance of the planned sector as an anchor, and to continued robust saving and investment. Some summary reform indicators of the overall process over fifteen years are given in Table A.1.

Three models of reform

It is possible to contrast the Chinese dual-track approach with two alternate models of reform. The first model is the "rationalizing reform" that guided reform efforts in the 1960s in the European command economies (ECEs).[3] The second model is the "big bang" approach popularized in the 1990s, initially in Poland and then to varying degrees in Czechoslovakia and Russia. These three separate models or ideal types can cover virtually all attempts at serious economic reform in the socialist command economies.

European rationalizing reform

During the 1960s, significant economic reforms were attempted in nearly every European command economy. The results were uniformly disappointing. The most important characteristic of the 1960s reforms is that they were designed to make the command economy work more smoothly, and not to eliminate it or replace it with a market economy. It was hoped that reliance on scientific methods and sophisticated indirect steerage would improve planners' control of the economy. For this reason I call these tools "rationalizing reforms." Indeed, reform as rationalization was the only approach that

Table A.1 *Reform indicators*

	1978	1985	1988	1990	1993
Proportion of total retail sales					
Market Prices	3%	34%	49%	45%	95%
Guidance Prices	neg.	19%	22%	25%	
Fixed Prices	97%	47%	29%	30%	5%
Proportion of agricultural procurement					
Market Prices	6%	40%	57%	52%	90%
Guidance Prices	2%	23%	19%	23%	
Fixed Prices	92%	37%	24%	25%	10%
Ownership structure of industrial production					
State	78%	65%	57%	55%	42%
Collective	22%	32%	36%	36%	40%
Private	neg.	2%	4%	5%	9%
Foreign	neg.	neg.	1%	2%	7%

Sources: Prices: *Price* 1991: 466; Tian Yuan and Qiao Gang 1991: 203; Sun Xiangyi 1993: 10: Niu Genying 1994. Industrial Output: *Industrial Statistics*, various years; 1993 is estimated based on SSB 1994.

was ideologically acceptable before the 1980s. Rationalizing reform was never a strategy for transition to the market; rather, the object was to introduce some market-like elements in order to improve or "perfect" the planning system (Augustinovics 1975).

Both in its conception and in its practice, rationalizing reform maintained the fundamental framework of the existing system, most crucially the state monopoly over the critical core sectors of the economy. Reformers hoped to compute a set of optimal prices that could be combined with improved reward functions to create a planned economy with the efficiency of a market economy. They were after a "computopia" that would combine the best aspects of plan and market, and in which perfect computation would substitute for real competition.[4] The objective of rationalizing reform was to increase the efficiency of the state sector by instructing managers to behave like profit-oriented businessmen, while remaining within the framework of the state plan. In rationalizing reform, planners believed that by manipulating the objective functions of state-sector managers, they could reduce or eliminate conflicts of interest between the government and enterprise managers.

Rationalizing reforms were in practice taken the furthest in Hungary, and there is an extensive literature on the Hungarian reforms (Berend 1990; Friss 1969; Kornai 1986). The Hungarian "New Economic Mechanism" was characterized by the outright abolition of compulsory plans and material allocation. However, centralized allocation was replaced by a vaguely defined "horizontal cooperation" between enterprises that falls well short of true market coordination. Planners turned to the use of "indirect instruments" or price levers. Prices were adjusted and subsidies reduced, but prices remained controlled by planners explicitly in order to allow them to steer production and investment decisions. Capital charges were implemented to encourage enterprises to economize on capital and regulate their own investment demand. Incentive schemes were revamped, shifting attention from physical output targets to value targets such as sales, cost reduction and, ultimately, profits. Enterprises were allowed to finance some of their investment from retained funds, particularly profit, and from bank loans. Finally, some parts of the "second economy" were legalized, permitting private business in a narrow range of activity, typically including some petty trade and repair services, and some housing construction.

These were important changes in the 1960s, but the limitations on this type of reform are more fundamental than the changes that were instituted. We can identify three crucial limitations: First, planners never renounced the effort to guide all fundamental economic decisions. The market was intended to be an instrument in the hands of central planners, rather than an autonomously functioning institution. Even the recourse to self-financing by enterprises was seen as a modest softening of central control that would not obstruct the basic ability of central planners to choose large investment projects and determine the overall direction and rate of investment (Brus and Laski 1989: 76–77). This is a vision – rather than a plan – of a computopia, in which the economy is optimally steered through the control of prices. Second, prices were never set free to equilibrate supply and demand. Third, the administrative hierarchy that controlled the economy remained intact, and with it the state monopoly of crucial industrial sectors. Maintenance of this monopoly was quite explicit. As Friss (1969: 17) put it:

The dependence [of the enterprise] on the state is reflected in the principles that enterprises can be founded only by a minister or leader of a national authority or by the executive committee of a local council, and that the founder has the right to determine the sphere of activity of the enterprise, as well as to appoint and discharge its director and deputy director.

Even in the late 1980s, after several additional waves of reform, the state monopoly remained basically intact. Legal provisions restricted or prohibited transactions between state-owned firms and the private sector (Kornai 1990: 94).

It should be clear that these limitations are not mere accidental shortcomings. They represent a coherent and internally consistent attempt by planners to maintain state control over the price system and to maintain the state monopoly over crucial sectors that is inseparably related to that control. Individual prices could always be "rationalized," even adjusted to accord with world prices. But the overall structure of prices, of markets, and of the pattern of entry was to be firmly controlled by the same planners who had managed the pre-reform economic system. The objective was to prevent market prices from "autonomously" determining all the important income and resource distribution issues in the economy. Instead, planners wanted to maintain as separate realms, under their control, the determination of income distribution and the determination of the level and composition of investment. Prices could not be allowed to jointly determine all of these, as in a market economy (Klaus 1990: 68).

There is an overwhelming consensus that rationalizing reform in these countries failed. In Schroeder's (1979) memorable phrase, the Soviet economy was trapped "on a treadmill of reforms." Even in Hungary, where rationalizing reforms were taken the furthest, there is broad agreement that reform did not qualitatively improve, or even much change, the way the economy operated. Rationalizing reforms were designed to salvage the ideal of state socialism. Today, this model has been discarded by the very economists who were most influential in its development. Brus and Laski (1989:73–86) refer to "central planning with a regulated market – the flawed model" and link its fundamental failure to the desire to maintain control of investment in the hands of state planners. Kornai (1986) refers to advocates of this model in the earlier periods – including himself – as "naive reformers," and later (1990: 17, 57, 72) makes a fundamental distinction "between experiments in simulating a market by 'market socialism' and the introduction of a genuine free market." He concludes (1990: 58) that "the basic idea of market socialism simply fizzled out."[5]

Big bang reforms

Given gradual disillusionment with rationalizing reforms, the sudden removal of political constraints at the end of the 1980s was followed by the emergence of big bang reform strategies. These are exemplified by the Polish program adopted on January 1, 1990. Able for the first time to contemplate abandonment of the command economy, reformers were faced with the close interrelationship of every element of the traditional economic system, as described earlier. Their response was essentially that disentangling the elements of the system was impossible, and therefore it had to be destroyed at a single blow and replaced as quickly as possible. (Ironically, in the Polish case, household farming had survived, so reformers could not very well begin by decollectivizing agriculture.)

The big bang solution to the challenge of the interdependence of the elements of the command economy has been to stress the necessity of first trying to improve the quality of the price system in as short a time as possible (Klaus 1990; Gomulka 1991). This requires the removal of price controls on as many goods as feasible and, in most cases, adoption of some form of currency convertibility so that most domestic prices will conform to international prices. The urgency of these initial measures is heightened when, as in Poland, macroeconomic imbalances have severely distorted the economy, either through open inflation or through serious shortages (Lipton and Sachs 1990). In the Polish case, currency convertibility was combined with a fixed exchange rate, helping stabilize the economy.

In principle, big bang transitions aim to come as close as possible to a simultaneous transformation of as many aspects of the economic system as possible. For example, in cases where macroimbalance is serious, fiscal and monetary policies must be restructured simultaneously with price liberalization. In other respects, though, it is easy to overestimate the degree of simultaneity in the transition. Indeed, even if movement begins on all fronts simultaneously, liberalization of the price system will be achieved much more rapidly than other aspects of the transition (Gelb and Fischer 1991; Dhanji 1991). Even liberalization of the price system usually covers only product markets at first. In Poland, both the exchange rate and the wage rate were fixed by government fiat in order to provide "nominal anchors" to the economy. The nominal anchors help the economy converge to the appropriate price *level* while equilibrium price relationships are being worked out by the marketplace. Without some nominal anchors, the process of price determination would be confused and delayed by the uncertainty individuals felt about where overall price levels would end up. Even with these limitations, price liberalization takes place much more rapidly than institutional transformation and structural adjustment.

Institutional transformation refers to the complex set of changes relating to the creation of new economic institutions. Privatization is the most significant, but also the most difficult and contentious element of this transformation. Indeed, privatization is entangled with two other crucial elements of the transformation: demonopolization and restructuring of enterprise accounts and balance sheets to permit them to accurately reflect economic realities. Further institutional change is necessary in the banking system, the tax system, the legal framework for business – indeed, virtually every aspect of a modern economy. Almost inevitably, big bang transitions imply that the attempt to rationalize the state sector is abandoned. Market prices are to be followed as rapidly as possible by large-scale privatization, and the ultimate shift to a market economy characterized by mixed ownership forms dominated by private enterprise. As institutional transformation is unfolding, the economy, now guided by the proper price signals, will begin the difficult process of structural adjustment, referring to change in the mix of output that is produced. Command economies produce many goods that have no future in an open market economy, and producers must shift into a range of goods in which they have comparative advantage. This process of structural change unfolds gradually in the wake of the big bang deregulation of the price system.

Big bang strategies clearly can succeed in destroying the command economy and eventually creating a market economy. The controversy surrounding big bang strategies revolves around the question of whether it is wise to concentrate so many of the costs of transformation in the early stages. Early price liberalization and currency convertibility exposes domestic producers to dramatic change, increased competition and high levels of uncertainty with little preparation. The experience of Poland and other countries that have adopted this strategy shows that it is very costly in terms of forgone output and unemployment. Proponents of big bang approaches argue that these costs are inevitable, and better taken at the outset and all at once. They argue that the consistency of the old system, the entrenched behavior patterns of existing interest groups, and the need for a credible once-and-for-all transformation dictate a big bang strategy. Skeptics doubt whether populations with new and fragile democratic institutions will tolerate the exceptional short-run burdens placed on them, and worry that excessive economic disruption will erode long-term support for the necessary economic transformation.

China and Eastern Europe

Fundamentally, the Chinese reform pattern resembles big bang transitions more than the rationalizing reforms of Eastern Europe. Both Chinese dual-track reforms and the big bang lead ultimately to a market economy (even if this was not known in China at the outset). Both involve fairly quick acceptance of market-determined prices, and large-scale entry of non-state producers. Because of this dynamic, both involve a sharp decline in the government's direct control over resources, as measured by budgetary revenues as a share of GNP, and a concommitant increase in control over resources by households and enterprises. None of these characteristics was shared by rationalizing reforms.

Chinese reforms are sometimes lumped together with rationalizing reforms because both appear to be gradual or partial reforms. This is inappropriate. Gradualism is not in itself a defining characteristic of reform strategies, and in any case, rationalizing reforms were not necessarily gradual. The most important case – that of Hungary – involved the adoption of an integrated package on a single day, January 1, 1968. This was the "big bang" of its day. Chinese reforms are also confused with the European reforms because they often use a similar vocabulary to describe their aims. In fact, as this book will demonstrate, the apparent similarity of vocabulary disguises fundamental differences in approach. Indeed, the similarity of vocabulary can be readily explained by Chinese use of Eastern European concepts to justify early reforms, and by the need to reassure conservatives that reforms would not lead to economic disorder. The fundamental objectives and processes of rationalizing reforms differ so much from Chinese dual-track reforms that it is quite inappropriate to put them in a single category.

To be sure, Chinese reforms do share with European rationalizing reforms the maintenance of the administrative hierarchy that manages production and, even worse for China, the continuance of Communist Party power. As unfortunate as this is, the context within which economic management takes place has been so profoundly altered by the steady introduction of market forces and competition that the negative effects of continued government oversight in China have been greatly attenuated. In addition, China's reforms differ from the big bang approach primarily because Chinese leaders were unwilling to undergo extreme short-term shocks to the economy. Big bang transitions inevitably involve large short-run adjustment costs, generally including discontinuous changes in the price system and sharp increases in unemployment. By contrast, the Chinese leadership has acted as if it were constrained to maintain both inflation and open urban unemployment within fairly narrow limits. The Chinese have acted as if minimizing short-run adjustment costs (at the expense of prolonging the overall adjustment process) were an important argument in their overall transition strategy. Doubtless this is related to a sense of precariousness among some (at least) of the Chinese leaders – lacking the firm popular backing that, for instance, the early Solidarity government had in Poland, the Chinese leaders have felt that it would be unwise to impose drastic adjustment costs on a population that is already somewhat alienated from the government. Maintenance of a planned sector allows the government to use direct controls over finance and investment to begin restructuring output. More specifically, it provides a degree of stability during the transition process, and China thus clearly differs from the big bang approach in the pace of change. Finally, the absence of significant early attempts to privatize large state-owned firms distinguishes China from some of the big bang cases.

Success and failure

Generally speaking, the Chinese reform process has been a success, and in this book, reform is generally treated as a success story. But there are many aspects of Chinese reform that have not succeeded, and there are competing definitions of what success is. Nevertheless, when the Chinese reform process is viewed as a whole, what is most striking is the succession of incremental, steadily accumulating measures of economic reform that have gradually transformed the economy in a fundamental way. By the end of the 1980s, the Chinese economy had become open to domestic market forces and world market opportunities in a manner without precedent in the socialist world. Indeed, after initial successes in the early 1980s – especially obvious in the agricultural sector – the period from 1984 through 1988 emerges as a second period of successful transformation, this time most apparent in the fields of industry and foreign trade. Clearly, gradual – indeed, often piecemeal – approaches to economic reform can meet with substantial success. Other approaches to economic reform may also be viable and indeed under some circumstances may be preferable. But the argument that reform must be rapid and discontinuous because that is the only feasible path does not stand up to scrutiny in light of the Chinese experience.

Comparative experience shows us that no reform strategies are perfect in practice. All wind up seriously distorted by the need to accommodate political realities, by the long and difficult process of building new administrative capabilities, by the legacy of past development choices, and by the unavoidable fact of human error in policy choice. China's experience is interesting in part precisely because reform has been adapted to the limitations imposed by primitive political institutions and the problems of underdevelopment and poverty. China's reform program has been extraordinarily *robust* under difficult circumstances. Always improvised, never clearly formulated in advance, the program has nevertheless been shaped by a distinctive logic and set of circumstances that have given it considerable coherence. China has experienced substantial marketization, liberalization, and opening to the outside world, all in the context of rapid economic growth.

It has been, in short, a success. Therefore, the Chinese approach to economic reform needs to be taken seriously and put in the context of other socialist reform processes.

Underlying this assessment is of course the fact of economic growth, and the undeniably better living standards that the majority of Chinese enjoy after fifteen years of reform. Of course, growth in itself cannot be the only criterion. A short-term acceleration of growth, purchased at the expense of macroeconomic imbalance, environmental degradation, external debt, or other costs, might not be an adequate standard. Growth must be sustainable to confirm an economic strategy: The ultimate criterion is broad-based development. Clearly, the measurement of China's development is beyond the scope of this book, but certainly by most measures, China's development is quite broad-based and reflected in substantial sustained improvement of living standards. Broad-based growth is the key to China's success.

There is a view – more prevalent in the media than in scholarly accounts – that whatever success Chinese reforms have encountered comes from the performance of the non-state sector. In this view, agricultural households, and subsequently rural enterprises and foreign investment, have driven continued economic growth. State-run enterprises, however, remain stubbornly unreformed, and the government as a whole has failed to adapt to the needs of the reform era. A more sophisticated version of this approach describes the Chinese reform process as "surrounding the cities from the countryside" (Findlay and Watson 1992). While this view, by stressing the growth of non-state sector, contains a kernel of truth, it is simply not adequate to describe the entire reform process. First, it ignores evidence of improving performance in the state sector. Second, it sees the state and non-state sectors as being essentially independent phenomena, when the evidence is strong that they are both interdependent and in competition. Third, it is essentially enterprise-based – that is, it ignores all the other institutions in the economy that must be reformed.

Moreover, such views simply do not "add up." We can do an experiment. If one took all the rural enterprises and foreign-invested firms, and stripped them away from the remainder of the economy, how fast would the remainder of the economy be growing? Relatedly, we could mentally detach China's five most dynamic provinces, all of them along the coast – Guangdong, Fujian, Zhejiang, Jiangsu, and Shandong. This would mean subtracting the provinces with the fastest growing industry, accounting for almost a quarter of China's total GNP. Moreover, it would mean subtracting about two-thirds of the foreign investment and rural industry. What happens to China's economic growth rates when these dynamic areas are conceptually amputated from the rest of the economy? Between 1978 and 1991, the official real GNP growth rate for all of China was 8.6% annually. When the "gold coast" areas are removed, the real GNP growth rate for the remainder of China falls, but only to 7.7%. The key feature is across-the-board high growth rates, *not* regionally concentrated growth (see also Denny 1991).

Conversely, another view attributes success primarily to the policies adopted by Chinese leaders. Needless to say, the most energetic purveyors of this view are in the Chinese propaganda apparatus. In this semi-official view, Chinese leaders adopted cautious, experimental reforms. Policies were tried out first in local experiments, and policies that worked were spread nationwide. Reforms began in rural areas, and achieved great success. As a result, a second stage of urban reforms was attempted and, although this was harder, it also eventually achieved success. Reforms succeeded because Chinese leaders were flexible and pragmatic. This is a highly sanitized account of the reform process, sufficiently misleading to count as misinformation: It distracts us from the real dynamics of the reform process in favor of an oversimplified morality tale. The official view centered on leaders and policies veers from oversimplification to dishonesty when it deals with changing policies and leaders in the past, since it seeks to always justify the current leadership. For example, in 1992 a comprehensive *Encyclopedia of Chinese Reform* was published in China (Tong Wansheng and Zuo Xiangqun 1992). This remarkable multi-volume work, totalling almost 5,000 pages, manages simultaneously to generally attribute reform successes to enlightened policymaking and to never once mention the name of Zhao Ziyang, who was in fact the most important single leader in the reform process, but was purged after the Tiananmen incident. The continuing flow of misleading information coming out of Beijing inevitably ends up distorting the interpretation of the reform process.

In fact, through much of the reform period, Chinese policymakers have failed to achieve consensus about or articulate a vision of the post-reform economic system. One of the reasons China's reforms were *gradual* was simply because so much time was *wasted* pursuing dead ends and even regressive policies. The Chinese leaders have never been able to articulate coherent visions of, for example, ownership structure, or a fully renovated financial system. Thus, for significant parts of our period, Chinese leaders have not so much been systematically groping for stepping stones in order to cross a river as they have been slogging around in a swamp.

Moreover, such a perspective cannot account for the very significant failures of the Chinese reform process, even with respect to issues that were viewed as critical by top government leaders. Indeed, the reform process during the 1980s was marked by four fundamental, closely related failures. These were the failure to create a new fiscal system, the failure to clarify or restructure property rights, failure to put real accountability into the investment system, and repeated and excessive delays in reforming some of the more distorted aspects of the price system. All four of these failures were the result of a continuing inability of the Chinese government to design and carry through coordinated or rationalizing reforms. At first, so many changes needed to be made that it was acceptable to defer the tasks that were most difficult administratively and ideologically. Later, it was easier to make these changes, because there was a far broader market context that could be used to shape these changes. Today, so many of the other changes have now been accomplished that the deferred rationalization and restructuring of the system is now the most immediate, pressing task. Thus, the Chinese political and economic systems continue to be profoundly challenged.

I view Chinese policymakers as weakly rational. The Chinese government, like governments everywhere, made vital economic decisions with inadequate information, often in near-crisis situations, and subject to numerous economic and non-economic constraints. As a result, the reform process was reactive and disjointed rather than smooth. The administrative capability of the government was strained to the limit during a process of wide-ranging change, and the government rarely had the ability to design and then carry out long-term, multi-stage reform programs. Moreover, improvised policy responses were made within the bounds of ideology, factional rivalries, and bureaucratic power and interests. But once economic policy choices were made, they met with varying degrees of success depending upon the nature of the underlying economic conditions. Policies that failed economically left their advocates extremely exposed: They tended either to abandon the policies or found themselves replaced by individuals willing to try other approaches. Successful economic policies tended to bring political success to their patrons. Thus, I argue that economic issues became part of the contemporary political agenda mainly for economic reasons that are readily understandable, and major policy shifts have usually occurred in response to changes in economic conditions that we can trace. That is to say, there was an economic logic to Chinese economic reform that is quite strong.

If this perspective is correct, it means that over the longer term the pattern of reform was shaped more by economic conditions and the interaction between economics and politics than it was by ideology or politics. Indeed, the Chinese reform kept evolving in ways that policymakers didn't anticipate, and they had to scramble to catch up with the changes they had unleashed. Indeed, this is another sense in which the title of this book may be understood. The reform process has typically unfolded in ways very different from those envisioned by reformers in the early phases. Unexpected consequences and accidental events proved important. In that sense, the economy and its reform both developed "out of the plan." The Chinese approach is in some ways the path of least resistance, traced on an economic landscape by a political organism with limited abilities to map the terrain and chart a path on its own. This fact is part of what gives the Chinese experience a more general interest. Some features of the Chinese case will be repeated in other socialist and developing countries undergoing reforms as they struggle to cope with difficult and rapidly changing economic realities.

Synopsis of the book

The book follows a modified chronological organization. This introductory chapter presented some of the main themes and describes the basic ways in which China's distinctive economic reform differs from the reforms instituted in Eastern Europe and the former Soviet Union. Chapter 1 describes the Chinese economy on the eve on reform. It is emphasized that although China's economic system was basically similar to that of the Soviet Union, an important difference was that China's economy was relatively underdeveloped. Partly as a result, the economy was not subject to the same high degree of centralized administrative control as in the Soviet Union, and there was more "space" for autonomous economic activity to emerge once liberalization began. Chapters 2 through 4 describe the first of three periods into which the reform era naturally divides. Each covers the period 1979 through 1983 from a different perspective, and together they describe the three most important processes of this early period: the reorientation of development strategy, institutional reforms, and liberalization and the growth of the non-state sector. Chapter 2 describes the crisis of the command economy at the end of the 1970s, and the initial response to that crisis. It asks why China initiated economic reform, and finds that the crisis was one of development strategy, and that the initial response to that crisis was a reorientation of development strategy (with significant macroeconomic consequences as well). Chapter 3 describes the earliest system reform measures that accompanied the reorientation of development strategy. It is stressed that these early reforms were carried out not so much *without* a blueprint as with a vague version of the rationalizing reform blueprint from Eastern European reform of the 1960s. Chapter 4 covers the initial liberalization that modified the state monopoly over the industrial sector, and permitted substantial entry of non-state producers, particularly in rural areas.

These early reforms, significant as they were, did not appear to be leading to a successful approach to continued reform. The rationalizing reform approach was simply not working. Chapter 5 discusses some of the crucial debates that grew up over reform strategy as experience in reforms (both successful and failed) was accumulating in the mid-1980s. While debate does not correlate exactly with policy change at the top, a crucial shift in policy did occur in 1984. Subsequently, the period between 1984 and 1988 emerged as the second and crucially productive phase of Chinese reform. This was the period in which the distinctive Chinese approach to reform, which I have called "growing out of the plan," emerged fully. This period is covered in two chapters: Chapter 6 describes the fundamental institutional changes that were at the heart of this reform process, while Chapter 7 describes the macroeconomic dynamics that brought the period to a temporary close with the inflationary crisis of 1988–89.

A third period can be said to emerge after the Tiananmen incident in June 1989, and this is covered in Chapter 8. Marked by initial hardline dominance of policy, it gradually passed into a third period of reform, which ended with the economy ultimately growing out of the plan. This period also reflected a new approach to reform strategy, as transition to a market economy became the explicit aim of reform. Chapter 9 attempts to draw some of the main theoretical and practical lessons from the Chinese experience.

Because of the chronological organization, some economic issues are treated in more than one place, and some continuous time-series data is relevant to several chapters. Chapters 2 and 7 both cover macroeconomic issues, and have much in common. Chapters 3 and 6 both focus on reform policy, with an emphasis on state-owned industry. Some continuity is lost by separating the treatment of closely linked topics that occur in different periods. Because Chinese data often requires some manipulation to be meaningful, there is a statistical appendix at the end of the book, to which the reader is occasionally referred.

1

The command economy and the China difference

China before reform operated a command economic system along the model borrowed from the Soviet Union. Command economies share certain fundamental characteristics, and thus the problem of transition from a command to a market economy poses similar challenges whether carried out in Eastern Europe or China. But China also differs from the European socialist countries, most fundamentally by being a much poorer country. China's lower level of development shaped the character of its pre-reform economic system as well as its reform options and growth prospects. This chapter begins with a brief discussion of the command economy, including the way its interlocking institutions make the problem of economic reform extremely difficult. It then describes the features of the Chinese command economy that served to differentiate it from the Soviet model. On balance, those features tended to make the Chinese planning system less centralized, though decentralization was tempered by rigid controls on economic activity in other respects. The performance and prospects of the Chinese economy are discussed at the end. It is stressed that China's economy was performing poorly on the eve of reform, but that its prospects for growth acceleration were arguably quite good.

The command economy

The Chinese economic system pre-reform was one of the class of Soviet-style economic systems often called command economies. Command economy is a good label, because it captures two of the most basic characteristics of Soviet-style economic systems. First, resource allocation decisions are made in response to commands from planners rather than in response to prices. The most important signals in the system are commands from the administrative hierarchy, rather than prices from the market. Second, command economies concentrate a large volume of resources in the hands of planners,

Table 1.1. *Characteristics of Soviet-type economic strategy*

1. High rate of investment, over 25% of GNP
2. Priority to heavy industry and military
3. Priority to investment in goods-producing capital, neglect of services
4. Investment in basic needs: health and education
5. Preference for autarky: limited importance of foreign trade

allowing them to assume command of the economy as a whole. More specifically, command economies evolved as the result of efforts to redistribute resources into the investment program controlled by the planners. These two basic characteristics fairly accurately define the command economy, and other features are not really necessary to *characterize* the command economy. But in fact the command economy comes with a great deal of baggage – a series of other features almost always appear along with the command economy, and these features shape the prospects and trajectory of economic transition. The command economy is an interlocking whole, and the specific way the elements interlock is a crucial part of the story of how the system can come to be disassembled. In practice, command economies share a common development strategy, common systemic features, and common macroeconomic characteristics.

Development strategy refers to the broad patterns in which resources are actually used in the economy: Investment policy is the central feature of any economic strategy. Historically, the commitment to a specific development strategy preceded the creation of the command economy system. The "big push" industrialization strategy adopted in the Soviet Union after 1928 led to the evolution of the command economic system. The strains and crises brought on by forced draft industrialization led to a series of ad hoc responses that eventually brought the economy under nearly complete bureaucratic control (Grossman 1983). The objective of planners was simple: to pump the maximum volume of resources into investment in heavy industry. The command system evolved as planners took steps to guarantee their control over resources. The system only makes sense from this perspective. All subsequent command economies have followed development strategies that stress high levels of investment and priority to heavy industry. A list of generic characteristics of Soviet-type economic strategy is given in Table 1.1 (compare Dernberger 1982, Ward 1980).

Table 1.2. *Characteristics of Soviet-type economic system*

1. Public ownership of productive enterprises
    a. State ownership of large-scale industry and wholesaling
    b. Collective ownership of agriculture
2. Material balance planning
    a. quantitative output commands
    b. allocation of commodities to match sources and uses
3. Nomenklatura system controlled by Communist Party
4. "Monobank" extends credit passively to accommodate plan
5. Material incentives (except in China during the Cultural Revolution) and hard budget constraints for households

This development strategy was designed to achieve maximum growth of industrial and military capacity as rapidly as possible. A massive flow of investment was directed into capital-intensive productive facilities and concentrated in the goods-producing sector. The development strategy depended on a number of "shortcuts" in that it attempted to maximize growth of industry while deferring costly development in other areas. Social services – particularly basic health and education – were provided broadly at an early stage of development, but subsequently there was a tendency to neglect provision of higher-level services. This development strategy was adopted in both the Soviet Union and China. But a heavy-industry centered strategy was not in harmony with China's initial economic endowment, as it arguably was in the Soviet Union. China was rich in labor power, but desperately short of land and capital. Early development of labor-intensive manufactures – as other East Asian economies did – would have been more appropriate to China's factor proportions. But partly because of the prestige of the Soviet Union in the socialist world, and partly because of their own great power aspirations, the Chinese leadership adopted a Soviet-style development strategy.

The overwhelming stress given to industrial development under this strategy made a redistributive system extremely appealing. Since the objective of pumping resources into heavy and military industries was paramount, the system that could pump over the maximum volume of resources was the most suited to the needs of the leaders. Government ownership of most productive resources guaranteed control of resources, while a planning apparatus was set up to directly steer resources to planners' priority uses. Those were the principles that shaped the Soviet-type economic system, the major characteristics of which are summarized in Table 1.2. "Economic system" here refers to the institutions that are used to make specific resource-allocation decisions in individual instances. It includes the distribution of authority, the structure of incentives, and the types of information that shape individual resource use decisions. Public ownership, in the form of state ownership of large-scale industry and commerce and "collective" ownership of agricultural production units, allows the state to maintain direct-authority relations over most of its output. The ownership structure permits a command system to function unimpeded. Command over materials is the most important in an immediate economic sense.

Material balance planning is the main technique used to actually run the economy. The term "material balance" refers to the computation of sources and uses of an individual commodity that a planner "balances" in allocating all supplies. It is the single most characteristic – indeed, diagnostic – element of the command economy, and has three components – an output plan for individual producers, a supply plan that transfers resources among producers, and a schedule of material usage coefficients or norms that links inputs and outputs for individual producers. These three interlocking components make it possible to treat the planning of society's output as an elaborate arithmetical exercise. The output plan shows total available output, or total supplies. The norms show the inputs needed for each unit of output (for example, each ton of steel produced requires 0.9 tons of coal). The supply plan is then the solution to the problem of how to provide all the needed inputs for each producer, and then allocate remaining net output for final consumption and investment. When all producers in a given sector are aggregated into a single producer, this problem can be reduced to a single input-output matrix. "Solving" input-output problems – that is, attaining consistency between output and uses – is not a particularly difficult problem.

In a real command economy, however, solving the problem of consistency is difficult, because supply plans must be drawn up for each individual producer. Given that producers differ, their material usage norms will also differ, and the real problem is vastly more complicated that even the most elaborate input-output matrix. The supply plan is generally worked out in the form of "material balances," in which sources and uses of each individual commodity, expressed in physical quantities, are equated. Thus, a planner in Moscow or Beijing attempts to get all the potential sources of copper, for instance, to balance with all the potential needs. At this level, the problem cannot be solved as a mathematical problem. However, planners can in fact "muddle through" because they have the experience of the previous year's outcomes. Instead of solving the entire set of relations each year from scratch, planners simply plan increments to the previous year's solution.

This allows the current year problem to be approximately solved, relying on ingenuity and flexibility at the enterprise level. Even with these shortcuts, the information requirements are large, and the coordination problem is difficult.

Other types of control are used to reinforce control over materials. Control over personnel is exercised through the nomenklatura system. The nomenklatura is a list of jobs controlled by the Communist Party, which thereby serves as the personnel department of the entire public sector. Communist Party committees at each administrative level control the appointment of personnel at the next lower level. They propose candidates to higher levels, and vet lists of candidates proposed by lower-level Party committees. As a result, control of career paths, and thus of the ultimate incentive structure, rests with the Communist Party. Finally, control over financial flows and credit is also exerted from the top, typically through a state monopoly banking system (or "monobank") that audits compliance with state directives. Monetary flows are passive – that is, they are assigned to facilitate completion of the plan (specified in physical quantities), rather than shaping resource allocation flows themselves.

In a sense, the authority over materials, manpower, and money is redundant. Real decisions are made by determining material flows, and controls over manpower and money serve primarily to ensure compliance with the material balance plan. But in another sense, these overlapping and redundant controls are the necessary counterpart of the high degree of discretion that planners have achieved over resource use. In pursuit of maximum state control, planners created a system in which property rights were vague or non-existent, and as a result many potentially separate income streams were merged into a large "river" over which planners had discretionary control. Therefore it was essential for planners to prevent that same kind of discretionary control from being exercised lower down in the hierarchy. Weak property rights imply that opportunities for misuse of public resources or outright corruption are rife. Therefore the command economy imposes a highly restrictive and rigid set of constraints over the behavior of economic agents throughout the economy. The objective is to maintain as much as possible of the discretionary power concentrated at the top of the economic system.

The redistributive command economy also has a distinctive set of macroeconomic characteristics. This refers to the pattern of the main economic aggregates, particularly the distribution of income and of total saving and investment. Macroeconomic characteristics are listed in Table 1.3. With ownership and control over allocation guaranteed, all income streams from

Table 1.3. *Macroeconomic characteristics of the command economy*

1.	Household income is modest share of national income, typically less than 60%. Large share of income accrues directly to state or state enterprise sector
2.	Household saving is small, and bulk of national saving is carried out by state-owned enterprises
3.	State carries out most investment, financed by transferring state enterprise revenues to the budget. Tax system is implicit in government control of price system
4	Bank lending restricted to short-term finance of trade and inventories
5.	Persistent shortages of goods

government-controlled resources are simply combined into a single huge income stream, representing government revenues. The government share of national income is large, while the household share of national income is quite limited. Households controlled 55% of disposable national income in China in 1978 and less than 60% in the Soviet Union (Cheng Xiaonong 1991; Zoteev 1991). By contrast, in market economies, household income – before taxes and transfers – is typically around 90% of national disposable income. This is true for the United States and Japan, and true for Sweden, which finances its generous welfare state primarily by taxing private incomes. In some market economies, the share of incomes accruing initially to households is lower, but rarely less than the 80-85% accruing to households in Korea (UN 1990). Government services are then provided in market economies by taxing private incomes and transactions; in command economies, government activities are financed by the large share of national income that accrues to government enterprises in the first place.

Control over the price system is essential to maintaining the large state share of national income. The state maintains terms of trade between the state enterprise sector and the household sector that are favorable to state enterprises. The "markup" on consumer goods is large, while wages are controlled at stable, relatively low levels. This markup is protected by the government's monopoly on consumer goods production and over industry as a whole. Prices don't make much difference at the microeconomic level, in determining specific resources uses, but they are important at the macro level, for chaneling resources to the government. The income streams, or surpluses, of government-controlled firms are lumped together in a single huge income stream that makes up government revenue. The source of any particular income stream is unimportant, since it is an artifact of government prices; in a similar fashion the taxation system is not explicitly developed, but is rather implicit in the price system as a whole.

In the early years of such regimes, the terms of trade between the state and household sectors are determined primarily by agricultural price policy. At the early stages of development, most households are in rural areas and are engaged in agriculture. Thus, the setting of (relative) agricultural prices is the most important part of the determination of the terms of trade between the state and household sectors. The earliest discussion of this issue was the debate about the "scissors gap" in the Soviet Union during the 1920s. Advocates of "opening the scissors gap," such as Preobrazhenski (1965 [1926]), called for low agricultural procurement prices relative to state industrial prices. That is, they advocated turning the terms of trade in favor of state-owned factories and against the majority of household residents in the countryside. Under Stalin, Preobrazhenski's policies were carried out with the added twist that the inflationary spiral set off by Stalin's industrialization drive rapidly eroded the real income of urban workers as well.

In later years, socialist regimes in the Soviet Union and Eastern Europe moved to improve the relative income of rural residents. The income gap between urban and rural workers shrank dramatically, and by some definitions the "scissors gap" was narrowed. Certainly, these states did not extract such a large volume of resources from the agricultural sector. However, the terms of trade between the household sector as a whole and the state sector were stabilized, but not fundamentally altered. State-owned units continued to earn large surpluses, which were channeled to the government budget for redistribution. Household incomes remained meager: household saving was low, taxes on household income minimal, and the supply of consumer goods grew relatively slowly. This demonstrates that the fundamental relationship is that of the terms of trade between the state and households, rather than between the urban and rural sectors. It also illustrates the crucial importance of state control over the price system. While prices in such systems are often described as distorted, it should be recognized that the pattern of distortion is not random. The price system as a whole is designed to channel resources to the state sector.

Control of household income is important to planners because the market for consumer goods is one in which households with independent choice and hard budget constraints determine demand for goods. As a result, a rough balance must be struck between household demand for consumer goods and their supply. This balance is, in most command economies, quite imperfect.

Shortages and queues for individual goods are common. These shortages seem to arise from two sources. First, the government simply channels so many resources into investment and heavy industry that there is little left for households. In order to keep shortages within certain limits, the government tries to maintain a tight control over household income as well, but this is not its highest priority and it never does a particularly good job. Second, shortages result from the soft budget constraints of enterprises. Most enterprises are quite profitable, and they face no risk of bankruptcy. As a result, firms seek growth without restraint, and they have an almost unlimited desire for investment. Thus, when enterprises are given modest amounts of autonomy, their demand for inputs tends to expand until total demand runs up against the total available supply of resources. Command economies have a built-in tendency to become "shortage economies" (Kornai 1980).

Command economies are extremely coherent. While they do not work well, they do work, in the sense that the elements of the systems are reasonably well coordinated. There is a high degree of consistency between the mechanisms that govern the resource allocation process. Indeed, this is perhaps the most fundamental problem of economic reform. The high degree of consistency of the system makes it very difficult to alter or improve individual aspects while keeping the system as a whole intact. This means that command economies have less flexibility and adaptability than market systems. While the command economy provides enormous discretionary authority to the top leadership, this power does not necessarily include the ability to alter particular aspects of the system, while leaving the whole intact. The institutions of the command economy are consistent but rigid, and obstruct the adaptability of the economy. This is true both in a short-term economic sense – these economies adapt poorly to changing economic conditions, such as changes in the relative scarcity of energy resources – and also for the process of economic reform. Incremental reforms are difficult because of the inadaptability of the system.

The problem of reform

The core problem of economic reform is the transformation of the predominant resource allocation mechanism from the plan to the market. Reform is the replacement of one coordination mechanism – an inefficient one based on administrative commands and quantitative targets – with the more efficient market-price mechanism. But economic reform is also much more than this, since it necessitates the creation of new institutions and new macroeconomic relationships. The coherence and interlocking nature of the command economy institutions makes reform difficult. Five specific consequences of the command economy system tend to complicate the reform process.

1. The central position that state-owned industry occupies in the economic system as a whole makes industrial reform an especially complex and contentious process. State industry is the focus of development strategy, it is the exemplar of the planning system, and it is the pivot of the macroeconomic balances in the economy. The first two of these statements should be self-evident: State industry is given the highest priority in the forced industrialization strategy, and material balance planning is at its most elaborate and complete in determining the flows of materials among state-owned factories. It may be less immediately apparent that state industry is also the pivot of the macroeconomic balances of the economy, but this is in fact the case. The huge volume of revenues accruing to state industry makes it the locus of the bulk of national saving, even while it is also the recipient of the majority of national investment. As a result, the balance between saving and investment – the crucial component of macroeconomic balance in any economy – takes place primarily within the state industrial sector.

Certainly, because the system is redistributive, it is the case that state industry saving is first transferred to the budgetary authority and then redistributed back to industry (without reference to the individual sectors from which revenues came). But ultimately it is the volume of saving and investment within state industry that provides the key to overall macroeconomic policy. In spite of the concentration of development policy on industrialization, state industry is on balance a surplus sector. In China in 1978, the modern industrial sector generated a surplus (total tax and profit) equal to a remarkable 25% of GNP. Virtually all of this was remitted to the budget, and most of that was channeled back into industry. But even after all state investments in industry are subtracted, industry remitted a net 6% of GNP to the budget (Naughton 1992). Even after the concentration of development policy on industry is taken into account, state industry remains an important source of aggregate saving for the economy as a whole.

State industry thus functions as a kind of "cash cow" for the government and for the economy as a whole. State-run industries in command economies therefore have very different financial positions from state-run firms in developing market economies. State-run firms in countries such as Brazil or India generally run large deficits. Even if they make a profit on current operations, they are in deficit once state investments are taken into account (Floyd, Gray and Short, 1984). On balance, they absorb saving from the rest of the economy. Of course, the surplus position of state-run industry in command economies is not due to their superior economic efficiency. It is simply an artifact of the price system, in which the terms of trade have been shifted strongly in favor of state industry.

Because of these factors, reformers of state industry must keep in mind the impact of changes they seek in three different dimensions. They must ask: What are the implications of these changes for development strategy? How will it affect the system of industrial decision-making? And how will it affect the balance between saving and investment in the economy as a whole? The complexity of these interrelated decisions makes reform of the state industrial sector an extremely difficult task.

2. Manipulation of the price system to ensure profitability to state industry is used as a substitute for a taxation system. All developing countries experience difficulty in building an adequate taxation system to support government services. By concentrating revenues in a relatively small number of state-run factories, command economies solve this problem. This is particularly evident in China, where the creation of this system during the 1950s rapidly terminated a prolonged period of government weakness and inability to shape economic conditions. Through the 1930s, Chinese central governments controlled a miniscule few percent of gross national product, reaching a maximum of perhaps 4%. Revenue of all levels of government, even by the most generous estimates, did not exceed 10% of GNP (Rawski 1989: 12–27). National disunity and conflict were both cause and effect of this weak central government. But after 1949, a central government apparatus was rapidly created that effectively united the country and operated reasonably efficiently with a high degree of centralization. Already by 1954, 30% of GNP was being channeled through the budgetary system.[1] There were several reasons for this striking turnabout, including the relative freedom from corruption of the new government, the willingness of the government to use unlimited coercive force against its domestic political opponents, and the help of the Soviet Union in quickly setting up administrative organizations and procedures. But the most important factor was the ease with which the new economic system could be implemented and used to concentrate resources in the hands of budgetary authorities.

As far back as the 1920s in the Soviet Union, Preobrazhenski (1965: 111) noted the ease of collecting revenues from the modern, state-run enterprise sector. Indeed, in China, in the 35 years from the founding of the PRC through 1985, exactly half of all budgetary revenues came from a few thousand large state-run factories (Industrial Census 1987). Many developing countries are effectively able to tax only a few modern enterprises and foreign trade, and in this sense the command economy model is merely a more extreme version of a typical developing country strategy. Indeed, the pre-

Communist government in China also derived taxes almost entirely from the large-scale urban sector, at that time privately owned (Rawski 1989: 30). The difference is that the post-1949 government used its control over the price system to concentrate much more revenue in the modern enterprise sector, so that a larger share of national income was available for taxation.

The implications for economic reform are enormous. Reformers must develop a new taxation system to replace that provided by state-run industry. But the administrative capability and human skills needed to do this are not present. So command economies in the course of reform face a problem of developing fiscal resources – a problem typical of developing economies, but one that they had previously avoided.

3. Because of the large mass of undifferentiated resources that had been flowing through the system, command economies developed overlapping and redundant control mechanisms to guard against corruption and appropriation of resources. The consistency of these mechanisms means that change of any one control mechanism, by itself, is likely to be ineffective. Financial decentralization – unaccompanied by reform of the material allocation system – will accomplish little. Similarly, providing profit incentives for managers will mean little if managerial career paths are still determined by Communist Party personnel departments (nomenklatura system) in which achievements are evaluated by a different yardstick. As a result, system change must simultaneously alter the control systems that affect materials, manpower, and money. Initial stages of changes will have only modest impact. Ultimately, however, changes in various areas may have a cumulative and self-reinforcing impact, and may result in rapid change in the behavior of the economy.

4. Ultimately, reformers are required to make decisions that will affect the distribution of total national income. The very large share of national income accruing directly to the government will be changed. It can be changed through widespread privatization, remanding ultimate control over income streams to households, or to intermediate institutions that are themselves owned by households (such as pension or mutual funds). This problem is the converse of the taxation problem. Just as a government tax system must be developed to substitute for state control of industrial enterprise revenues, so the remainder of the state surplus must ultimately be redefined into financial flows that are more firmly anchored in the ownership of productive resources. Eventually, this will require some kind of ownership reform.

5. Finally, just as the administrative and human resources necessary to operate a modern fiscal system are lacking, so are the human skills necessary to run a market economy in short supply. Command economies operated a kind of short-cut strategy of modernization, focusing most investment on physical assets, basic education and health, and some types of science and technology. As a result, skills in finance, auditing, and statistics – to say nothing of entrepreneurship – are woefully underdeveloped. Institutions for transmitting economic information are inadequate and hampered by secrecy requirements. The development strategy has economized on these re-sources, but this economization will no longer be feasible if market coordina-tion is to expand. New institutions and skills must be built, and this will inevitably be a protracted process.

These five implications of the command economy all represent serious obstacles to the process of economic reform. Different reform strategies should be interpreted as different approaches to resolving the problems presented by the interlocking features of the command economy. Reformers must not only change the economic system. They must also devise coherent development strategies and ensure a modicum of macroeconomic balance. The command economy provided a "cheap" version of all these things. The institutions were not of high quality, but they achieved the bare minimum necessary without an extensive use of resources. Mass production and rigid controls worked for a while. Transforming the economic system creates a need for more effective, higher quality institutions. It requires real resources to build up this higher quality set of institutions, and effective economic policymaking during the transition. The challenges are formidable.

The different approaches to economic reform described in the previous chapter can each be seen as a response to the overlapping nature of the command economy mechanisms and to the particular challenges of reform. Adherents of the big bang approach to reform essentially look at the interde-pendent and overlapping institutions of the command economy and argue that it is hopeless to think of gradual transitions. The system cannot be picked apart, and therefore must be smashed to bits. In their view, this will allow a new system to grow up as rapidly as possible. Adherents of rationaliz-ing reforms look at the same interdependent institutions and argue that they can be made to work through further perfection of instruments and use of indirect levers for steering decision-making. They do not attempt to disman-tle the system, nor do they tackle any of the fundamental issues about whose preferences run the system, or whether prices should be allowed to reflect anything other than planners' preferences and calculations. Adherents of the Chinese approach to economic reform look at the interdependent institu-tions and argue that moderate changes can touch off a far-reaching process of change precisely because so many features of the command economy are related to other features. Although the economic system is knit into a single fabric, removing a stitch may cause that fabric to unravel. In particular, the reliance of the system on the state's monopoly control over industry means that elimination of that link may initiate changes in all aspects of the economic system.

China in particular: The pre-reform economic system

China before 1978 was undeniably a command economy (Ward 1980). The discussion in the previous section applies to China as well as to the Soviet Union and the Eastern European countries during the pre-reform periods. But the Chinese system was not an identical twin of its Soviet relative and ancestor (Granick 1987). China differed in the pattern of resource and skill endowment it possessed on the eve of socialist development, and – partly because of this difference – in many of the specific forms of its economic system. The most important factor separating China from the Soviet and East European socialist systems was that China was much poorer. In the early 1950s, China was one of the poorest countries in the world, and even in the 1980s it ranked among the poorest third of countries. As a result, the structural transformation of the Chinese economy was much less advanced than in the ECEs, and the rural sector was much larger.

A little over two-thirds of the Chinese population is rural. As a result, the rural economy is correspondingly more important to the fate of reform, and the industrial economy less important. As we have seen, industry is the sector in which the overlapping controls of the command economy are most significant. The smaller relative size of industry might therefore mean that reformers have more flexibility to experiment with different approaches to reform before or during the difficult attempt to reform state-run industry. Moreover, the rural population in China has never had the same income guarantees that were implicitly extended to urban populations in both China and the ECEs. Indeed, in the former Soviet Union, development had proceeded far enough that even farmers were often given income guarantees, and worked for wages on state farms. This was never really the case in China. As a result of their somewhat more precarious economic position under the old system, Chinese rural dwellers may be less averse to the economic uncertainties implied by economic reform. In any case, the rural population came to be a more fertile soil for entrepreneurship and economic innovation than did the urban population.

At the same time, China still has a severe problem of underemployment. At a low level of development, China remains a "labor surplus" economy. In contrast to the ECEs, where demand for labor has long outrun the supply of labor at going wages, China faces a chronic problem of potential and real unemployment. This creates an opportunity for economic reform, but may also strengthen resistance to it. Workers in state firms in China may face a particularly sharp drop-off in their incomes if they quit or were laid-off, and this makes them cling to their state positions and resist reforms.

China's poverty was also manifest in much lower levels of output per worker in agriculture and industry than in Eastern Europe. More broadly, China's poverty meant that it was weakly endowed with the whole range of skills needed to operate any economic system, including the command economy. It is true that, by comparison with other less developed countries, China had a number of clear advantages, particularly its entrepreneurial traditions, relatively high levels of literacy, and familiarity with large-scale organizations. But compared with the other countries that were engaged in socialist planning in the 1950s, China was very weakly endowed. Communications and transportation infrastructure were underdeveloped, precious skills were spread thinly through the population, modern work habits were far from universal, quality of output was poor. China faced all the problems of an underdeveloped country, and the operation of its socialist system must be seen in that context. The Soviet Union certainly faced some of these problems during the 1920s, but it was far more richly endowed with agricultural land and other resources than was China.

The relatively low level of Chinese development was not merely a function of China's poor endowment at the starting point. As a result of the Cultural Revolution, the gradual accumulation of human and administrative skills was interrupted. Until the late 1960s, China followed the Soviet example in rapidly increasing the supply of certain kinds of basic skills necessary to the operation of an industrial economy, while simultaneously increasing the degree of administrative control of the economy. But this process was halted, and in some respects reversed, after the late 1960s. China's human and administrative resources – relative to the size of the economy – actually deteriorated during the 1970s.

One indicator of this process, shown in Figure 1.1, is the share of engineers and technicians in the industrial labor force. Through the mid-1960s, China rapidly increased its stock of technical personnel, and the number of technicians surpassed 4% of the industrial labor force. However, the paralysis of the education during the Cultural Revolution created a steady slide in this measure, which reached a low point of only 2.6% of the industrial labor force in 1976. Indeed, even with renewed attention to technical training during the reform era, it was not until 1987 that the level of technical manpower again reached the level of 1965. The Chinese use the same defini-

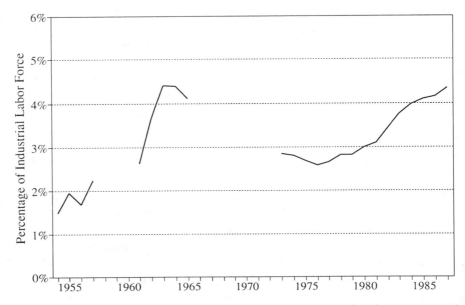

Figure 1.1. Engineers and technicians: share of state industry labor force. Source: *Labor* 1949–1985:39; *Labor* 1978–1987:49.

tion of technical personnel as do the Soviets, so comparison is straightforward. The definition of technicians in particular is quite broad, including graduates of technical middle schools. By contrast, in the Soviet Union, this ratio had already surpassed 8% in the 1950s, and 12% by the 1970s.

The fact that China was largely rural and low-skilled inevitably had an impact on its economic system. These factors must be considered in conjunction with the obvious fact that China is a very big country (the same size as the United States). Moreover, its geography is quite rugged, such that it tends to divide into separate economic regions to a greater extent than did the larger Soviet Union. Because of these factors, China's industrial structure was more heterogeneous than in the Soviet Union. In the Soviet Union, production was concentrated in a small and declining number of state-run factories, totaling just over 40,000 by 1979. Moreover, factories with over 1,000 workers accounted for 74% of Soviet industrial output and 75% of the industrial work force (Ferris 1984: 9). By contrast, in China where factories with over 500 workers accounted for a little over 40% of industrial output, there were many more small and medium-sized factories. China had 83,000 state-run factories in 1978, plus 100,000 urban collectives, and some 700,000 rural collective factories (Chapter 4). Both in

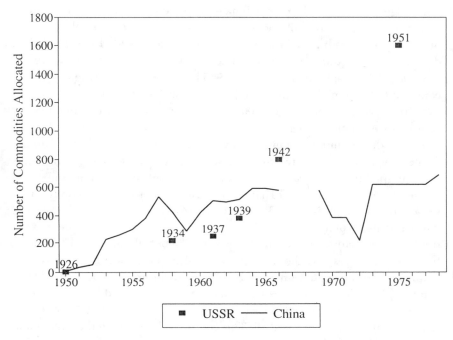

Figure 1.2. Materials allocated in China and the USSR. Source: CMEA 1982; Zaleski 1980:97–100; 287.

size and ownership, China's factories were far more diverse than those in the Soviet Union.

We would expect to find that large size and diversity, a high rural share, and relatively low skill levels would be correlated with relatively low degree of centralized administrative control, and this was indeed the case in China. One indicator of the level of administrative control exercised by the central government can be found in the number of commodities subject to central government allocation. This measure, by specifying the degree of fineness to which planners partition total output, can measure the degree of detail incorporated into material balance planning. Figure 1.2 shows the development of this indicator in China and the Soviet Union. In both, the number of commodities planned increased steadily during the early years of operation of a planned economy. Beginning in 1926 for the Soviet Union and 1950 for China, the number of commodities planned increased from 0 to about 600 in fifteen years. It increased more rapidly in China's early years than in the Soviet Union's, which is to be expected: China rapidly created a planned system on the basis of extensive Soviet advice and assistance. However, after 1965 in China – compared with 1941 in the Soviet Union – the experience of the two economies diverged completely. The number of commodities allocated in China stagnated after 1965. Indeed, it declined sharply during the immediate post-Cultural Revolution years before recovering approximately to the 1965 level. By contrast, the number of commodities planned in the Soviet Union continued to increase through the 1970s, when as many as 60,000 separate commodities were allocated by central government agencies.

The modest number of commodities subject to material balance planning shows that planning was relatively "coarse," in the sense that commodities were lumped into large categories. In addition, central government material balances were "incomplete." That is, authority over crucial commodities that the central authorities planned was divided between the central and local governments. Commodities such as coal, rolled steel, and cement were produced by factories under local government control, and the allocation of those commodities was the privilege of local governments. The division of authority became significant after 1970, and by the mid-1970s, over 50% of cement, 40% of coal, and 25% of finished steel was allocated by local governments. This large proportion of output simply did not enter into central government allocation plans at all. This contrasts sharply with the situation in the Soviet Union, where the central government maintained monopoly control over commodities that it plans. While the Soviet economy was highly centralized, the Chinese economy has long been partitioned into a large central portion and a substantial locally controlled portion.

Because the Chinese central material balance plan did not aspire to reconcile all supplies and uses of individual commodities, there was no particular requirement that those balances be precise. Users might be able to locate additional supplies from locally controlled resources, and so central planners could "leave gaps" in their allocations. Given the technical difficulties of reconciling a large number of sources and uses of individual commodities, and the weak Chinese information processing capacity, it is not surprising to discover that Chinese planners did precisely that. Although information is scarce, indications are that central planners frequently created plans with shortfalls of up to 25% of the commodities being allocated built into them. In China, material balances didn't balance. By contrast, while Soviet planning was often inaccurate, there is no indication that Soviet planners intentionally created supply plans with large shortfalls, at least after the 1930s.

The inaccuracy of planning at the central government level was paralleled by a reduced importance for output plans at the enterprise level. In the Soviet Union, enterprise output plans were generally "taut," in the sense that enterprises exerted substantial effort to fulfill their plans, and rarely exceeded those plans by more than 10%. In contrast, it appears that in most sectors of the Chinese industrial economy, enterprise plans were set at modest levels, and enterprises frequently exceeded their plans by large margins. There is little evidence that enterprises were under pressure to fulfill their plans (Granick 1987: 117–23).

Decentralization of the material balance planning system was paralleled by financial decentralization. Enterprises and local governments were left in control of substantial sums of so-called extrabudgetary funds, which were available for investment at the local level. Funded primarily by retained depreciation allowances, but also by profits of rural enterprises, these extrabudgetary funds accounted for fully 30% of total investment by the later 1970s (on the eve of the Chinese reform program). Financial and material decentralization reinforced each other, providing local governments with substantial leeway in making economic development decisions. Thus, the weakly centralized Chinese system permitted the de facto development of local government property rights. Local governments had not only a presumptive claim on the allocation of output of locally run factories, but also first claim on the profit stream generated locally. Local governments took an interest in local economic development, and had instruments available to shape it (Wong 1985).

Yet there were also severe limits to the amount of decentralization that occured in China. This was by no means an economy without central controls. In fact, central government was never prepared to allow local governments to operate in an independent manner before the reform era. The central government wished to maintain control over the general direction of local development, and it wished to maintain the basic parameters of the planned economy. As a result, precisely because of the weakness of traditional command economy mechanisms, the central government imposed crude blanket controls over the economy. These across-the-board controls were designed to substitute for the more precise direction of the economy promised by traditional instruments, and to keep the economy from veering outside the bounds designated in Beijing. Three kinds of central control were particularly important: ideologically exerted controls over development strategy, tight controls over labor mobility and remuneration, and central control over commerce and agricultural procurement.

Ideological guidelines required that localities replicate central government development priorities (development strategy) at the local level. Local governments were instructed to develop heavy industries, particularly those that produced inputs for modernization of agriculture. This meant a stress on developing the "five small rural industries" (cement, coal, hydropower, fertil-izer, and agricultural implements), all heavy producer-goods industries. De-velopment strategies that emphasized production of consumer goods with high markups were forbidden by strictures against "putting profit in com-mand." Moreover, the government maintained monopoly control over agri-cultural procurements: In a moderately developed economy like China's, most consumer goods required some agricultural raw materials, and local governments were not given control over those resources (Wong 1989). The central government wished to maintain its priority control over the distribu-tion of resources through the state monopoly over industry. It was willing to allow local governments to share in this control to a limited degree, but not to do anything that would fundamentally change the system.

In addition, China maintained very strict controls over labor and remu-neration. Migration to cities by rural individuals was forbidden. Only a modest intake of rural workers into the industrial economy was permitted through tightly restricted recruitment programs. This small flow into urban areas was more than overbalanced by the draconian program of rural rustica-tion. 17 million urban school-leavers were sent to the countryside to work. All were sent down for indefinite periods, perhaps permanently, and most in fact worked in the countryside for many years. Within the cities, labor mobility was virtually non-existent. For most state workers, a system of permanent employment evolved (only a group of casual workers, amounting to about 15 percent of total employment, was outside this system). Perma-nent employees not only stayed in a single enterprise for life; they could often pass their jobs on to their children when they retired. It was illegal in principle and impossible in practice for firms to fire workers, and quits were also almost unknown. During 1979, there were only 22,000 total quits and fires of state employees – 0.03% of the labor force. Death was seven times more important a cause of job-leaving than were quits and fires together (*Labor* 1990: 218). All workers were assigned to a specific job classification, and enterprises had no authority to reclassify workers. Chinese wages were essentially frozen after the beginning of the Cultural Revolution. Bonuses and piece rates were folded into base wages, and workers no longer received any material reward for superior performance. Promotions occurred only when the national government legislated a nationwide promotion quota, in the course of which individual enterprises were generally instructed what type of worker to promote. All this was in marked contrast to the situation in the Soviet Union, where 88% of industrial workers received some kind of piece-rates or bonuses. Moreover, Soviet workers frequently changed jobs and urban labor markets were well-developed. The fact of substantial labor mobility meant that workers in fact searched for more lucrative jobs, and factories were forced to respond to a modest extent to supply-and-demand conditions on the labor market. Labor markets existed in the Soviet Union, whereas they were abolished in China (Granick 1987; Pryor 1985: 241).

The draconian restrictions on labor and wages in China can be seen as a response to the general dilemma that faced Chinese planners. Their detailed control of the economy was much weaker than that of their Soviet counterparts. Yet they could not afford to lose control over employment and income. The Chinese lost control of the economy once before, during the Great Leap Forward: The migration of 30 million prime workers from agriculture to industry put unbearable stress on national food supplies and led to widespread famine. Unable to accurately manage gradual increases in the labor force and household incomes on the basis of individual enterprise needs, planners were forced to resort to crude blanket controls. These controls "succeeded" in preventing a reoccurrence of the Great Leap Forward catastrophe, but the cost in diminished incentives and misallocation of labor was tremendous.

The Chinese command economy traditionally operated with a strong centralized monopoly over commerce. Monopoly purchase of grain actually preceded agricultural collectivization in China (unlike the Soviet Union), and even during the Cultural Revolution when much of the industrial management system was being decentralized, central control of agricultural procurement and distribution of key consumer goods continued uninterrupted. Virtually all commercial personnel worked for units organized into the state Ministry of Commerce system. At the end of 1978, there were 5.2 million employees of the Ministry's urban commercial system, and only 173,000 workers in commerce who were not part of that system (Commerce 1984: 541–43). In rural areas, most commercial transactions were carried out by the Supply and Marketing Coops – nominally an organization of cooperatives but in fact a heavily bureaucratized organization that functioned as the rural wing of the Ministry of Commerce. Peasants were forbidden to bring produce into the city to sell, and all urban free markets had been closed since the beginning of the Cultural Revolution.

To be sure, not all petty entrepreneurship had been stamped out. There were still 30,000 rural periodic markets, and urban dwellers sometimes rode the bus out to suburban markets to purchase supplies unavailable in town. But even these rural markets were tightly controlled, and it was forbidden to transact goods such as grain and cotton, over which the Ministry of Commerce had a monopoly. In some places with strong entrepreneurial traditions – such as Wenzhou in Zhejiang – peasants smuggled vegetables into the city to sell furtively at black markets (Zhang Guisheng 1981). Small urban collective factories sometimes sold their output directly to the market, and state factories set up retail shops for the convenience of their own employees. But on balance, the state monopoly over commerce remained unshaken.

As might be expected, this extraordinarily tight monopoly was accompanied by extremely severe shortages. The shortages of basic consumer commodities in China at the end of the 1970s were much worse than those in any of the European command economies. Indeed, all the ECEs ended formal rationing during the 1950s, but rationing of basic commodities remained a daily fact of life for Chinese urban dwellers. The most important ration was that for staple grains, but a whole range of other commodities were subject to quantitative limits. Monthly ration coupons were required at least part of the year for cooking oil, tofu, coal, soap, meat, eggs, good quality cigarettes, and sugar, and ration coupons for cloth were distributed annually. For special purchases, such as a good quality bicycle or sewing machine, sesame oil or special Chinese New Year foods, households were required to wait for distribution of coupons from the work unit. Even when purchasing ordinary manufactured items, each household had to bring a passbook in which purchases were recorded to guard against speculative buying. According to one Guangdong source, the number of rationed retail commodities had reached a maximum of 77 in 1976 (Wang Qiren 1981). Certainly, in some of these cases, lower quality or more expensive versions of the goods could be freely purchased. But more than half of total outlays of the typical urban household were affected by some kind of quantity restraint. Even when supplies were available, shopping was extremely inconvenient. The commercial monopolists had organized retail sales into an ever smaller number of large outlets, and steadily reduced the number of small shops. By 1978, there was only one retail outlet per 914 residents, compared with 331 in 1957, and one retail sales worker per 214 residents, compared with 114 in 1957 (Commerce 1984: 539).

Evaluation of the economic system in China

Was it an advantage for China to have a weakly planned, relatively decentralized economic system? There are obvious advantages to decentralization, and these advantages might become more evident throughout the course of economic reform. But on the eve of economic reform, it appears that the Chinese economic system was performing *less* well because of its relative decentralization. There is substantial evidence suggesting that China's system was performing relatively poorly, even in the command economy context. This is not due to the decentralization in itself, but rather to the fact that decentralization was incomplete and poorly implemented. There were few clear principles that governed the distribution of authority between central and local governments (Riskin 1987).

Decentralization without clear principles for dividing authority led to chaotic authority relations. Throughout the 1970s, China continuously sought a workable set of principles for decentralization, with the result a restless shifting among different schemes for the division of authority, and chaotic and conflicting authority relations at the enterprise level. This story can be traced through any of the major management systems. Direct authority over even the largest enterprises was decentralized in 1970. Subsequently, local governments had direct control of personnel and managerial decisions in those enterprises. Simultaneously, control over material allocation was decentralized, and a new fiscal system introduced that gave local governments substantially greater control over financial resources (Wong 1986). A full description of this period is beyond the scope of our discussion. The crucial point is simply that no stable or effective system for dividing responsibility between governmental levels was ever developed.

The evolution of the material allocation system exemplifies this point. When enterprises were placed under local control, local governments were supposed to take responsibility for supply plans, but local governments did not have the administrative capability to do so for the largest enterprises. Of 2,600 very-large enterprises placed under local control after 1970, more than 2,000 continued to have their supplies planned by central government ministries. Unable to shift to a decentralized planning system on an enterprise by enterprise basis, China's planners attempted to decentralize on a commodity by commodity basis. They attempted to create a material balance planning system in which provinces were the fundamental planning unit, and central planning only accounted for net transfers of resources between provinces. Each province balanced sources and uses of the given commodity within its borders, and central planners would then manage a sort of "foreign trade" among provinces (Economics Delegation 1979). But planners were never able to successfully implement this system either. Region-based planning was tried with cement, coal (but only in 20 out of 29 provinces), and with several commodities simultaneously in four experimental provinces. By the late 1970s, authority over material allocation was fragmented in different ways in different provinces and for different commodities, and it was clear that the system was not working (People's University 1979: 230; CMEA 1983). A similar process of ceaseless change went on with the fiscal system. Lines of authority between the central and local governments were repeatedly redrawn during the 1970s (Oksenberg and Tong 1991). There was wide-

Table 1.4. *Control of Sichuan enterprises*

	Personnel (nomenklatura)	Production planning	Material allocation	Investment planning
Center	9	14	60	56
Province	49	44	5	9
Municipal	7	7	0	0

Source: SRC/ER 1990: 333.

spread agreement among Chinese planners and financial officials that none of these fiscal systems performed adequately.

At the enterprise level, this failed decentralization created a chaotic situation in which enterprises were subordinate to many different governmental bodies, with the lines of subordination differing acccording to the type of decision under review. Table 1.4 shows, as of the late 1970s, the subordination relations that evolved for 65 large enterprises that were decentralized to Sichuan province beginning in 1970. Typically, control over material supply and investment (capital construction) was exercised by a higher governmental body, while direct authority over personnel and management decisions (the nomenklatura) was exercised by a lower-level body. It is most striking, however, that not a single one of these enterprises was subordinate to the unified control of a single governmental level. Each enterprise had to contend with multiple authority figures who could, and did, issue conflicting commands to the enterprise. Such organizational confusion was not a characteristic of the economic system in the Soviet Union.[2] Consider the implications for the planning problem of having production and supply planning in different hands: It is impossible for the interlocking components of production and supply planning to be coordinated. Clearly there is no way to create consistency among sources and uses of commodities in this situation. The system has no other recourse but constant "muddling through."

The chaotic state of the administrative system was exacerbated by the chronic factionalism of the Cultural Revolution. Both in the enterprise and higher up the administrative hierarchy, opposing factions had contended for control since the late 1960s. In many cases, authority had seesawed between different groups, but because of China's permanent employment policy, winners and losers remained trapped together in a single administrative unit. Decision-making had become more and more difficult, and the system was close to paralysis. (For a vivid description, see Walder.) Matters were made even worse by the absence of a system of material rewards that could be used to motivate workers and managers to meet planners' goals. The Chinese administrative economy was in a state of progressive devolution in which even the tasks to which the command economy was best suited became difficult.

The relative inefficiency of the system can be measured in terms of the system's own goals. It is a commonplace that Soviet-type systems make relatively inefficient use of the goods that they produce. While such systems have respectable records in terms of the growth of total output, lack of response to market demands and clumsy coordination of industrial needs lead to uneconomical accumulation of stockpiles of goods and incomplete investment projects. Because statistical systems differ so greatly, it is hard to compare Soviet performance with that of market economies, but such comparisons, when attempted, invariably show that the Soviet Union operated with much greater levels of inventories and incomplete construction than do market economies (Campbell 1958; Kohn 1970). The similar statistical systems operated by China and the Soviet Union facilitate comparison between these two countries. When the comparison is made, it turns out that China in the late 1970s carried a much larger volume of inventories and incomplete construction than did the Soviet Union.

By the late 1970s, China was carrying huge quantities of inventories. Between 1976 and 1978, total inventories in the state-owned economy ranged between 95% and 98% of net material product (NMP).[3] Essentially, China had an entire year's worth of production piled up in warehouses. Figures on total inventories in the Soviet Union do not appear to be available, but it is possible to compare inventories in the industrial and material supply (industrial wholesaler) systems in the two countries. During the 1960s in the Soviet Union, inventories in these two systems ranged between 19.5% and 22% of gross industrial output value (Schroeder 1972). By contrast, in China in the relatively good years 1975 and 1978, the comparable figures were 41% and 39% (*Statistic* 1989: 26, 265). Chinese industrial inventories were almost twice the level of Soviet inventories.

A similar picture emerges when we examine incomplete construction. During the 1950s and 1960s, incomplete construction in the Soviet Union ranged between 15% and 20% of NMP. By contrast, during 1976–77, incomplete construction in China amounted to well over 30% of NMP. Moreover, this comparison is actually biased in favor of China, since it excludes incomplete construction associated with investment outside of capital construction, which was significant in China but trivial in the Soviet Union. Why was incomplete construction so large in China? Explanations can be found both in the economic system and in the development strategy followed by China.

Table 1.5. *Planned and actual output for 1975*

	Plan	Actual	Fulfillment[1]
	(million metric tons)		
Steel	35–40	24	−36%
Grain	300–325	285	−9%
Coal	400–430	482	+16%
Electricity	"surpass England"	–	−28%

[1]Fulfillment is difference between actual output and mid-range of plan targets.
Source: Li Zhining 1987: 417–18.

China's decentralized economic system had no mechanism for coordinating investment in different regimes. Local governments would begin investments to establish a claim over a new activity. Such projects could sometimes not be completed, due to shortages of supplies or uncertainties about jurisdiction. Even more important was the legacy of a failed investment strategy. During the late 1960s and early 1970s, China invested huge sums in remote regions of the interior in an attempt to develop industry in militarily secure areas. This program, called the "Third Front," purposely dispersed productive facilities into relatively inaccessible areas (Naughton 1988). The scale of construction was ambitious, and as the inevitable delays and cost overruns began to mount, China's leaders discovered they could not complete the program. In the mid-1970s, planners drastically cut the flow of investment resources to the Third Front regions, refocused investment strategy on coastal regions, and began a program of complete plant imports. By the late 1970s, *neither* of these ambitious investment programs had been completed. The Third Front projects languished in comparative neglect, while few of the newer coastal projects had yet been completed. China's investments were thus spread over an enormous number of projects. The limited resources available for each individual project inevitably meant that construction periods stretched out, and the stock of incomplete construction grew.

Thus, by 1977–78, China's planners were struggling with a system that was carrying massive amounts of underutilized resources. Their challenge was to come up with a strategy that would permit these resources to be utilized. In the sphere of investment, they had to draw up a program to either complete some of the many investment projects in a reasonable time period, or else recognize that they had little potential economic value, and cancel them, thus reducing the drain on other projects that did have potential value. To do the first, they would have to dramatically step up investment; to do the second, would require tremendous political will (Naughton 1991b). Chapter 2 describes the fashion in which planners tackled this problem.

Command economies may not serve consumers well, but they do reasonably well at providing military and heavy industrial output that planners want. But in the case of China in the 1970s, the command economy was not really delivering these goods either. For years, planners stressed "taking steel as the key link," and the entire planning exercise was organized around the desire to maximize steel output. Yet during the Fourth Five Year Plan (1971–75), steel production was more than 30% below the plan target (Table 1.5), growing only 6% annually compared with the planned 15%. Subsequently, steel output actually declined for two years, before beginning a spectacular recovery in 1978. The other priority item in planners' efforts was grain: Actual output in 1975 was about 10% below the planned figure.

Even products that exceeded their plan targets reveal a more complex story upon closer inspection. Coal output was more than 15% over the target, but this reflected two factors. A low growth rate had been planned for coal as part of the expected conversion of the economy to a greater reliance on petroleum. And much of the increase came from small-scale local mines that filled the gap when the conversion could not be made at the pace projected by planners (Li Zhining 1987: 417; *Coal*). It is striking that the products that had the highest priority in the eyes of planners were the items for which plans were underfulfilled by the largest margins. This is very much counter to our ordinary understanding of Soviet-type economies. Planners gave commands to the system, but what actually emerged bore little resemblance to those commands.

The inability to get the economy to respond to planners' directions was matched by a profound instability in the economy. Some of this instability can be attributed to political conflicts surrounding the death of Mao. But purely economic factors were of great importance. Planners repeatedly put the brakes on the economy because the growth of investment and industrial production threatened to outrun the capacity of the agricultural and mining sectors to support that growth. The economy was locked into persistent stop-and-go cycles. Annual fluctuations in investment growth were much greater in China than in the USSR (Naughton 1991b).

Performance and prospects of the Chinese economy

The previous section showed that the Chinese economic system had some serious operational problems. What can be said about the ultimate growth performance of the Chinese economy, and its prospects for future growth as of the late 1970s? Over the long term, Chinese growth was respectable. Between 1952 and 1978, net material product grew at a 6% annual rate, which, with population growth at 2% annually, yields an annual growth per capita of 4%. Industrial output growth was particularly robust: Between 1957 and 1978, Chinese official figures show real industrial output growing at the rate of 9.7% annually. Inadequate statistical practices inflate these figures somewhat, but there is no doubt that industrial growth was rapid. Life expectancy–the most comprehensive indicator of population well-being–grew steadily, reaching 65 years by 1978. Thus, the Chinese system was able to deliver the basic goods: increased output and better living standards. It was certainly not an abject failure (Naughton 1991a).

Yet a further look at this performance reveals numerous paradoxes. In particular, a central characteristic of the Chinese development experience between the late 1950s and the late 1970s was a relatively slow growth of living standards. Slow improvement in living standards attests to the severity of the choice of development strategy, which stressed expansion of industrial and military capacity above all else. But the contrast between vigorous output growth and slow improvement in living standards is so large that it also testifies to the magnitude of the waste described in the previous sections. Equally important was the relatively slow growth of agricultural output. In a careful study of China's agricultural development, Lardy (1983) demonstrated the slow growth of agricultural output in per capita terms and the attendant stagnation in agricultural incomes. Lardy also clearly explains the reason for this poor performance, giving particular stress to misguided policies that stressed grain production in all areas; regional self-sufficiency policies; and inefficient planning based on quantity and acreage targets to the neglect of price policy. Table 1.6 shows the trends in per capita production of four key agricultural commodities. After more than a decade of stressing grain production, grain output per capita increased only 5% from the 1950s, although it was up 16% from the period following recovery from the worst of the Great Leap Forward disaster. Cotton production declined and oilseed production plummeted, although this was partially offset by an increase in meat supplies. The last column in Table 1.6 shows that Chinese agriculture turned out to be capable of much higher productivity. After reforms, output of all four commodities surged.

In an economy as poor as China's, slow growth of agricultural output inevitably implies slow growth of living standards. The bulk of the population lives in the countryside and earns its livelihood through agriculture; food has a large weight in the consumption basket of all residents at low income levels; and agricultural raw materials are required for a large propor-

Table 1.6. *Per capita production of agricultural products*

	1955–57	1964–66	1977–79	1983–85
	(kilograms per capita)			
Grain	303	274	318	376
Edible oil	7.5	4.9[1]	5.4	12.3
Meat	6.2[2]	7.6[3]	9.3	15.1
Cotton	2.4	2.8	2.2	4.8

[1]1964–65 only
[2]1957 only
[3]1965 only
Source: Statistic 1989: 198–99, 213.

tion of non-food consumption goods, particularly clothing. The slow growth in availability of consumption goods was made even more conspicuous by the persistance of rationing described earlier. Moreover, there is abundant evidence that China's leaders were deeply concerned about the mediocre performance of agriculture in the late 1970s. The desire to strengthen an enfeebled agricultural sector shaped the course of early reform efforts. Thus, slow growth of agriculture ranks with deterioration of the industrial planning system as a major chronic problem that faced Chinese leaders at the end of the 1970s.

How do we assess this growth performance and the potential for the future? On the one hand, the Chinese economy appears to have strong growth potential regardless of system. Even before reforms, China's economy was growing at respectable rates. More generally, China should be seen as an economy with a relatively high human capital endowment (for a developing country) combined with very low wage rates (even for a developing country). Life expectancies and educational levels in China's cities and advanced coastal provinces are not far below those of the ECEs, while living standards are far below those countries. This reflects the success of socialist policies, particularly in the countryside, but also the inefficiency of socialist production:

It is often said that modern China's levels of health and literacy are unusually high for its level of national income, yet the inescapable converse of this observation is that China's level of national income is unusually low for its given level of "human resources" (Eberstadt 1986: 291).

Moreover, China's age structure is relatively favorable for rapid growth. With a young population, particularly a young labor force, but with relatively few dependent minors, the economy has an unusually high proportion of productive and adaptable workers. The young population provides abundant labor power necessary to fuel economic development, and probably makes the country more responsive to reform-induced changes. Thus, unlike the situation in the European socialist countries, it appears reasonable to think of China as having strong economic growth fundamentals, and being poised to achieve acceleration.

Moreover, China is adjacent to the East Asian economic region, the fastest growing economic region in the world. Technology transfer can be rapid, and international markets are expanding quickly. Theory and practical experience tell us that the combination of a skilled labor force, low wages, and proximity to large and growing markets should lead to rapid growth. The potential of international trade in the reform process was enhanced by the fact that China traded primarily with market economies even before reform. Although China's exposure to foreign trade was very low in 1978, 86% of that trade was conducted with predominantly market economies, and only 14% with other planned economies. Even before reform, Hong Kong played a major role as a middleman in facilitating China's exports to market economies, taking more than a quarter of total exports (*Foreign Trade* 1984: IV–11). This trade orientation – which dates back to the Sino-Soviet split of the early 1960s – provided China with some opportunities to learn about world markets. Many of these early exports to market economies were light manufactures, particularly textiles and food products, precisely the commodities in which China had long-run comparative advantage. Learning about world markets was concentrated in the most important sectors. The experience of cooperation with Hong Kong capitalists also paved the way for the expanded role that they played in the Chinese economy during the 1980s, once direct foreign investment was allowed. In this respect, too, China appears, in retrospect, poised for rapid growth.

Conclusion

At the close of the Cultural Revolution era, the Chinese economy faced enormous chronic problems. In addition to the problem of slow growth of agriculture and living standards, equally significant chronic problems existed in industrial development strategy and industrial management. By 1977, Chinese planners confronted an economy that was not under their control and did not produce the products they wanted. Only a handful of their priority investment projects were near completion, and they had consistently failed to achieve their priority output targets. Unwanted goods and incomplete investment projects were accumulating. Planners lurched from crisis to crisis, and they had little prospect of getting the decentralized system that had been envisioned through most of the 1970s up and working. That the economy managed to work at all, muddling through and growing steadily, may seem miraculous, until it is recalled that the Chinese still had in place the most fundamental tool of the command economy, a redistributive mechanism that steadily pumped resources into new investment. Investment continually augmented the capital stock and caused total output to grow. But planners no longer had control over this process. The system needed overhauling.

At the same time, many of the fundamentals for economic growth were in place. The population was relatively healthy and well-educated, and a huge amount of productive capital had been created over the previous thirty years. Even the dysfunctional decentralization of the economy might be converted into an advantage if some reasonable principles of division of authority could be developed. The leaders felt, almost instinctually, that the economy was capable of greatly accelerated growth in spite of its short-run problems. Thus, as China emerged from the Cultural Revolution, the leaders were anxious to remake the economy into a system that functioned successfully. Their first response was not to engage in economic reform, but rather to rebuild the planned economy. Rebuilding the planned economy seemed initially to be quite compatible with a range of "reforms" designed to improve administration. It would take further economic crisis before the concept of reform would be reformulated to encompass a serious transition to a qualitatively different economic system.

Phase one

The bird in the cage, 1979–1983

2

Crisis and response: Initial reorientation of the economy

By the late 1970s, Chinese leaders had been grappling with chronic economic problems for many years. Yet the decision to initiate a program of economic reform came remarkably suddenly. Within the span of a single year – between July 1978 and July 1979 – nearly every aspect of Chinese economic policy was recast. Major shifts in development strategy were accompanied by institutional changes that were quickly and vigorously implemented. Why did China move so rapidly to reverse its previous policy direction and move toward fundamental reform? The search for origins has an intrinsic interest, but it takes on additional significance in the Chinese case. Because reforms were begun without a clear reform objective, the initial measures determined the trajectory of reform and shaped the entire reform process. The origins of reform are thus inseparable from the story of how reforms managed to take hold and ultimately succeed.

In this chapter I argue that the driving force behind change in 1978–79 was a reorientation of Chinese development strategy. When one examines the entire spectrum of economic policies adopted between 1979 and 1981, one is struck above all by the vigor and consistency of the policies to reorient economic development strategy, rather than with the profundity of institutional reforms. The initial commitment to reform was, in a sense, a side-effect of that reorientation and can only be fully understood in that context. Initial reforms were tentative and exploratory, but they took root and persisted, and this was largely the result of reorientation. The policy of reorientation itself grew out of a special set of circumstances. After the death of Mao in 1976, Chinese leaders were finally free to deal with the chronic problems created by the Cultural Revolution. They did pretty much what one might expect – they returned to the familiar and set about rebuilding the centralized planned economy. But their attempt to rehabilitate the planned economy failed. Out of that failure, came an acute short-run crisis of development policy, and this crisis in turn led to a reorientation of economic policy of much greater long-run significance.

After China's leaders were compelled to abandon the attempt to re-centralize the economy, the logic of economic circumstances drove them into a particularly thorough recasting of development strategy. Reorientation of the economy involved a dramatic reduction in industrial investment and a shift of resources toward the household sector. It included significant efforts to restructure the capital stock and to reintegrate human resources into the economy. This shift of economic development strategy was remarkably broad-based. While it was implemented most dramatically during 1979–81, it continued to determine the basic parameters of economic policy through 1984. As such, the policy of reorientation determined the basic conditions under which other policies unfolded, including economic reform in the state sector (described in Chapter 3) and liberalization of the rural economy (Chapter 4). Because change began on such a broad front, changes in different areas reinforced and supported each other. The rigorously implemented reorientation of the economy in 1979–82 created a more relaxed, "slack" environment that sharply lowered the cost of pursuing reform. As a result, essentially ameliorative and exploratory reforms survived long enough to show economic results. The contrast is particularly sharp with the Soviet Union: Gorbachev's reforms were begun as part of an attempt to accelerate economic growth after years of stagnation. While Soviet reforms began as part of an effort to do more, Chinese reforms began following a recognition that planners had to do less. This initial difference helps to explain the sharp contrast between initial Chinese success and initial Soviet failure in economic reform. The reorientation contributed a favorable environment to the development of reform. At the same time, reorientation of development strategy strengthened China's growth prospects, and encouraged a continuing interventionist role for the government during the rest of the reform era. Economic reorientation is essential to an understanding of the origins of China's reform era.

Why did China initiate a program of economic reform?

The origin of Chinese economic reform presents something of a puzzle. Despite its deep-seated problems, the economy had clearly not exhausted its growth potential under the old system. From the perspective of the Eastern European economies, the shift to reform in China seemed "premature." Hewett (1985) points out that demand for reform in command economies typically becomes widespread only after a certain stage of economic develop-

ment is reached. In the early stages of "extensive development," high investment and forced draft industrialization succeed in creating growth through
rapid structural change, and this is simply too attractive to Communist planners for them to contemplate serious reform. Hare (1988: 58) attempts to
resolve the issue:

Why [should] China embark on major reforms at its present stage of development[?] . . . The economy as a whole has grown very rapidly since 1950, with
industry doing especially well . . . Moreover, China is so poorly integrated into the
world economy and so self-sufficient in essential materials, that the arguments for
reform based on foreign trade efficiency . . . carried very little weight. But China's
traditional central planning system had failed to achieve any significant advance in
popular living standards since the early 1950s, and it is this glaring failure which the
present reforms are seeking to rectify.

Certainly this contains a grain of truth: Leaders turned to reform in part
because they were seeking to deliver more of the rewards of economic
growth to the Chinese people in order to solidify their political position.

But there were many ways to increase living standards besides radical
reforms. Soviet leaders engineered a significant increase in living standards
after the mid-1960s without fundamentally altering their economic system.
Many policies – reorganization, better planning, import of technology, better incentives – might be expected to address chronic problems in the economy. We are left unable to explain why such a drastic shift to fundamental
reforms occurred so suddenly. For example, slow growth of living standards
can be traced primarily to sluggish growth of agricultural output. But many
of the most obvious causes of agricultural retardation could be addressed
within the framework of the traditional system. By abandoning regional grain
self-sufficiency policies, raising agricultural prices, and giving greater flexibility and autonomy to agricultural collectives, China's leaders could have expected to see a significant rebound in agricultural production (Lardy 1983).
Indeed, as a result of decisions made in the early 1970s, China's production
of chemical fertilizer was already poised to increase rapidly (it more than
doubled between 1976 and 1980), and this increase would produce a significant increment to grain output. This is just one example of the difficulty of
explanations based on chronic economic problems.

The most common alternative is to stress political factors. As Harding
(1987: 39) argues:

What distinguished the political situation from the economic arena, however, was the
immediate acute crisis in politics resulting directly from the trauma of the Cultural
Revolution . . . The objective problems at the time of Mao's death still do not explain
the extent of the reforms that have occurred under Deng Xiaoping. Indeed, Mao's
immediate successor, Hua Guofeng, seemed convinced that fairly modest changes

would be sufficient to restore political normalcy and economic vitality. The immediate cause of reform was the existence of a reform faction within the Chinese Communist Party, its successful struggle to gain supremacy over more conservative rivals, and its skillful strategy for launching and sustaining a bold program of political and economic renewal.

Of course, this is also the official Chinese version, in which the triumph of Deng Xiaoping, with his determination to "seek truth from facts," initiated the entire reform process.

There is a sense in which this is true. Clearly, if Mao Zedong or some other highly ideological leader had remained in control, there could not have been serious market-oriented reforms. In that sense, the coming to power of leaders with a significant amount of pragmatism is a necessary precondition for meaningful reform. But this fails to explain both why these particular reformers – wielders of awesome power in an authoritarian political system – chose to follow a fairly profound model of reform, and why they were able to assemble a pro-reform consensus at the top of that system. In practice, two individuals among the top leadership dominated the initial process of reform and adoption of new economic policies: Deng Xiaoping and Chen Yun. The assertion that Deng Xiaoping was always a proponent of economic reform, waiting for a chance to push his agenda, simply does not fit the available facts very well. When Deng was in power up through 1978, he was part of a broad consensus in support of rapid heavy industrial development (Bachman 1985: 60; Halpern 1985: 390–92; Naughton 1994). As for Chen Yun, subsequent events showed that his conception of reform was extremely narrow – much narrower than the path China actually trod. The evidence is overwhelming that at the end of 1978, Deng and a number of others in the top leadership began to support economic reorientation and reform, even though for many this involved abandoning earlier policy positions. As one political scientist has commented: "Conservatives and reformers acted as one at the Third Plenum to thwart Hua and his economic policy" (Crane 1990: 28). The real challenge for a political analysis is to explain why a large majority of China's veteran revolutionaries moved to transform a system of which they were the traditional beneficiaries. One part of that answer may be that Deng Xiaoping and his allies were able to present themselves as the "new" post-Cultural Revolution leadership, and they were eager to improve living standards rapidly in order to enhance their popular legitimacy. But that is only part of the story.[1]

International factors certainly eased China's approach to reform, and some argue that they were decisive (Cumings 1989). In the late 1970s, China was engaged in bitter strategic rivalry with the Soviet Union that led it into a de facto alliance with the United States and its allies, and events during 1977–78 pushed China closer to the United States just before the shift in Chinese economic strategy.[2] Strategic shifts were accompanied by economic cooperation, including import of U.S. technology and possible U.S. participation in developing Chinese mineral resources, especially petroleum. Indeed, the desire to import advanced technology from the outside world had long motivated China's leaders, and the desire to increase foreign-exchange earning capacity led to early attempts at reform in the export sector even before the beginning of the reform era (Li Zhining 1987: 615). Finally, recognition of the dynamism of Asian capitalism – particularly the rapid growth of the "little Chinese" economies of Taiwan, Hong Kong, and Singapore – combined with awareness of the technological changes that had been transforming world capitalism. Deng Xiaoping pointed out in March 1978:

Profound changes have taken places and new leaps have been made in almost all areas. A whole range of new sciences and technologies is continuously emerging . . . we have lost a lot of time as a result of the sabotage by Lin Biao and the Gang of Four . . . Backwardness must be recognized before it can be changed. (Deng Xiaoping 1984: 103, 106.)

International factors made the capitalist economies more attractive models, and it helped the course of reform that problems with the command economy could be blamed on having copied the Soviet Union, now seen as a dangerous adversary.

But it is important not to make too much of these factors. A turn toward the capitalist world was entirely feasible within the framework of a centrally planned economy. Indeed, nothing could have been more ordinary at this time. Through the 1970s, the Eastern European countries – and even the Soviet Union – turned to the capitalist world to import new technologies and equipment, frequently tapping world credit supplies and incurring deep debt. China was simply following the path that had already been trodden by Poland, Romania and Hungary. For these countries, import of Western technology was an *alternative*, not an inducement, to economic reform. Indeed, China's leaders probably thought that their opposition to the Soviet Union would give them even more liberal access to technology and aid from the capitalist powers, without requiring them to relinquish any of their control over the domestic economy. Many see the import of Western technology as the first stage of the reform process; actually, it was not until the Chinese recognized that Western technology was not an economic panacea that they could accept the need for radical reform.

Thus, neither chronic economic nor acute political factors can explain the initiation of reform, nor does it make sense to see some fraction of China's veteran leaders as being innately reformist. Instead, initial Chinese attempts to overcome the chronic economic problems left by the Cultural Revolution were quite conventional and firmly bounded by traditional socialist ideology. But in the course of cobbling together a program of economic recovery, planners stumbled into an economic crisis of their own creation. This man-made crisis put Chinese policymakers in some serious dilemmas, and they opted for vigorous reorientation of development policy and modest experimentation with reform as a way out of those dilemmas (see Solinger 1991: esp. pp. 11, 26–30, 80–82). China's leaders responded effectively to the challenges before them, but they should be seen as reacting to a set of problems that constantly threatened to slip out of their control.

In coalition with a group of veteran Communist Party leaders, Deng steered the elite into a reform process, and was able to assemble an effective consensus. For better and for worse, this created the conditions for radical economic reforms within the context of political continuity, and avoided the possible alternatives of dissolution or chaos. Subsequent economic reforms unfolded under constraints imposed by this aging oligarchy. They revealed themselves to be highly averse to both inflation and urban unemployment, and they therefore constrained the reform process to a gradual and exploratory path. Why they accepted the necessity of a reform path at all is the subject of the following sections.

Recovering from the Cultural Revolution: The twin strands of policy

The death of Mao in 1976 finally brought to an end a ten-year period of political conflict and administrative deterioration. The economic system was in a shambles – everything needed to be done. Yet paradoxically it was not in crisis, because there was every reason to believe that a little bit of repair work would fix up the economic system and permit a rapid acceleration of growth. The initial Chinese response to the degraded state of their economic system was to emphasize the rehabilitation of the command economic system. They began to rebuild the institutions that had deteriorated during the Cultural Revolution, and these measures on balance tended to increase the degree of centralization in the economy. Through 1977 and 1978, China's economic system became more like that of the Soviet Union. Planners progressively liquidated many of the unique features of the Maoist approach to economics, a process that sometimes required frontal assaults on the ideological legacy of Maoism. But none of the changes implemented were in any sense outside the realm of normal Soviet practice. Central planning organs were strengthened. Material incentives were revived. The institutions of the Chinese economy converged toward the Soviet model.

Careful rehabilitation competed with another response to the frustrated development plans of the Cultural Revolution era: the desire to dramatically accelerate economic growth. As recovery began, impatience with moderate growth rates grew. One approach to acceleration was to expand reliance on a traditional Maoist policy: mobilization of massive amounts of labor power. But as the central planning organs were reestablished, the drive for acceleration increasingly focused on a plan for construction of huge investment projects in heavy industry, typically based on imported Western and Japanese technology. Maoist mobilization and investment in heavy industry megaprojects coexisted in a peculiar mixture, the common theme of which was a desire to accelerate growth. As China prepared to throw ever larger amounts of labor and capital into the struggle for production growth, the atmosphere increasingly came to resemble a new version of the Great Leap Forward.

Between Mao's death in 1976 and the end of 1978, the twin impulses of rehabilitation and accelerated growth interacted to create an increasingly unrealistic and unsustainable set of policies. It was more difficult for the Chinese to overcome the legacy of institutional deterioration than it initially appeared. Reestablishing control over the economy was not simply a matter of creating new institutions. It required as well the rebuilding of administrative capabilities, information networks, and human skills, and the ability to draft details and coherent plans for the future. But the drive for acceleration overtook these difficult, long-term processes. The result was the overambitious and infeasible Ten Year Plan adopted during 1978. When those policies collapsed dramatically at the end of 1978, the field was clear for the introduction of a dramatic set of economic reform proposals.

Rebuilding and recentralization

During 1977–78, the Chinese labored to reconstruct the sturdy and generally familiar mechanism of the generic Soviet-style centrally planned economic system. Planners began to rebuild the crude material allocation system inherited from the Maoist era. Rehabilitating the system involved rebuilding each of the three interlocking elements of material balance planning: increased material allocation, more detailed enterprise production plans, and material use coefficients linking supplies to output. Planners abandoned region-based planning. More than 1,000 of the largest enterprises were returned to central control in 1978 and incorporated in central supply plans (He Jianzhang 1979). The national Material Supply Bureau was reestablished and the number of commodities allocated by the central government increased steadily. Commodities allocated by the planning organs (as opposed to production ministries) jumped from 52 in 1977 to 210 in the plan for 1979 (CMEA: 61–3; 74). Enterprises were drawn more tightly into the planning system. Material usage coefficients, which had fallen into disuse during the Cultural Revolution, were revived, beginning with fuel and power. Planners drew up new norms for stockpiles, and attempted to enforce them on enterprises. New controls were imposed on the interregional barter trade that had grown up during the Cultural Revolution (CMEA: 65–6, 70). In a curious ideological twist, Cultural Revolution leftists were condemned for undermining state plans by ignoring price controls, and encouraging enterprises to develop and market output independently (Commentator 1977: 9; Tong Zhimin 1979). These charges, otherwise incomprehensible, show that planners were attempting to reverse the de facto decentralization of the Cultural Revolution. Repeated directives were issued stressing that state fixed prices had to be followed. National work conferences were convened in succession to rectify agriculture, railroads, and industry, and new regulations were issued for industrial enterprise management (Li Chengrui and Zhang Zhuoyuan 1982: 16–17).

Financial controls were strengthened: Enterprise bank accounts were frozen, audited, and gradually unfrozen. Bank supervision of cash accounts was strengthened and lending procedures tightened (Xu Yi and Chen Baosen 1982: 11; Li Zhining: 440–41). The power to remit or reduce enterprise taxes, which had been given to local governments during the Cultural Revolution, was reclaimed by the central government (Wang Chengyao 1983: 69–70; Qiao Rongzhang 1988: 46). Financial recentralization occurred when enterprises were required to hand over half of their depreciation allowances to the budgetary authorities. Firms had been retaining these locally since 1971, and they had funded investment equal to 4% of GNP, an unusual decentralization measure for a command economy (Naughton 1987a). These measures greatly strengthened the state budget and increased the volume of resources under the direct control of central planners. Aided as well by the reviving economy, budgetary revenues in 1978 reached their highest level ever as a share of national income.[3] By the end of 1978, on the eve of reform, the Chinese economy was more centralized than it had been for over a decade. But, as we shall see, the centralized control apparently achieved was in fact extremely fragile.

Acceleration and the Ten Year Plan

By late 1977, pressures to accelerate economic growth were building. It was obvious that agriculture was the bottleneck holding back the economy. The response was to revive Maoist mass mobilization of labor and an old plan to "basically realize agricultural mechanization by 1980."[4] Armies of peasant labor were set to work building irrigation networks and factory farms: The target was to increase the proportion of sown area mechanically plowed to 70% from the 41% prevailing in 1978. Huge rallies were staged to whip up enthusiasm for work: 3.5 million peasants were summoned to one mass meeting in Xi'an. Nationwide, by November 1977, one-fourth of the rural labor force, 80 million peasants, was at work on rural construction projects. The slogan of the day was "mobilize the entire party, resolutely struggle for three years, basically complete agricultural mechanization," the title of a major address by head planner Yu Qiuli in January 1978 (Li Ping'an: 416, 420, 426; Li Zhining: 440, 442; Chung 1993: 270–76).

Agricultural mechanization required the rapid development of heavy industry, particularly the steel industry. As the economy revived during 1977, planners' aspirations began to focus on a still more grandiose program of industrial development, the Ten Year Plan for Economic Development 1976–85. Originally drawn up in 1975, when Deng Xiaoping was last running the economy, the plan had been put aside during the political chaos of 1976. The Ten Year Plan emphasized the priority to heavy industry that had guided Chinese development since 1949. It was explicitly centered on 120 mega-projects in industry and transport, including 10 integrated steel mills, 30 electric power plants, 10 petrochemical plants, 10 synthetic fiber plants, 10–20 fertilizer plants, and even 10 new oil fields (Li Chengrui and Zhang Zhuoyuan 1982: 17; Fang Weizhong 1984: 590). The Ten Year Plan was as close as China ever came, after the 1950s, to explicitly following Stalinist development priorities, with their stress on gigantic enterprises as well as heavy industrial construction. In late 1977, planners began to raise output targets above the already ambitious goals in the original plan draft. The Ministry of Coal proposed raising the 1985 coal target 20% to 880 MMT, and then raised it again to 900 MMT. In response, the Ministry of Metallurgy pushed the steel target up 10% to 60 MMT, and suggested an additional "struggle target" of 70 MMT. Plans for synthetic fiber production were increased by two-thirds (CCPW 1987: 384–85; Li Zhining 1987: 441). Table 2.1 shows the main output targets for 1985, and the implied growth rates. Overall, industry was slated to grow at about 10% per annum, a return to historically high industrial growth rates that was not completely unreasonable. The

Table 2.1. *Planned and actual output for 1985*

	1980 output	Ten-year plan target	Sixth FYP target	1985 output
	(million metric tons, billion KwH, annualized growth rate)			
Steel	37	60	39	47
		(10.2%)	(1.1%)	(4.9%)
Coal	620	900	700	872
		(7.7%)	(2.5%)	(7.1%)
Oil	106	250	100	125
		(18.7%)	(−1.2%)	(3.4%)
Electricity	301	500	362	411
		(10.7%)	(3.8%)	(6.4%)
Grain	321	400	360	379
		(4.5%)	(2.3%)	(3.4%)

Sources: Fang Weizhong 1984: 591; Sixth Plan 1984; *Statistic* 1989: 198; 298–99.

unrealistic features of the plan were rather some of the individual output targets and the large number of huge new investment projects.

The Ten Year Plan focused overwhelmingly not just on heavy industry, but specifically on energy, materials, and transport. Of particular significance was the projected development of chemical-based industries designed to substitute for scarce agricultural land. Massive development of fertilizer production would increase output from existing land, while large-scale chemical fibre production would substitute for natural fibres, freeing up land for more food production. Synthetic materials – including plastics, artificial leather, and synthetic rubber – would play a major role in the future development of industrial and consumer goods. In a sense, this was a heavy industrialization strategy that was designed to break the agricultural bottleneck. Complementing and going beyond the agricultural mechanization strategy, it would free industry from its dependence on agricultural products. But in order to do this, the Chinese industrial structure, already dominated by heavy industry, would have to become even more energy intensive.

The Plan centered on the import of complete industrial plants. The version of the Plan approved in early 1978 called for the import of 22 mega-plants, costing $12.4 billion (China's total exports in 1978 earned $9.75 billion). Of the import contracts actually signed during 1978–79, 95% were for energy, materials (including synthetic fibers), and military industries. It is striking that China was opening to the outside world, but was importing virtually nothing related to electronics, telecommunications, precision machine-building, transportation machinery, or agriculture (Chen Huiqin 1981). This was a program to improve the technology of existing heavy industry rather than to introduce new high-tech sectors.

Petroleum was the key to the entire plan. Petroleum was to be the crucial incremental earner of foreign exchange to pay for imported plants. The Ten Year Plan called for exports of petroleum to double by 1985 (from 13.5 to 30 MMT), providing several billion dollars in annual foreign exchange revenues. Moreover, many of the new plants were designed to utilize petroleum either as primary energy or as feedstock. Planners calculated that the 22 imported mega-plants alone would require more than 5% of China's total energy consumption in 1978. Thus, petroleum was required both to pay for the plant imports and to supply the shift in the industrial structure toward a more energy-intensive profile with a large chemicals sector. China's petroleum sector had been one of the few success stories of the Cultural Revolution era: Output had grown by 20% annually between 1969 and 1977, and planners were projecting that rapid increases would continue. Moreover, the key technocrats drawing up the plan (most notably Yu Qiuli, the head of the Planning Commission) had come directly out of the petroleum sector. In projecting that petroleum output would reach 250 MMT (5 million barrels per day) by 1985, planners were stating that China would approach Saudi Arabia's position as the world's third largest petroleum producer (behind the Soviet Union and USA). Though ambitious, such plans could not be automatically dismissed. The Chinese were attempting to repeat what the Soviet Union had accomplished betweeen 1957 and 1965. The question was whether they possessed the same vast reserves that the Soviet Union enjoyed.

The Ten Year Plan, then, was an ambitious development program that reflected an internally consistent strategy for breaking through the constraints holding back rapid growth. It relied on the massive increase of inputs into industrial production in order to break or circumvent bottlenecks in agriculture, industry, and transport. It reflects remarkable optimism about China's growth potential, optimism that is hardly compatible with a strong desire to transform the economic system. But the plan was implicitly based on a number of faulty assumptions about the nature of the Chinese economy. It was assumed that China was rich in oil, and that China's planning apparatus could administer a massive program of industrial plant import and construction. More fundamentally, it was assumed that agricultural output was basically given; that agriculture was basically constrained by limited land endowment, and that only massive new industrialization could ease this constraint. As a result, incentives and organization were irrelevant in agriculture – there was no point in trying to get more farm goods by improving incentives, and conversely there was no danger in continuing to squeeze farm incomes for several more years. Finally, and perhaps most unrealistically, it was assumed that jobs could always be found for China's massive population, even if agricultural mechanization made millions of rural dwellers economically redundant. Everything was being gambled on a program of economic acceleration. As it turned out, virtually all of the assumptions on which that program was based were wrong.

The bubble bursts

In retrospect it is not surprising that the assumptions on which the Ten Year Plan was based were flawed. As it turned out, the Ten Year Plan was built on sand. The actual preparatory effort underlying the ambitious targets and investment projects was shabby or nonexistent. Planners had not prepared feasibility studies or determined the total costs of projects; they had not verified reserves to cope with contingencies. The Ten Year Plan was a wish list, rather than an economic development program. Because each component of the plan was arbitrary, there was no mechanism to prevent individuals or organizations from taking on one more grandiose project. In the course of 1978, individual ministries put forward ever expanding claims on the economy's resources, as they jockeyed for position with competing megaprojects. This process led to an increasingly unrealistic and dangerous short-term economic situation.

Through 1978, the situation gradually spiraled out of control. The 1978 investment plan was twice revised upward during the course of the year (Li Fuchen 1981: 25). Planners were unable to obtain consistency in the 1979 economic plan, which was adopted in September 1978 with shortfalls in fuel, finished steel, cement supplies, and budgetary revenue targets (Li Zhining 1987: 444; Capital Construction I:245). The general inflation in claims occurred in individual projects as well. A famous example is the Baoshan steel mill outside Shanghai. The central government originally approved in November 1977 a project to build a port and a 5 million ton iron smelting facility, to supply iron to Shanghai's existing steel mills. By September 1978, five successive design changes had expanded the project to 6 million ton capacity iron and steel mills with continuous casters, a seamless pipe mill, and hot and cold rolling mills. From an ordinary large investment, the project had been pyramided into a completely integrated state-of-the-art steel mill, with virtually all technology and equipment to be imported from Japan. Foreign exchange requirements more than tripled from about $1.8 billion in the original version, to $5.7 billion in the September 1978 version. Virtually all of this inflation occurred without the direct oversight of central planners (Liu Jingtan and Hong Huiru 1981; Weil 1982).

As 1978 progressed, Chinese buyers stepped up their negotiation with foreign suppliers. At one point, literally hundreds of billions of dollars worth of contracts were under discussion. Not all discussions were serious: In some cases, the Chinese were engaged in exploratory discussions with competing suppliers. There was no clear delineation of which Chinese agencies were allowed to commit themselves to projects, so Chinese buyers had a strong motivation to conclude agreements as quickly as possible in order to lock their own government into commitments. It culminated in a buying frenzy during the last ten days of the year – contracts worth $3.1 billion were signed – when it must have been clear to insiders that the tide was already beginning to turn (Chen Huiqin 1981). The Chinese government faced the very real danger that within a matter of weeks, organizations under its nominal command would commit it to the further outlays of scores of billions of dollars. Increasing foreign exchange obligations were particularly ominous. This was an unfamiliar world of hard budget constraints in which national creditworthiness was at stake. Traditionally unwilling to incur debt, China in the course of 1978 nevertheless incurred future foreign-exchange obligations that were $10 billion greater than revenues. By year end, China began to indicate it would consider accepting foreign loans. Thus, by the end of 1978, the grandiose Chinese growth plans were in danger of coming apart at the seams. While the economy was growing rapidly, claims on economic resources were inflating at an even more rapid pace. It would take the removal of only one element to bring down the house of cards.

Petroleum was to have been the source of hard currency to pay for technology imports. For twenty years, production had grown steadily as output from the Daqing oilfield (accounting for half of the total) was matched by that from several smaller and newer fields. The Ten Year Plan called for the development of ten additional oilfields on the scale of Daqing's million barrels a day. But, incredibly, petroleum planners did not know where those fields were to be found. There were promising locations, but reserves had not been verified. Planners merely assumed that their string of successes in developing new fields during the early 1970s would continue: there seemed to be oil everywhere in China. But suddenly, during 1978, luck ran out. Chinese teams drilled 6.5 million meters of oil wells, without locating a single new producing field. Drilling was stepped up in 1979 to 8.2 million meters, but only a single small field was found. In 1980, drilling remained at an intense pace of 6 million meters (Li Juwen 1981; Du Ang and Chen Qizhang 1981).

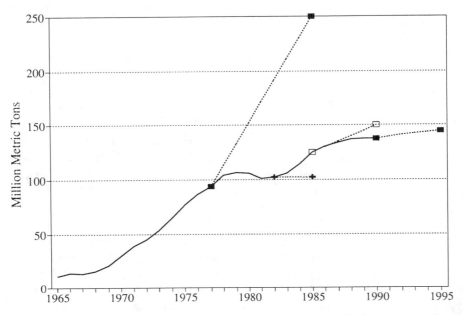

Figure 2.1 Petroleum: actual and planned output. Dashed lines link plan targets with production in the year the plan was set. Source: Brown 1986: 27; *Statistic* 1992; Seventh Plan; CCP 1991.

Without new finds, the rapid growth of petroleum output came to an abrupt halt.

1978 was the last year in which petroleum output grew rapidly. Natural gas production peaked in 1979, and did not surpass that year's output until 1989. The effects of astonishingly poor planning were concentrated in a short period of time because of a run of bad luck. Every strand of petroleum development collapsed simultaneously. New onshore oilfields didn't exist, Sichuan gas reserves turned out to be overestimated, and petroleum officials were forced to recognize that their decade-long effort to develop offshore oil on their own had failed (Brown 1986: 33). But behind the apparent bad luck, in each case, lies a failure to perform the simple verification of resources and examination of alternatives that is the essence of even the simplest planning.

Figure 2.1 shows actual petroleum output (solid line) as well as projected output (a broken line linking a future plan target with the actual output the year during which the plan was drawn up). Four plan targets are shown, and three of these can be compared with actual outcomes. The figure displays the inaccuracy of Chinese planning. The initial 1978 plan for 1985 was *double* actual 1985 output, and the 1982 revision of the plan was more than 20% *below* actual output in 1985! Moreover, in all four cases where the plan targets are known, they are simple extrapolations of the growth rate from the preceding three years.

This is quite a remarkable record. It implies that plans contain no information that could not be inferred by an outside observer who has access only to past trends. But if plans contain no useful additional information, it follows that no additional information was effectively utilized in drawing up the plans. As far as we can judge, no information about reserves and investments coming on stream were incorporated into projections of petroleum output in China. Small wonder that plans turned out to be inaccurate.

The situation was even worse than just failure to find new oil. The rapid expansion of petroleum output during the 1970s had been achieved by overexploitation of available fields. In many cases, current output maximization had been accomplished at the cost of damage to long-term productivity. Output at major fields peaked out in the late 1970s (Yang Jisheng 1981). The case of Sichuan natural gas involved bungling on a colossal scale. China invested billions in industrial facilities on the assumption that surpluses of Sichuan natural gas could be shipped to neighboring provinces. A gas pipeline was built hundreds of miles through the mountains of Sichuan to the province of Hubei, and was to be extended first to Jiangxi, and subsequently all the way to Shanghai. Five imported fertilizer plants were erected in the provinces surrounding Sichuan, and all were to use Sichuan natural gas as feedstock. But it turned out that Sichuan didn't have any surpluses of natural gas after all. Once again, reserves had not been verified. The huge pipeline out of Sichuan was halted in the middle of nowhere, and it now supplies home cooking gas to the small city of Xiangfan in Hubei. The fertilizer plants had to be converted, at great expense and with lower efficiency, to petroleum feedstock barged in on the Yangtze (Xu Yi 1981; Li Juwen 1981). By the end of 1978, China's planners faced the uncomfortable reality that the most successful element of their pre-1978 industrialization drive – and the crucial centerpiece of their plan to accelerate industrialization – was in ruins.

The common thread that runs through the gathering crisis of 1978 is the extreme weakness of Chinese planning. Chinese leaders were able to regularize and recentralize the economy, but they were mistaken if they believed they had created an adequate planning process to guide that economy. Both the inability to control the steady inflation of claims on the economy and the colossal failure to carry out long-term development of the oil industry are manifestations of a weak or incompetent planning process. As 1978 proceeded, economic planners were increasingly overcommitted, and it was inevitable, given the absence of reserves and backup capabilities in the plan, that something would go wrong. The fact that petroleum exploitation collapsed was in fact extremely lucky. The abrupt shift in petroleum output trends (the failure to find any new oil in 1978) presented the Chinese leaders with a warning signal they could not ignore. Rather than proceeding down a road that ultimately led nowhere, Chinese leaders were forced to contemplate a drastic recasting of development strategy.

Here then is the economic crisis that triggered the beginning of the reform era. An increasingly precarious planning process led to a virtually unsustainable commitment of the economy's resources to an enormous range of projects. When the central prop of that strategy, petroleum development, was removed, the entire edifice collapsed. To persist in this program would have led quickly to economic disaster, and China's leaders abandoned it quickly and completely. With the collapse of the grandiose plans, the economic outlook of China's leaders swung toward pessimism. They saw that they could not so easily rebuild the powerful apparatus of the command economy, not so easily pump ever increasing amounts of petroleum from the ground, not so easily import the latest in Western technology. If China's economy could not leap forward, it might instead have to pause, or even take a step backward, to address serious problems before it could resume forward motion.

The turning point: The Third Plenum

By unanimous agreement, the Third Plenum of the Eleventh Communist Party Central Committee, in December 1978, marks the decisive break with the past and the begining of China's reform era. It was at this meeting that Deng Xiaoping effectively replaced Hua Guofeng as the paramount leader, thereby creating the potential for more flexible and pragmatic policies across the board. But why was this meeting so decisive for economic policy? The meeting itself passed few concrete resolutions, and adopted no significant administrative reforms. At the meeting itself, leaders were preoccupied with the political reconfiguration taking place, with the job of rehabilitating thousands of purge victims, and with normalization of relations with the United States. Deng himself said nothing about economic policy, and most concrete economic decisions were deferred. The meeting even ratified "in principle" the flawed annual plan for 1979 that had been part of the Ten Year Plan strategy.

But a fundamental change in economic policy was nonetheless signaled at the Third Plenum by the return to power of Chen Yun and his assumption of responsibility over economic policy. It was Chen Yun who moved onto the supreme organ of political power (the Politburo Standing Committee) at the Third Plenum, Deng having already attained that height in August 1977. The crucial change at the Third Plenum was thus not simply Deng's emergence as top leader, but also that as part of Deng's assumption of this role, he made common cause with Chen Yun and decisively repudiated the previous economic policy. For Chen Yun was a known quantity. He had been a top Communist party leader since the 1940s, and he specialized in economics. Chen made his reputation by taking over economic policymaking after economy had been damaged by unsustainable "leaps forward." Chen was famous for taming inflation in the early years of the PRC, and for repairing the economy after reckless growth spurts in 1956 and after the Great Leap Forward. Tough, conservative, and with little apparent personal ambition, Chen Yun had a reputation for speaking frankly and implementing his policies forcefully when given the opportunity, but also for fading quickly into the background when his policies were out of favor.[5] During the preparatory meetings for the Third Plenum, Chen had already spoken of the need to stabilize the situation in agriculture, not to import too many projects at once, and not to leave gaps in material supply plans (Li Zhining 1987: 446; Wang Mengkui 1991).

Chen Yun's overhaul of development strategy began with agriculture. The Third Plenum itself made significant decisions to increase the flow of resources into agriculture (but *not* to reform agricultural institutions). The Plenum resolution, calling agriculture "seriously damaged," argued that the first priority of development had to be increasing agricultural production, and that in order to do that more resources had to be put into agriculture. To channel resources to rural producers, the Plenum adoped a 20% increase in agricultural procurement prices, to be combined with decreased prices for agricultural inputs, and increased state investment and bank credit for agriculture. The Third Plenum resolution held that the situation in agriculture was critical – it was "gasping for breath" – and needed an infusion of resources immediately. Policies of this magnitude would be important in themselves, but they were particularly significant because they represented such a complete break with the assumptions underlying the Ten Year Plan. The Ten Year Plan was in essence a huge end run around agriculture, designed to increase agricultural output eventually, but on the assumption that the peasants themselves could be starved of resources for a few more years. Now the Plenum was declaring that agriculture could not be starved of resources for a moment longer. At the same time, Chen Yun had already argued that resources were stretched overtight in the pursuit of the Ten Year Plan. Projections of increased petroleum output were collapsing. Where were the resources to come from to ease the situation in rural areas? All the assumptions on which the Ten Year Plan were based were now declared to be unsound, and the Plan was in a state of collapse.

On January 1, 1979, Chen Yun instructed planners to revise and lower the 1979 annual plan: "There should be no gaps [inconsistencies] in the plan: Better to lower targets, better to reduce the number of projects under construction" (Li Zhining 1987: 448). In February the Chinese suspended $2.5 billion of contracts with Japanese suppliers (Kim: 108; Weil 1982: 374). In March, Chen became head of the Economics Leading Group, making him economic policy "czar," with Li Xiannian, another of China's veteran leaders specialized in economics, as his deputy (on Leading Groups, see Hamrin 1992). Chen and Li pushed through the adoption of policies of "readjust-ment," or reorientation of the economy. During April, a central government work conference formally adopted a four-part slogan to describe the new policy orientation: readjustment, reform, rectification, and improved stan-dards.[6] While this slogan also gave its blessing to initial reforms, it was clear that the most important component was a fundamental reorientation of eco-nomic development strategy. The basic idea of reorientation was to reduce heavy industry investment and shift resources to agriculture and consump-tion, thereby also moving the economy onto a more moderate growth path with less strain on available resources.

The reorientation of development strategy

The logic of economic events drove China's planners to a particularly thor-ough implementation of the policy of reorientation. The Ten Year Plan also had had an internally consistent logic, based on tight control of consumption and accelerated industrial investment. But once that program collapsed, a new way had to be found to balance the pressing economic imperatives that pushed in upon the Chinese leaders. A compromise policy simply wouldn't work. Reorientation of the economy was attractive because it provided a way to cope simultaneously with several problems, any one of which had the potential to reach crisis dimensions. The main three problems were agricul-ture, energy and employment.

The first imperative was to stimulate growth in the lagging agricultural sector. Clearly, the new economic leadership perceived agriculture differ-ently than formerly dominant central planners. They saw peasants as will-ing to respond to the promise of higher incomes through harder work and greater agricultural output (and conversely, they appeared afraid that peas-ants might reduce output if their economic conditions did not improve).

China's leaders believed agricultural problems could be addressed through a two-pronged approach: liberalizing rural economic policy and improving the terms of trade of agriculture. More liberal rural policies involved keeping the agricultural collectives and communes as the fundamental rural organizational forms, but allowing them greater freedom to organize work and market output. In order to improve agricultural terms of trade – raising government procurement prices for agricultural products while allowing peasants to sell more at higher market prices – the government had to be willing to release resources that had previously gone to heavy industrial development. Reorientation would slash government inputs into heavy industry, thereby releasing financial and material resources that could be used to stimulate agricultural production.

Next, with the collapse of petroleum, planners faced a serious energy crisis, which would limit the speed of industrialization. There are two possible responses to an energy shortage: increase energy production or reduce energy consumption. China had tried the first approach in the Ten Year Plan. It had failed, and was no longer feasible. Under reorientation, by shifting the structure of industrial output away from energy-intensive investment goods production and toward labor-intensive and energy-frugal consumption goods, the consumption of energy availability would become less binding and industrial growth could continue. The benefits would come from a "lighter" economic structure. Because so much of China's prior development had been concentrated on energy-intensive heavy industry, the scope for saving in this area was very great. Substantial increases in industrial consumer good production could occur without increases in energy supply, so long as some reductions in heavy industrial output occurred.

Finally, there was an employment problem. The Ten Year Plan had completely neglected the pressing problems of employment. China had a chronic problem of rural underemployment, but in addition, a serious crisis of open urban unemployment developed during 1978. The urban labor force was entering a period of rapid growth as the large cohorts of young people born after 1962 began reaching working age. The problem was pushed into immediate crisis by the fact that the ongoing political relaxation was allowing millions of urban youth, sent down to the countryside during the 1970s, to return to their urban homes. The official urban unemployment rate surged to 5.3% at the end of 1978. Jobs had to be provided for these people, and the most effective way to provide jobs was through the rapid expansion of the labor-intensive light manufacturing and service sectors. In these sectors, jobs could be provided at relatively little investment cost per job, and, since these sectors had been consistently neglected for twenty years, there was substantial unsatisfied demand for their products.

Clearly, the policy of reorientation was very coherent. In fact, the various elements of the strategy were mutually dependent. Efforts to stimulate agricultural output with better incomes and incentives could only succeed if there was a large expansion in the availability of consumer goods. Consumer goods were initially in short supply, and, as described earlier, often rationed. If agricultural incomes increased without a corresponding increase in consumer goods supply, the result would only be increased shortages and consumer discontent. Conversely, increases in agricultural output, if achieved, would provide more food and more agricultural inputs to industry (food products, beverages and tobacco, textiles, wood and paper products), permitting a rapid expansion in consumer goods industries. It was this expansion that would absorb excess labor in city and countryside, permitting continued growth despite the energy bottleneck. Together, these changes would allow substantial increases in living standards that would reverse a decade of near-stagnation and provide legitimacy to the new Dengist leadership.

However, because of the interdependence of the various components of reorientation, there was also a danger that the policy could fail. New rural purchasing power would be created almost immediately, but the supply of both agricultural and manufactured consumer goods would take some time to increase. If increased rural incomes merely created inflation, then imbalances would be accentuated and the hoped for output increases might not occur.

In order to ensure that this negative scenario could be avoided, China stepped up its import of agricultural and manufactured consumer goods. China's grain imports increased, even as policy was becoming more friendly to agriculture, and soared to a record high of 16 million tons by 1982. The decision to allow these imports naturally increased the effective demand for foreign exchange, which was already stretched to the limit by the splurge of plant purchases at the end of 1978. The only way to provide adequate foreign exchange was to ruthlessly cut back the plant import program. A half-hearted readjustment would fail, while a radical reorientation could succeed. For the policy to succeed, planners had to devote resources both to improving agriculture, and to substituting for agricultural production in the short run. Only later would the recovery of agriculture provide additional foreign exchange earning capacity through the export of labor-intensive manufactures made with agricultural raw materials.

Thus, in order for reorientation to succeed, the big push of the Ten Year Plan had to be drastically chopped back. But there were other potential benefits to a rigorous reduction in new investment projects. The collapse of the Ten Year Plan left planners without a plan and – more crucially – without a backlog of good investment projects. There were no projects in the pipeline, and it takes time to draw up and coordinate project plans. At the same time, China had many deferred investments – internal debts – that were desperately needed. These included both deferred consumption investments – housing and urban services – and investment in depth in production facilities, like coal mines and oilfields, necessary to sustain productivity over time. With the pressure to throw available resources into current output expansion drastically reduced, planners could spend time on designing better projects for the future, and resources could be spent on paying back long-deferred "internal debts," laying the groundwork for sustained growth in the future.

Reorientation could be either a medium-run or a long-term strategy. The overwhelming economic fact facing China is its abundance of labor and shortage of good land. Under such circumstances, the loss from foregoing labor intensive production, where that is possible, is huge. Capital-saving and labor-intensive light manufacturing should be an early component of China's development strategy, as it was in other labor-rich East Asian countries. Thus, by adopting the policy of reorientation, China was in the position of quickly picking up huge economic benefits that it had neglected earlier due to its insistence on a big-push growth strategy. At the same time, the "premature" development of heavy industry made development of light industry that much easier. Over the long term, and as capital becomes more abundant, resumed development of heavy industry would be essential, not only because of the importance of heavy industry in development of technological capabilities and national defense, but also because of the need for heavy industries to provide substitutes for agricultural land and agricultural products (fertilizer, synthetic fibers, building materials). Some of China's leaders saw reorientation of the economy as a medium-term expedient – a tempering of excesses rather than a fundamental change in strategy – to be followed by a resumption of heavy industry centered growth by the 1990s (Ludlow 1981). Others argued that the objective of development under socialism should be improvement of living standards, and that China should thus make a permanent shift to a more consumer-friendly growth path (He Jianzhang and Zhang Zhuoyuan 1981). A politically sensitive debate about the ultimate objective of socialist development obliquely dealt with these questions of long-range strategy (Fang Sheng 1981; Wang Yongjiang 1981).

The rectification of economic policy during 1979 took place behind closed doors. There is no programmatic document that clearly expresses all the strains of policy. Yet the speeches by Chen Yun and Li Xiannian on readjustment in the spring of 1979 touch on nearly all these main points (CCP 1982: 74–79; 109–47). Chen's speech is compressed and sometimes elliptical, but the main points are there:

> On one hand, we are very poor; on the other hand we wish to carry out the four modernizations within twenty-some years. This is a contradiction. It's not easy to raise living standards with such a large population; modern production units use few people, so employment is difficult . . . the target of 60 million tons of steel in 1985 is absolutely impossible (*genben zuobudao*) . . . the disproportions in the economy are far more serious than those of 1961–62 . . . It won't be easy to carry out readjustment, because we owe serious [internal] debts from the past ten years.

The way in which "readjustment" was actually carried out is the subject of the remainder of this chapter.

Implementing economic reorientation

Economic reorientation was multi-stranded. The central feature of the reorientation policies was the shift in resources away from investment and heavy industry and toward consumption, light industry, and agriculture (Solinger 1991: 127–62). This change in the proportion of total output to investment required accompanying changes in the distribution of income among households and governments, as well as in the composition of investment. Changes in the proportions of current income streams going to different end-uses were at the heart of Chinese discussions of what they called "readjustment," implying the reestablishment of a harmonious relation among these ratios. In addition, reorientation included active government interventions to redefine priorities, restructure the existing capital stock, and reintegrate into the labor force those who had been excluded under the old development strategy. Moreover, reorientation had important macroeconomic policy implications as well. The following discussion begins with the reorientation of current flows (cutting investment) and follows with restructuring of the capital stock and the supply of labor. Macroeconomic policy is discussed in a later section.[7]

Cutting and restructuring investment

The clearest indicator of reorientation policies is the changing role of state fixed investment in the economy. Figure 2.2 shows the shifts in state fixed investment in the years following 1978 (see Statistical Appendix). Between 1978 and 1981, certain types of state investment were slashed, subsequently

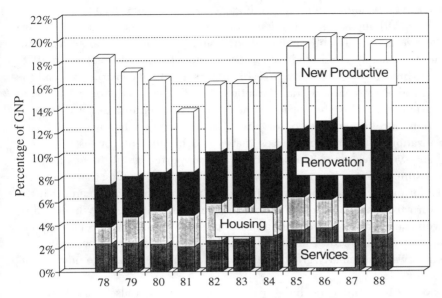

Figure 2.2. State fixed investment. Source: *Fixed Investment* 1949–1985; 66–67, 220, 330; 1986–1987: 69, 167, 256; 1988–1989: 61. 164, 243. See Statistical Appendix.

leveling off and displaying rough stability between 1982 and 1984. Our discussion here is primarily concerned with the dramatic reductions in investment through 1981; however, the general impact of the reorientation policy clearly carried through into 1984.

Total state fixed investment declined as a share of GNP annually from 1978 through 1981, dropping from 18.6% to 14% of GNP, before recovering to 16-17% for the period 1982 through 1984. Changes in the components of state investment were even more dramatic. The category showing the largest change is that of capital construction for "productive" investment – that is in investment in new facilities producing goods and productive services.[8] In 1978, such investment accounted for well over half of total state investment and 11% of GNP. Such investment was drastically cut back, reaching a low point of 5.3% of GNP in 1981, before recovering to a about 6% of GNP in the 1982–84 period. This key component of investment was chopped in half, falling by 5% of GNP.[9]

Other components of investment increased to make up for some of the reduction in productive capital construction. Productive "renovation and replacement" investment, which consists primarily of upgrading and expansion of existing enterprises, held steady from 1978 through 1981 at around

3.7% of GNP, and then increased its share to 4.5–5% of GNP in the 1982–84 period. Although such investment can include some large projects, the average size is considerably smaller than capital construction, and such investment is usually controlled by local governments or enterprises. In 1978, three-quarters of productive investment was in capital construction, and the remainder in technical transformation; by 1982–84 the proportions were nearly 50-50. This shift of investment to existing enterprises was popular with both reformers and conservatives. Reformers were happy to see decentralization of financial resources that would permit enterprises to finance their own investment. Conservatives also supported a shift to smaller-scale investment, but on more narrowly technical grounds, arguing that the potential for expanded output from existing facilities was quite large and that the return to small investments in existing facilities could be very high. Thus, even conservatives were willing to accept modest financial decentralization, since it was a practical means to fund technical upgrading, the urgency of which was particularly great given the cancelation of grandiose new investment projects.

While investment declined overall, its composition also shifted. Investment in consumer industry increased, and reductions were concentrated on heavy industrial investment, although an attempt was made to shield the energy and transport sectors from the overall reductions. Investment in textiles and food processing had been 7% of capital construction investment in 1978, and this surged to 13.5% in 1981 and 1982. Figure 2.1 shows that the share of investment going for housing doubled, from 1.4% of GNP in 1978 to 2.8% in 1981. A large share of enterprise-retained profits went into housing construction during these years: Perhaps 60% of total urban housing was financed by enterprise funds. Investment in services (health, education, and government administration) remained roughly constant in the early years, but increased slightly at the end of our period. Housing and services together increased from 3.8% in 1978 to 4.9% in 1981, then between 5.5 and 6% in the 1982–84 period.

Distribution of national income

As discussed in the previous chapter, households had direct control of a comparatively small proportion of total national income at the beginning of the reform process. Households claimed 55% of national disposable income. The remaining 45% was either government income or the net income of enterprises or non-profit organizations. (See Statistical Appendix: National Income data.) The distribution of national income changed dramatically in the years after 1978. By 1981, household income had reached 66% of national income, a level it generally sustained subsequently. The household share of national income pushed briefly higher in 1983–84, when it reached 70% of total disposable income. Reorientation implied transferring control of 10-15% of national income out of the direct control of the state, and into the hands of households.

This change in the distribution of national income was fully accounted for by changes in the share of income accruing to rural residents. The share of income accruing to urban wage-earners has changed relatively little. Between 1978 and 1980, urban wage-earners did increase their share of national income by about 2%, increasing from 18% to 20% of national income. Thereafter, there was a modest decline through 1983, and the long-run trend is for a constant share of around 20% of disposable income. By contrast, farm household income jumped from about 30% of national income in 1978 to nearly 40% in 1981, and then continued to climb slowly to reach 44% of national income in 1984.

This remarkable change in the economic status of rural households is the most striking feature of the initial period of reorientation. The rising rural household share is due to three factors: the shift in the terms of trade in favor of agriculture, the rapid growth in agricultural output following the adoption of the rural responsibility system, and the rapid growth in non-agricultural output following relaxation of the rural economic environment (Sicular 1991). One of the results of increased household income, particularly in rural areas, was a sharp increase in household saving (Chapter 4). Increased saving was certainly a response to the new opportunities provided by economic reform. But it required an increase in the absolute amount of income available as well. In this sense as well, reorientation opened up the possibility for broader processes of economic change.

Government budget

Changes in income distribution can also be traced by directly examining the state budget share of national income, shown in Figure 2.3. State revenues, including all types of subsidies, declined from a little more than 35% of GNP in 1978 to 27% of GNP in 1982. Moreover, since the decline included an increase in the share of GNP laid out for subsidies, effective resources under the control of budgetary authorities decreased even more sharply. If we assume that subsidies represent a prior claim on state resources, we can see that effective state resources declined by an even larger amount. Revenue net of all subsidies declined from 32% of GNP in 1978 to 21% of GNP in 1982.

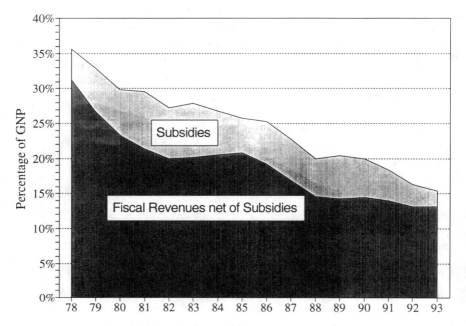

Figure 2.3. Fiscal revenues: subsidy and net revenues. Source: *Statistic* 1993: 219; Liu Zhongli 1994; See Statistical Appendix.

Subsidies reached a peak of about 8% of GNP in 1981, from a 1978 level of only about 4% of GNP, and remained between 7% and 8% of GNP through 1983. Almost all the increase in subsidies was the result of a decision by planners not to pass on the increased costs of agricultural procurements. Urban consumers continued to purchase most agricultural products at low, state-set prices, and the subsidy burden increased rapidly. Moreover, price policy initially shielded industrial enterprises as well from the impact of rising agricultural prices – for example, the increased procurement price for cotton was not passed on to state factories. Subsidies to unprofitable factories actually declined. In 1978, most subsidies had been for industrial enterprises, reflecting primarily the burden of a relatively small number of egregiously inefficient enterprises, particularly the small state-sponsored rural enterprises set up during the Cultural Revolution. As the worst of these enterprises were shut down, and basic measures were taken in industry, industrial losses (and subsidies) declined. Overall industrial losses/subsidies declined from about 3% to under 1% of GNP. However, the decline in industrial subsidies was more than offset by the increase in commercial subsidies.

In general, the government responded to the rapid decline in budgetary revenues by cutting outlays. There was a large deficit in 1979 – when a war with Vietnam and substantial non-recurring costs relating to the first stages of reorientation swelled outlays – but thereafter budgetary deficits were controlled at a little less than 2% of GNP. From the discussion in the first section of this chapter, it is easy to determine how planners kept the budget in balance. State outlays for investment (both fixed and inventory accumulation) and for the military declined steeply throughout this period. Budgetary outlays for investment were 16.2% of GNP in 1978 and only 7.7% in 1982. Military outlays were 4.7% of GNP in 1978 and only 3.4% in 1982. By contrast, civilian current outlays remained constant at around 10% of GNP (*Statistic* 1991: 215–16).

Three striking conclusions follow about the changes in the sectoral distribution of income that occurred between 1978 and 1984. First, they were large. A very substantial proportion of national income was removed from the control of budgetary authorities and given to households and enterprises. Second, they were consistent. The state reduced its expenditures in line with reductions in its revenues. Moreover, the reorientation of the economy was very much in step with the changes in income distribution: Increases in the supply of consumer goods met the increased demand from larger household incomes. Finally, they were monotonic. The state share steadily declined, and the household share steadily increased, from 1978 through 1984. Overall, macroeconomic policy was remarkably successful in managing a shift toward a more balanced growth path, with greater stress on raising living standards and a diminished role for state redistribution and investment.

Redefining administrative priorities

Because the Chinese economy was still largely administrative and characterized by recurrent shortages, the shift in financial resources, to be fully effective, had to be accompanied by a change in priorities for the distribution of scarce materials. Beginning in 1980, the government reversed the traditional priorities that had guided micro-allocation of resources. Traditionally, priority access to materials was given to heavy industrial sectors such as steel and petroleum. At the beginning of 1980, priority was explicitly shifted to consumer goods production, with the declaration of six types of priority for consumer goods. The six were priority access to (1) raw materials and power; (2) small-scale investment funds; (3) capital construction investment funds; (4) bank loans; (5) foreign exchange; and (6) transport capacity. These administrative mechanisms facilitated the shift in output structure that was driven by changes in the distribution of income and demand. It was a remarkable reversal. Planners were using the planning system to achieve goals perhaps best reached by markets.

Heavy and light industry

With investment declining and consumption demand surging, and backed by the new priority to consumer goods, light industrial production growth far exceeded that of heavy industrial growth, reversing long-established patterns. Light industrial growth surged during 1980–81, while heavy industry decelerated, and indeed stagnated during 1980 and 1981. In essence, the economy pivoted on a fixed output of energy and heavy industrial goods. While heavy industrial output declined 2.8%, light industry increased output by 36% over two years.

Writing down the capital stock

The changes in the level and distribution of investment described in the preceding section were relatively easy for planners to carry out once they became convinced of the need to do so. In general, all that was required was for planners to announce a policy, permit a decentralization of control over resources, and accommodate that decentralization by reducing their own investment. But reorientation of the economy also required that planners restructure the existing capital stock as well. In many cases, this required the exertion of a powerful government to control decisions made on local levels. The record of the central government in this area, as might be expected, was mixed. Yet the decisiveness with which the government made a number of difficult economic choices is quite striking. Planners moved to close down extremely inefficient small plants, to cancel large numbers of investment projects under construction, and to shrink the military industrial sector.

The industrial development strategy during the Cultural Revolution decade had fostered the development of numerous plants of uneconomically small scale (Wong 1982). Moreover, numerous errors had been made in the design and construction of industrial plants. A substantial amount of industrial fixed capital already in production had a zero or negative value and had to be written off. Closings that took place in 1979–80 focused on small iron and steel plants and small fertilizer plants. These plants were closed primarily because they had exceptionally high energy consumption per unit output. In many cases, they were also money losers, but this appears to have been a secondary consideration. From the beginning of 1979 through mid-1981, 276 small iron

Table 2.2. *Large investment projects under construction*

	Under construction	Completed	Minimum number canceled
1978	1,723	–	–
1979	1,610	128	309
1980	1,106	82	201
1981	893	79	162

Source: Fixed Investment 1953–85: 155. Minimum canceled is number canceled if no new projects were started in that year.

and steel plants – 59% of the total – were closed down or converted to some other use (SEC 1982). Hundreds of small coal mines in the south of China were shut down (Du Zhenbiao 1980). Overall, some 3,600 factories were closed down in 1979, and probably twice that number in 1980 (Lin Senmu et al 1982: 59). According to one careful account, industrial energy consumption was reduced by 3% in 1979, and fully one-half of the saving was achieved by shutting down small iron and steel and fertilizer plants (Liu Junlian 1980).

Cancellation of investment projects under construction was even more dramatic. Reorientation began with the cancellation of Japanese projects just beginning to be imported. But this was merely the tip of the iceberg. The huge volume of incomplete construction projects had to be dealt with in some way in order that it not become an indefinite drain on resources. In fact, there was a dramatic drop in the volume of incomplete construction between 1978 and 1981, amounting to over 10% of GNP. This drop did not come about because projects were finally finished and put into operation. Rather, the decline is almost entirely due to the decision to cancel projects and write-down useless assets.

As one would expect, this was an extremely difficult political task. During June 1979, a meeting of the Finance and Economics Commission decreed a large-scale cutback in existing investment projects, including the 22 super-large imported projects. But through the remainder of 1979 and most of 1980, patrons of existing projects maneuvered furiously to protect their pet projects, and virtually no progress was made. Finally, in December 1980, as part of a shift to further reorientation, the three most powerful leaders in the economic sphere, Deng Xiaoping, Chen Yun, and Li Xiannian, issued an emergency document insisting that projects be shut down. They declared, "We must be utterly miserly, and not provide a dime for these projects" (Wang Hongmo 1989: 183–86). Table 2.2 shows the changes in the number of large investment projects during these years. The number of large projects under construction was nearly halved between 1978 and 1981, but more than twice as many projects were cancelled as were completed. This deserves to be called "the great write-off". Many billions of dollars worth of wasted investment were officially acknowledged by the Chinese government.

Finally, Chinese planners moved rapidly to reorient the military industrial complex away from its exclusive focus on military production. Military industry had taken about 10% of industrial investment in the years up until the late 1970s. Not surprisingly, data are scarce on this sector, but it is clear that its claim on resources was large. Planners cut back military industry in two ways. First, they reduced investment in military production as such. Second, they encouraged military plants to convert to the production of civilian products, and they provided investment funds and raw material supplies to firms that were able to make the conversion. By 1986, it is estimated that military industrial capital had declined to 5–6% of the industrial capital stock (Folta 1992; Maruyama 1990).

Investment in depth

We noted in previous chapters that a characteristic of Soviet-style economies was a tendency to concentrate investment on directly productive investments, which frequently implies skimping on what we have called "investment in depth." These are investments that do not immediately result in increased output, but rather lower the costs and raise the productivity of future investment. Investment in human skills or knowledge is one example of investment in depth. The rehabilitation of the education system occurring during this period was by far the most important example of such investment, but that is outside the scope of this book. Similar shifts were taking place within industry, and a particularly important case was that of the energy industry. Consider petroleum. Past investment in the petroleum industry had been concentrated on output expansion – on drilling and pumping new wells. Exploration and verification of new reserves had been slighted, with the result that the return to investment plummeted to zero. In this case, there was literally no choice: Investment in depth had to be made in order to locate new exploitable resources. A similar situation had developed in the coal industry, with the difference that it had not quite reached the point of final crisis. Coal mines had been overexploited, with extraction of coal outrunning the construction and strengthening of new mine shafts and tunnels. This led to declining productivity and increasingly unsafe conditions, affecting 22% of large mines in 1979 (CCP 1982: 113). As part of the reorientation policy, resources were taken from direct extraction of coal and redirected to strengthening and expanding existing mines, to tunnel reinforcement and better safety. As coal production stagnated between 1978 and 1980, existing investment projects were suspended. Potential new capacity equal to more than 10% of output was put on hold. About 5% of capacity was judged irreparably dangerous and decommissioned through 1980. There was widespread concern that production would drop sharply (Li Dazheng 1989a: 23; Li Dazheng 1989b: 18). The actual result was a short-run decline in coal output of about 2% between 1979 and 1981 (Figure 2.4). The decline and subsequent stagnation in coal production was most significant in the large, centrally run coal mines, which barely increased output at all between 1979 and 1983. Overall primary energy production also declined 2% between 1979 and 1981. Petroleum output declined because the oil was simply not there, while coal output declined because excess extraction from individual mines had to be cut back to rectify long-standing problems. In both cases, past failure to invest in depth had to be rectified at the cost of foregoing current output.

Reintegration of human resources

Reorientation of the economy included important initiatives to utilize China's abundant human resources more effectively. In the preceding chapter, I described the extreme rigidity of China's labor control system under the pre-reform regime. Restrictions on mobility, rustication of urban youth, and political oppression all contributed to an enormous waste of human resources. Economic reorientation, combined with the political liberalization of 1978–79, began the process of reintegrating millions of potentially productive individuals into the economy. From a purely economic standpoint, this meant that the supply of human skills available increased significantly, enhancing productivity. Moreover, the economic aspects were only part of a much greater human drama. During 1978–79, China was undergoing the initial stages of a process of de-Maoization that was comparable in many respects to the de-Stalinization that took place in the Soviet Union in the 1950s. As is the case with other aspects of economic reorientation, this involved short-run costs as well as long-run benefits, and required active intervention by the government. Most significantly, reintegration made China's chronic problem of surplus labor and unemployment temporarily more acute.

One of the most remarkable Chinese policies during the 1960s and 1970s had been the rustication of urban youth. Beginning in the 1960s, more than a million urban school-leavers had annually been sent to the countryside to participate in agricultural labor. By the end of 1977, a cumulative total of 17

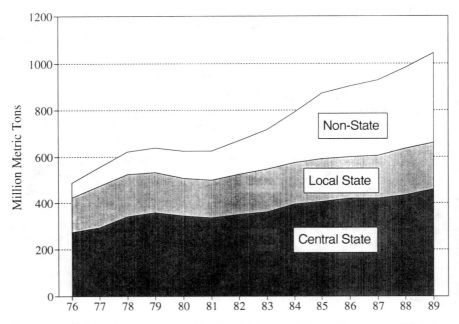

Figure 2.4. Coal output by ownership form. Source: *Coal, various years, Table 5.*

million urban youth had been sent to the countryside; a little more than half of these had returned to the cities through various channels over the years, leaving 7.6 million still in the countryside. The overwhelming majority of these – a total of 6.5 million individuals – returned to the cities during 1978 and 1979. The immediate result was a sharp jump in unemployment. There were over 5 million registered urban unemployed annually between 1978 and 1980, with the official unemployment rate peaking at 5.4% at the end of 1979.[10] Moreover, unemployment rates were particularly high in China's largest cities, where unemployment was most visible and politically sensitive. The official unemployment rate at the end of 1978 was 8.7% in Shanghai and 7.8% in Tianjin (*Labor* 1949–85: 110; *Labor* 1978–87: 109–11).

Nearly every aspect of labor policy was stretched to accommodate the returnees. Early retirement programs that rewarded retirees with generous pensions and with guaranteed jobs for their offspring were instituted. As a result, some 7 million state workers retired between 1978 and 1981, compared with a few hundred thousand annually in previous years. Many returnees were absorbed into new types of employment in the service sector (Chapter 3). Five million urban jobs were created in 1978, then 9 million in both 1979 and 1980, and 8 million in 1981 (Taylor 1986: 254–59; Feng Lanrui and Zhao Lukuan 1982). Job creation at this pace clearly involved substantial amounts of make-work: Two-thirds of new jobs were in the state sector. The state was actually *strengthening* its employment guarantee to urbanites.

The economic impact of political rehabilitation was nearly as great as that of the return of rusticated youth. During 1978, the top leadership devoted an enormous amount of time to rehabilitating political victims. Beginning with their old friends who had been victimized during the Cultural Revolution, Deng Xiaoping and his allies gradually broadened the political amnesty to millions of ordinary victims. Class labels that had been affixed to landlords, rich peasants, and capitalists during the 1950s were removed, and many returned to productive work. The number of people involved in this process is so large that the economic consequences must have been significant. In rural areas, the removal of landlord and rich peasant labels affected more than 20 million people. In the cities, class labels were removed from nearly a million "capitalists." Another million who had been classified as "rightists" in 1957, including a large proportion of China's non-Communist intelligentsia, were rehabilitated. Even within the Communist bureaucracy a large number had been scapegoated – 17% of the 17 million full-time administrative cadres, or nearly 3 million people, had some kind of legal charge or accusation pending against them, nearly all of which were dropped by the early 1980s (Wang Hongmo 1989: 151–68).[11] An unknown number of people – certainly in the millions – were released from prison during this period. While China's gulag did not disappear, it disgorged millions back into society. A beginning was made to repair one of the most colossal wastes of human resources in history. As these people returned to society, they began to contribute knowledge and creativity that had previously been squandered.

The urban labor force of 95 million (at the end of 1978) was augmented by the participation of about 5 million rehabilitated people and the return from the countryside of 6 million young people. Almost all of these people had relatively high levels of education and intellectual, administrative, or entrepreneurial skills. In total, this process must have resulted in a substantial increase in the overall productive capacity of China's urban economy. Occasionally, individuals were ideally suited for critical niches in the economy – for example, Rong Yiren, a Shaghai capitalist who had cooperated with the Communist government during the 1950s. Beginning in 1978, he was rehabilitated and compensated, then given government sponsorship to develop CITIC, the China International Trust and Investment Corporation. This unique organization has since played an important role as an interface between China and international business activity. CITIC facilitates some types of foreign investment in China, and raises and invests capital on its own outside China. Its unique style of operation, for better and for worse, depends on the individual character and connections of its founder, Rong Yiren. In the short run, reintegration of individuals like Rong Yiren into the economy was costly. Direct monetary compensation to rehabilitated victims came to over a billion yuan in 1979.[12] More important, real resources were devoted to ensuring employment to most of these individuals. By 1983, registered unemployment had been brought down below 3 million (2.3% of the labor force), and most of these were recent graduates awaiting their first job assignment (*Labor* 1978–87: 109). A huge volume of human resources had been reabsorbed into the economy.

Macroeconomic slack

One of the initial objectives of economic reorientation was to create "slack" in the economy by reducing the pressure of excess demand on available resources. In the heavy industrial sector, that objective was fulfilled fairly quickly. The sharp reduction in investment spending reduced demand for many producer goods, an effect particularly evident in the machinery sector (see Chapter 3). More broadly, the reduction in demand for heavy industrial products reduced the overall demand for energy, permitting continued economic growth despite the fallback in energy production. In a similar fashion, reducing the number of investment projects under construction allowed the government to concentrate the flow of investment resources on a smaller number of projects, enabling these projects to be completed more rapidly. Thus, initial slack in the heavy industrial sectors permitted the government to achieve its early objectives.

However, it was more difficult to achieve slack on the consumption side. The rapid increase in household income that followed the new rural policies increased demand for consumer goods. Similarly, pro-consumption policies in the cities resulted in sharp increases in household income. The increase in household income was of course intended by government policymakers, but it occurred more rapidly than they had anticipated. There was a tendency for programs that increased household income to be "overimplemented," spreading more rapidly than initially envisaged. The first-stage urban reforms, discussed in the next chapter, fit this pattern, and their rapid spread contributed to surging urban incomes. Increased household income combined with de facto price liberalization led to inflation during 1980. The urban consumer price index jumped 7.5%, by far the highest inflation rate since the early 1960s. During 1979–80, reorientation succeeded in releasing resources from investment and heavy industry to consumption, light industry, and agriculture. But because the demand for consumer goods increased so rapidly, the policies were unable to create abundant supply of consumer goods across the board. Supply of some key commodities responded quickly to liberalization – prices on farmers' markets declined 7% during 1978 and 5% during 1979. But the emergence of across the board consumer price inflation during 1980 showed that the fundamental problem of balance of supply and demand for consumer goods had not been solved.

Other signs of continuing macroeconomic imbalance emerged during 1980. The rapid spread of enterprise reforms contributed to the erosion of budgetary revenues (again, an intended outcome, but occurring more rapidly than anticipated). There had been a large budget deficit in 1979, but this had been due primarily to one-time only events, such as the war with Vietnam and the immediate costs of liquidating the Ten Year Plan projects. Therefore, conservatives were alarmed that the overall governmental deficit declined only moderately between 1979 and 1980, and that the central government deficit actually *increased* from 13 billion to 14.5 billion yuan (*Budget* 1950–88: 149). Signs of continued macroeconomic imbalance led to stricter implementation of the reorientation policy at the end of 1980 and during 1981. Investment was cut further, and policymakers got tougher on recalcitrant local governments. From the perspective of investment and heavy industry, this was a simple continuation and intensification of the policies already adopted in 1979–80, and those policies have been described. However, policy shifted with respect to consumption. Growth of household income, and particularly urban wages slowed markedly (see Figure 3.1). Policy shifted from being proconsumption across the board to linking support for consumer goods production with strict controls on the growth of consumer demand – that is, with slow growth of household income. This policy succeeded in slowing the growth of demand and creating generally abundant supply in relation to effective demand. Beginning in 1981, policymakers succeeded in creating a slack demand environment across the board for a significant period. Consumer price inflation fell to the 2-3% range, and remained there through 1984.

The creation of a relaxed macroeconomic environment was aided by the many light industrial projects begun in 1979–80 that were now coming on stream, delivering a sustained flow of new consumer goods to the marketplace. Wang Xiaoqiang (1993) argues that this is a characteristic of the reform process as a whole: There is a "golden age" of reform characterized by the rapid creation and expansion of consumer goods industries, especially consumer durables, that had been neglected under the previous economic strategy. Certainly that seems to have been the case in China. During 1982–84, consumer livelihood improved despite the stagnation of money incomes because goods became more available and rationing was reduced (discussed further in Chapter 3). Creation of a relaxed economic environment also reduced pressure on planners: It gave them time for institutional experimentation and resources to take care of unfinished business.

Conclusion

The supply side policies adopted during 1979–81 would have improved the long-run performance of the economy even in the absence of any accompanying economic reform. Many more of China's human and material resources were brought to play in the production process, wasteful processes were eliminated, and the interrelations among different sectors were coordinated more effectively as part of the reorientation of economic strategy. In part, it was simply that planners stopped doing a lot of silly, wasteful things. But it went far beyond that. Everywhere we look, we see active government measures that were designed to increase long-term growth potential, and which almost certainly had that effect. Thus, if it is appropriate to see China before 1979 as an economy already with substantial growth potential, it should be evident that that potential was substantially enhanced by the policies followed in the early 1980s.

Yet planners were most decidedly not aiming at acceleration of the growth rate in the short run. Quite the contrary. They believed that the measures they were taking would reduce the short-run growth rate, but were necessary anyway. The contrast between the origin of economic reforms in China and the Soviet Union is particularly striking. The Soviet Union faced a crisis of declining growth rates and general stagnation. The command economy apparatus was in place and functioning, but the economy as a whole faced a "crisis of effectiveness" (Bialer 1980). As a result, Soviet economic reforms in the mid-1980s were closely associated with attempts to accelerate economic growth and social change across the board. Reform coincided with an effort by the central government to do more, maintaining or increasing investment while reforms proceeded. The economy ran into severe problems because decentralizing reforms increased overall demand precisely at the time when planners were trying to increase investment as well. The result was severe imbalances and inflation (Aganbegyan 1988; Aslund 1991; Hewett 1988). In contrast, Chinese planners had been forced to discard their programs of economic acceleration before reform began, and so entered the reform era with a focus on restructuring the economy, increasing employment, and increasing consumption goods availability. In terms of current output growth, reform coincided with an effort by the central government to do less, restructuring and decreasing investment while reforms began. As a result, China avoided the pitfall of acceleration, and reforms could unfold in the decidedly more favorable economic environment created by the policy of reorientation.

In some respects, the Chinese reorientation corresponds to the decline in output that follows on the big bang. Production of heavy industrial and military goods, required for the old, but unwanted in the new, development strategy, drops. In China, this reduction in output was masked by the growth of new consumer goods production, and the entire process was carried out under government control.

The character of early reform era was inevitably shaped in other ways as well by the commitment to reorientation. Reform began with an increase in employment, strengthened government guarantees of employment to urban dwellers, and increased living standards. Moreover, the most fundamental imbalances in the system were rectified under the old administrative system. Excess demand pressures were greatly reduced. As a result, the "big bang" policies combining macro-stabilization with liberalization were not relevant. It was not essential to soak up excess demand pressures through a traumatic episode of sudden price decontrol. There was no temporary period of unemployment and falling incomes to weather before institutional reforms could take hold. As a result, economic policy won many adherents to the policies of Deng Xiaoping, who firmly consolidated his political leadership. Reform began with successes that enabled the process to survive in the face of later reverses and occasional failure.

Reorientation was marked by direct government intervention in many aspects of the economy. This intervention was often successful. Thus, reorientation contributed to a characteristic of the Chinese reform process that was quite enduring: continued government intervention in the development process. For better and for worse, government kept trying throughout the reform era to develop investment policy, restructure enterprise incentives, and devise new and appropriate institutions. There was never a period of hands-off policymaking in the Chinese reform. Activist government persisted through the 1990s.

Finally, because of the collapse of ambitious investment programs, planners were not much inclined to squeeze out initial economic reforms. Contrast the experience of abortive reforms in Eastern Europe, where initial partial reforms led to macroeconomic imbalances that caused planners to strengthen material controls (Nuti 1979). Generally, planners have little difficulty convincing themselves that they have vital projects the importance of which overrides any reform initiatives. But that was much less true in China where planners found themselves temporarily without vital projects to pursue. The importance of slack markets is closely related. With supply surpassing demand, planners were encouraged to leave certain decisions to the market, since the market-driven resource allocations were not threatening to their interests. As a result, reorientation created a situation where initial exploratory reforms, no matter that they were tentative and not well thought out, could be sustained. Reorientation reduced the conflict between resources needed to establish reform and resources needed to carry out the planners' project of rapid industrial growth. Reorientation created an environment in which the costs of economic reform were quite low. Because the costs were low, reforms were able to survive long enough to produce economic benefits and justify their continuation.

It is in this sense that we may be considered to have answered the question of why China undertook an ambitious program of economic reform. Reforms could begin first of all because the economic system was already in a state of flux. Constant incremental changes continued to alter the system, just as they had for decades. Yet it was equally true that incremental change was not the same as fundamental reform, and indeed incremental changes tended to move the system back toward the pattern of its more centralized Soviet relative. This was all changed by the need for economic reorientation. Reorientation was good policy that conformed well to China's underlying economic conditions, and responded well to China's long-run economic challenges. But the sudden and dramatic shift to policies of reorientation can be traced not to a gradual rethinking of China's economic strategy, but rather to the sudden and dramatic collapse of an alternative development strategy. Economic crisis was created by planners, and provided strong incentives for the leadership to adopt reorientation. Forced to respond to a nearly overwhelming set of challenges, Chinese leaders finally moved dramatically to change development strategy and restructure the economy. This change in turn created a favorable environment in which initially modest and uncertain economic reforms could become well entrenched in the economy. The combination of change enacted over a broad range of strategic and systemic areas and an initially weak administrative system meant tentative reforms could take root and succeed. In that sense, economic reorientation explains both why China's leaders began reform, and why reforms persisted.

3

State sector reforms, 1979–1983

During 1979 and 1980, the Chinese government began a vigorous reform program in the state sector. Reforms centered around the twin initiatives of expanding enterprise autonomy and combining plan and market, and they quickly spread to encompass much of the state sector. In the context of economic reorientation, reforms took root rapidly, and along with liberalization of the rural economy discussed in the next chapter, these initiatives mark the beginning of China's reform era. Reform was energetically promoted until the end of 1980, when policy suddenly changed direction. A much more conservative policy emerged in 1981, skeptical about rapid reforms and insisting that planning was necessary. The government then backed away from state sector reforms until the early months of 1984. The 1979–83 period thus emerges as a classical policy cycle, in which a phase of energetic reform policy was followed by a phase of cautious retrenchment.

Actual change in the economic system, though, did not fit so neatly into phases of reform and retrenchment. First, even during the activist reform phase, implementation was extremely unbalanced. Although reformers were quickly able to decentralize and introduce more flexibility into the system, their attempts to rationalize prices and financial relations were largely unsuccessful. The retrenchment beginning in 1981 partially reflected the inability of reformers to develop an overall program of reform that was both coherent and practical. Conversely, the conservative policies post-1981 had a number of unanticipated consequences that had a positive influence on the further development of reform. Reforms developed with a certain logic of their own, not entirely dependent on the policy orientations of the central government. In a sense, these first phase industrial reforms failed, but in the course of failing they touched off fundamental changes that laid the groundwork for future successes. By 1984, after both a reformist and a retrenchment phase of the policy cycle, the time was ripe for a reassessment and renewal of reform.

This chapter is primarily concerned with the actual reform measures and their impact upon the economy, but also examines briefly some of the most important reform ideas. It begins by briefly considering the origins of Chinese industrial reforms, and then moves to reform implementation. Reforms began simultaneously in industry and agriculture, but the most significant early reforms were in industry. This may seem surprising, since most accounts hold that Chinese reforms began in the countryside.[1] In fact, the historical record is quite clear that initial reforms in the agricultural sector were rather modest, and that it took two to three years for rural reforms to gain momentum. But rural reforms, after accelerating in 1981–82, reaped outstanding successes by 1984. Industrial reforms, despite their early and promising start, still had a troubled and uncertain status as of 1984. It is not surprising that in retrospect, Chinese publicists wanted to claim that reforms had begun in agriculture.

The first stirrings of reform

Reform ideas began to appear in the Chinese press during 1978. However, the earliest expressions of reform ideas were sketchy and disjointed. China's community of economists had been devastated during the Cultural Revolution, unable to do serious work for years. Moreover, economists had been isolated, not merely from all of Western economics, but even from recent trends in economic thought in Eastern Europe. After the economics institutes were reconstituted, beginning in 1977, economists were pressed into service waging ideological warfare on Cultural Revolution radicals. Their first job was to rehabilitate economic ideas that had been rejected in China during the Maoist period, but that were utterly conventional by the standards of the rest of the socialist world. Employing Marxist vocabulary, economists argued for the merits of "socialist profit" and economic efficiency, for the rehabilitation of the "law of value," and for the principle that income should be received acccording to labor contributed. Economists were engaged in vindicating orthodoxy. Small wonder that as Halpern (1985: 404) suggests, "[Academic economists] were minimally involved in the initial decisions to carry out reform."

During 1978, two principles of reform were commonly advanced: expanded enterprise autonomy and increased use of economic levers (as opposed to administrative means). Reference to the need to adjust distorted prices was occasionally made (Hu Qiaomu 1978; Xue Muqiao. 1978b). In addition, the need to boost exports to pay for plant imports led to some early changes in the foreign trade sector. In October, Zhao Ziyang, later Premier and chief architect of concrete reform measures nationwide, introduced a program of expanded enterprise decision-making in six factories in Sichuan (Halpern 1985: 404–7; Li Zhining 1987: 444, 615). Expanding enterprise autonomy was a good place to begin tinkering with the system, because it was relatively noncontroversial. Even the most committed planner might agree that a management system would perform better with more autonomy at the base level. In fact, these early ideas and measures were being advanced at a time when the main trend was toward recentralization of the economic system and toward a new "big push" for industrialization. They were compatible with a wide range of minor modifications of the traditional economic system, and in particular compatible with a process that would simply bring China back into the socialist mainstream after its long Maoist interlude.

The vagueness of initial reform ideas reflected the fact that China's reform began not only without a blueprint for how to reform, but without even a sense of what the ultimate objective of reform should be. In contrast to Poland's reformers in 1990 – who declared at the outset that their objective was a market economy with a government sector similar in size and function to that of Western European countries – China's reformers sought merely to improve the operation of the economic system, through whatever means seemed appropriate. Indeed, at this time, proposals to end the planned economy and make a transition to a market economy were, for the majority of economists and politicians, simply unthinkable (Chen Yizi 1990). Only gradually, through the process of reforming, did the objectives of reform become clear. Initial efforts took place under two main initiatives: expanding enterprise autonomy and combining plan and market.

Expanding enterprise autonomy

Industrial reforms began rapidly and made substantial progress during 1979. Characteristically, reformers simultaneously began taking concrete measures and thinking about an overall program of reforms. Following on Zhao Ziyang's enterprise experiments in Sichuan, central government leaders discussed in April a program to select a group of enterprises nationwide to implement expanded autonomy. On July 13, 1979, five documents on expanded enterprise autonomy were officially issued (SRC 1984: 182–88). The documents specified that enterprises selected for expanded autonomy would have the right to retain a share of profits, enjoy accelerated depreciation, and have the right to sell above-plan output. This step marks the beginning of China's nationwide urban reform. Enterprise autonomy proved to be extremely popular, since it included profit retention. Although the program as initially proposed was for a small number of experimental enterprises, by the end of 1979 it had been adopted in 6,600 mostly large enterprises, accounting for 60% of the output and 70% of the profit of state factories under the state budget (see Statistical Appendix for industrial categories). Government officials quickly saw the benefits of profit retention in their subordinate enterprises, and the program was over-implemented (Naughton 1985; Shirk 1993: 200–04).

At about the same time, economists and specialists from the bureaucracy were brought together to study future directions for China's economy. This was China's first attempt to draw up a blueprint for economic reform. Four working groups were established under the Economics Leading Group, the two most important of which were to research China's economic structure and a future economic reform program. These groups were the ancestors of various "think tanks" set up by the central government during the 1980s, and were a crucial first step in building independent policy research capabilities in the government. The guiding spirit of the reform group was Xue Muqiao, active as a socialist economist since the 1930s, and converted into a vigorous reformer by his post-1949 experience in economic affairs. Under Xue, the reform group worked fast and drew up successive reform programs in December 1979 and August 1980.[2] But these reform documents mostly described problems with the existing system of economic management. A few concrete measures were proposed, almost all relating to expanded enterprise autonomy, with complementary reforms in price, taxation, and planning to follow later. Reform should be carried out in phases: detailed reform planning and initial implementation in 1980–81, complementary reforms in stages from 1982–85, and "comprehensive reform" in 1986. But the outlines acknowledged that there was no agreement about the content of comprehensive reform (SRC 1988a: 1–36). China was attempting to draw up a reform blueprint, but the process was proving difficult.

Despite the lack of coherence for these long-range reform plans, enterprise reform in China perhaps carried a volatility that it did not have in the Soviet Union. Because of the weakness of the planning apparatus, the implications of expanded autonomy were potentially greater. The limited strength of China's control mechanisms meant that in practice many enterprises had significant freedoms to engage in outside plan activity and deflect the implementation of government commands in ways that suited their interests. Thus, the loosening of bonds on enterprise behavior carried with it the possibility of rapid system change – a "fast and dirty" approach to reform. At the same time, in other respects, Chinese firms had less autonomy at the beginning of reforms than did enterprises in the ECEs. The rigidity of the labor and compensation systems greatly surpassed that in East European countries, and the direct authority of the Communist Party was much greater. Thus, nobody was sure how far the concept of enterprise authority might be taken, and the most innovative writings of this period discussed the implications of substantial expansion in enterprise autonomy. Dong Furen (1979) proposed an expansion of the concept of public ownership, and a much greater role for collective firms as opposed to state-owned firms. Jiang Yiwei (1980) argued for an "enterprise-based economy," which would have some features in common with Yugoslav-style worker management. With limited labor mobility in China, Jiang argued that reform should grant workers in a state-run firm a corporate interest in their firms. Sympathy toward worker management was present in much reform policy of this time. Actual reform implementation proceeded in an environment of uncertainty over where reform would lead.

Financial reforms

The first set of enterprise financial reforms included enterprise profit retention and initial rationalization of the financial system. A group of experimental "expanded autonomy" enterprises were to begin profit retention immediately, and simultaneously begin to implement comprehensive reforms of the enterprise financial system. These enterprises were to pay fees to the budget for fixed capital and to the banks for working capital. In addition, depreciation rates were to be raised (SRC 1984: 182–88). At the same time, planning officials were to gradually transform budgetary investment grants into repayable, interest-bearing loans (SRC 1984: 713–14). Later, but as soon as possible, a broad realignment of state fixed prices would be carried out.

As noted, profit retention was rapidly implemented. By September 1980, moreover, the government announced that this system would be made universal in state industrial firms during the following year (SRC 1984: 209–14). The amount of profit retained by a firm was based on the total funds it had been granted in the previous year for worker welfare, bonuses, and new product development, training, and research. The percentage of total profit that this sum represented then became the firm's profit sharing ratio. The firm was required to deposit retained profits into three separate funds – welfare, bonus, and production development (investment). The firm was to control the use of funds within each fund.

Profit retention was only a first step, pending price reforms. But rationalizing measures – payment for capital, transforming grants to loans, and price adjustments – were implemented only partially or not at all. This failure is discussed further later, but the interrelation between these measures must be discussed here. There is a general relation between expanded autonomy and the quality of the price system. Clearly, if enterprises are responding to the wrong prices, then increasing their decision-making power and increasing their responsiveness to profit does not necessarily improve the performance of the economic system as a whole, and can easily harm it. In China, there were huge variations among profit rates in different industrial sectors at this time, reflecting the distorted price system. But there is also a simpler, more mechanical relationship between profit retention and financial rationalization. This comes from the fact that large enterprise surpluses were channeled into the state budget.

As noted in Chapter 1, industrial enterprise profits were an enormous sum. In 1978, industrial profits amounted to 17% of GNP (industrial taxes were another 9% of GNP). "Profits" were a large, undifferentiated sum of money that included a number of income streams unrelated to profit narrowly defined. Important among these were the returns to past investment (the government did not charge for its investment, but instead claimed control over resulting profit streams), implicit taxes, rents to land and mineral resources and false profits caused by underaccounting of real costs such as depreciation. Perhaps most important, profits included the rents that accrued to industrial firms because of state price controls combined with barriers to entry in the industrial sector. A sense of what this meant for profit retention can be gained by comparing total profit and total wages. In 1978, state industrial profit was 2.4 times the total state industrial wage bill; since bonus and welfare funds were initially intended to be around 15% of wages, the retention ratio for these funds averaged only 6% of profit. Total retention rates would go higher as firms were allowed to retain profit for productive investments as well. But in any case, enterprise profit retention could only mean granting the enterprise rights over a small proportion of "paper profits."

The ultimate objective of reform therefore was an enterprise taxation system that would permit enterprises to exercise greater autonomy within the framework of a clear, consistent set of rules; but this could only be achieved once paper profits were redefined, divided into their economic components, and shrunk in absolute magnitude. Profit retention could not wait until comprehensive financial rationalization had been carried out, because quick results were needed. Simple rules of thumb were established to determine enterprise profit retention. Enterprise retained profit was set by some variant of the following general formula, in which P is profit and R is retained profit:

$$R = a*P_{t-1} + b*(P_t-P_{t-1})$$

The initial scheme implemented was the simplest possible: a=b, so that the enterprise retained a simple percentage share of total profit, with that percentage based on the previous year's performance. This scheme had the advantage of simplicity, and the absence of ratchet effects. But it provided very weak incentive effects, because the marginal retention rate was very low. In 1980, in-budget industrial enterprises on average retained 12.6% of total profits. With a equal to b, marginal retention equals average retention, so that an enterprise that increased its profits by one dollar would only retain an additional 12.6 cents on average. Moreover, marginal retention rates varied enormously emong enterprises. The higher were profits per worker, the lower were marginal retention rates, so the most profitable factories had the weakest incentives. Conversely, factories that did poorly in the base year might enjoy very high marginal retention rates, and experience windfall gains as profits recovered.

Some tinkering with the formulas was tried to remedy these problems. One approach was to set a higher rate for retention out of incremental than of base-year profit (that is, b > a). In many cases, this incremental sharing ratio was set at 20% (Zheng Derong *et al.* 1987: 68–69). This modification increased marginal incentives slightly for most firms, while equalizing marginal rates across firms. The system as modified could be applied to low-profit enterprises, and even to chronic loss-making firms (for which a < 0). Nevertheless, marginal incentives remained weak, and further progress seemed to await financial rationalization.

Wages and bonuses

With the institution of profit retention, worker bonuses grew rapidly and became a major component of employee compensation. By 1980, bonuses amounted to 9% of total state wages, and the institution of bonuses accounted for the bulk of the 14% increase in real urban wages between 1978 and 1980 (Figure 3.1). Profit retention also permitted a rapid increase in worker welfare funds. These funds were used to finance investment in housing and in clinics, clubhouses, and cafeterias that served the workers. The effect of enhanced funding for worker welfare was most evident in the accelerated pace of urban housing construction. From substantially less than 30 million square meters annually before 1978, housing construction jumped to over 100 million square meters by 1982, and sustained that level through the 1980s (*Fixed Investment* 1950–1985: 154, 272). Thus, for over a decade,

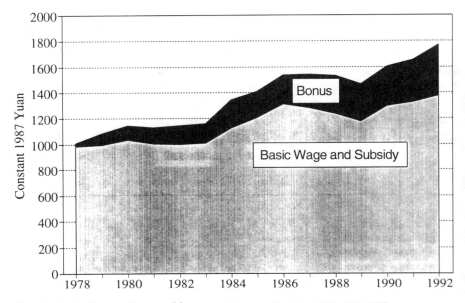

Figure 3.1 Real state wages and bonuses. Source: *Statistic* 1993: 132, 237.

China annually added one half a square meter of housing for each urban resident, an impressive achievement. About 60% of this urban housing was financed by enterprise retained funds (*Economic* 1982: V-42). Thus, enterprise retained funds used for bonuses and collective facilities were the specific mechanism by which the reformers implemented their pro-consumption policies in urban areas.

Bonus and welfare funds were not intended solely to improve the life of Chinese workers – they were also supposed to make them work harder. The extreme rigidity of the Chinese wage system was described in Chapter 1, and despite the revival of worker bonuses in 1978, the overall wage system remained much less flexible in China than in the ECEs. The enterprise had no control over promotion or firing, so distribution of bonuses was the only significant mechanism for motivating labor.[3] As an incentive mechanism, bonuses had many shortcomings. Two factors limited the usefulness of bonuses. First, the enterprise had no significant internal motivation to restrain bonuses. From the enterprise's standpoint, the more bonuses it could pay, the better. Factories had soft budget constraints and were often able to evade specific financial regulations, particularly during periods of rapid reform implementation. For example, a Shenyang report found that during 1980 two-thirds of the factories studied had paid bonuses in excess of regulatory ceilings, with one factory managing to double its average wage in a single year (Pu Shumian 1981). As a result, planners worried about the macro-economic consequences of uncontrolled increase in bonuses, imposed ceilings on total bonuses per factory, and stepped up monitoring of bonus ceilings. Those ceilings were initially set at one and a half months base wage, but were gradually raised and then stabilized at the value of two and half months base wage (thus from around 9% to about 15% of total income, including wage, bonus and cash subsidies). The better-run factories were thus soon in the position of annually paying out the maximum amount of bonus allowed, so that further improvements in productivity could not increase bonuses.

Second, workers colluded to blunt the incentive impact of bonuses. Where bonuses were already at the ceiling, workers correctly perceived that bonus distribution was a zero-sum game. Bonuses could be differentiated to make them work harder, but could not increase average levels of compensation. As a result, workers tended to push for egalitarian distribution of bonuses. Moreover, workers had the means to enforce their preferences. Some of this was institutional: Bonuses were reviewed annually by Workers' Congresses which had the right to veto managerial distribution plans. More important still was the impact of the permanent employment system. Managers and workers were condemned to long-term coexistence. Unable to fire workers, managers were nearly helpless if a group of disgruntled workers chose to disrupt production through slowdowns or absenteeism. Managers and their families usually lived in factory-run residential quarters along with workers and their families, who thus had many informal ways to pressure managers.[4] Finally, the permanent employment system meant that more productive workers had no credible threats to enforce their claim to larger bonuses. They could not leave the factory and find a better job, so they were forced to accept the preferences of the average worker.

Overall, reform of the wage system in the early 1980s was important in increasing urban income and living standards. It thus served the goals of economic reorientation, as well as the political objectives of China's leaders. As an incentive mechanism, bonuses were weak at best. Like the profit retention system as a whole, bonuses provided some incentives for better work, but those incentives were not very powerful.

Growth of enterprise investment

Expansion of enterprise investment in housing and worker facilities was only a part of a broader pattern of increased enterprise investment. Fig-

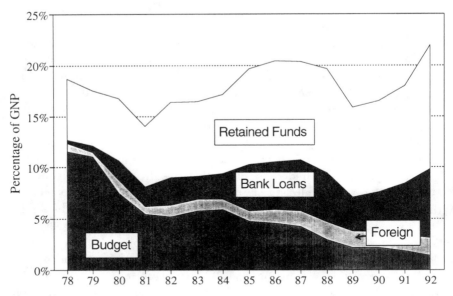

Figure 3.2 Finance of state investment. Source: Naughton 1987a: 80; *Fixed Investment* 1949–1985: 69, 218, 329; *Statistic* 1993: 150.

ure 3.2 summarizes changes in the finance of fixed investment in the state-run economy. Before the initiation of reforms, in 1978, investment was financed out of two tranches. Over 60% of investment came from the state budget, while almost a third came from retained enterprise funds, predominantly depreciation funds. Foreign loans (also channeled through the budget at this time) and domestic bank lending played a minor role. Thus, there was significant financial decentralization in the prereform economy, but the types of finance were quite limited. The reform program swelled decentralized investment financing in two ways. Retained profits joined retained depreciation funds as a major source of enterprise retained funds. Gradual expansion of bank lending for fixed investment lending also contributed to enterprise resources. During this period, the bulk of bank lending was for small, light industry projects, and the recipients were generally existing enterprises or local governments. By 1982, enterprise retained funds accounted for almost half of all investment financing, while budgetary grants had fallen to 30% of the total. Thus, the financial decentralization of investment – already significant before reforms – quickly became an important trend in the reform process overall (Naughton 1987a).

Authority relations

The effort to expand enterprise autonomy makes it seem as if it were clear who exercised decision-making power in the enterprise. But the enterprise was actually a subdivision of a hierarchical bureaucracy. The internal organization of the enterprise was generally required to correspond to that of the economic bureaucracy. Managers did not have the authority to shape the enterprise into a unique or idiosyncratic organization to match the output, market, or personality of that unit. Indeed, it was unclear whether managers had any autonomous authority at all. The enterprise was permeated by authority relationships from outside the firm itself, shaped by commands that did not go through the firm's "head office" at all. For example, the labor section of the enterprise was required to follow instructions from the municipal labor bureau. The enterprise was in this respect not an autonomous business organization at all, but was rather knit into the fabric of the bureaucratic economy (Komiya 1987).

Among these external authority relations, by far the most important was that exercised by the Communist Party. For a while during the Cultural Revolution, the Party had simply run the enterprises directly. By the late 1970s the formal structure of authority was "factory manager responsibility under the leadership of the Party committee." In theory, the factory manager was in charge of day-to-day operations, but with the presumption that the Party was the ultimate arbiter of important decisions. In practice, according to one account: "The current system is that the party secretary is the number one man, and the factory manager is the number two man. Even when the number one man doesn't give direct orders, the number two man has to secure his agreement when managing production and administrative work" (Yan Chongzong 1980: 26). The Party had direct control over personnel and employment. Party committees controlled the *nomenklatura* – the appointment, promotion, and dismissal of all significant managerial posts. Moreover, Party control over political work explicitly included authority over income distribution and the distribution of welfare benefits and housing. Party secretaries had offices and secretaries working for them, and thereby had the means to intervene in decision-making when they chose.

Any significant expansion of enterprise authority required a diminished Party role in the enterprise. Early reforms began to address the problem, but reformers at this time hesitated to grant full authority to factory managers, fearing creation of excessive personal authority (the Soviet system of "one-man management" in factories had long been criticized in Maoist China). One prominent proposal was to give factory managers authority under the overall guidance of the Workers' Congress. The reform blueprint of September 1980 called for "factory manager responsibility under the leadership of the Workers' Congress," and said the Party would withdraw from day-to-day decision-making. Implementation of this system was tried in a few selected enterprises (SRC 1998a: 29–30; Han Xiugang 1981: 4). Thus, Chinese reformers flirted with the adoption of institutions for worker management, similar to those in Yugoslavia. A competing proposal was however championed by Deng Xiaoping himself, in a major speech of August 1980:

[We must] progressively and with preparation change the system of factory manager responsibility under the leadership of the party committee, and, after testing, gradually implement the system of factory manager responsibility under the leadership of the factory management committee or board of directors. . . . This reform will take the party committee out of day-to-day affairs, and allow it to concentrate on political and ideological work and organizational supervision (CCP 1982: 531).

Deng's approach was no less significant in removing the Party from enterprise management, but it meant much more authority to the manager, and less to the workers. The manager would have substantial direct influence over the management committee, which he would chair, and would include representatives of junior management as well as Party and labor union representatives. This approach was also tried out in selected factories during 1980, and seemed to gain favor and be on the verge of general adoption by 1981 (Commentator 1981).

Further enterprise reforms

Experimentation began in 1980 with further enterprise reforms that had as their objective the full commercialization of state enterprises. The Chinese called this "responsibility for profits and losses," and it involved rationalization of the enterprise financial system as well as a dramatic expansion in independence. In January 1980 a new system was tried out in a handful of enterprises and labeled "tax for profit" because it involved the reclassification of a substantial portion of enterprise profits as tax revenues. Firms paid "four taxes and two fees." The fees varied between regions: In Shanghai, enterprises were to pay a 9.6% annual charge on fixed capital financed from budgetary grants and a 5.04% annual fee on working capital so financed. Enterprises were to pay a 50% income tax, taxes on real estate (1.2% annually for structures plus an urban land fee of .72 yuan per square meter) and vehicle taxes. Even with these three taxes and two fees, profits pending price reform were still quite uneven, so enterprises were subject to an "adjustment tax," essentially a profit-sharing ratio set on after-tax profit (Zheng

Derong *et al.* 1987: 66). This approach substantially rationalized the distribution of after-tax profit, but still implied that profitable enterprises ended up with relatively low marginal retention rates because of the adjustment tax. Similar programs, though with lower capital charges, were also implemented in a few enterprises in Sichuan and Guangxi.

This was a natural next step in the enterprise reform program, and a promising step in economic reform overall. By the mid-1980s, reformers were hoping that tax for profit schemes would become the main financial form of Chinese enterprises. Clearly, the central idea was to take the large undifferentiated mass of accounting profits and reclassify it into several economically more meaningful categories, most of which could be labeled as taxes. Moreover, by redefining some profit as tax – by definition a legally instituted financial responsibility of the enterprise – the enterprise could have substantially greater autonomy in the disposition of the part of profit that was not included in tax. The idea was to combine this financial reform with the conversion of enterprises into independent business units, and limit their obligations to the state to tax payments.

Combining plan and market

Enterprise reform by itself cannot achieve much unless there is an adequately functioning market environment in which the enterprise can operate. The initial impetus to rehabilitate the market, like so much policy in the early period, came in a speech by veteran leader Chen Yun. In March 1979, Chen reiterated his long-held view that the market should have a role in the socialist planned economy (CCP 1982: 68–71). The objective of "combining plan and market" quickly replaced the ideal of "using economic levers" as a prime reform slogan. Chen had long advocated a subsidiary role for markets under socialism, particularly for sideline production of rural households and other small scale commodities, and in 1979 he probably did not really envisage markets as a substitute for planning. Instead, he probably expected the combination of plan and market to mean both more plan and more market: more plan because more realistic planning would result in more accurate and authoritative plans, and more market because planners would not bother to set targets for myriad small commodities.[5] By legitimating market operations, Chen put his stamp of approval on the growth of new markets, and also touched off a broad-ranging discussion on the meaning of combining plan and market.

In these early discussions, two conceptions of how to combine plan and market emerged as the main contenders. The first of these tended to be favored by the planning commission and relatively conservative economists (Xu Yi 1981; Gui Shiyong *et al.* 1980), and can be seen as an extension of Chen Yun's ideas. It envisaged economic activity divided into "blocks" (*bankuai*): Compulsory planning would guide a sphere of state-owned, large-scale industry; markets would guide small-scale activity. Conservatives essentially saw the market as a concession to Chinese reality, that of a large developing country. Because planning could not be comprehensive, allowing the market to govern relatively unimportant economic decisions would remove a large burden from planners. But planning was still seen as the most essential activity directly guiding the country's development and modernization. The alternative concept was held by most of China's reform economists. This concept envisioned plans and markets that "permeated" (*shentou*) one another. The entire economy would operate according to market principles but the market would be shaped and guided by a state plan. The highest form of planning was state manipulation of "economic levers" or price parameters, such as tax, interest rates, and price.[6] The expansion of enterprise autonomy and the enterprise's self-interested desire to increase its profit would improve microeconomic efficiency; but macroeconomic coordination and effective development strategy would still require indirect government control.

> This means that the state must by means of administrative intervention and various economic levers, mainly in the form of prices, taxes and interest rates, direct the economic results of individual units, so that they are identical to those of the whole society (He Jianzhang and Zhang Zhuoyuan 1981).

Planning would indirectly guide the market.

The idea of combining planning and market according to this second concept is not a native Chinese creation. Rather, it looks back to the idealistic concept of reform socialism that was prevalent during the 1950s and 1960s in Europe and that provided the intellectual underpinning for rationalizing reforms in Europe in the 1960s.[7] In the Introduction it was argued that the rationalizing reform model proved inadequate to guide the transition to a market economy in Eastern Europe, and this reform model was to prove equally inadequate in the Chinese reform. But in the very early stages of reform, it was an attractive model because it promised a thorough rehabilitation of market forces throughout the economy: It was by far the more radical of the two concepts of plan and market. It also had the advantage that many contentious issues could be deferred until a later stage of reform. The immediate task was to create a functioning market environment through price and financial reforms. Exactly what planning would accomplish in the new environment could be determined later. The reform camp thus still united economists with a wide spectrum of ideas. A few advocated immediate abolition of compulsory output planning and limiting government activity to macroeconomic stabilization. For others, government intervention should continue and the government should determine income distribution, set the level of investment, choose the main growth sectors, coordinate regional development, and so forth. But whatever their concept of the ultimate government role in the economy, it was clear that the immediate priority was price reform. All those holding to the reformist concept believed in rapid price reform, conceived as realignment of state-set prices. For conservatives, price reform was less pressing: After a few ameliorative reforms, they could return to the job of planning economic growth.

The plan in practice

While theoretical debates proceeded, the practical reality was that plans were still important and that planning had to be adapted to rapidly changing economic conditions. For three years in a row – from 1979 through 1981 – the state plan was revised and targets signficantly lowered months after the plan had already been delivered to production units. Changes in economic policy coming in rapid succession made it impossible for planners to keep up with feasible, consistent plans. Changes in investment strategy from 1979 through 1981 had their biggest impact on the machinery industry. Virtually every feature of economic reorientation tended to reduce machinery demand: Overall investment was reduced, defense production was slashed, and the remaining investment was shifted toward housing, which required no machinery. In 1979, compulsory plans given to the large machinery enterprises in the First Ministry of Machine Building system amounted to 86% of total output. In subsequent years, as central government investment was slashed, the compulsory output plan covered only 54% of output in 1980 and only 20% in 1981 (Ding Changqing 1984; Yu Youhai 1982). With output planning slashed and excess capacity everywhere, it made little sense to continue allocating most machinery products. Beginning in 1980, the government continued to list 157 types of machinery nominally subject to allocation, but in fact only 7 were actually allocated by the Material Supply Bureau or the Machinery Ministries (SRC 1988b: 453). Machinery firms and their customers were left to arrange their own transactions.

These changes had a significant impact on the evolution of the Chinese planning system overall. The early enterprise reforms had been compatible with a goal of strengthened but rationalized central planning, and even as enterprise reforms were beginning, planners continued their efforts to make the material allocation system more precise and more complete. The list of commodities nominally subject to distribution by the Material Supply Bureau was increased in both 1979 and 1980 to reach a total of 256. But in fact, only some 60 commodities were actually allocated in both 1979 and 1980, and in 1981, as cutbacks intensified, even fewer commodities were centrally allocated – perhaps as few as 30 in all (Economics Delegation 1979; CMEA: 75, 92). In the face of this buffeting from the winds of economic change, the impetus to strengthen the traditional material balance plan gradually faded. By 1980, the Material Supply Bureau itself was proposing that the number of commodities subject to centralized allocation be cut to 68 (Xinhua 1980), a proposal to recognize and stabilize the contemporary reality, rather than reduce the number of commodites actually allocated. Thus, by the end of 1980, serious efforts to rebuild the traditional planning system were essentially dead.[8]

Changing economic priorities during 1979–1981, while cutting demand for most producer goods, did increase demand for many consumer goods. At first this had the paradoxical result of *increasing* the degree of planning for consumer goods industry. Planners provided light industry with priority access to raw materials and fuel and power, so they understandably intensified their oversight of light industrial production. Central government output plans covered 30% of light industry output value in 1978, but this had increased to 53% of output value by 1982 (Wang Zhong 1983: 68–69). Thus, some of the changes in planning were merely a shift in focus: As industrial machinery became a surplus commodity and manufactured consumer goods became shortage commodities, the attention of planners simply shifted to manufactured consumer goods. But in any case, throughout the early 1980s, the disparity between the theoretical and actual condition of material balance planning persisted. After 1982, as industrial growth resumed, planners undoubtedly resumed allocating a few more heavy industrial products. But the number remained extremely modest, and the character of the planning system did not fundamentally change. Planners continued to list 256 commodities subject to allocation, but in fact, through 1984 they never allocated as many as 40 (Zhong Zhiqi 1984).

The market for producer goods

Already in the pre-reform system, something like a market for producer goods existed based primarily on small scale and rural firms. A large proportion of standardized producer goods was controlled by local governments and small-scale producers. In practice, these agencies participated in market-type transactions, including sale and barter. In regions such as Jiangsu province, where rural industry was already significant, market-like transactions accounted for about one-quarter of the supply of key raw materials in 1978 (Shen Yi 1979). Weak administrative coordination of the economy was combined with the presence of material and financial resources under the control of local governmental organizations, and this led inevitably to the growth of primitive forms of market-like exchange. One such type was interregional trade, conducted between local governments. Crucial limitations were that explicit profit-seeking activity was taboo (it occurred anyway) and that enterprises were required to go through government sponsors to operate outside their region. In some cases, rural enterprises operated on the market completely independently, usually because of the absence of a competent government sponsor. Prices were in theory always controlled, but this control was frequently exercised at the local level, and locally set prices often diverged from centrally set prices. Thus, there was a large volume of materials, and a set of habitual practices, already in place that could contribute to the development of a genuinely market-oriented extra-plan sector. Mostly this involved swaps of standardized producer goods, such as coal, cement, and iron (Wong 1985, Wu Jinglian and Zhao Renwei 1987). As the number of small-scale producers grew with reform, this market-like sector grew.

Similarly, the machinery industry, which had to adapt its products to the needs of hundreds of thousands of individual factories, had some market-like operations even before reform. For example, during the mid-1970s, the Shanghai machinery industry – the most important in the country – undertook extra-plan tasks that amounted to 10-20% of its total output (Zhang Pinqian and Xiao Liang). Markets for machinery products grew dramatically after 1979, following the reduction in the central plan. While central investment was being cut, financial reforms in industry were increasing the financial resources of enterprises, and this created a new decentralized demand for investment goods. Given the really serious difficulties the machinery industry faced, planners responded by giving machinery enterprises maximum flexibility. They were encouraged to find their own customers, and with the rapid increase in decentralized investment resources they were often able to so. As a result, new linkages were created, and actual output declined far less than the plan. The whole machinery industry was thrown onto a *predominantly* market basis in a remarkably short time. Constant change eroded planning, because planners could not respond quickly enough to draw up consistent plans, while reforms allowed production units considerable flexibility in responding to the deterioration of the planned economy. Enterprises increasingly learned to operate outside and without plans, and increasingly in the market. During the early 1980s, a dual-track plan and market system sprang up, but one without clear legal sanction or rules of operation. Its emergence was the unintended consequences of repeated shifts in economic priorities, and the more rapid response of market-like institutions to these shifts.

The expanded autonomy provisions of 1979 allowed large enterprises in other sectors to enter these quasi-markets for the the first time. Large enterprises were given the right to sell their above-plan output. In essence, the provisions allowed enterprises to locate their own customers when output plans were set below capacity. These provisions ultimately became quite important. Even in the early stages, enterprise self-sales were often beneficial to the enterprise. If the enterprise produced consumer goods, it could pocket the commercial markup on its direct sales and thereby increase revenues. Producers of scarce producer goods also benefited by having a proportion of output under their direct control. They could provide goods in exchange for access to other materials they needed, even while price controls were respected. Enterprise supervisory authorities gave enterprises the power to sell a small portion of their output independently, precisely in order to give them a few economic benefits and an additional measure of flexibility. In addition, producer goods markets were established in large cities, including Shanghai, to facilitate transactions (Byrd 1991). Statistics on direct sales by large enterprises in steel and cement are given in Table 3.1.

During the early 1980s, then, a market sector for industrial producer goods developed. This sector consisted of the small enterprises, which had never really been integrated into the planning system, the machinery sector, and "fringe markets" for above-plan output of industrial raw materials. The market sector added some flexibility to the industrial supply system. But large enterprises were required to follow state-set prices when they sold above-plan output. The provisions were more flexible for small-scale local and rural firms, but there was no commitment to the principle that outside-plan transactions of state enterprises should take place at market determined prices. As a result, after an initial spurt in outside-plan marketings, a process of creeping recontrol of state-controlled materials appeared. As economic conditions revived, and industrial materials appeared relatively scarcer, planners cut back on the proportion of goods large enterprises were allowed to market directly (visible particularly in steel in Table 3.1). It was unclear whether this market sector would be a temporary accompaniment of economic reorientation, or whether it represented the first stage of a more profound economic transformation.

Table 3.1. *Direct enterprise sales by keypoint enterprises*

	1980	1981	1982	1984
	(percentage of total output)			
Steel	11	20	14	10
Cement	6	7	8	9

Source: Ren Tao 1982; SRC 1988: 452; Byrd 1991: 52.

*The market for consumer goods: Ending the state
commercial monopoly*

In order to create a functioning market for consumer goods, it was essential to
eliminate the near monopoly over consumer goods distribution that was exercised by the state commerce system. The impetus to relax the commercial
monopoly came from two sources. First was the desire to introduce more
flexibility into the system to improve incentives for producers and better meet
consumer needs. This was the area where Chen Yun's call to combine plan and
market was most salient. Chen Yun clearly envisaged maintaining the state
monopoly for a few crucial commodities (such as grain and cotton), while
abandoning it for a diverse range of less important commodities. Second, the
pressure of urban unemployment strongly encouraged planners to allow the
creation of new commercial organizations. Jobs in commerce were much
cheaper to create than jobs in industry because they required a much smaller
initial investment. The urgent shortage of retail services combined with large
numbers of unemployed suggested an obvious marriage of convenience: Start
up new commercial outlets quickly as a solution to both problems. Beginning
in 1979, the commercial monopoly was substantially relaxed, and eventually –
by the mid-1980s – eliminated. The rules that tied factories to the state commercial system for distribution were gradually relaxed. New commercial outlets, at first sponsored by city governments and enterprises, but soon by
individuals as well, transformed the environment for commercial transactions.
The result was an increasingly flexible commercial system that did much to
improve the quality of life for Chinese households.

Industry-commerce relations

The traditional command system had tied commercial and industrial units
together with little autonomy for either side. State-run factories were re-

quired to sell all their consumer goods output to state commerce, which was
required to buy it all. This system was formally abolished in mid-1980. In
general, state commerce maintained right of first refusal of factory output,
but if state commerce declined to purchase output, factories were allowed to
sell on their own if they could locate customers. The previous system of
monopoly procurement by commerce was replaced by a diversified system in
which four categories of procurement were recognized. By 1982, the proportion of total manufactured consumer goods procured through different systems was as follows (Liu Yi 1982):

Monopoly purchase	32%
Planned contract	28%
Ordered	12%
Selective purchase	28%

The old monopoly system covered only one-third of consumer manufactures.
While the planned contract system may have provided only marginally more
autonomy, some 40% of consumer manufactures were now procured according to negotiated contracts. State commerce still had priority access to the
goods of state factories, but increasingly factories were able to first sign
contracts with state commerce and then orient the remainder of their production to the market (Lu Chaorong 1981).

Conversion from supply plans to voluntary contracts has been a staple of
reform programs in other socialists countries, including Hungary and the
Soviet Union. China's conversion seems to have been somewhat more successful than in those countries, for two reasons: First, macroeconomic policy
reduced the degree of shortage, thus really affecting the incentives of both
contracting parties; second, a rapid proliferation of retail outlets and distribution channels encouraged serious demonopolization. This is discussed in the
next section.

Diversification of commercial network

The first and easiest departure from the strict commercial monopoly came
when the prohibition on peasant markets in urban areas was dropped. Several thousand outdoor markets for fresh produce quickly sprang up, and
urban planners facilitated the revival of these traditional institutions by setting aside space and building simple shelters. The share of direct peasant
marketings in total urban retail sales climbed steadily from 4% in 1978 to
10% by 1982.

The most important step in the diversification of the commercial network

Table 3.2. *Labor service company workers*

	1979	1982	1984	1986
	(million)			
Total	1.52	4.91	8.31	9.80
Training or temporary work	1.10	2.17	2.74	2.80
Placed in collective enterprises	0.42	2.74	5.57	7.00

Source: Taylor 1986: 257; *Economic* 1986: V-52; *Economic* 1987: V-41.

came with the attempt to create a large number of new jobs. A peculiar Chinese institution was adapted to accommodate the large demand for employment of urban young people. During the 1960s and 1970s, the Chinese had allowed state-run firms to sponsor "collectives" in order to create employment for the sons and daughters of state workers. Neighborhood organizations had also sponsored collectives. (These are described in Chapter 4.) These had generally been in light manufacturing – 97% of commercial employees had been part of the formal state system. With the increase in employment pressure, policymakers shifted to strongly encouraging these sponsored collectives to engage in commercial activity. These new entities were generally called "labor service companies," and their number expanded rapidly beginning in 1979. At first, nearly all were sponsored by state-run enterprises and non-profit organizations for the children of their own workers (they faced strict quotas on hiring new state employees). Gradually municipal and neighborhood governments also became important sponsors through the Municipal Labor Bureaux. Labor service companies were an important part of handling the short-run employment problem as well as liberalizing the commercial sector. All labor service companies combined absorbed between one and two million labor market entrants annually. At any given time, up to 2 million of these entrants were either undergoing training or engaging in temporary work (often make-work). Gradually, these entrants were shifted into permanent employment in collective enterprises set up as part of the labor service companies. In the early years, virtually all of these collective enterprises were engaged in commerce, especially retail sales and catering. By the mid-1980s, though, an increasing number of small manufacturing establishments were operated by the labor service companies as well. As Table 3.2 shows, these organizations had grown steadily and developed into a significant presence in the urban economy by the mid-1980s.

As these enterprises expanded in scale, they came to constitute a large-

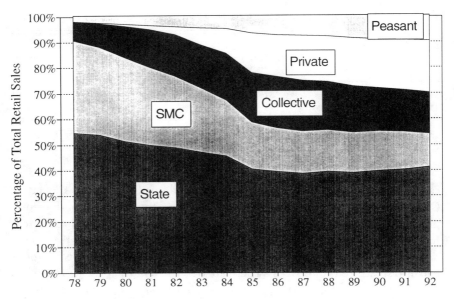

Figure 3.3. Retail sales by ownership. Source: *Statistic.* Various years, Table 14-25; Commerce 1984: 503.

scale commercial network not under the control of the commercial monopoly administered by the Ministry of Commerce. They were forced to carve out a place for themselves by dealing with wholesaler and production enterprises directly, operating as relatively independent business entities, and contracting for supplies in an ordinary business fashion. By the time the large number of new job-seekers was accommodated, a large new commercial sector had been created, amounting to 36% of total urban commercial personnel at the end of 1982 (Wang Hongmo 1989: 265). Within four years, more than 3 million people were absorbed into commercial activity in urban areas outside the commercial monopoly. By the end of 1982, 2.08 million workers were employed in collectively run commercial firms not subordinate to the Ministry of Commerce, and slightly over a million private peddlers had gone into business in urban areas. In addition, another three-quarters of a million commercial workers were in operation either as sales agents for factories, or in sponsored organizations with state worker status (Commerce 1984: 543).

The result of this process was a substantial diminution of the commercial monopoly (Figure 3.3). By the early 1980s, multiple supply channels were generally available both for manufactured consumer goods and for agricultural produce. The initial steps in this upwelling of "entrepreneurship" had, however, been taken by municipal governments. Concerned above all to provide employment for their own children, they summoned up a new commercial system in the process. Gradually the process expanded to create a diversified commercial system characterized by different ownership forms.

Summary of initial reform program

Chinese enterprise reforms began with a remarkable burst of activity during 1979–80. Virtually every aspect of the enterprise control system was addressed, and liberalization moves begun. Moreover, through most of 1980, reforms were gaining momentum. In August 1980, the government called for the universalization of enterprise autonomy measures beginning in 1981 (SRC 1984). Yet reformers also found that enterprises were far more deeply enmeshed in the bureaucratic economy than they had anticipated. While each element of reform introduced a bit more flexibility into decision-making at the enterprise level, enterprises continued to be bound by the overlapping control mechanisms that restrained them within the bureaucratic economy. In order for the initial enterprise reforms to have an impact, they would have to be reinforced by additional changes in the economy. But before that could happen, the government called a temporary halt to enterprise reforms.

Retrenchment of reforms

By the end of 1980, some of China's leaders became increasingly concerned at a loss of control over the economy. This concern was fueled initially by macroeconomic considerations. As described in the last chapter, readjustment had reduced excess demand in the producer goods sector of the economy by cutting investment; but rapid growth of household income had outrun the expanding production of consumer goods and led to inflation. Moreover, investment had not been reduced as rapidly as expected, because enterprise investment had increased nearly as rapidly as central government investment had declined. But these problems did not lead just to a shift in macroeconomic policy, because conservatives argued that overly rapid implementation of reforms was the major cause of economic problems. Financial decentralization had swollen enterprise coffers, contributing to an erosion in budgetary revenues and growth of decentralized investment. Informal relaxation of controls on pricing had allowed macroeconomic imbalances to translate into open inflation. As a result of these concerns, the pace of reform was drastically slowed.

The crucial person in this policy shift, as in the initial adoption of reorientation and reform in 1979, was the old economist Chen Yun. Chen throughout his career was a consistent advocate of moderate growth policies: His opposition to the Ten Year Plan led to reorientation of the economy in 1979, and in 1980–81, Chen displayed a similar aversion to overly rapid growth of demand caused by rapid reforms. But though Chen's hesitancy about reform was initially prompted by macroeconomic considerations, Chen used the opportunity to lay down some ideological principles about the nature of the socialist economy, and in particular about the primacy of planning. Chen's statement on combining plan and market had opened the door to productive reforms and fertile discussion, but now Chen slammed shut the door he himself had opened. He began to insist that the plan must be primary, and the market merely a secondary or supplementary element. Moreover, an indispensable part of the plan must be compulsory production and allocation targets. One of Chen's closest followers wrote with great explicitness:

Sure we want to enliven the economy, but we must be careful not to enliven the planned economy out of existence . . . Compulsory plans are a basic characteristic of the socialist planned economy . . . The state manages the important enterprises that affect the lifeblood of the economy; the state controls the commodities which affect the people's livelihood, and it carries out compulsory planning over this production which makes up a large proportion of total industrial and agricultural output. This proves that our economy is basically a planned economy (Deng Liqun 1982).

The conservative interpretation of combination of plan and market was made orthodox during 1982–83 (Fang Weizhong 1982). Chen Yun's own pronouncements were more elliptical, but there was no doubt that he was the main patron of these conservatives. On December 2, 1982, he chose a striking metaphor to display his own distrust of spontaneous market forces:

Enlivening of the economy should be under the direction of the plan. It's like the relationship between a bird and a cage. You can't just hold a bird in your hand, for it will die. You have to let it fly, but you can only let it fly in a cage. Without a cage it will fly away. The cage has to be the right size, and the cage itself has to be adjusted regularly. But no matter what, there has to be a cage (Li Zhining 1988: 474).

The veteran reformer Xue Muqiao was criticized for overly enthusiastic advocacy of reform ideas, and economists were forbidden to publicly advocate the abolition of compulsory planning. Public debate about combining plan and market ground to a halt (Xue Muqiao 1982; Yu Guangyuan 1982).

Retrenchment cut deeply into enterprise reforms as well. Plans to spread profit retention schemes to all state-run enterprises in 1981 were canceled, and there was to be no further expansions of reforms in the short run. For a brief period, even financial resources that had already been assigned to enterprises were blocked: Enterprise bank accounts were frozen and bank investment loans suspended (Yang Peixin 1981). There was even a temporary decline in rural free markets, as peasants reacted cautiously to the new policy winds blowing from Beijing (Xue Muqiao 1981). Proposals to remove the Communist Party from enterprise management were abandoned. Support for various forms of worker management seemed to wane sharply after 1981, and the proposals dropped from sight. Indeed, in a remarkable display of ideological clout, conservatives managed to censor Deng Xiaoping himself. When Deng's Selected Works were published in 1983, the passage on factory manager responsibility cited earlier in the section on Authority Relations was edited out (Deng Xiaoping 1984: 322–24). Orthodoxy had triumphed, and the flirtations with worker management and reduced Party control were seemingly forgotten. Factory manager responsibility did not return to the reformist agenda until after 1984. Indeed, activist promulgation of reform measures in the state economy virtually ceased until 1984.

Reforms were vulnerable in part because no consensus had been reached on the objective of reform. Some well-known socialist reformers, including Czechoslovakia's Ota Sik (then visiting China) warned that the worst possible course of action was to keep instituting reforms without any goal (Rong Jingben *et al.* 1981). Perhaps a pause in reform implementation would give time to draw up a more coherent strategy of reform. In other areas, the low quality of personnel – a legacy of the Cultural Revolution – seemed to impede reform progress. For example, in many enterprises, the Party Secretary was still the dominant authority figure. In such enterprises, a central government policy subordinating the Party Secretary to the manager was unlikely to succeed, and managers with decent working relations with the Party secretary were said to be reluctant to support disruptive changes (Lin Ling 1981). Further personnel changes might reasonably be required before the transition away from Party control was accomplished. After a period in which reform implementation ran ahead of reform theory, a delay in implementation might give theory a chance to catch up.

An important change took place around this time in the economic leadership. It should be apparent that Chen Yun was the dominant economic policymaker during the first year or two of the reform era. Not only was he in charge of day-to-day policymaking, his personal influence can be discerned behind both of the crucial turning points in economic policy of this time. But during 1980, the 75-year-old Chen Yun turned over day-to-day management of the economy to the 61-year-old newly installed Premier Zhao Ziyang, who took over the Economic Leading Group. Chen withdrew to a "second tier" position as a Communist Party elder. Even from the second tier, Chen was powerful enough to put across the policy shift at the end of 1980, and to lay down the ideological law in 1981–82. But from this time on, the nature of his influence began to change. Chen was willing to see a younger generation take over the work, as long as it could be counted on to carry out the principles laid down by elders like himself. Zhao, upon his accession to the Premiership, accepted the need for retrenchment, and his initial policy measures were cautious. Chen commented approvingly that since Zhao had come to Beijing from the provinces to become Premier, he had "begun to speak like a Beijing native" – that is, he had accepted the interests of the central government as paramount. Indeed, Zhao was a careful, flexible and pragmatic leader who kept the interests of the nation as a whole in mind. In subsequent years, he also came to have an increasingly firm commitment to the objective of a market economy and a more open society. As Zhao dealt with the economy on a day-to-day basis, his pro-reform ideas become solidified and radicalized. On the other hand, in retirement, Chen Yun's ideas became increasingly rigid, and after 1981 he made no constructive contribution to Chinese economic policy. Watching from the sidelines, but with considerable residual power and influence, he would occasionally raise obstacles to the reform process. By the end of the 1980s, Chen Yun and his fellow conservatives would experience increasing disquiet about the pace and direction of reform, leading to conflict with the increasingly radical ideals of Zhao Ziyang.

Unanticipated consequences of retrenchment 1: Further financial decentralization

The dramatic cuts in investment in early 1981 threw the economy into a sharp recession. Planners, regardless of their attitude toward reforms, were soon faced with a pressing problem: how to manage the economy out of recession. Frozen funding sources were unblocked within a few months. Planners had to find ways to manage enterprises facing renewed uncertainty and large reductions in their plans. Their solution was to adapt profit retention into a new form that gave them enhanced control over the enterprises. Planners pushed for the adoption of "profit responsibility systems" throughout history. The predominant feature of profit responsibility systems was the establishment of a profit delivery target for the year, combined with a high marginal retention rate – frequently 80% – for profit above the target. The emphasis of responsibility systems was on providing high-powered incentives to managers, to induce them to deal energetically with difficult economic conditions. Various kinds of enterprise profit responsibility systems were put in place in more than 30,000 in-budget state industrial enterprises – 80% of the total – during 1981. Similar systems were adopted in 35% of the larger state-run commercial enterprises (SRC 1988a: 76).

In the earlier profit retention schemes, baseline remittances were determined according to the enterprise's profit in the previous year. In 1981, this baseline was removed. As enterprise profits plummeted during the sharp early 1981 recession, enterprises and their superiors reopened negotiations on profit delivery obligations. Enterprises argued, usually successfully, that since central government policies were depressing profitability, they could not be penalized for not achieving 1980 profit levels. Without a universal rule for determining enterprise profit remittances and retention, virtually any argument could be advanced. An enterprise with large investment needs could be given a lower base delivery figure; another enterprise could be penalized by having its base figure increased. Thus, the financial relation between enterprise and superordinate body became primarily a bargaining relationship; as Kornai has observed for Hungary, financial bargaining replaced plan bargaining as the predominant interaction between enterprises and their superiors. Moreover, the classic problem with such bargaining – concern with ratchet effects – became prominent. That is, enterprises had less incentive to do exceptionally well in a given year because of their fears that their base figure would be raised in response. While in a static sense marginal incentives were strengthened, incentives may actually have been weakened once the dynamic impact of the ratchet effect is taken into account. Managers were comfortable with the system because of its flexibility; but it was apparent that it represented real regression of the objective of rationalizing reform and the creation of impartial rules to guide enterprises.

An amazing variety of specific schemes for determining profit retention were tried out beginning in 1981. One description of financial reform in Beijing blandly describes the success they achieved in establishing seven different financial systems between 1979 and 1984 (Ge Peng 1988). The fundamental reason for this restless shifting among systems was the continued unresolved tension between incentive effects and the impartiality of rules. Without a level playing field, no single system could effectively provide incentives to all firms. Pending fundamental rationalization of the financial system, managers within the industrial system attempted to improve on responsibility systems and guard against ratchet effects. They set explicit long-term – but still enterprise-specific – terms for profit sharing. The most common form of this was to establish a multi-year agreement in which base figures would increase by a fixed annual amount. By building in a certain increase in obligations that would be credible and accepted by the enter-

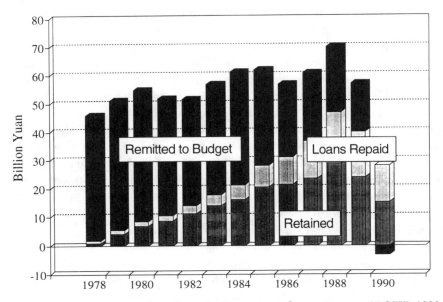

Figure 3.4. Disposition of profits in-budget state industry. Source: SRC/ER 1990: 645; *Abstract* 1993: 82.

prise, the true marginal retention rate (after discounting for ratchet effects) could be raised. This system (*ticeng baogan*) was popularized by the Capitol Iron and Steel Works and publicized as an incentive scheme that was compatible with the existing management system. Thus, there was a tendency for the bargaining relationship to evolve in specific directions: toward longer-time period, increasingly explicit bargains with a more complex content. These tendencies were to become especially important in the second phase of reforms.

As the economy revived after mid-year, the relatively high marginal retention ratios set by these systems ensured that enterprises would continue to retain relatively large amounts of aggregate profit. 1981 and 1982 were conservative years insofar as overall policymaking is concerned. Yet, during those years, retained profits increased 23% and 32% respectively, even while total profits declined. As a result, the share of profits retained jumped from 13% in 1980 to 22% in 1982 (Figure 3.4). Total profits grew very slowly over the entire period between 1978 and 1989, particularly considering the rapid growth of industry and persistent moderate inflation (we will return to this point in Chapter 6). Nevertheless, both retained profits and profits repaid to banks increased steadily. Indeed, the share of total profits retained by enterprises increased *every* year between 1978 and 1989, as did the share of profits paid to banks. Profit retention developed a cumulative momentum: from an initially modest program, financial decentralization gradually swelled to significant proportions.

It is striking, moreover, that the increase in profit retention bears no apparent relationship to progress in reforms in other dimensions, or to reform orientation at the top of the political system. After the introduction of "responsibility systems" in industry, it became clear that the division of profits between enterprises and their superiors was determined by the distribution of bargaining power between enterprises and the bureaucracy. In the early 1980s, Chinese enterprises demonstrated that while they had little autonomy, they had substantial bargaining power.

Unanticipated consequences of retrenchment 2: Decline of planning and rise of the market

The intensification of retrenchment policies in 1981 cut sharply into the growth of household incomes. Urban wage growth slowed drastically after 1980 (see Figure 3.1). At about the same time, the products of rapidly growing light industry began to appear on the marketplace. Texitles were a particularly important case. Supply of textiles grew rapidly as synthetic fiber production expanded and better cotton harvests were reaped. At the end of 1981, as a relative oversupply of synthetic fabric developed, planners twice cut the initially high price of synthetics (in 1981 and 1983) while raising the low fixed price of cotton textiles. Increased cotton textile prices, combined with sluggish income growth, reduced the demand for cotton fabrics, and oversupply spread to include cotton cloth. Trying to limit its expenditures on unsalable cloth, the Ministry of Commerce ended its existing arrangement to purchase all output of cotton textile mills, and instead began signing contracts for specified amounts of output. Textile mills were then allowed to sell uncontracted output independently, beginning in late 1982. Factories responded by setting up retail companies, sending salesmen to rural areas, and negotiating contracts directly with garment factories, hotels, and other bulk users. The state commerce monopoly on textile sales crumbled during this period of abundant supply. From 1983 through 1987, 29% of total textile sales were made independently by textile factories (SRC 1988b: 367).

Textiles had been the most important manufactured consumer good subject to rationing, which had been in place since the mid-1950s. At China's level of development, textiles make up a large part of the consumption bundle: 15% of urban consumer outlays in 1981. After 30 years of rationing, textiles were becoming freely available. With ample supply and stable prices, ration coupons gradually lost their value. Stores stopped demanding them, consumers stopped using them, and most localities stopped issuing them in 1983. Cloth rationing faded away. The spread of weak demand conditions to consumer goods markets thus produced the same effects as it had in producer goods markets. Slack demand for commodities weakened the demand for planning. In each case, markets seemed preferable as long as shortages were not a serious problem.

Reorientation policies undermined the justification for the plan and prepared the ground for an unanticipated growth in market-like transactions. Similar effects were apparent in the marketing of agricultural products as well. Every time a bumper crop came in, state commercial organs were overwhelmed, and a new arena for peasant marketing opened up (Wang Hongmo 1989: 262–63). Intensified macroeconomic austerity tended to spread the market elements already introduced.

The legitimacy of market prices remained uncertain. Price controls on outside-plan marketings by state enterprise remained in place. There was significant price flexibility in practice, but market prices had no formal standing in the system. Reformers did succeed in defining one unambiguous area for market prices. During 1982–83, price controls were eliminated on more than 500 small consumer items. Shoelaces and buttons were henceforth to be priced by the market. This was a small step forward, but important as the first unambiguous commitment to market prices, particularly since it was successful. After decontrol, price reductions outweighed price increases by a ratio of eight to one (*Jiage Lilun* 1983:5, 39–40; 1983:6, 45–49).

Unanticipated consequences of retrenchment 3: Support for the non-state sector

Early reform proposals were overwhelmingly concentrated on the problem of expanding autonomy for existing firms, especially state-owned enterprises. But with the slowdown in state sector reforms, and rapid growth of the non-state economy (Chapter 4), especially in rural areas, reform-minded politicians began to see non-state enterprises as a potentially successful component of reform overall. Beginning in 1982, growth of the non-state sector began to be presented as one of the main accomplishments of reform, and an important constituent of the reform process overall (SRC 1988a: 58). This was very much in contrast to earlier proclamations, in which growth of rural enterprises had never been mentioned. The idea of reform gradually began to include the spread of a diversified ownership system. Reformers were reacting to new information: the already emerging dynamism of rural industry in contrast to the difficulty of reforming state firms. They may also have been responding to purely political imperatives: Zhao Ziyang and First Party Secretary Hu Yaobang were both under pressure to show results, to provide evidence of some kind of forward motion. With progress in state-sector reforms stalled, the embrace of non-state enterprises could provide them with a welcome success story.

Distorted implementation: The failure of rationalization

In the early stages of the reform, reformers had hoped to rationalize important financial and other parameters as part of the early stages of reform. But after several years, every attempt at rationalization had failed. Three forms of rationalization are considered here: financial rationalization, price realignment, and the design of an overall reform program.

Financial rationalization

From the beginning, it was intended that enterprise reforms would be accompanied by a restructured financial system. Financial rationalization was to go along with financial decentralization. But the attempt to carry out financial rationalization never succeeded. Despite a series of explicit government decrees, no systematic reform of the enterprise financial system was ever carried out. The fate of the attempt to institute capital charges exemplifies this failure.

All the European socialist economies had implemented new enterprise financial systems in the 1960s that included charges to the enterprise for the use of fixed and working capital supplied by the state. But China's path had diverged from the other socialist countries by the early 1960s, and China never went through the 1960s stage of rationalization. As a result, China was the only socialist economy without fixed capital charges. The price of capital to state-owned industrial enterprises was usually zero: Fixed capital investment was provided primarily through the state budget and was costless to the enterprise, and the same was true for most working capital (though a portion was financed through bank loans at low interest rates). Generally, the only cost of capital was the opportunity cost an enterprise experienced when it used its own retained funds to purchase new assets.

With the onset of reform, the government tried to establish a positive price for capital. It proposed that enterprises pay a fixed percentage capital charge on the value of the state-supplied fixed assets they possessed, and that all future state investments would be made in the form of interest-bearing loans.[9] Three times between 1979 and 1982, the government issued categorical directives or regulations announcing the beginning of fixed asset charges, and not one was ever implemented. The initial reform package of July 1979 stipulated that all enterprises practicing profit retention would pay capital fees. Finance Minister Wang Bingqian specified on September 1, 1980, that fees for allocated working capital would be collected beginning with the first half of 1980 and that fees on fixed capital would be collected beginning in 1981 as part of the universal implementation of profit retention. These plans fell victim to the reform retrenchment at the end of 1980. Subsequently, financial regulations of December 26, 1981, proclaimed that all industrial enterprises would pay fixed and working capital fees beginning in 1982 (Zheng Derong *et al.* 107–8; 187). This regulation also had no effect. By the end of 1982, in spite of three unambiguous national regulations requiring all factories that practiced profit retention to pay capital charges, a system had emerged in which nearly all enterprises retained profits and none paid capital charges.[10]

The initiative to transform new investment from budgetary grants into repayable loans was nominally implemented, but never succeeded either. Investments were initially made repayable only for projects that were expected to be highly profitable. A few experimental projects were set up in November 1979, and the program was to be gradually spread after 1980 (Li Ping'an: 467; Zheng Derong *et al.* 1987: 81). Not until the end of 1984 was a determination made that all state investments ought to be on a repayable basis. As a result of this pattern of implementation, projects were never under any serious pressure to repay funds unless they were highly profitable and could easily repay them: The program could not screen projects on the basis of their profitability. Between 1980 and 1986, a total of 70 billion yuan in repayable investments was made, only one-third of budgetary investments. Moreover, only 8% of the loans had explicit contracts specifying the terms of repayment (Qi Guan 1987). By the end of the 1980s, many projects were in arrears, and a tiny proportion of total investment had actually been repaid (CIC 90:10, 37; 91:1, 26–31). Transforming budgetary grants to interest-bearing loans played no role in improving the allocation of capital.

The situation was not quite as grim as it appears. Although the system of state supply of capital remained stubbornly unreformed, financial decentralization implied that the budgetary system was of decreasing importance. By 1983, 15% of investment in the state sector was funded by bank credits and 45% by enterprise retained funds. In the case of retained funds, there were no interest charges or repayment obligations, but enterprises did have to weigh the opportunity costs of their finances, since they were now the owners of the funds being used. The majority of state investments were coming from decentralized funding sources that had an opportunity cost. But, remarkably, within the state system that was the core of the command economy, planners were unable to command enterprises to pay capital charges in exchange for the privilege of profit retention.

Price realignment

It was taken for granted among China's economists that comprehensive re-alignment of state-set prices would be a central and early component of industrial reforms. Moreover, as described earlier, advocacy of price reform was almost a defining characteristic of reformist economists. Visiting economists from Eastern Europe and the West urged that price reform be made the key to further reforms (Rong Jingben *et al.* 1981). China's two most eminent economists, the theoretician Sun Yefang and the policy-oriented reformer Xue Muqiao, both supported price reform as the central measure of reform overall. Moreover, the largest distortions in the price system were obvious to all: Energy, some raw material, and transportation charges all needed to be increased. During 1981, plans were made to realign some of the most obviously distorted prices, but this proposal apparently fell victim to the newly conservative atmosphere described before.

During 1981, a Price Research Center was established with the job of calculating a full set of "optimal" prices for the economy. It decided to follow the procedures of Czech reformers in 1966–68 and compute a full set of prices based on an input-output table. These would be cost plus markup prices. The methodology could produce one of a spectrum of prices depending upon how "surplus value" (profit) was distributed.[11] The Price Center labored for two years. It built a 253 sector I-O table and delivered several variant sets of prices in mid-1983 (Lu Nan 1982, Lu Nan and Li Mingzhe 1991; Tian Yuan and Qiao Gang 1991: 321–56). But despite this accomplishment, the Price Center model wasn't able to answer the really important questions about price reform. The I-O table was inaccurate, requiring ad hoc adjustments to achieve consistency. Questions about how to price natural resources (apparently the most distorted prices) were unanswered. The Center had no strong argument for the superiority of any of the variant prices it had computed. Most crucial was the question of how to handle the financial redistributions required by price adjustments. It seemed that any price adjustment scheme would require the state to compensate losers, imposing substantial costs on the government. After the calculation of optimal prices was finally complete, there were few compelling reasons to accept it, and it was discarded.

As the difficulties in computing optimal prices became increasingly apparent, doubts about the value of cost-plus prices were also growing. Cost-plus prices were not equilibrium prices, which could only be determined by explicitly incorporating demand into the price-setting mechanism. Increasing familiarity with the market made economists more comfortable with equilibrium prices, and they became familiar with economic models that could compute market prices, including programming and general equilibrium models. The objective of creating an "optimal" set of prices was gradually discarded. By some accounts, Zhao Ziyang had given up on the computation of optimal prices by mid-1984, and accepted the necessity of prices that equated supply and demand. Under these circumstances, planners were left to adjust individual prices one at a time. Progress was slow, though there were occasional successes. It remained true that price reforms were expected to begin with industrial raw materials and other producer goods, rather than the politically sensitive consumer goods. Reform plans in early 1984 called for a simple realignment of prices based on pushing up the prices of energy and raw materials, to be combined with taxation reform (SRC 1988a: 50, 121–22). Five years after the beginning of reform, the price realignment once seen as a crucial and early component of reform had not materialized and had little prospect.

Designing a reform plan

The failure of rationalization was mirrored by a continuing inability to draw up a coherent vision of the objective of the reform process. Between December 1979 and February 1984, seven reform programs were drawn up and officially adopted. Yet all of these reform programs shared a common feature: each outlined a set of measures and priorities for the following year or two. In each case, a further unspecified state of "comprehensive" reform was to begin in three to five years. It was assumed that additional practical experience and further discussion would lead to some practical content for the phase of comprehensive reform, and thus it was left unspecified. But each subsequent reform document continually pushed back the date at which "comprehensive" reforms would begin. None of these programmatic documents contains any indication of what comprehensive reform would actually look like (SRC 1988a: 1–125). Indeed, the reform programs contain a number of rationalizing reforms that never made it even to the initial stages of implementation, including an independent national taxation authority to be set up in 1982, and a social security fund to be set up by 1983 (SRC 1988a: 46, 71). Unquestionably, the change in the political environment after Chen Yun's pronouncement in 1981 is partially responsible for the vapidity of some of these documents. But it is also clear that exercises in reform design were simply not succeeding in producing consensus or making reform measures more concrete. China's reform without a blueprint did not unfold because of a commitment to atheoretical empiricism. Rather, policymakers began groping for stepping stones to cross the river only after attempts to build a sturdy framework for a bridge had failed.

Making the best of it: Institution-building, 1982–83

With broad progress on reform impossible because of the obstruction of Chen Yun and other conservatives, and rationalizing reforms failing consistently, the overall pace of change slowed down during 1982 and 1983. Yet a steady incremental process of institution-building continued. Institution-building was in some ways a direct continuation of the rehabilitation of administrative structures that had been going on since 1977, but the process was tilted in a reformist direction by the increased prominence of Zhao Ziyang in day-to-day decision-making. More capable institutions were to contribute to further reforms in the latter half of the 1980s.

Enterprise institutions

Enterprise management on the eve of reform had been chaotic, and the limited success of initial enterprise reforms showed how deep-rooted the problems were in state firms. From early 1982 through 1985, planners carried out a program of enterprise rectification that had two goals: rebuild and regularize the management institutions of enterprises, and promote a new group of younger, better educated managers. Targeted at the largest enterprises, enterprise rectification was in some respects profoundly conservative, because management structures were made more similar, rather than more diverse. But the turnover in personnel that took place as part of enterprise rectification was ultimately more important. As one politician put it, "The crux [of enterprise rectification] is the rectification and reconstruction of enterprise leadership groups. Now the most important question is to get the old cadres to retire smoothly, and promote a group of younger cadres." (Li Ping'an 1987: 506). Managerial personnel at all levels became younger, better educated, and with much greater representation of technical personnel. While the gerontocratic leadership held onto a piece of power at the very top, through most of the Chinese administrative structure, management

Table 3.3. *Percentage of enterprise-level leadership with college education*

		1978–79	1985
249	Large machinery enterprises	14%	n.a.
2,900	Large industrial enterprises		
	Managers	49%	89%
	Party secretaries	11%	81%
1,402	Large industrial enterprises	20%	64%
All	Large industrial enterprises	n.a.	52%

Sources: Yu Guangyuan 1985; SRC/ER 1990: 529; Yi Daren 1989.

passed to a new generation, and to a relatively well-trained and competent segment of that generation.

The 1985 Industrial Census revealed that the educational level of China's managerial personnel overall was woefully inadequate. Surveying enterprise "leadership personnel" (the top three to ten managers in each firm), the census found that a mere 11.5% had college educations, 7.6% had technical school degrees, and only 19.3% even had high-school diplomas. More than 60% of enterprise leaders had less than high-school educations. However, the situation was somewhat better in the large and medium enterprises. In these enterprises, 52% had college degrees and 79% had at least high-school diplomas. Moreover, 73% of all leadership personnel were younger than 50 (Industrial Census 1987: 9). Available comparisons (summarized in Table 3.3) suggest that the relatively good qualifications of large enterprise managers was the outcome of rectification. Of course, there was no guarantee that more highly educated managers would do a better job of managing. But it is clear that there was substantial turnover of managerial personnel, with an effort being made to promote younger and more qualified individuals. Similar changes were occurring in government administration above the enterprise level. A ministerial shuffle in 1982 increased the percentage with college educations from 37% to 52%. By 1986, engineers were playing a large role in management at all levels, with 45% of ministers and 64% of mayors having engineering degrees (CBR July-August 1982; Hong Yung Lee 1990; Li and Bachman 1989). The composition of China's managerial elite was changing, becoming younger and more technocratic. Indeed, China's post-Tiananmen leaders, Premier Li Peng and First Party Secretary Jiang Zemin, were both engineers who were promoted during this period. Not all engineers are good leaders. But on balance, there is little doubt that the promotion of younger and better educated managers during this period substantially improved the operation of the economy as a whole.

Building banking institutions

The banking system began to play a more important role in the Chinese economy almost immediately with the beginning of reforms in 1979. The system began to diversify away from the initial "monobank" role characteristic of command economies. In the early stages, reform of the banking system was primarily linked to the creation of a new system for financing fixed investment. Faced with difficult budgetary problems and a situation in which the state investment plan was overcommitted to a variety of large, long-term projects, central planners turned to the banking system to give them additional flexibility in funding investment. In the early years, 1979–80, virtually all new bank credits went to create new capacity in light, consumer goods industries, generally in small or medium-sized projects. The expanded role of bank lending allowed planners to increase resources for light industry without going through the politically contentious process of redirecting budgetary investment away from existing projects: An entirely new funding mechanism was created. Bank lending, which funded only 1.6% of state fixed investment in 1978, increased rapidly to 12% of such investment in 1980. In this case, the small-scale, relatively dispersed and relatively profitable nature of much of this investment made it a particularly suitable object of bank financing (Naughton 1987a).

In order to make the transition to a more flexible banking system suited to a more diverse economy with greater market elements, substantial restructuring and institution building was required (Byrd 1983). The People's Bank of China (PBC) was nominally designated a central bank in 1983, and its commercial banking functions were delegated to a new institution, the Industrial and Commercial Bank. A new institutional structure was created in which the PBC presided over four main specialized banks: The Agricultural Bank, the Industrial and Commercial Bank, the Bank of China, and the Construction Bank. The Rural Credit Cooperatives were granted much greater autonomy. New financial institutions that included several hundred Trust and Investment Companies, four new domestic banks, and urban credit unions were authorized. These changes did not begin to really affect the banking system until the transition to central bank functions began in earnest in 1985. But once again, a crucial preparatory stage of institution building was required, precisely because China's administrative capability was so low at the beginning of the process.

Priority investment program

The structural problems described in Chapter 2 required institutional solutions. In the short run, slow growth of energy could be managed by cutting investment and shifting to a lighter economic structure, but in the long run, investment in energy and infrastructure had to be provided for. Energy consumption was virtually stagnant through 1982, but it was clear that the economy could not continue to grow unless energy supplies increased (*Energy* 1986: 12). Moreover, given the uncertain progress of reform, it was clear that government would have to take direct responsibility for maintaining such investment. During 1982, agreement was reached within the government on the need for a priority investment program.

Priority investment partially reflected the gradual rehabilitation of the planning apparatus after the collapse of 1979. Planners were able to draw up a Sixth Five Year Plan by 1982, though it was more meaningful as an expression of caution and growth pessimism than as an actual plan. More important, lists of key projects – largely concentrated on energy and infrastructure investment – were developed and given priority. The existing material allocation plan was drawn on to support these projects. Guaranteed supply of materials and strict government controls were put in place to support construction of keypoint projects. Projects financed by Japanese government and World Bank development loans were incorporated into the list of priority projects (Lin Fatang 1984). During 1983, nearly 2% of GNP was channeled into this core central government investment plan.

The priority investment program was the result of a modest but significant improvement of the planning apparatus. Instead of undermining economic development, planners were beginning to contribute to it. The priority investment program was overwhelmingly focused on energy, transport, and a few heavy industrial materials industries. Of total outlays through 1985, 42% went to the energy sector, 19% to transport and communications, and 35% to materials industries (predominantly steel and chemicals). In total, 96% of priority outlays went to these sectors (SSB 1991: 138–41).[12] Planners were concentrating their activities on the areas where they could arguably do some good.

The significance of the priority investment program in 1982–83 was not that it represented any kind of institutional innovation – it didn't – but rather that it provided a means for agreement about the immediate objective of central government plans and investment. Earlier in this chapter we discussed the differences between concepts of plan and market held by conservatives and reformers, and the difficulty of reconciling those theoretical views. But while theoretical agreement proved elusive, practical agreement about actual plan priorities was fairly easy to achieve. Indeed, reform made it easier to achieve agreement about real priorities. With agriculture and light consumer goods industry beginning their reform-induced booms, it was clear to all that central government activity had to be concentrated on energy and infrastructure, or these areas would rapidly reemerge as critical bottlenecks. All sides could agree that for now, a smaller but more focused investment plan was best for the economy.

Conclusion

Fundamental changes reshaped the Chinese economic system during the years 1979–83, but many of these changes were not foreseen by China's leaders or reformist economists, and in some respects must have been discouraging to them. While many positive changes had occurred in the economic system, the initial approach to economic reform was now in a shambles. The economic system had been reshaped by increased market orientation, and the gradual strengthening of institutions that were at least minimally adequate to function in the new environment. But in other respects, the economic system had proven alarmingly resistant to reform. None of the rationalizing reforms advanced at the beginning of the process had been implemented. Nor could reforms that expanded enterprise autonomy be considered a success, since it was clear to all observers that most enterprises remained very effectively subordinated to the bureaucratic apparatus.

A wide network of subsidiary markets had been allowed to emerge around the state planned economy. Markets of some kind existed for ordinary intermediate goods, industrial machinery, many light manufactured consumer goods, and most farm products. Markets were particularly widespread in rural areas, where new programs of rural industrialization had begun to bear fruit. Yet these changes did not represent a conscious strategy of reform, nor were they necessarily envisioned by China's leaders at the beginning of the process. Instead, they were the result of a series of ad hoc adaptations to a powerful series of economic changes. These adaptations were made possible by the relatively flexible attitude of the top leadership, but were also mandated by the inability of the old administrative system to respond with adequate speed and flexibility to new circumstances. The weakness of China's planned economy was converted from a hindrance to an advantage, as that very weakness allowed a significant opening up of the economy.

There were serious limitations to the process set in motion. Since the authority to engage in market transactions had been granted on an ad hoc basis, there were neither clear limits to nor adequate protection of that authority. It was conceivable that after the economy adjusted, the new market elements would be reintegrated into the planned economy. Some of China's leaders clearly envisaged "regularizing" temporary institutions as the economy stabilized and planning institutions were strengthened. Moreover, large state industrial enterprises participated only weakly in this partial marketization. Though some exceptions had been created as a part of industrial reforms, most large enterprises continued to be obliged to provide output to the state material supply and planning organs. As a result, many high-technology industrial goods generally did not enter into markets at all. Thus the process of marketization set in place remained fundamentally a "fringe" process. While far larger in size and with much more ideological legitimacy than the inevitable black and grey markets that spring up in all command economies, these markets still coexisted uneasily with the planned economy which remained dominant, at least in the industrial sphere. These were not mere cracks in the edifice of the planned economy – a whole network of fissures had opened up – but the edifice remained in place.

Thus, by the end of 1984, a very peculiar pattern had emerged in China's industrial reforms. While widespread and important programs of financial decentralization had taken place, every single element of the program of financial rationalization had been defeated. Factor prices were unreformed, product prices had not be realigned, the investment mechanism had not been reformed. From the standpoint of rationalizing reforms – which was the intellectual heritage that had been brought to bear on the problem of reform – the process had been a failure. The notion of increasingly rational price parameters being used to steer the economy began to appear hopelessly irrelevant. But many good things were happening in the economy as well. The liberalization that had accompanied rationalization was having some favorable impact. Even more favorable processes were developing in the rural areas, and are the subject of the next chapter.

4

Growth of the non-state sector

The flowers I planted did not blossom;
But the willows I never wished for now throw cool shade over my garden.

—traditional Chinese poem

One of the most striking and important elements of the Chinese reform process has been the rapid and sustained growth of the non-state sector. The broad liberalization of the conditions under which non-state sectors could begin economic activity must be seen as the third crucial element of the early reform period, along with reorientation and the beginnings of institutional reform. This liberalization created the conditions for large-scale entry of new producers, in time fundamentally reshaping the Chinese economy. In a growth process taking place predominantly in rural areas, thousands of new township and village enterprises went into business, manufacturing goods, building houses, and shipping and selling goods around the country. Entry of new non-state producers transformed the industrial sector, greatly expanding the range of goods and services available on the market, and creating competition for existing state firms. The expanding output of these firms made an important contribution to China's rapid economic growth during the 1980s. At the same time, following on the heels of the successful decollectivization of agriculture in the early 1980s, the growth of rural enterprises suggests that China's countryside was a fertile breeding ground for economic reforms, a source of entrepreneurship and resources that could create alternatives to the existing state system.

China's rural enterprises have attracted a great deal of attention, but also considerable misunderstanding. This chapter describes the growth of the non-state sector, and particularly the township and village enterprises (TVEs), within the broader context of China's economic system transformation. It argues that many of the institutional conditions of the command

137

economy in transition created a kind of hot-house environment for growth of non-state industry. The high profitability of industry, ultimately traceable to the state monopoly over industry and the associated price system, strongly supported the growth of the non-state sector. Thus, the rapid growth of the TVEs can only be understood as part of the overall system transformation.

The chapter begins with a broad look at the shift in rural policy at the end of the 1970s, and then focuses on the transformation of rural industry. While agricultural policy is strictly speaking outside the scope of this book, the shift in rural policy was a fundamental step in creating the conditions for growth of the non-state sector, and must be briefly considered. I stress that the main objective of the new rural policy was to raise rural incomes by improving prices and transferring income-generating activities to rural areas, rather than radical system reform. The policy shift had three unanticipated consequences: family farming, increased household saving, and rapid growth of rural industry. Rural industrialization was a complex phenomenon in which initial liberalization played a catalytic role. After a detailed look at rural industry, the chapter draws back to again consider the position of non-state industry in general in the context of the Chinese industrial economy as a whole.

Agricultural reform

Chinese policy toward the rural areas was radically transformed following the Third Plenum at the end of 1978. Concerned that agriculture was being "starved of resources," that it was weak and potentially fatally undermined by extractive policies, the leadership engineered a major change of course. This major change of economic strategy included a radical change in the volume and direction of intersectoral resource flows. It did *not* initially include a radical change in institutions. The shift in economic development strategy, as it affected the rural areas, created a space for a broad liberalization of rural policy. Once this general relaxation was carried out, it was met by three significant economic responses, all more or less unanticipated: the return to family farming, a rapid increase in household saving, and rapid growth of rural enterprises. The changes were conceived of as an attempt to shift resources into the rural sector without fundamentally changing the institutions that determined how decisions were made in the countryside. But the ultimate outcome was profound institutional change. As Kelliher (1992: 56–57) notes: "What is striking about the initial reform program is how little it anticipated the more radical changes it set in motion . . . In fact, the state initially outlawed what were to become the most important reform measures. Foremost among these was the most fundamental change of all, family farming, which the Third Plenum specifically banned."

The primary measures of the new policy were raising agricultural prices (which included reducing taxes and stabilizing compulsory procurement quotas) and providing greater autonomy to agricultural collectives. The Third Plenum stressed the inviolability of economic rights of collectives (they were not to be subject to arbitrary exactions) and expanded the scope of permissible payment schemes for peasants within the collectives. Policymakers believed that peasants *in collectives* would respond to prices and incentives and to an amelioration of their living standards. The dominant view of agriculture at this time was simply that the government had tried to squeeze too much out of agriculture: The policy statements describe agriculture with words like damaged, recovery, panting for breath.[1] Policymakers believed that existing price policies made agricultural production unprofitable at the margin: Rural collectives were being forced to maintain high levels of output that actually reduced their incomes because the marginal cost of modern inputs was greater than the value of the incremental output at state prices (Tong Wansheng and Zou Xiangqun 1992; Wiens 1982). Raising state prices would return such production to profitability and make it less difficult to enforce output targets. In short, more liberal rural policies could be contained within the framework of the traditional rural economic system.

Yet in spite of the limitations of the initial measures, they set off a complex series of interactions between peasants and government leaders that eventually led to the "rural responsibility system" and the widespread adoption of family farming. There is substantial debate as to whether these interactions should be seen as primarily "bottom up" or as "top down" [Kelliher (1992) and Watson (1983) stress the bottom up aspects; Hartford (1985) and Unger (1986) stress the top down.] From our standpoint, it is perhaps most important to see that the regime made a crucial first move by relaxing rural policy generally. This relaxation included a reduction in the degree of extraction from rural areas: by raising agricultural prices, reducing taxes, and increasing state investment into agriculture, the government was clearly reducing the effective tax rate on the rural sector. This component of policy was rather similar to that carried out in the Soviet Union at the end of the 1960s and early 1970s. The Soviet government at that time raised agricultural procurement prices and began to pump significant investment resources into the countryside. But the results were disappointing. The crucial difference from the Soviet Union in the 1970s may have been that the Chinese relaxation also included a substantial commitment to a degree of institutional flexibility. Institutional experimentation was not intended or expected to lead to household farming, but it did permit a range of solutions to the question of how to organize collective production. The leadership thus created a presumption of permissiveness in the countryside that encouraged further experimentation. The point is sometimes made that Chinese peasants, unlike Russian peasants, still had a memory of household farming, which had existed until 1955. It is less often stressed that Chinese peasants had even more recent memories of experimentation with the proper forms of organizing and compensating work within the collective. This experimentation had continued virtually unceasingly through the 1970s, and had included in particular fairly radical experiments with household farming in the early 1960s (Liu Yishun 1987; Unger 1985). In any case, the peasants responded vigorously with forms of organization that differed from the standard collective model.

The peasants quickly went beyond the boundaries that seemed so clear to the leaders. They began dividing land up to individual households. Kelliher (1992: 67) cites a Hubei newspaper report of peasants saying, "As long as you're letting us divide into work groups, why not just leave everything to us?" It was a question for which the government did not have a ready answer. As the peasants took advantage of the greater latitude given them, and local leaders demanded guidance, policymakers tried to stabilize the situation. In September 1980, the Party classified rural areas into three regions: *poor and mountainous regions* could carry out family farming, *intermediate regions* should preserve the collectives but organize more flexible work groups, and *advanced regions* should preserve the collectives but develop specialized agricultural and non-agricultural households in addition (SRC 1984: 123–26). Family farming was to be forbidden in all but the backward regions, but otherwise there should be a kind of peaceful coexistence between different organizational forms.

This policy was acceptable to conservatives because it seemed to maintain the idea that collective forms of organization were more "advanced" – only the really backward areas were allowed to regress to household farming. But the policy also implied, almost inadvertently, that the appropriate institutional form depended on the degree of government extraction. Backward areas were so poor that they really did not sell any agricultural product to the state in any case, and the state could thus afford to let them do as they pleased. Controls over institutional form would be maintained only in those advanced areas where state procurements were significant. But this formulation was profoundly subversive. In the past, collective ownership was the

Table 4.1. *Rural household responsibility system*

Percentage of households participating at year-end.	
1979	1%
1980	14%
1981	45%
1982	80%
1983	98%
1984	99%

Source: Lin 1992: 38.

only best form; now, no institutional form was best in all circumstances. Any institutional form could be acceptable, as long as it was compatible with continued state procurement of adequate levels of agricultural produce. If household farming could produce as large a marketable surplus as collectives, it might conceivably emerge as the best form.

Some important leaders tacitly supported and protected – if indeed they did not actually sponsor – initial moves to adopt family farming. It was widely known that in Sichuan, under Zhao Ziyang, and in Anhui, under Wan Li, some peasants had begun dividing land up for individual household cultivation. During 1980, Zhao Ziyang was made Premier and Wan Li became Vice-Premier in charge of rural work. At this point, it must have been clear to individuals lower down the political hierarchy that they could not suffer, and could conceivably benefit, from encouraging household farming in their jurisdictions. At the end of 1980, still only 14% of Chinese farmers had adopted household farming (*baogandaohu*). But the new permissiveness associated with the ascension of obviously pro-reform leaders, while never explicitly permitting the spread of household farming, was interpreted as allowing virtually anything anywhere. Change accelerated in 1981 and 1982 (Table 4-1), and the government then retrospectively gave formal blessing to the change-over.

Once the household responsibility system was adopted, the output response was phenomenal. Agricultural output growth soared, peaking with the phenomenal bumper harvest of 1984. Accelerated growth was aided by rapid increase in modern inputs and by the abandonment of economically irrational policies that forced all regions to achieve grain self-sufficiency. But there is no doubt that the return to household farming was one of the main causes, if not the main cause, of output acceleration (Lardy 1983; Lin 1992;

McMillan et al. 1989). Such spectacular success provided a powerful support for reform in the non-agricultural economy. The desire to claim credit for this success also spawned the subsequent claim that Chinese economic reform had begun in the countryside.

Rapid growth of household saving

As described in Chapter 2, reorientation of the economy increased the share of national income going to households by ten to fifteen percentage points. In general, saving propensities of households are much lower than those of enterprises or the state. Thus, we would normally expect that increased control of income by households would result in much lower national saving overall and – in the absence of significant foreign funds – an equivalent reduction in investment. But national saving and investment has remained robust throughout the 1980s. This occurred because Chinese households dramatically increased their propensity to save.

Total household saving – including both in-kind and financial saving– jumped rapidly from 7% of household income in 1978 to 17% in 1982. Along with the increase in household income as a share of disposable national income, this implied that household saving jumped from 4% of national income to 11%. Even more crucially, financial saving tripled, increasing from 2.3% of household income in 1978 to an average of 6.8% in the years 1980– 83. The household share of total national saving increased from 11% in 1978, surpassing 35% in 1981 (Cheng Xiaonong 1991,, ESRRI 1987). Changes in the composition of saving are shown graphically in Figure 4.1. The figure shows that the changes in the aggregate level of saving in the economy between 1978 and 1984 were relatively modest, whereas the change in the structure of saving was large. As saving of government and enterprises dropped, households picked up the slack and increased their saving sharply. This minimized the adjustment to the economic system that was required on the supply side, because investment could be maintained at relatively high levels notwithstanding the drop in government saving. Thus, Chinese households provided the key element to the macroeconomic stability that prevailed during these years. As a result of these changes, China's financial system began to diverge from the standard command economy model, and resemble that of most market economies. Saving surpluses in the household sector were transferred through the banking system to fund investment in the enterprise and government sectors. Flows of this kind amounted to 20% of total saving by the early 1980s.

Why did Chinese household saving increase so rapidly during the reform

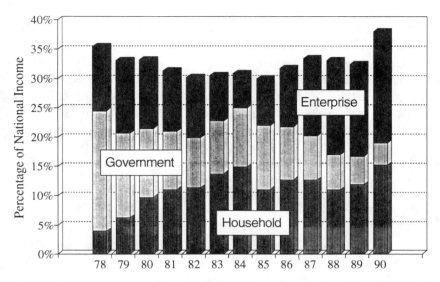

Figure 4.1. Sources of national saving. Source: ESRRI 1987; Cheng Xiaonong 1991.

era? The suggestion that this represented increased excess demand and monetary overhang is not plausible. The period in which saving was increasing most rapidly was the same period (discussed in the last chapter) in which rationing was being greatly reduced and in which prices on free markets for agricultural produce were stable or declining. Increased saving reflected rapid remonetization of the household economy. As households effectively disengaged their household businesses from the agricultural collectives, their need for currency increased. Under the collectives, all intermediate transactions had been carried out by the collective and settled through bank clearing accounts: Households received only the final net income at the end of the agricultural production cycle.[2] After the resumption of household farming, though, households had to settle in cash most purchases of agricultural inputs, as well as the sundry obligations to local government officials. The household became fully incorporated into a monetary economy, whereas previously its participation had been buffered by the collectives.

Moreover, under the collective system, household choice had been strictly limited in a number of respects. Most important were restrictions on household ability to purchase big-ticket items for consumption or investment purposes. Households were rarely able to build new or expand existing housing under the old system; lavish life-cycle celebrations – weddings and funerals – were severely discouraged. With the removal of such constraints, households quickly resumed such activities. Similarly, with the relaxation on constraints in non-agricultural businesses, households found many new opportunities for productive investment. As we shall see in the next section, those investments were often extremely profitable, particularly in the initial phase of liberalization. In order to respond to these new consumption and investment opportunities, households had to engage in preparatory saving. Investment opportunity leads to increased saving (as stressed in McKinnon 1973). These changes occurred in urban areas as well, but they were most striking and most important in the rural areas that are home to the bulk of Chinese households.

Rural enterprises

The early evolution of policy toward rural enterprises should be seen as part of the same broad shift in rural policy that created the conditions for rapid decollectivization. Support for rural industrialization was originally conceived of as part of a structural policy, rather than as a system reform policy. Support for rural industrialization would shift some income-earning opportunities to the countryside, but not fundamentally alter the existing institutional framework. Indeed, existing rural enterprises were firmly integrated into the rural collective structure: "Commune and brigade industries" were seen as one of the most outstanding achievements of the rural collective setup. As a result, rural industrialization, as originally conceived, could be expected to *strengthen* the collective system by providing it with additional resources. But as in the case of household farming, the shift in development strategy led to unanticipated institutional changes with profound consequences. To understand these changes, it is essential to take a broad look at rural industrial development before the onset of reform.

It is surprising how *unimportant* rural industrial output was on the eve of reform. Of China's total industrial output in 1978, only 9% was produced in rural areas. Even non-state industry was a majority urban: 60% of non-state industrial output was produced by urban collectives, 40% by rural collectives. Rural residents were overwhelmingly engaged in agriculture: Fully 90% of the rural labor force were agriculturalists in 1978. This figure is high in comparison with other countries at China's level of development, and particularly surprising in light of China's history: The traditional rural economy was highly diversified and rural areas produced a very large part of total industrial production (Blank and Parish 1990; Zelin 1991). In fact, the countryside had become deindustrialized under the command economy. During the early years of the People's Republic, state policy had drastically re-stricted rural industrial production. As the rural population was organized into agricultural collectives, non-agricultural production declined signifi-cantly, and the state itself took over virtually all manufacturing production (Fei Hsiao-tung 1989). It is not hard to understand why this occurred. In order to maintain control over the price system and concentrate revenues in the industrial sector, the state had to establish a monopoly over agricultural procurement and manufacturing activity. This it achieved during the 1950s and 1960s. Indeed, the proportion of rural residents engaged in agriculture seems to have reached a peak in 1965, when it was three percentage points higher than in 1978 (*Labor 1949–85:* 80; *Labor 1978–87:* 103.)

The late 1960s and early 1970s saw some relaxation of this drastic policy and the beginning of a wave of state-sponsored rural industrialization. The agricultural collectives and the communes that had been organized during the Great Leap Forward served as platforms for industrial development, and, from a very low base, output grew rapidly through the 1970s. Indeed, this rapid growth attracted a great deal of attention during the 1970s, since it seemed to be part of a unique Chinese approach to economic development (Perkins *et al* 1977; Riskin 1971). In fact, Chinese rural industry did have many innovative characteristics, but the attention given to it created the misleading impression that the Chinese countryside was characterized in general by high levels of industrial activity, when in fact the reverse was the case. Rural industrialization in the 1970s was actually concentrated on a narrow range of heavy industrial products. Policy at the time stressed the "five small" rural industries, producing iron and steel, cement, chemical fertilizer, hydroelectric power, and farm implements. The factories involved were small relative to urban factories, but rather large compared with work-shops and factories in most countries. After all, these were capital-intensive industries usually thought to be characterized by significant economies of scale. These factories made a dramatic sight among the rice fields, but did not absorb a significant part of the rural labor force.

The crucial fact about this 1970s rural industrialization was how removed it was from traditional types of rural industry, which was organically connected to the rural economy through multiple linkages. Although rural industry was exhorted to "serve agriculture" during the 1970s, this was interpreted nar-rowly to mean supplying producers' goods to agriculture. Very little agricul-tural produce was supplied to rural industry, and rural industry in no way interfered with the state monopoly on the procurement of agricultural pro-duce. In 1978, only 17.5% of the gross value of output of commune and brigade industries was derived from the processing of agricultural materials, while for urban industry the figure was 29%. Only 39% of rural light industry output consisted of processed agricultural materials, compared with 68% for urban industry (*Agriculture* 1980: 367; *Industrial Statistic* 1949–84: 101). In other words, rural industry actually made substantially less use of agricultural produce than did urban industry, so all-encompassing was the state monopoly over agricultural procurement. Unlike non-farm rural employment in most developing countries, China's pre-1978 rural industrialization was not based on the processing of agricultural products. The Chinese countryside lacked the dense network of small-scale, non-agricultural activities that characterize prosperous rural areas in the rest of developing Asia.

Rural industries in the 1970s were miniature replicas of the state's command economy. They replicated the heavy industry-based development strategy, and tried to replicate the command economic system as well. Rural collectives at the commune and brigade level (later township and village) were subordinate to the government that created them, rather than being autonomous firms. Although overall rural industry was quite profitable, local leaders did not hesitate to develop unprofitable industries if those conformed to the command development strategy. According to the first nationwide survey of rural enterprises in 1980, 13.5% of commune-level enterprises operated at a loss, and thus required continuous subsidization (Cao Chengneng 1981). Although rural industries were not included in national plans, they weren't quite free to engage in market transactions either, and they were forbidden to "put profits in command" (though of course some did). In spite of these handicaps, rural industries were growing rapidly. Between 1970 and 1978, rural industrial employment grew at a 20% annual rate. But the countryside, was still relatively deindustrialized, and the potential for recovery growth of industry was great.

Thus, on the eve of reform, China's non-state sector was plagued with many of the same problems as the state sector. Firms lacked autonomy and incentives and were expected to act in furtherance of the objectives of their superior organs. Yet this sector was growing considerably more rapidly than the state sector and had the advantage of generally not being integrated into state planning. Perhaps most critically, these firms responded to the interests of a geographically dispersed group of local officials, whose interests could be as easily linked to the economic success of the firm as to the command of national policymakers. Nevertheless, it would have been hard to foresee the catalytic role these firms would play. They were not that different from state firms in their overall organization and subordination to government authorities, but they had far fewer skilled employees, and less technology and capital, than state firms.

Changing policy toward rural enterprises

During 1979, government policy toward rural enterprises went through important changes that greatly enhanced state support for rural industrialization. The crucial shift in policy was not support for "rural industry" per se – for the state had been actively supporting rural industry since at least 1970, and rural industry had been growing rapidly during the intervening period (Xue Muqiao 1978a). Rather, the change was the abandonment of the restrictive model of rural industrialization that had confined its growth during the 1970s primarily to a few agricultural producer goods. This general liberalization included a proposed relaxation of the state monopoly on purchase of agricultural materials, making them available to rural enterprises for processing. The new policy adopted in 1979 was: "Whenever it is economically rational for agricultural products to be processed in rural areas, rural enterprises should gradually take over the processing work." In addition, urban firms were encouraged to subcontract work to rural enterprises when appropriate (SRC 1984: 114, 97–104). These changes were thought of as a planned adjustment in development strategy. For example, provincial governments were to determine whether individual state-run factories processing agricultural materials should be turned over to rural management. In fact, changes of this sort, by themselves, would have been inadequate to spark the explosive growth of rural industry, because the agencies that controlled agricultural procurement were unlikely to share their lucrative raw materials with rural enterprises simply because a government document encouraged them to do so. But once rural industries were encouraged to take over agricultural processing, they were simultaneously being encouraged to produce for consumer markets and, more generally, were set free to engage in whatever form of profitable activity they could find. From an initially highly restrictive model of rural industrialization, rural industrialization was now encouraged in response to multiple rationales: processing agricultural goods, producing energy, export products, and so on – in practice to whatever the market would support. A presumption of permissiveness was created.

Development of rural enterprise was seen as one more policy – like the increase in state investment or the reduction in tax burden – that would increase the volume of resources available in rural areas to develop agriculture. Moreover, rural industrialization had the additional advantage that it would strengthen the rural collective system by providing an infusion of new resources. Rural enterprises were firmly ensconced in the existing collective organizational structure in the countryside, and their very name – commune and brigade enterprises – reflected their origins and close interrelation with the rural collective structure. Revenues earned from rural enterprises were regularly channeled by community governments not only for public works projects, but also for specific aid-to-agriculture projects and even payments to raise the value of work points, on which collective payments to agricultural workers were based (Wong 1988: 18–21). In a sense, the objective was to take part of the income earning potential created by the state's monopoly over industry and share it with small-scale rural collectives cum governments. From the standpoint of state industry, it was a radical decentralization of control, but from the standpoint of rural policy, it could be expected to strengthen the rural collectives, the most "socialist" part of the countryside.

The policies adopted in 1979 laid out a series of stimulative measures and envisioned rapid growth. The crucial State Control document on township and village enterprises in 1979 says: "We should raise the share of commune and brigade [township and village] enterprises in the total gross income in the three-level rural system from 29.7% in 1978 to around 50% in 1985." (SRC 1984: 98). The arithmetic of this statement is such that if agricultural income were to grow by a moderate 4% annually, township and village enterprise income would have to grow by 18% per year to reach the 1985 target. If agricultural income grew more rapidly, rural enterprises would correspondingly have to grow even faster. This was a rapid growth rate, although in practice it was exceeded: Rural industrial output grew by 21% annually between 1978 and 1985, and maintained this rapid growth rate through the early 1990s as well. Clearly, policymakers *did* anticipate the rapid emergence of a large number of enterprises run by villages and townships.[3]

What policymakers did not anticipate was the profound changes township and village enterprises would make in the economy as a whole. Indeed, as the liberalization of rural policy deepened, throughout 1981–82, the very commune structure within which the rural enterprises were embedded began to come apart. Most communes were abolished during 1983–84 and their functions divided between townships that assumed responsibility for governmental operations and local economic committees that took over economic management. Local economic committees enjoyed relatively more autonomy than the old communes, even though they were still government bodies. This freed rural enterprises to become more independent, profit-oriented entities. The change in name from commune and brigade to township and village also dates from this momentous change. From here on, we will use township and village exclusively, if occasionally anachronistically.

Causes of rapid growth of rural industry

The favorable policies toward rural enterprises were highly successful. Why were rural industries able to grow so rapidly? What were the forces that propelled rapid entry of new industrial firms? There is no single answer to these questions. Rather, a combination of six favorable factors contributed to rural industrial success.

1   Fundamentals: Factor price ratios reflected China's true factor endowment

China's basic economic situation is created by its abundant labor force, limited land, and relatively scarce capital. One of the greatest irrationalities created by the command economic system was that urban factories faced factor prices that were sharply at variance with the relative scarcity of the factors of production. Total worker compensation was quite generous: Although money wages were not necessarily high, the full package of compensation, including food subsidies, free medical care and social security, and highly subsidized housing was substantial. Many of these costs were borne by the enterprise, although sometimes in hidden forms. Conversely, capital was supplied to urban firms either cost free, or at highly subsidized interest rates. Thus, urban firms faced cheap capital and expensive labor, while factor endowments would have indicated the reverse.

Rural enterprises faced factor prices much more in line with China's real factor endowment. The cost of labor was much lower: By 1989, rural enterprise workers earned 1230 yuan per year on average, 63% of the wages of urban collective workers, and 58% of state enterprise workers (Li Weiyi 1991: 130). Since subsidies to TVE workers were small, the total compensation package was much less than half that of urban workers. Similarly, TVEs only occasionally had access to highly subsidized capital. The bulk of TVE capital was provided at near-market interest rates, or came from internally generated funds with a high opportunity cost. As a result, the ratio of labor to fixed capital in TVEs was nine times that of state-run industry (Findlay and Watson 1992). Similarly, TVEs paid near-market prices for energy and raw materials, not having access to the extensive subsidization from which state-run firms benefited. Facing realistic factor price relationships, TVEs had incentives to locate the production relationships that were most appropriate in the Chinese economy and that over the long run gave them an advantageous competitive position. Economic fundamentals were on the side of the TVEs.

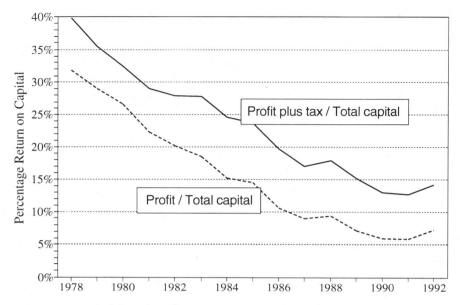

Figure 4.2. Profitability of rural enterprises. Source: *Statistic* 1993: 396–97.

2 *Rural industries were extremely profitable*

Rural enterprises were remarkably profitable in 1978: The *average* rate of profit on capital was 32%. If we include tax revenues created – in order to reflect the fact that TVEs were often developed by local governments that had a claim on tax revenues generated – the total rate of profit and tax per unit of capital was 40% (capital is here defined as the value of depreciated fixed capital plus all inventories). The high rate of profitability was not simply, or even primarily, the result of the better factor proportions and consequent lower costs, described in the previous section. Indeed, the fact that TVEs did not enjoy many of the subsidies granted to state-owned firms must have meant that their measured costs were often higher than state firms. Moreover, in subsequent years, even as TVEs developed a broader network of supporting services and many TVEs began to achieve economies of scale, profitability declined steadily and precipitously (Figure 4.2).

What can explain this pattern of rapid growth combined with steadily declining profitability? It seems clear that early TVEs were in a position to benefit from the protected market created for state-run factories. By easing the state monopoly over industry, the Chinese government allowed TVEs to enter this previously protected market and share in a portion of the monopoly profits. First, mover advantages were large, big enough to repay early entrants with windfall profits. In this situation, continued entry only gradually created competition. State firms scarcely noticed the competition at first, because they were protected by a cushion of high profits. As long as they could gain access to low-price raw materials, they were indifferent to a few TVEs producing similar products. But gradually, as entry continued, competition among TVEs and between TVEs and state firms began to compete away monopoly profits and erode profit margins (see Chapter 6 for additional evidence on this point).

Second, the existence of empty niches also contributed to this pattern of high initial profits, followed by steadily declining profitability. Empty niches existed for two reasons. Certain commodities – particularly miscellaneous consumer goods – had simply not been provided by the inefficient command economy, and TVEs jumped in to meet needs until then largely unmet. For example, this response explains much of the early success of the Wenzhou region, where small-scale rural firms specialized in such items as buttons, ribbons, and elastic bands in a variety of colors and specifications: Producing these items for a market of one billion led to explosive growth. In addition, a whole series of new markets were created by the sudden growth of rural incomes and the relaxation of rural economic policy. For example, rural housing construction took off, and new rural industries developed to supply building materials to this new market. In both situations, early entrants could expect windfall gains, and the presence of potential windfalls naturally induced extremely rapid entry. Gradually, entrants created competition that eroded the exceptional profits available early on.[4]

3 Taxes were low on rural industry

Rural enterprises enjoyed very low tax rates, and particularly low tax rates on profit. By contrast, state-run industrial firms benefited from government price policy, but they also paid the price in a very high tax rate – sometimes 100% – on profits. Rural enterprises enjoyed the benefits of price policy without the corresponding high tax burden. This unbalanced treatment seems peculiar unless we recall that during the early phase of reform China's leaders conceived of rural enterprises primarily as a device to increase the resources available to agriculture. As a result, they were not so much interested in taxing such firms as they were in ensuring that a significant proportion of the net revenues of such firms went to local projects that supported agriculture. This could include purchase of agricultural inputs for the collective, or construction projects, including irrigation and transport, that could benefit agriculture. Thus, the government decreed tax breaks for rural enterprises, but also tried to direct after-tax profits toward these uses that were supportive of agriculture.

One of the very first reform measures taken was a reduction in the tax rates of TVEs. In December 1978, the government decreed that all new TVEs could be granted three-year tax holidays. Moreover, when taxation began, profits would be taxed at the flat rate of 20% of profits above 3,000 yuan (Wang Chengyao 1983: 62). As the government realized what a huge tax break it had created, it began backing down from these generous provisions. By 1983, all TVEs were supposedly back on the tax regime that applied to all collectives, in which a progressive profit tax was collected, with top rates rising to 55%. Nevertheless, the average rate of profit tax collected from TVEs remained very low: In 1978, it was only 8%, and by 1980, it had declined to only 6%. It then gradually climbed to around 20% by 1986, where it remained subsequently (*Statistic* 1992: 390). It is true that TVEs have paid out substantial sums to "support agriculture," in what could be considered a local tax. In the early 1980s, firms at the township and village levels paid out between 30% and 40% of their total profits to local governments to "support agriculture," and significant sums may be paid to local governments as "management fees" (which show up as extra-budgetary revenues of local governments, rather than profit tax). Thus, rural firms at the township and village level typically have about half or less of their gross profits available for reinvestment.

Still, this regime results in a light tax burden for the rural enterprise sector as a whole. First, as private and cooperative rural firms increased in importance, they benefited from low explicit taxes, while the government did not directly control their profits and therefore could not divert money to "support agriculture." As these ownership types are now more than a third of total rural industry, the overall tax burden is correspondingly lowered (Wong 1988). Second, the definition of "support agriculture" is fairly elastic. Many localities are not eager to divert large sums to agriculture uses, and instead mislabel a wide range of activity as "support agriculture." These funds are actually transferred among industrial enterprises under the local government's control, and the locality as a whole enjoys a low tax burden on its industrial activities. There can be little doubt that the rural enterprise sector as a whole enjoys a substantially lower tax burden than do state-run urban enterprises.

4   Capital was available

China's township and village enterprises turned out to be an effective form of channeling investment capital to new enterprises. In part, this was due to the combination of high profit rates and low tax rates described in the previous sections, which allowed successful rural enterprises to rapidly snowball. In addition, the sponsorship of China's township and village enterprises by local governments greatly enhanced the access to capital of these new businesses. By contrast, the experience of other transforming socialist economies has been that new start-up businesses proliferate, but that such businesses have difficulty getting access to capital, and as a result remain small, undercapitalized, and dependent on informal capital markets. In China, local government officials acted as intermediaries and guarantors, reassuring local agents of the banking system that their loans would ultimately be repaid. Indeed, in some cases, local government officials actively pressured local branches of the banking system to provide funds to their firms.

Clearly, if local government officials were able to act as guarantors to TVEs, it follows that TVEs did not have completely hard budget constraints. Government sponsorship served to spread the risks incurred by these new start-ups, essentially by having the entire local community absorb the cost of failure. But it is unlikely if perfectly hard budget constraints for start-up businesses would be optimal – a certain amount of "insurance" provided by local governments would almost certainly enhance social welfare. By underwriting a good portion of the risk of entry, local governments enabled start-up firms to enter production at a larger size, starting with some mechanization, and exploiting the economies of scale that come when there is movement away from the smallest form of petty production. Undoubtedly there was some cost to this kind of sponsored entry, but it seems to have been more than balanced by the benefits to rapid entry.

With local governments facilitating the flow of capital to rural enterprises, those firms were able to take advantage of China's relatively abundant household saving. Chinese traditional credit clubs and other forms of informal credit markets were put to good use. As Chinese rural household saving skyrocketed during the 1980s, the supply of funds to the local Rural Credit Cooperatives (RCCs) expanded drastically. The RCCs, nominally independent, locally controlled financial coops, were in fact part of the state-run financial system, and had been used before reform primarily to transfer the modest rural savings to urban uses. With the onset of reform, the RCCs had much more money, and they also were allowed to lend a much greater proportion of it locally.[5] The result was that the RCCs emerged as an important source of finance for TVEs. In 1978, loans from the RCCs and state banks were only 7% of the total capital of TVEs (depreciated value of fixed capital plus circulating capital). That increased steadily to 27% in 1986, and then leveled off. Nominal lending of RCCs to TVEs increased at a 39%

annual rate between 1978 and 1991, and by the end of the 1980s, RCCs were providing two-thirds of the total bank funding to TVEs. Thus, local government sponsorship of TVEs combined with existing rural credit institutions to channel funds into TVE development.

5   *Proximity to urban areas and state firms fostered rural industrialization*

The growth of China's rural industries has occurred primarily in regions that might more properly be termed suburban – or at least, in areas that are part of the immediate hinterland of cities. Some perspective on the degree of concentration of rural industries can be derived from statistics on China's urban areas. Most Chinese cities have administrative authority over a belt of rural or suburban territory outside the boundaries of the city proper, and statistics are available on production in these city-administered rural areas. In 1987, cities and their subordinate areas included 58% of the total national population, and, not surprisingly, accounted for the overwhelming bulk of state industrial production – 91%. More surprising is that these same areas accounted for almost the same proportion of total non-state industrial output – 87%. Of the non-state output, the type we would expect to be most purely "rural" – is the village collectives and "below-village" cooperatives – and private businesses were almost as concentrated: 77% were in this urban-influenced region (*Urban* 1988: 7, 10–11; Perkins 1990). Moreover, rural industries are also highly concentrated regionally, with coastal areas containing a disproportionate share of rural industries. In 1988, three coastal provinces – Jiangsu, Zhejiang, and Shandong – accounted for 17% of China's rural population, but 43% of total rural industry, and exactly half of all township and village-level industrial output (*Rural* 1989: 51; *Abstract* 1989: 37).

To some extent, such geographical concentration is entirely natural. The fact that there are cities in these regions means that they are economically more productive. Not only is productivity a precondition for urban growth, cities also provide transport networks, communications, markets, technology and other conditions that boost productivity throughout the cities' hinterlands, as well as in the cities themselves. Therefore, it is not surprising to find that "rural" enterprises are more likely to thrive in regions where they can benefit from the spillover effects of the urban economies. Nevertheless, it is striking how *little* the general regional distribution of rural enterprises differs from that of urban enterprises. Rural industries do not grow up where there are no urban industries. They grow up in the same general regions that urban industries grow. That suggests that urban and rural industry are complementary, rather than being substitutes for one another. It also suggests that rural industrial growth might be best analyzed as part of a broader process of metropolitan industrial growth.

The growth of rural enterprises in peri-urban areas was facilitated by direct cooperation between urban state-run firms and rural factories, primarily in the form of subcontracting. In the three province-level municipalities of Beijing, Shanghai and Tianjin, an estimated 60–80% of rural industrial output was produced by firms subcontracting with large urban factories (*Industry* 1949–1984: 50). The proportions were only slightly lower in nearby provinces such as Jiangsu or Zhejiang, where linkages with Shanghai firms "played a decisive role in the development of township and village enterprises in southern Jiangsu" (Tao Youzhi 1988: 100). In 1985 in the southern Jiangsu town of Wangshi, every one of the 93 rural enterprises had some kind of subcontracting or joint venture relation with an urban enterprise, mostly in Shanghai. In the Changshu district under Suzhou city, out of a total of slightly over 3400 township and village enterprises, over 1500 had "horizontal economic links" with Shanghai. In the Wuxi municipal district, 2055 entities linked rural producers and urban firms: Over 60% of these had Shanghai urban partners. In the Suzhou municipal district in 1985, out of 11,302 projects that linked rural and urban enterprises, 63% involved Shanghai partners (Zhou Yuan 1985; Tao Youzhi 1988: 90, 99–100). These horizontal links were primarily long-term subcontracting and marketing relationships, but included a large variety of forms of cooperation ranging up to equity joint ventures.

In the early years, such arrangements were facilitated by family relations – rural people who had migrated to the cities and urban youth sent from Shanghai to the countryside during the Cultural Revolution helped rural firms get started. Later on, rural firms purchased talent from the cities, especially by paying high salaries to technicians and retired urban workers (Zhou Yuan 1985; Tao Youzhi 1988).

Why do urban, state-owned firms cooperate closely with rural enterprises? One motivation is diversified supply. For instance, some processing was moved into the countryside around Shanghai in an attempt to diversify textile supplies for export – though both procurement of the materials and export of the finished product remained government monopolies (Shen 1990). Another motivation is profit. As state firms have gained a greater interest in profit they have sought to reduce costs, and subcontracting operation to rural enterprises became increasingly attractive (particularly important in the garment industry). A third motivation is that such relationships allow urban firms to escape from some of the tight constraints of the state-run industrial system. Urban firms in a position to expand often found themselves restrained by restrictions on construction, land procurement, or hiring. By entering into relations with rural firms, state firms could gain access to the resources they needed (particularly land). It might also be advantageous to a state firm manager to have control over some funds in the collective sector, where accounting standards and supervision were somewhat less strict than in the state sector. In other words, the presence of the rural enterprise sector gave state firm managers a certain amount of flexibility to escape the rigid controls of the state sector. A manager could use that flexibility to evade some of the most irrational controls and to achieve some of the autonomy and independence denied him by the system.

6   Organizational diversity accommodated growth

In reality, there is no single pattern of rural industrialization. But neither were rural enterprises confined to a single organizational form. Indeed, different "models" of rural industrialization grew up, each plausibly suited to a different set of economic conditions. The "Southern Jiangsu" model relied primarily on collectively owned township and village-level enterprises. Strong in the provinces around Shanghai where the collective organization was strong, such organizations facilitated links with the state economy – this is where subcontracting was most important – as well as close ties with local governments. A contrasting model was the Wenzhou model, where rapid growth occurred on the basis of individual household businesses. Wenzhou experienced explosive growth with a high degree of private enterprise and intensive marketization (Nolan and Dong 1989).

Many of the township and village enterprises became de facto private operations in the course of the 1980s (Wong 1988). Rural governments continued to register enterprises in the traditional categories, because this was ideologically more secure. In practice, though, the entire countryside was going through a massive process of privatization, and this affected rural industry as well. Many township and village enterprises effectively devolved to private entrepreneurs who made cash payments to local governments, the former "owners." Indeed, many private start-up firms were allowed to register as collectives (*guapaizi*) in return for payment of management fees and other considerations to local officials. In some cases, local officials themselves took advantage of these opportunities to become entrepreneurs; in other cases, local officials benefitted from the ambiguous legal status of private firms to peddle influence and protection. Local officials formed alliances with entrepreneurs – sometimes for mutual benefit, sometimes more predatory in nature – as rural industrialization spread. The result was that by the latter 1980s, many rural firms that were nominally collective had in fact become private firms operated with the cooperation of local officials (Byrd and Lin 1990). Policy toward private business was gradually liberalized. During the first wave of reform – in 1979–1980 – private businesses were allowed to reemerge, but there were still limitations on the size of private business that were enforced during the retrenchment of 1981–82. Thereafter, gradual liberalization resumed. Restrictions limiting individual businesses to local areas were abandoned, first for rural entrepreneurs and subsequently for urban businessmen (*Economic* 1984: IX-55). Individual entrepreneurs were allowed to engage in wholesale trade, transport goods across provincial lines, and purchase machinery and trucks. During 1984–85, restrictions limiting private businesses to a maximum of seven employees were informally allowed to lapse. Still, it was not until 1988 that legal sanction was given to large private businesses, with the promulgation of a law on private firms.

The diversity of organizational forms taken by rural enterprise enabled it to adapt to a wide variety of economic conditions. In many cases, TVEs were firms owned by local governments. But in other cases, large and small private firms and true cooperatives emerged as well. Local government ownership had certain obvious advantages and disadvantages. Most importantly, continued government interference, inadequately specified property rights, and inappropriately defined incentive systems are described as disadvantages of local government ownership. Conversely, it is argued that local governments could operate like diversified corporations with relatively hard budget constraints at the community level (Byrd and Lin 1990; Nee 1992; Weitzman and Xu 1993; Whiting 1993). But perhaps it was most important that TVEs were not constrained to a single organizational form, but were rather allowed to adapt as comparative advantages and disadvantages became clear.

Conclusion

Rural enterprises grew up in the interstices of the command economy system. It should be clear that their successful growth cannot be understood in isolation from that system. The command economy, having destroyed the traditional rural economy in the 1950s and 1960s, then created the distinctive conditions for the emergence of a new diversified rural economy during the 1980s. The influence of the command economy is particularly clear in the profitability of early rural enterprises, the differential tax treatment accorded rural enterprises, and the close links between emerging rural enterprises and the existing state-run urban economy. Moreover, the semi-public character of rural enterprises – a characteristic unique to China – may plausibly have assisted in the supply of capital to these firms. These "artificial" conditions were the most powerful proximated causes of the explosive growth of rural industry in the 1980s.

Yet rural enterprise growth would not have taken root had it not been favored by additional, more fundamental considerations. Of these, the basic fit between rural enterprises and China's underlying factor endowment is the most important. Next in importance is the fact that the rural sector became a fertile ground for organizational experimentation in which the entrepreneurial energies of the Chinese population were given ample expression. In addition, the chance factor of China's huge size may have played a crucial role. The simple fact that China has some 2,000 counties, over 40,000 townships, and almost 1 million villages was crucial to the success of rural industry. For although each of those townships and villages may have originally tried to operate a miniature state-run economy, the fact was that ultimately producers in each were subject to competition from thousands of other villages. In this fundamentally competitive environment, each township or village found that it faced a relatively hard budget constraint, and had to make its own enterprise economically successful. Rural enterprises created competition for state firms, but they were themselves ultimately shaped by the competitive process as well. Ultimately, this may have been adequate to overcome some of the disadvantages under which rural enterprises labored due to local government control and the distortions of the economic system as a whole.

Rural output structure: Three case studies

Rural industrial output is remarkably diverse, and nearly every industrial sector is represented. Indeed, diversity and rapid growth are the two most significant characteristics of rural industrialization (Byrd and Lin 1990). However, certain patterns in the structure of rural industrial output can be discerned. Detailed sectoral data on township and village level industries is available beginning in 1986, and show that the sectoral profiles of township and village industries were fairly similar. The largest sector was building materials: Nearly 9 million workers, fully 30% of rural industrial employment, worked in clay and stone mining and building materials, predominantly brick-making. Machinery and metal fabrication employed 4.4 million workers, 14% of the total. Textiles and clothing accounted for 4 million workers, or 13% of the total, mostly in township enterprises. Food products were of modest importance, accounting for less than 6% of total employment, reflecting the continuing importance of state procurement of agricultural products, as described earlier.

The importance of building materials is not difficult to explain. A housing boom has been going on in China's countryside since the initiation of rural reforms in 1979. The demand for housing created by rising incomes has been added to the repressed demand for housing accumulated over thirty years in which private rural construction was subject to a near blanket prohibition. The rural industrial sector is in a position to supply materials for rural construction. Indeed, any visitor to the Chinese countryside will have been struck by the brick kilns, stone quarries, and lime kilns, and by the volume of building materials being transported on the roads. This sector uses many backward production techniques, and output is often of low quality; moreover, pollution can be serious. But the new building materials firms are meeting hitherto unsatisfied demand, and the creation of this sector has been almost purely a benefit to the economy.

The textile industry – the third largest source of rural industrial employment – might be a case in which output diversion from existing state firms is significant. Some comparisons can be made between textile production in township enterprises and in the state sector, for which detailed 1983 data are available (RDSG 1987: 240–41). Township textile output grew by 39.6% annually between 1979 and 1983 (total textile output grew 12.6% annually). Compared with state firms, township enterprises have a lower capital-output ratio, but they require nearly two and a half times as many workers to produce a given net output value. For a reference net output, the state sector used 6.3 workers and 43,668 *yuan* worth of fixed capital, while the township enterprises use 14.3 workers and 32,336 *yuan* worth of fixed capital. Even if we value workers at the low rural wage of about 600 *yuan*, the interest rate would have to be over 42% in order for township production to be more efficient. Since this is implausible, we must conclude that the rapid growth of township level textile production represents the more rapid growth of the less efficient producers. To the extent that this is true, the increasing role of township production represents a reduction in overall economic efficiency.[6] Rural textile production also has the surprising characteristic that it is concentrated in provinces with state-owned textile mills, rather than in raw material producing areas. Over 80% of rural cotton spindles are in Shandong, Jiangsu, Zhejiang, and Shanghai (Xu Gongfen 1987). If it is true that the rapid growth of rural industry has been driven partly by the opportunity to appropriate monopoly rents previously accruing to state producers, it is inevitable that there will be some cases where rent-seeking leads to a net reduction in social welfare. It is possible that in some cases the growth of township textile production might fall into this category.

The rapid development of rural coal mining also presents an interesting picture (see Figure 2.4 for a summary of the changing ownership composition of coal production). In this case, the absence of clearly specified property rights over mineral resources contributed to rapid growth. In China, as in other socialist countries, all mineral resources theoretically belong to the state. But China permitted free access to coal resources in an attempt to solve its energy problems, but without ever addressing the question of property rights. This was possible in part because China's complex geological history has created small coal deposits over a remarkably broad range of the country: 1,349 of China's 2,200 counties have some coal resources, and every province except Shanghai and Tianjin produces some coal. By 1987, there were almost 2 million full-time miners in the non-state sector, and another 1 million seasonal mine workers. More than 200,000 of these worked in privately run mines. Many of the non-state mines, and virtually all the private mines, were simply shallow pits and tunnels worked with pick and shovel, with an average output per mine of less than 5,000 tons. 95% of private mines lacked even the most rudimentary safety equipment, such as fans, pumps, gas meters, and lights, and they had accident rates ten times those of central government mines – which are not noted for safety – and three to four times those of rural collective mines. Moreover, the easiest way for a private miner to locate coal was to dig in the vicinity of a state-run mine. In Henan's Zhengzhou mine district, private miners broke into state tunnels thirty-five times between 1984 and 1989, and caused two cave-ins in 1987 that killed nine people. Sometimes state or collective mines were unable to continue tunneling because the surrounding district had been honeycombed with small-scale private mines. At times, the result was a kind of "coal rush" reminscent of the mining free-for-alls of the American West or the interior of Brazil (Yu Boren 1988; Zhang Jiwu 1989).

By the mid-1980s, China's coal supply was improving significantly, in no small part because of the rapid expansion of output from small mines. Nevertheless, the government began to take a stricter attitude toward small-scale mining, and closed 8,500 mines in 1987, about one-tenth of the total number. New laws requiring safety equipment and licenses were passed, but they were scarcely enforceable (Yu Boren 1988; Zhang Jiwu 1989). After 1987, the growth of rural collective and private mines dropped sharply, but they continued to supply one-third of total output.

As these examples show, the presence of distortions and potentially large appropriable rents shape the development of rural industry in complex ways. In some cases, such as the growth of building material production, large-scale entry seems to be almost entirely beneficial. In the case of rural coal mines, the picture is a complex one created by unspecified property rights. Finally, if the data on textile production are adequate to support the comparison, this may be a sector where large-scale entry has actually reduced social productivity. Overall, there can be little doubt that the process of rural industrialization overall has contributed immensely to China's development during the 1980s. But rural development has also been marked by multiple distortions imposed by the old economic system. Not surprisingly, a phenomenon of this breadth and complexity provokes a wide range of reactions.

Contention over rural industry

There has been subtantial sustained controversy about the role and assessment of rural industry in China. In spite of the initial consensus in favor of rapid development of rural industries, conservatives quickly came to recognize the disadvantages of rural industrialization and began to advocate restrictions on rural enterprise development. Rural enterprises were a potential threat to state revenues. They were a threat not because they were necessarily more efficient than state firms, but rather because their very existence signaled the end of the state monopoly over lucrative industrial sectors, and meant that monopoly profits would inevitably be competed away. Conservatives never expressed their opposition to rural enterprises in quite these terms. They argued instead that rural enterprises competed with state firms to buy raw materials, and created wasteful duplication of "processing" facilities. Conservatives also liked to point to the low tax rates and relatively lax financial supervision enjoyed by rural enterprises to suggest that their rapid growth resulted from unfair advantages and behavior.

During the first reform retrenchment, beginning in 1981, conservatives tried to cut back on rural enterprise development by scaling back tax breaks and trying to integrate rural processing of agricultural products into province-level plans. Conservatives particularly targeted a few sectors with very high profits or taxes: Cigarettes and cotton textiles were singled out to be closed down if they could not be integrated into state plans (SRC 1984: 140). High tax rates actually stimulated development because local governments knew that they could share a portion of the tax revenues generated. Hundreds of new cigarette factories had sprung up during the first years of the reform policies (Wong 1985: 268–78). The conservative efforts were well targeted in the sense that they put the spotlight on sectors where rents were particularly large, and where incentives to tap into those rents – whether in the form of profits or taxes – were correspondingly great.

But the problem with which conservatives were grappling was much larger than a few lucrative sectors. Lowered entry barriers naturally induced entry into those sectors where profitability was highest. But in the new environment, in which most prices remained fixed and profitability differentials large, opportunities to enter produced widespread investment in the most profitable industries. This phenomenon was unavoidable, given that entry barriers were reduced while monopoly rents to industry were still large. Even though existing capacity might be adequate to process all the available cotton or tobacco, local factories could still be profitable if they could gain control over some portion of the raw materials. Indeed, even if they were less efficient and less profitable than existing factories, they could still be profitable to the localities. Capture of monopoly rents would more than offset the effect of higher costs. This phenomenon would persist as long as the government maintained control over the price system and did not carry out financial rationalization.

Clearly, there are real social costs to this process. The presence of monopoly rents induces potential entrants to expend real resources, even if they don't actually increase production. Costs of this rent-seeking behavior (showing up as excess capacity plus expenditure of influence resources to gain control over raw materials) will persist until entry and competition realigns prices and eliminates the potential rents. In some sectors, these processes occur fairly rapidly, and without large social costs. For instance, electric fans happen to be a high mark-up item initially, and fan producers proliferated. In the large city of Wuhan, the number of factories producing electric fans jumped from 1 pre-1978 to 47 in the course of 1979. Nationwide, over 1,500 factories nationwide were producing electric fans in that year. But by 1984, only some 300 brands of electric fan had survived (Zhao Xiangyang 1980; Tao Youzhi 1988: 113). A number of the surviving firms – now sophisticated and with national markets, and some producing a range of related consumer durables – were township and village enterprises. A couple of significant producers in Jiangsu and Guangdong stand out.

In other cases, it took much longer for rents to be competed away. For example, in the textile sector, profitability only gradually declined as the state's control over textile raw materials was eroded during the course of the 1980s. Competition for raw materials led to a series of "wool wars," "silk wars," and so on, as entrants with processing capacity contended for inputs that remained underpriced (Watson, Findlay and Du 1989). Capital utilization rates in the state sector dipped and profit rates fell dramatically. Overall productivity grew slowly or not at all, as these transitional inefficiencies offset technological improvements and modernization in the textile sector. Supporters of rural enterprises correctly pointed out that the phenomenon of entry was not limited to rural enterprises. Local government sponsored "state-run" firms were also competing away monopoly rents, and in some sectors these were the more important entrants (Zhang Yi and Huang Guangshu 1981). This shows that the question of lowered entry barriers was a general one that confronted the entire Chinese economy during the transition process. It was not limited to rural enterprises, and a fundamental solution to the problem would have required the revision of the price and tax system to reduce the impact of monopoly rents in the system. But, as described in the previous chapter, finance and price rationalization was beyond the capacity of the Chinese government at this point. Instead, steady entry combined with price liberalization gradually competed away the available monopoly rents (see Chapter 6).

Indeed, government policy toward rural enterprises began to swing back toward positive support almost immediately after the crackdown of 1981. After the conservatives succeeded in reaffirming the state monopoly over a few of the most lucrative sectors (such as cigarettes), central government policy again became favorable to rural enterprises. Subsequently, the general revival of overall reform in 1984, discussed in the next chapter, included a clear tilt in favor of rural industrialization. Support gradually expanded to include explicit recognition for the role of private and "new cooperative" enterprises. The policy support given to rural enterprises reached a peak during 1987–88. A 1987 Central Party document (No. 5) gave explicit support to the important role played by private business, specifically in the transfer of labor from farming to non-agricultural occupations (Ma Jisen 1988). By late 1988, Zhao Ziyang was even calling on state enterprises to emulate some of the management methods of rural enterprises. Yet hostility toward rural enterprises remained. During the period of conservative dominance immediately after the Tiananmen incident, Premier Li Peng declared, somewhat priggishly, "We do not agree with comrade Zhao Ziyang's inappropriately exaggerating the role of rural enterprises" and argued that most rural enterprises owed their existence to "relatively preferential conditions and the support of cheap labor." (Li Peng 1989). But this period of hardline dominance proved to be relatively short-lived. Within a year, even conservatives such as Li Peng were discovering that rural enterprises had some desirable features.

Non-state industry and the national industrial economy

It is essential to draw back and place the growth of non-state industry, including rural industry, within the broader context of the national industrial system. Non-state industry was already significant on the eve of reform, pro-

Table 4.2. *Industrial output by size and ownership categories*

	1978	1985	1991
	(percentage of total output)		
Large-scale sector	41.5	42.3	43.6
[State]	[41.5]	[41.9]	[40.6]
[Other]	[0.0]	[0.4]	[3.0]
Urban medium/small	49.4	38.8	25.2
[State]	[35.8]	[22.9]	[12.2]
[Collective]	[13.6]	[15.9]	[13.0]
Rural medium/small	8.7	14.6	20.6
[Township]	[4.8]	[7.8]	[10.3]
[Village]	[3.9]	[6.8]	[10.3]
Very small scale	0.4	3.4	7.8
[Urban]	[0.0]	[0.3]	[0.7]
[Rural]	[0.4]	[3.1]	[7.1]
Other: medium/small	0.0	0.8	2.8
Total	100.0	100.0	100.0

1978 at 1970 constant prices; 1985 and 1991 at current prices.
Source: Statistical Appendix.

ducing almost a quarter (22.7%) of total industrial output in 1978. Virtually all non-state output was accounted for by enterprises that were nominally "collectively owned," mostly in cities. Through more than a decade of explosive growth, the non-state sector has been transformed. It is now primarily rural, predominantly market-oriented, and with an important private sector. In 1992, the industrial output value of the non-state sector surpassed that of the state sector for the first time. The growth of the non-state sector is therefore significant not only for its sustained rapid growth over a period of more than a decade, but also for the transformation of its character during this period. More generally, the growth of the non-state sector is part of the changing size structure of Chinese industry.

Changes in the size structure of Chinese industry are summarized in Table 4.2, where industrial output is classified into four categories. The first category consists of Chinese "large and medium" sized firms, nearly all of which have over 500 employees (see the Statistical Appendix at the end of the book). The second category consists of "small" urban state and collective firms: As discussed next, these are in fact medium-sized firms by international standards, nearly always having more than 50 employees. A similar, third category of medium-sized rural firms can be constructed by summing township and village level output. Although a few of these firms might have fewer than 50 employees, this would be a very small proportion of the total. Finally, a "very-small" category, consisting of private firms and independent (non-government sponsored) cooperatives, rounds out the comparison.

In 1978, on the eve of reform, Chinese industry was characterized by an unbalanced size distribution of industry. China resembled the Soviet Union and other ECEs – though not in as extreme a fashion – in having a prominent large-scale, state-run industrial sector. 41.5% of industrial output was produced by the large-scale state sector – large for a developing country, but considerably less than the 74% of industrial output that was produced in the Soviet Union by firms with over 1,000 workers (Ferris 1984). Even more striking, perhaps, was the large reliance on urban, mid-sized industry. Almost exactly half the output was produced by smaller state and urban collective firms. These firms, although classified as "small" in Chinese statistics, were mostly medium-sized. The very-small industrial sector, which plays a significant role in most developing countries was virtually absent.

These medium and small urban factories were peculiar, intermediate creatures. Too small to reap economies of scale, yet too large and bureaucratized to respond flexibly and efficiently to scattered economic opportunities, this sector was the most characteristic product of the Chinese decentralized command economy. Most were state-run (36% of total output) and incorporated into local planning. The urban collective factories (14% of output) accounted for the bulk of non-state output, and had complex origins. In theory, urban collectives should have a great deal of autonomy. They were originally created as worker-owned cooperatives, and the workers should therefore have the right to dispose of after-tax profits. But in practice, most urban collectives were, by 1978, rather like state firms, and had little operational autonomy. The payment of post-tax profit as dividends to workers had been abolished in 1967, at the beginning of the Cultural Revolution. The large majority of collectives were subordinate to some other organization – most often a local government organ or another enterprise – that had created it and controlled its revenues. Most collective firms were thus something like community enterprises: They were free from central planning, but subject to control by local governments or state-owned units.

Urban collectives fell into three categories with different histories and somewhat different characteristics. The largest category consisted of the light industry cooperatives formed during the 1950s through the forced participation of handicraft workers. By 1978, these accounted for slightly over half the workers and 56% of the output of urban collective industry.

Over the years, most of these cooperatives had lost their marginal independence and became subordinate to the local Second Light Industry Bureau,
to whom they turned over their after-tax profits. In about three-quarters of
these firms, workers got a better benefits package and factories didn't have
to worry about profitability: These firms were called "big collectives." By
1980, almost half of these firms were at least partially mechanized. (Wu
Dongyan 1981; Ma Hong 1982: 218). The second category consisted of
collectives created by neighborhood committees, often called "street industries." These were usually small workshops initially established to provide
employment for urban housewives, and later to provide work for unemployed youth. By 1978, they employed almost a quarter of all urban collective industrial workers, but because they were relatively undercapitalized
they produced only 14% of urban collective output. Nearly all of these were
"small collectives," forced to be self-reliant because of a lack of resources.
The third category was collective firms established and managed by large
state-owned factories. Initially called "May 7" factories – after a speech by
Mao Zedong that called on citizens to combine productive labor with other
activities – they were primarily established to provide employment for de-
pendents of state workers. It would not be unusual to visit a state-owned
steel mill within which there was a collective garment factory employing
primarily female labor. Collectives of this type employed about a quarter of
all urban collective industry workers (Wu Dongyan 1981; Sun Dejun 1981).
Only a quarter of urban collective industrial workers – those in the neighborhood firms – were clearly in independent businesses. The others had
bureaucratic patrons and supervisors who could be counted on to bail them
out of economic difficulty and shape their behavior in the interests of the
superior organ. All urban collectives are placed in the urban medium/small
category shown in Table 4.2.

The almost complete absence of the very small scale firms in China is
readily traceable to the virtual non-existence of the private sector before
reform. Large private firms had been nationalized in the 1950s, and most
small producers and merchants had been organized into cooperatives. A few
stubborn, mostly elderly, individuals continued in private business, but
these accounted for less than 0.2% of the urban labor force in 1978. In rural
areas, all residents were nominally members of village collectives, so that
there were in theory no private businesses at all (residual private businesses
were classified as "sideline" activities of collective members). By contrast, in
other developing countries – and in China before 1949 – this sector has
played a vastly more important role. For example in Indonesia in 1975, 76%
of industrial workers were in household businesses or small workshops; the

comparable figures for India (1973) and the Philippines (1975) were 60% and 53%, respectively (Anderson 1982). By contrast, even after a decade of reform in China, this proportion remained well under 20%.

We must assume that the regular occurrence and survival of a very-small sector in a wide range of market economies reflects a true competitive advantage for small firms in certain activities. In a spectrum of industries ranging from the lowest to the highest technologies, very small firms play a crucial role. In the face of vigorous competition with giant corporations, small firms survive and reproduce themselves. This must correspond to some real competitive advantage. There are, in industrializing economies, pervasive niches that are commonly filled by small firms. In China, as in the ECEs, these niches were largely empty. This meant, first, that the economy was experiencing substantial losses in efficiency, since it was forgoing forms of production that were much lower cost. Conversely, the potential for rapid efficiency gains was that much greater.

With this background in mind, the changing size structure documented in Table 4.2 will be easy to interpret. Overall, the rapid growth of non-state and rural industry has changed the size and ownership structure of Chinese industry in important ways. The state share has shrunk, and rural production grown rapidly. But the largest state firms have continued to grow. Overall, the state share of industrial output has shrunk, but as Table 4.2 shows, the share of the largest firms has remained approximately constant. The extraordinary success of rural industry has led many observers – inside China as well as outside – to conclude that the large-scale state sector has performed poorly in comparison. In fact, the data show that the shrinkage in the state share is entirely accounted for by the decline in the importance of the medium/small state sector. Small state enterprises accounted for 35.8% of total output in 1978, but only 12.2% in 1991. By contrast, large state enterprises accounted for 41.5% of total output in 1978, and 40.6% in 1991, an insignificant change. Moreover, the rapidly growing large-scale "Other" sector, primarily consisting of foreign-invested enterprises, has begun to have a significant presence in the late 1980s.

These trends should not be surprising, and are in fact somewhat reassuring. The large state enterprises are heavily concentrated in producer goods and raw material production in which economies of scale are significant. It would be very surprising if rapid industrial growth could be sustained without significant increases in large-scale sector output. With a few exceptions, the newly entering firms are small-scale, and have not had the opportunity to reach anything like ample scale economies. Instead, rapidly growing sectors have displaced the portion of state output that had no obvious economic advantages to begin with. The proliferation of state firms too small to reap scale economies but too bureaucratic to exploit the advantages of smallness was a peculiar characteristic of Chinese development patterns. In the most competitive environment of the 1980s, those firms were largely swept away by the more vigorous rural firms.

Indeed, urban collective firms have merely maintained their share of total output. The 20 percentage point decline in small state firms has been mainly taken up by an 11 percentage point increase in the share of rural township and village enterprises, and a 7 percentage point increase in the very-small scale sector, most of which is also in the rural areas. Thus, two important changes have occurred in the structure of output. First, about half the small-scale production has moved out of the cities and into the countryside. Second, an entirely new very-small-scale sector has grown up. From virtually nothing in 1978, this sector now produces 7% of output. If international experience is any guide, however, there is still substantial room for expansion of this sector. The growth of rural, non-state industry is part of a more general process in which Chinese industry is losing its peculiar characteristics, and approaching a more normal size distribution that makes it more similar to other industrializing nations.

Conclusion

The successful emergence of the non-state sector was obvious by the year 1984. It was most visible for agriculture, the output of which soared during 1983 and 1984 to unprecedented levels. Yet the vigor and economic rationality of the household response to the newly liberalized environment was evident in other respects as well. Rapid growth of rural industry was clear to all, and the growth of household saving had guaranteed the maintenance of macroeconomic balance that was clearly so important to China's conservatives. Thus, the vigorous non-state response became crucial in allowing the reform process as a whole to go forward. The consequences of this liberalization were almost entirely unforeseen at the outset. Of course, even within the state sector, the reform process was full of unanticipated consequences. But the growth of the non-state sector created unanticipated consequences of a wholly different magnitude: Not only was the speed and breadth of growth unanticipated, but also the political and economic impacts of this growth were more profound than anyone predicted.

The emergence and growth of the non-state sector is one of the most important elements of China's economic reform. But this is so not because the *performance* of the non-state sector has been so outstanding but rather because the emergence of the non-state sector introduced a competitive market environment to China. That market environment, in turn, is the key to understanding changing behavior and performance in both the state and non-state sectors, as well as the changing macroeconomic behavior of the economy. It is not the case that rural industries represent the sprouts of the new economy growing up in the wastelands of the old state-run economy. Rather, the rapid growth of rural industries changed the entire economic ecology, creating a fundamentally new environment in which both state and non-state firms operate.

In some respects, the growth of rural industry should be understood not as "surrounding the cities from the countryside" (Findlay and Watson 1992), but rather as spillover of the urban economy, and spill out from the state-run economy. The reality is that both state and non-state sectors have grown rapidly and both have been subject to continuing distortions in their behavior because of the persistence of elements of the traditional system. More importantly, the rapid growth of the non-state sector can only be understood within the context of the traditional system, which ironically provided many of the conditions for the spectacular growth of non-state industry.

In a broad sense, these processes should be replicable in all transitional economies. It is true that China seems to have an advantage in the promotion of rural industry simply because it has so much more rural area in which to promote it. But the fact is that China's rural industrialization has been concentrated in those parts of the countryside that are close to cities, that is, in the parts of the countryside that are more like the countryside in the ECEs. There are unique organizational features to the collectives, and they may have helped the process of rural industrialization. Not every economy can expect such a rapid increase in household saving in response to early reforms. The elements for non-state growth certainly came together well in the Chinese context, and that growth reshaped the entire reform process. The rapid entry and speedy growth of new businesses is a fundamental part of the transition process, wherever it occurs.

Phase two

Reforms take off, 1984–1988

5

Reformulation and debate: The turning point of 1984

The peculiar combination of success and failure in China's economic reforms during the period from 1978 through 1983 triggered a reassessment of China's economic condition and the proper approach to economic reform. Accomplishments had been considerable. The most important goals of economic reorientation had been achieved, ameliorating imbalances and building reserves. The vigorous growth of the non-state sector had contributed substantial dynamism to the economy. As a result of these economic changes, the overall outlook of the leadership swung from pessimism to optimism. At the same time, the unbalanced progress of reforms in the state sector led to intensified debate about the proper way to reform. The rationalizing reform approach had failed. This approach had failed in the generic sense – that of not having qualitatively changed the behavior of state-run enterprises. But even more important was that the government had discovered itself unable to carry out the basic prerequisites of rationalizing reform, in the form of the initial rationalization of the financial and price systems. The model of reform was a shambles, but reform itself – in the form of vigorous growth in agriculture and non-state enterprises – was alive and successful.

This peculiar combination of success and failure touched off a process of reassessment and reformulation among the Chinese leadership. Since Zhao Ziyang was increasingly making the key decisions about individual reform measures, he was also the central figure in this process. He first assembled an eclectic version of reform in order to regain momentum for the reform process as a whole. But almost immediately, this eclectic program began to raise new questions about the direction and ultimate objective of reform. In response to those questions, a new and increasingly sophisticated debate about Chinese reform strategy emerged beginning in 1985. In this chapter, we first consider the mixture of positive and negative experiences that led to reformulation of the ideal of economic reform during 1984. Next we examine the actual mix of reform proposals that emerged during 1984, giving stress to

Zhao Ziyang's advocacy of three initiatives: a comprehensive reform program, an altered role for the planning system, and the program of financial rationalization called "tax for profit." Finally, we examine the continuing debate about what practical lessons for future policy could properly be drawn from China's attempt to develop a reform strategy. The chapter following describes the way these efforts then coalesced into a distinct and coherent strategy.

From pessimism to optimism

Chinese reforms had begun at the end of the 1970s in a near crisis atmosphere, and highly pessimistic assessments of the economic situation were dominant through the drafting of the Sixth Five Year Plan (6FYP) in 1981–82. The initial reorientation of the economy was driven by perceived economic necessity, and reforms themselves were vulnerable to retrenchment at the end of 1980 when it was felt that reforms were conflicting with unavoidable economic restructuring. The Sixth Plan was supposed to cover 1981–85, although it was actually not completed until 1982 ("Sixth Plan" 1984). It projected continued low growth through 1985, based primarily on continued pessimism about the energy sector (see Table 2.1 and Figure 2.1, showing projections of aggregate growth and petroleum development). Economic growth began to pick up after 1982, but policymaking remained steadfastly conservative, even as economic conditions improved.

By late 1983, unmistakable notes of optimism began to creep into policymakers' speeches. This optimism was well founded: The two most important bottleneck sectors holding back the Chinese economy – agriculture and energy – were showing signs of greatly improved performance. Agriculture turned in a spectacular performance between 1982 and 1984. Large successive annual increases in crop output seemed to promise a permanent end to agricultural scarcity, allowing the economy to finally escape from the single most important problem that had hobbled it for decades. Steadily increasing output – based on higher productivity – increased rural incomes and loosened the agricultural supply bottleneck, always one of the most pressing concerns to Chinese policymakers. Simultaneously, forecasts of near-zero growth of primary energy output were confounded after 1982 by an upturn in state coal production reinforced by rapid growth of township and village coal mines. Petroleum output increased, and the petroleum ministry was increasingly confident of its ability to deliver future increases. Increasing output in the two most important bottleneck sectors promised a less crisis-ridden economic environment, and promised a turn to stable and rapid growth.

More rapid growth on the supply side was accompanied by the beneficial effects of continued restraint on the demand side. Three successive years of near-zero wage growth had combined with a growing supply of consumer goods to create substantial slack in the economy. Prices were stable. Indeed, some food prices on the free market were declining, and cloth rationing had been eliminated. Moreover, the largest bulge in urban job-seekers had now been accommodated, and measured urban unemployment had fallen to 2.3% by the end of 1983. Macroeconomic balance was showing up in the foreign trade accounts as well, and foreign exchange reserves were increasing. Export promotion activities between 1978 and 1981 had brought some success, and planners put tight limits on imports during the 1982 downturn in world trade. The result was a moderate trade surplus and a larger current account surplus that pushed foreign exchange reserves from $4 billion to $14 billion during the two years 1982 and 1983 (*Banking 1952–87:* 155, 158). Reorientation of the economy had achieved both of its main goals – restructured production and macroeconomic stability – and policymakers had successfully coped with the economic crisis of 1978.

Economic optimism began to affect policymaking in 1984, as it became clear that output in 1984 and 1985 would substantially surpass the targets of the Sixth Plan. A new series of planning exercises were begun to project the development of the economy through the year 2000. This was a new type of planning for China, based on projections of potential growth paths, rather than simple output targets (Hamrin 1990; Naughton 1990).[1] Generalized optimism was given specific form in the drafting of the Seventh Five Year Plan (1986–1990), which began in 1984 and was completed during 1985. In the Party "Suggestions" for the plan, first priority was to be given to continued agricultural growth, second to consumer goods industry, and third to completion of keypoint projects in energy, transport, communications, and raw materials (CCP 1985: 13–15). The political leadership was here giving its blessing to a program of balanced growth. As has rarely been the case in China, the emphasis was neither on coping with crucial bottlenecks to development, nor on accelerating growth through new leaps forward. Linkages between various sectors of the economy were acknowledged, and broad-based, harmonious growth was the clear objective.

Technocrats drawing up the actual plan proceeded very much in this spirit. They coordinated the drafting of the Five Year Plan with a forecasting exercise in China's economy in the year 2000 (China 2000). A similar but smaller-scale exercise was carried out by the World Bank (World Bank 1986), and members of the two teams exchanged views. The Seventh Five Year Plan that emerged from this exercise turned out to be one of the most realistic and sound plans ever promulgated in China. It projected GNP growth of 7.5% annually, a rapid but attainable pace. Exports and imports were slated to increase rapidly. While there were a large number of output targets for specific commodities, these were put forward as reference targets, rather than commands. Projections of population growth, student enrollments, and growth of hospital beds were all included, bringing the plan even further from past plans with their stress on heavy industrial development.

Particularly striking was the absence of concern about energy bottlenecks. Energy supply and demand were seen as being basically in balance, with energy savings of about 2% annually being targeted to ensure consistency between energy and aggregate output targets. Moreover, investment priority in the energy sector was given to electricity rather than primary energy. Reflecting the strong recovery in primary energy between 1982 and 1985, energy sector officials were now projecting moderately rapid growth. This was accurate for coal, but petroleum ministry officials predicted a 1990 output of 150 MMT, which turned out to be over-optimistic (actual output was 138 MMT). Nevertheless, both the energy and aggregate output targets were generally realistic, and realized energy output growth would have been adequate if aggregate economic growth had conformed to the plan projections ("Seventh Plan" 1986).

Thus, during the crucial 1984–85 period, Chinese economic policy-making moved out of the crisis mode and toward a concern with broad-based economic growth. Resolution of crisis did not lead, on balance, to an attempt to reignite unsustainably high growth rates. Instead, increasing optimism about the economy was reflected in an attempt to lay the groundwork for a sustained economic expansion and in a willingness to accelerate economic reform.

Zhao Ziyang's initiatives: What model of reform?

But what model of reform would be attempted? As described in Chapter 3, early theoretical discussions of reform tended to yield two camps. The conservative camp advocated the continuing primacy of planning over key sectors of the economy, combined with an increased role for market forces for less important sectors and smaller enterprises. The reformist camp, though including many diverse viewpoints, basically drew its inspiration from the model of European rationalizing reform. Reformists rejected the separation of the economy into different sectors with different operating mechanisms. They advocated, rather, shifting state control of the economy toward economic levers – requiring comprehensive reform of prices, taxes, and interest rates – and the impartial application of these economic parameters to all enterprises. Presumably such a reform would involve the abolition of mandatory planning, but the precise role of the government was not clearly described.

Intervening events had undermined the rationale for *both* these approaches to reform. The conservative approach had been undermined by the successful recovery of the economy. The appearance of macroeconomic slack, first in producer good markets and subsequently in consumer markets, greatly reduced the force of the argument for across-the-board planning. If goods were not scarce, there was little need for rationing and compulsory allocation. More specifically, the critical bottlenecks in energy and agriculture that provided planners with their *raison d'être* had been substantially relaxed. In the case of energy and transport bottlenecks, the relaxation had been achieved not through greater economy-wide planning, but simply through better targeting of government resources on critical projects. The success in agriculture was even more telling: The unprecedented appearance of agriculture abundance was indisputably the result of institutional reform and increased market forces. Moreover, the success of household farming was almost equaled by the vigorous growth of non-state enterprises and the rapid increase in household saving. In these conditions, it was difficult to argue that what the economy needed was more planning and less market.

Yet the argument for rationalizing reforms had been even more seriously wounded. As described in Chapter 3, a whole string of rationalizing reforms, essential to the overall project, had failed to be implemented. China was still unique even among command economies in not charging enterprises for state-supplied fixed investment. Equally striking had been the failure to carry out significant price realignments. The rationalizing reform model requires that the government steer the economy through manipulation of economic levers; but if the government had proven impotent to correct a handful of the most obviously distorted prices, how could it possibly hope to harmoniously steer the economy through the use of economic levers? Reformist economists gradually began to move away from their previous acceptance of rationalizing reform, and to the advocacy of market determined prices.

Under these circumstances, Premier Zhao Ziyang, in charge of economic policymaking, cobbled together a practical reform program that combined elements from these competing approaches. With this syncretic program, Zhao was able to gain support – or at least acquiescence – from all the major political forces in China for major reforms during 1984. Like many political compromises, Zhao's initial measures were not intellectually elegant. Indeed, they included mutually contradictory elements. But they gained him the freedom to maneuver and the ability to launch major new reform initiatives, initiatives that could support the new-found dynamism of the economy. Through most of the 1980s, Zhao Ziyang was an extremely cautious reformer. From 1980 through 1983, he never challenged Chen Yun's reimposition of economic orthodoxy, even though it was clear he favored a bolder approach to reform. Zhao might be likened to a defensive driver, maintaining a space cushion around his policy vehicle. In 1984 for the first time, Zhao managed to create a large enough space for maneuver to give himself the freedom to implement significant economic reforms. During the period from 1984 through 1988, Zhao was the dominant force in the leadership shaping the path of economic reform, and he initiated the most creative period of Chinese reform (cf. Lam 1989).

Zhao kicked off this dynamic period during 1984 with three main initiatives. First, he used the vocabulary of rationalizing reform to gain the assent of the older generation of leaders, particularly Chen Yun, to a program of comprehensive reform. Second, he took a page from the planners' book and accepted the division of the economy into plan and market spheres. However, he did this in a way that radically reinterpreted the conservative conception and shifted the balance sharply toward the market sphere. Third, he pushed for the rapid implementation of the program of financial rationalization called "tax for profit." Of these three initiatives, the first had a political objective that was achieved when the entire Communist Party approved the comprehensive reform document of October 1984. The second initiative had apparently rather modest aims, and these were quickly achieved. But it turned out to have profound consequences, and served as the basis for the subsequent "growing out of the plan." The third initiative failed to be successfully carried through, and was the last attempt to implement rationalizing reform. Its failure left the path open for alternative approaches that eventually coalesced into the distinctive Chinese reform strategy.

Assembling political consensus

On September 9, 1984, Zhao Ziyang sent a letter to the members of the Politburo Standing Committee outlining his ideas for economic reform. This letter went to the three most important Communist Party elders – Deng Xiaoping, Chen Yun, and Li Xiannian – as well as First Party Secretary Hu Yaobang. Each of them approved the letter, verifying the consensus among the top leaders.[2] This letter is an impressive piece of reformulation and redefinition. Zhao begins by reviewing recent reform work, and argues that since enterprise reform is already underway, the current challenge is to carry out a three-part reform of planning, prices, and government economic administration. Zhao strongly reaffirms that China practices a planned economy, not a market economy, and he reinforces the point by stating that "blind and spontaneous" market forces will only be relevant for a few minor commodities and agricultural sideline products. But, he immediately goes on, the planned economy does not mean that compulsory planning is the main instrument, and indeed China will gradually reduce the scope of compulsory planning and increase the scope of guidance planning. Guidance planning relies on economic methods, and planning and the law of value will be integrated. This is clearly different from a capitalist market economy, Zhao says, but he does not specify in what way it is different.

Zhao is here unmistakably using the vocabulary of rationalizing reform. He describes China as "a planned commodity economy with public ownership as the basic form," a fuzzy consensus formulation that was subsequently incorporated in the October reform charter. This formulation implied movement in the direction of a market economy, because all goods would be voluntarily transacted among independent enterprises, rather than allocated among subdivisions of the state. But at the same time, the formulation implied a goal well short of a market economy. The state plan would still control the really important economic variables – investment and the distribution of income – and "spontaneous" market forces would not be allowed to determine the allocation of resources. Closeness to the rationalizing reform model is further indicated by Zhao's argument that conditions are favorable for price reform, which should therefore be carried out immediately. The government should get out of the business of running enterprises and instead confine itself to administrative and regulatory functions.

Although we cannot know what was going on in Zhao Ziyang's mind at this time, it is hard to resist the impression that he is purposely using the vagueness of his concepts as a stratagem to overcome resistance to reform. He argues that since most planning will become guidance planning, it is no longer appropriate to say that "planning is number one, and the law of value number two". Both will be combined in guidance planning. Zhao is here politely and obliquely discarding Chen Yun's ideas on the primacy of planning, while being careful not to quote him directly.[3] Moreover, there are indications that by this time, Zhao had become disillusioned with the computation of optimal prices, and had come to accept the idea that prices should be determined by supply and demand. Indeed, this letter, after discussing problems in the price system, notes that multiple prices for some commodities have already developed, and "it is quite possible that the future trend in price reform will be (a) reduction in the scope of state-set prices and increase in the proportion of free prices, and (b) adjustment of state-set prices to be close to market prices" (CCP 1986: 537). Behind the rhetoric of rationalizing reform and the continuance of the planned economy, there are hints of a dual-track system with a shrinking planned sector and a growing market sector.

The October 1984 economic system reform document, ratified by a CP Central Committee meeting with all the top leaders in attendance, is universally recognized as the programmatic document for accelerated industrial reforms. It continues to use the vocabulary and formulations of Zhao's September letter. It sounds like a problem of rationalizing reform. The central idea is again that enterprise reform will be followed by comprehensive reforms. Enterprises should become self-managing entities responsible for their own profits and losses, with the authority to determine their own labor force, organizational, and reward systems and the authority to set their own prices – within the scope of the state plan. Coordinated reform of all the systems – planning prices, state administration, labor and wages – should follow and be completed within five years. Of these, the reform of the price system is the crucial determination of success and failure of the reform program as a whole. Hints of a greater role for market prices are included, but they are even more muted than in Zhao's letter (*Economic* 1985: I-4-6). Reading this document, an expert on Eastern European reforms notes, "the vision is virtually the same" as that of the Hungarian reform of 1968 (Hewett 1985: 34).

But in fact the October document turned out to be an astonishingly bad description of the reforms that actually followed. Immediately thereafter, reform policymaking turned in the direction of a very different strategy – that of increasing reliance on market prices and growing out of the plan. From 1984 onward, there was an increasingly profound divergence between the stated goal of reform, which, partly for political protection, continued to be a state-guided semi-market economy, and actual practice, which was to steadily increase the market elements in the economy at the expense of the planned elements. This divergence is probably due to Zhao Ziyang's political constraints: The most generous endorsement of reform he could achieve was in response to a reform model that stressed control and planning along with reform, and the rationalizing reform model was ideally suited for that purpose. Having achieved the desired endorsement, he was then able to set off on a course of policymaking that was much more eclectic, more shaped by economic reality and by political constraints, and ultimately more feasible than rationalizing reform would ever have been.[4]

Freezing the plan

The second of Zhao's initiatives involved the acceptance of a practical compromise about the role of the plan. It will be recalled that conservatives advocated the partition of the economy into plan and market segments in which the plan would cover all important products and large enterprises. As a normative theory of how to combine plan and market, this had little to recommend it, but as a positive description of how China's economy actually worked, it was roughly accurate. Central government planning covered only the larger enterprises and most basic commodities. Moreover, actual investment planning increasingly focused on the energy and infrastructure projects of the priority investment program. Conservatives wanted to "rationalize" the partitioning of the economy into plan and market sectors and develop some principles that would justify and guide the partition. But this was hard to do. Scattered small enterprises produced even the most vital commodities such as coal, and huge enterprises produced commodities in excess supply such as heavy machine tools. Zhao's eminently practical solution was to abandon the search for principles and instead base the size of the plan on past practice. After all, with the priority investment program in operation, the current rough division of labor was working reasonably well. Practical compromise was much easier than theoretical agreement.

However, this practical compromise was carried out in a way that radically shifted the balance of the economy toward the market sphere. During the course of 1984, economic bureaucrats gradually moved toward a concept that would freeze the size of the plan in absolute terms and thus guarantee that the economy would gradually develop a predominantly market orientation. Early in the year, the System Reform Commission proposed that the number of allocated commodities be further reduced, and that after this reduction "the proportion of important materials directly controlled and allocated by the state should be set strictly according to the needs of keypoint construction [priority investment] and keypoint tasks. It can be slightly raised or reduced according to changing conditions" (SRC 1988a: 114). In this formulation there is still some ambiguity: The "proportion" of allocated materials might be maintained constant, allowing the plan to grow along with the economy as a whole. The next step, as described by the Material Supply Bureau (which actually does the allocation), was: "Beginning in 1984, except for those needed to guarantee state keypoint construction and key production tasks, planned material allocations for ordinary needs were maintained unchanged at the level of allocation in 1984; beginning in 1987, we began to reduce allocation amounts for ordinary needs" (SRC 1988b: 454; Wu and

Zhao 1987: 312). This statement redefined the relationship of the compulsory plan to the vast majority of transactions between enterprises – those not directly linked to keypoint construction projects. The level of material allocations relating to those transactions would be fixed in absolute terms. Therefore, all new transactions would occur outside the plan. The crucial innovation came in the clarity of the definition of the central plan. It was explicitly tied to the central government's priority investment program, and for the first time, a clear boundary was drawn around the core central plan. While there could be some fluctuation in the level of the investment plan, such fluctuations could not be very large. The priority investment plan accounted for 3–4% of GNP, and even major fluctuations relative to that plan could not cause significant fluctuations in the size of the plan relative to the economy as a whole. For all other transactions, the plan was to be absolutely fixed.[5] For example, light industry was explicitly told that its raw materials allocations would be unchanged at the 1984 level; henceforth, increased production would not bring increased allocation (Nie Sibin 1988: 79). By the end of 1984, planners had accepted the fact that the absolute size of the compulsory plan would be fixed in subsequent years (Gui Shiyong 1984; Zhong Zhiqi 1984).

The compromise was thus based on the conservative's view of partitioning the economy into plan and market sectors, but did so in a way that condemned the plan to a steady decline in relative importance. As the economy grew, the plan share would decrease and the nature of the plan would change. Since the plan was oriented toward priority investment, it would increasingly come to resemble a set of contracts that the state signed to carry out its investment. Granted, these were not voluntary contracts – particularly initially. Rather, they were compulsory tasks, and because they had to be carried out at state-set prices, they represented a tax on the enterprise that fulfilled the responsibilities. Conservatives were willing to accept this compromise because it satisfied their deepest concern: They were guaranteed continued control over resources that would allow them to carry out their priority investment program and maintain the prerequisites for continued growth. More generally, it was clear to all sides that during the protracted reform process the government would have to take the lead on energy and infrastructure development. Perhaps it was not essential that the traditional planning apparatus be the instrument for energy and infrastructure development, but since it already existed, it was cheap and easy to continue using it for this purpose.

For the full implications of the new policy on planning to be evident, it was essential that the outside-plan portion of the economy be a well functioning market. Previous reforms had not clearly established the right of enterprises to buy and sell outside-plan products at market prices. But during 1984, that right gradually was accepted. By the end of 1984, officials at the State Price Bureau were declaring that it was impossible to control outside-plan price (Cheng Zhiping 1984), and market price quotations began to appear in journals. During January and February 1985, explicit authorization to firms to price outside-plan products according to the market was finally granted (Tong and Zou 1992). From this time forward, the dual-track system was formally in operation.

Tax for profit

The third initiative that Zhao undertook during 1984 was to push for the implementation of the tax-for-profit system. This was designed to be the centerpiece of enterprise reforms, creating an entirely new financial system that would serve as the basis for commercialization of all enterprises. Experimental implementation of tax-for-profit systems was described in Chapter 3. Zhao now pushed for the adoption of tax for profit across the board as the logical next step in the transformation of state-run enterprises. The fundamental principle was the same: reclassification of profits into a set of functionally differentiated revenue streams, most of which were designated as taxes. Profits would be divided into capital charges, resource taxes, sales taxes, and income tax. In theory, the enterprise could then emerge as the residual claimant on after-tax profit. At this time, tax-for-profit seemed to be the crucial reform initiative, on which reformers pinned most of their hopes (Naughton 1985).

It needs to be stressed that tax for profit was also the central measure in a program of comprehensive rationalization of the price and tax system. First, tax for profit was initially intended to be combined with price realignments. Without price adjustments, it would be virtually impossible to set tax rates at anything close to uniform rates. Realignment of producer goods prices was to accompany the implementation of tax for profit (SRC 1988a). Second, tax for profit was to be the basis for a comprehensive restructuring of the fiscal system. Not only would it place the financial relationship between enterprises and the government budget on a much sounder long-run basis, tax for profit was to serve as the basis for dividing revenues between the central and local governments. Certain taxes would be defined as central revenues, while others would become local revenues, ending the need to continuously bargain over revenue shares. With these thorny problems solved, enterprises would compete under much more equal conditions, permitting a fundamental expansion of enterprise autonomy.

In practice, however, the details of the tax-for-profit program had to be determined through a process of consultation and negotiation within the bureaucracy. The program that emerged from this process of negotiation was drastically diminished, and carried few of the theoretical advantages of the original program.[6] Preparatory work began on the tax-for-profit system in 1983. So-called "first stage" implementation in that year merely introduced a nominal income tax for enterprises. The key step was "second stage" implementation, which was to be carried out during 1984. Economic bureaucrats from different sectors and provinces caucused during 1984, and went through more than twenty proposed drafts of the program. Representatives of industrial interests, such as the State Economic Commission, and representatives of inland provinces pushed for lower tax burdens, while representatives of the Ministry of Finance pushed for higher taxes to protect central government revenues. The final program that emerged was barely recognizable as the tax-for-profit system.

Two crucial failures marked the program that finally emerged. Both price realignments and charges for fixed-asset use failed to be included in the final program. Price realignments failed for the same reason that early price reform proposals had failed. Worry about the impact of price adjustments on inflation and budgetary revenues was reinforced by the opposition of sectors that would be directly hurt by increased input prices. By the end of 1984, the proposal to begin price reform with producer goods had been abandoned, and a program to raise consumer food prices (thereby reducing government subsidies) was adopted in its place. Charges for fixed assets were part of the initial draft tax-for-profit, but in the course of negotiation over the final product, elimination of fixed asset charges was the price paid to reach a compromise document. Eliminating capital charges gave negotiators more flexibility to satisfy the various interest groups at the bargaining table.

What were the fundamental factors that made capital charges so difficult to implement? The variety of interest groups represented was daunting, and reconciliation of their views would have been difficult in any case. But the fundamental problem underlying the proposal was the huge divergence of profit rates among factories. Variations in profitability were particularly marked along two dimensions. First, the price system artificially lowered profitability for most producers of raw materials and mining products, including primary energy products. The most important example was the state-run coal industry, which earned almost no profit in the aggregate in 1984. Another important case, though, was that of military industries, which were in the midst of a difficult conversion to civilian production. Thus, variation of profitability across sectors was very large. Second, regional dispersion of profitability was also large. Advanced coastal regions with relatively skilled labor forces and superior infrastructure had much higher profit rates for given types of production than did inland provinces. The failure to carry out even rudimentary price realignment meant that the variation in profit rates among sectors remained large. Regional variations were even more difficult to cope with. Because they represented real differences in economic efficiency, a reform program that treated producers equally would place mainly inland producers in serious difficulty.

Tax for profit as originally designed had real teeth to it. Taxes were designed to be set high enough to put real pressure on most producers – pressure similar to that of the marketplace, that would prepare the firms to be released to the marketplace. But that implied that a political process – drawing up the actual program – had to be able to impose on individuals pressure equal to that of the marketplace. In practice, this was difficult to achieve. If tax rates (capital charges or product taxes) were set high, many producers of raw materials and many producers of all kinds in inland provinces would find all their profit taken by taxes. The government was not eager either to subsidize these newly loss-making enterprises, nor was it willing to start the process of mass bankruptcy. Therefore, all sides to the bargaining process (except for some profitable coastal industries) drew back from a solution that would impose large burdens on the weakest participants.

Moreover, opponents of capital charges had an additional argument in their arsenal. They pointed out that existing fixed assets had been allocated by the state, not purchased by the enterprise, which should not be responsible for these specific past decisions. Fixed capital had never been revalued in China, so any kind of fixed-asset charge would be based on a distorted accounting of fixed asset value based on past purchase prices. An apparent compromise was reached: Tax for profit would go forward without a capital charge, and a capital inventory and revaluation would be carried out later, permitting future assessment of fixed-asset charges (which never took place). Across the board, the solution was to set taxes of all kinds – fixed capital charges, product taxes, and resource taxes – at relatively low levels in order to protect backward producers.

Thus, the tax-for-profit scheme emerged from the bureaucracy without the crucial auxiliary rationalizations of capital and producer goods prices. Under these conditions, some enterprises were left with very high profit rates, and it was inconceivable that the government would be willing to allow them to retain the profit left over after income and product taxes were paid. The final solution was to require the most profitable enterprises to pay an "adjustment tax" that would be calculated to leave them with approximately the same amount of retained profits as they had enjoyed in the previous year. Naturally, this meant that in practice, final retention rates would continue to be set on an enterprise-specific basis – and would thus be negotiable – for the largest, most profitable state enterprises. At the end of the design process, officials predicted that the former volume of paper profits would be divided into four new categories:

new product taxes	40%
income tax	33%
adjustment tax	12%
retained profit	15%

But clearly the system would not attain its ambitious goals of converting the system of profit remittance into an impartial system of taxation (Naughton 1986a). In addition, the division of tax revenues between central and local governments was no longer such that a simple assignment of taxes among levels would be appropriate to budgetary needs.

The tax-for-profit scheme was not without some attractive features. Smaller enterprises that did not pay adjustment tax faced a more uniform set of regulations and also, in most cases, enjoyed somewhat higher retention rates. Moreover, it could be argued that this was a modest, incremental step in the right direction: Continuing efforts might nudge enterprises further along the road toward an impartial taxation system. Ultimately, though, the tax-for-profit scheme proved to be a dead end. Implementation was slow. By the end of 1986 – fully two years later – only 67% of state industrial enterprises had implemented second stage tax for profit (Liu Liang and Gong Zong 1987: 39). Even then it was unclear if enterprises that had nominally adopted the system had actually made any fundamental changes. It was easy for bureaucratic superiors to recompute the existing profit responsibility systems in ways that made them resemble tax-for-profit formulas. For the enterprises that paid adjustment taxes, it was hard to see what difference the system made. Moreover, in initial implementation, the system was to have been linked to a new formula for dividing revenues between the central and local governments, based on the distinction between different types of taxes. But with slow and uncertain implementation at the enterprise level, it proved impossible to make this change in the fiscal system as well. Ultimately, the tax-for-profit system had no strong patrons at the top of the political system. During 1987, policy shifted to favor a new system, and the tax-for-profit system became a dead letter. It became the final attempt at rationalization that was actually promulgated by the government, and the final example of failure.

Zhao's three initiatives

Did Zhao's initiatives add up to a coherent approach to reform? Certainly in terms of the old contending models of reform, they did not. For example, Zhao envisaged making the compulsory plan partial, covering only a delimited sector of the economy, but this undermined the goal of rationalizing reform with its ideal of having the state optimally steer the *entire* economy. Similarly, Zhao accepted market-determined prices for a very large sphere of the economy, but this undermined the rationale for adjusting state-set prices as steerage mechanisms. In other words, even as he was advancing the rhetoric of rationalizing reforms, Zhao's actions were undermining that vision. But if the objective were a market economy, these initiatives made sense. While the planning reform would permit the economy to grow out of the plan, the tax-for-profit reform, had it been successful, would have helped create a "level playing field" for continuing enterprise reform. But the failure of tax-for-profit opened up new questions about the appropriate reform strategy.

Debates on reform strategy

The changes of 1984 had a profound impact on discussions about economic reform. First, the renewal of reform implied a substantial liberalization of the grounds of debate. Moreover, there was increasing agreement among reform economists that the old models of reform were no longer applicable and that questions of strategy were questions about the transition to a market economy. While it was still ideologically uncomfortable to say so publicly, this increasingly became the fundamental objective that guided reform thinking and debates. Finally, the failure of tax-for-profit added increased urgency to the search for alternative strategies, and the interpretation of that failure became a key focus of dispute. Responding to these changes, China's economists began a new period of practical discussion and theoretical debate about the best way to reform.

Beginning in 1985, a debate about the proper strategy of reform engaged the best economists in China. In contrast to the vague and general economic discussions that took place between 1979 and 1981, this debate began from the premise that markets and material incentives were desirable. All participants agreed on the necessity of moving rapidly to a market economy, and the debate focused on the most effective strategies for making this transition. At an early stage, the participants identified and described the most fundamental choices and dilemmas facing reformers in the Chinese environment.

Indeed, the debate demonstrated the remarkable maturation that had occurred among China's economists after several years of practical experience in attempting reforms. The level of insight and analysis, and the identification of fundamental issues, showed that China's economists had leaped ahead of foreign observers in grappling with the most fundamental problems of economic reform in the Chinese environment.

Although a wide spectrum of views were presented, there were two main camps in the debate. It is commonly said, within China, that adherents of one camp advocated "price reform" in opposition to another group of advocates of "enterprise reform." These labels are adequate, but like any shorthand designation, can be misleading. Advocates of price reform believed that the basic objective of rationalizing prices and financial relations, which had been prominent during the first phase of reforms, had been correct. They saw the failure of rationalization as the primary obstacle that was holding back further progress on reform. As a result, they called for a comprehensive or coordinated reform, in which prices and taxes would be rationalized in a rapid preliminary stage. This could then be quickly followed by a shift to full market prices under conditions in which prices would be closer to their market-determined values initially, and in which conditions for equal competition would have been created by the rationalization of financial relations (Wu Jinglian and Zhou Xiaochuan 1988).

It is reasonable to label this group "price reformers" because they stressed adjustment of the parameters that affect enterprise behavior, of which prices are the most obvious. But from the beginning, their stress on adjusting parameters explicitly included reform of the tax system and the finance of enterprise capital. They stressed the fact that a true market system implied that enterprises were all impartially guided by the same set of price parameters, which were exogenous to the enterprise. They opposed special provisions or bargains for individual enterprises on the grounds that this would merely perpetuate the dependence of enterprises on the superiors with whom they were bargaining. On the other hand, they stressed the ability of the state to intervene in price-setting in the short run, because they relied on the state to adjust prices in a preliminary stage, in order to remove distortions caused by fixed prices and chaotic financial procedures. The price they paid for this was delaying the onset of real market guidance of enterprises until after this rationalization was carried out, with the danger that progress in reform would be held hostage to a difficult and often-delayed preliminary stage.

Advocates of enterprise reform approached the problems from a very different perspective that incorporated political as well as economic considerations.

Enterprise reformers were unenthusiastic about price adjustment, and sometimes openly hostile to it. However, the fundamental argument of enterprise reformers was not that price adjustments were undesirable, but simply that they were not feasible. They argued that the failure to carry out rationalizing reform in the early 1980s was not accidental, but instead reflected fundamental systemic features of the existing system. The failure of tax-for-profit schemes seemed particularly telling to them. Just as the bureaucracy did not have the capability to steer the economy effectively through administrative commands, it was in much the same way incapable of effectively adjusting prices to carry out some ideal rationalization. Thus the problem was not only or primarily that enterprises were guided by the wrong price signals; the bureaucratic economy itself was fundamentally dysfunctional. In their terminology, "the contradiction between a centralized method of price adjustment and a decentralized interest structure is a major limiting factor in price reform." (Hua Sheng *et al.* 1985:37). By this they meant that different elements of the bureaucracy would, during the course of price adjustments, systematically exploit their privileged access to resources and information. Precisely because they possessed effective local monopolies of information and control of resources, they were in a position to frustrate attempts at rationalization and turn any attempt at price reform to their own advantage. Enterprises would pass cost increases through to consumers by raising their own prices and shift financial costs onto the government by reducing profit remittances. Therefore, the attempt to adjust prices would never succeed, and should not be attempted (Hua, Zhang, and Luo 1988).

Instead, enterprise reformers argued in favor of the two-tier price system, stressing the importance of having market determined prices for outside-plan production. They argued that the two most important immediate measures were to expand the proportion of goods marketed independently by enterprises outside the plan, and to ensure that such marketings took place at uncontrolled, market-determined prices. This view had some points in common with the position of Western neo-classical economists, but it also differed in important ways. A neo-classical economist would be inclined to stress that no system of prices based on cost plus an assigned markup could ever be an adequate basis for determining resource allocation. Only flexible prices that equate supply and demand could serve this function. Since price adjustments would inevitably reflect some kind of cost-plus formula, they could never be entirely adequate, and the only feasible approach would be to move to market prices as quickly as possible. Enterprise reformers never stressed this theoretical opposition to price adjustment schemes. Instead, they focused on the behavior and incentives of enterprise managers.

Enterprise reformers argued that managers did not have sufficient economic interest in enterprise profitability to turn them into true profit maximizers. This was in part because of the need to build new human skills and give managers an opportunity to learn to be effective entrepreneurs and market-oriented managers, in part because of the need to create adequate incentives. If this was inevitably a prolonged process, it was arguably more important to begin building those skills and incentives than it was to fine-tune the parameters that would shape the decisions of profit-maximizing managers. A primary benefit of the dual-track system, then, would be that it would begin the process of getting managers accustomed (or reaccustomed) to operation in a true market environment. As the share of transactions taking place at market prices increased, managers would gradually but steadily be faced with the pressures and opportunities that came with a market economy. Indeed, enterprise reformers argued as early as the beginning of 1985 that this was beginning to occur (Hua Sheng *et al.* 1985). Above all, though, this required a secure link between enterprise performance and managerial reward. Thus, enterprise reformers stressed the need to create incentive systems that would give managers "high-powered incentives," in which their rewards would be highly variable and closely linked to enterprise performance. It was this emphasis that led this group to be termed "enterprise reformers." They saw the fostering of entrepreneurial attitudes as the necessary precondition for effective price reforms because only when entrepreneurial attitudes were in place would managers effectively adjust to the changing signals about resources scarcities that price reform was supposed to provide.

Finally, enterprise reformers argued in a frankly political vein that it was essential to create a political constituency for reforms in order for them to succeed. This had already been achieved in rural areas, where peasant smallholders and especially newly wealthy non-agricultural households could serve as a political support base for further reform. In urban areas, guaranteeing a successful reform process required that a class of managers be created with an interest in further reform. Controlling resources and opinion, those managers would then join with newly enfranchised peasants, an emerging class of individual entrepreneurs in both urban and rural areas, and reform-minded intellectuals to create a strong reform constituency. From this perspective, the program of comprehensive adjustment of prices at the outset was not feasible because it required a concerted administrative effort without a strong political base. It called for actions that would create opponents to the reforms – because any price reform would create potential losers – and had little in the way of short-run benefits to reward supporters. This political objective combined with the economic analysis presented here supports the argument that the crucial immediate task was the creation of a stratum of entrepreneurial managers.

Enterprise reformers argued that entrepreneurial managers could be encouraged by the creation of long-term quasi-property rights in their enterprises. For small enterprises, this could be provided by leasing to individual entrepreneurs. For large factories, multi-year management contracts (*chengbao*) with the potential of earning very large returns for managers were advocated. This school favored the rapid creation of "high-powered" incentives for managers, in which managers would guarantee some kind of minimum payment of taxes and profits to the state and then be the residual claimant on income and be responsible for losses. These residual gains and losses could then be shared to some extent with workers in the enterprise. Essentially, this position espoused providing managers with opportunities and obligations to bear risk in return for much higher compensation.

Subsequently, some enterprise reformers also began to point out that the dual-track system provided market prices at the margin. Since economic theory teaches that only marginal prices matter – inframarginal prices amounting ultimately to a fixed cost that will not affect current decisions – the emergence of the dual-track system meant that price reform had already occurred. This line of reasoning remained a secondary current in discussions within China, but the implications are nicely developed by Byrd (1989). In a sense, advocates of enterprise reform took as given the twin Chinese facts of weak administrative capabilities and a persistent material balance plan. Their objective then became to freeze that plan as much as possible and allow enterprises to operate in the market on the margin, as quickly as possible.

Opposition and common ground

Although there are important differences of emphasis, it would seem that there was considerable common ground between enterprise reformers and price reformers. Both sides agreed on the desirability of a market economy and both sides were raising important questions about the transition process that could hardly be ignored. It is obvious that transition to a market economy requires both price and enterprise reform; although individuals will have different views about which is primary, they might be able to agree on some compromise transition path. Indeed, a compromise might well be more effective than either approach on its own. A combined approach of adjusting price and financial levers, while also enhancing the incentive mechanism at the enterprise level – movement on multiple fronts – would presumably be most desirable and acceptable to both camps. Since the dual-track system already existed – having developed independently of any conscious reform design – we might expect that different schools would be able to reach agreement on ways to improve the operation of the dual-track system and make a transition to a better functioning market economy. Indeed, one of the early arguments enterprise reformers made in favor of the dual-track system was that market prices on the margin would make it easier to adjust plan prices at a further stage of reform (Hua Sheng *et al.* 1985: 42); moreover, this approach was subsequently incorporated into the 1985 Party suggestions for the Seventh Five Year Plan. In such a process, enterprises would be simultaneously learning to operate on the market and having the distorted incentives created by plan prices reduced. Pushing and pulling enterprises to the market might be more effective than only pulling (enterprise reform) or pushing (price reform).

In practice, the different schools were unable to agree on a common approach, and relations between different groups were often strained. The stress of competing for the attention of top policymakers was undoubtedly a factor in strained relations, as were personal and generational conflicts (enterprise reformers were a young group in general). But there were more fundamental reasons why the two schools regularly took opposite views on the crucial policy decisions of the day. These were the impact of divergent views on macroeconomic policy, the assessment of binding agreements made between enterprises and their superiors, and the influence of limited administrative capability.

Price reformers stressed the need to maintain a "slack" macroeconomic environment – in which aggregate demand was less than aggregate supply – in order to carry out price reform. In their view, an inflationary environment would make it impossible to adjust, and then to free, prices. Because they stressed the simultaneous adjustment of a large number of prices, the macroeconomic conditions that prevailed at the time of price adjustment were of tremendous importance. If the overall environment were inflationary at the time of price adjustment, enterprises would have the ability to push up their own prices and thwart the price adjustment by translating changes in relative prices into across-the-board inflation. In this sense, price reformers disagreed with enterprise reformers about the reason price adjustments could fail. Rather than locating the obstacle to price adjustment in the enterprise incentive mechanism, they located it in market conditions. In a slack macroeconomic environment, even relatively bureaucratic enterprises would face weak demand for their output and be forced to accommodate increases in their raw material prices without raising output prices. Price reformers gained inspiration from the positive effects on enterprises of the period of slack demand in 1981–82. In retrospect, they said that this would have been the best time to carry out price adjustments (Wu Jinglian 1987). Thus, the immediate recommendation of the price reform camp was to adopt conservative monetary and credit policies in order to moderate demand and create optimum conditions for reform. In practice, this often meant restraining the pace of financial decentralization, in order to control the growth of enterprise financial resources. Stabilization had to come first. Price reform and marketization would then follow.[7]

Enterprise reformers reached opposite conclusions on macroeconomic policy. First, they tended to believe that the economy was capable of vigorous growth. They argued that China was nearing a "take-off" stage of the development process, in which the effects of past investment in basic industries would combine with infusion of new technology and development of whole new industrial sectors to create a period of rapid growth. In order to promote this growth, planners should permit rapid growth of the money supply and consumption, without worrying too much about inflation (Zhu Jiaming 1985). Second, enterprise reformers believed that "shortage, or a sellers' market, is a chronic illness of our traditional structure . . . a systemic, not a policy phenomenon." (Zhang Xuejun 1987: 72). A fundamental change to a slack environment – a buyer's market – could not occur until after reforms had succeeded. Since enterprise reformers stressed that the changes in behavior required by reform could take place only over a prolonged time period, they concluded "it is necessary to be prepared to carry out the economic reform under *not very relaxed* conditions." (Zhang Xuejun 1987: 73). Enterprise reformers accepted Kornai's characterization of the bureaucratic economy as a shortage economy, caused by soft budget constraints at the enterprise level. Conservative macroeconomic policies could only alter the situation temporarily. Finally, they argued that it was essential to continue decentralization of financial resources in order to provide rewards and resources to the main beneficiaries of reform, the class of enterprise managers. They thus vigorously opposed any restrictions on the decentralization of financial resources. Since realistically, conservative macroeconomic policies required at least temporary restrictions on financial decentralization, they also opposed conservative macroeconomic policies.

The two camps also clashed on the desirability of individual enterprise reforms. Enterprise reformers tended to support measures that would expand the autonomy of enterprise managers on a contingent basis. They generally looked favorably on the practice of signing long-term contracts with managers, because they saw this as a way to enhance managerial status and transform managers into an "entrepreneurial stratum." Long-term contracts made the reward curve facing managers much steeper, providing them with high-powered incentives to improve enterprise performance. (Long-term contracts are discussed in Chapter 6.) Once such contracts were signed, it was important that the plan and plan prices be relatively stable, in order to free managers to operate on the market at the margin. Only if the plan and plan prices were fixed would managers truly face market prices at the margin. Otherwise the prospect of changes in the plan and plan prices would cause them to divert attention to bureaucratic maneuvers that would be crucial to protecting their financial position. In this framework, adjustment of state-set prices and financial regulations would require renegotiation of all long-term compacts, as well as reassessment of the impact of the plan on the enterprise's well-being. Enterprise reformers feared that reopening these issues would draw the attention and effort of managers away from the market, and to an all-consuming scramble to influence the outcome of price and plan revision. As a result, as the reform developed, enterprise reformers became indifferent or actively hostile to price revisions, viewing them as a harmful diversion from the enterprise reform process. Precisely because of these considerations, price reformers came to exactly the opposite conclusion about long-term enterprise contracts. Seeing that formal contracting would only make the process of price adjustment more difficult – since it would require an enterprise by enterprise renegotiation of contracts – they regarded long-term contracting as a step backward in the reform process.

A final reason that the two reform camps remained at loggerheads was the limited administrative capabilities of the Chinese government. The bureaucracy had difficulty carrying out more than one or two major tasks at a time. For example, the Ministry of Finance found it nearly impossible to devise and implement tax reforms while also concentrating on vigorous tax collection to slow the erosion of government revenues. Even more crucially, the hierarchical and unresponsive character of China's political system meant that virtually every important decision had to be made personally by one of a handful of top leaders. In practice, Premier Zhao Ziyang personally made virtually every important decision on reform policy that was formally adopted. A pattern emerged in which individual reform measures were taken up in series by the top leadership; nothing could be done without the approval of the top leadership, and the top leadership only had so much time and resources to devote to any given issue. Thus, it was impossible to move simultaneously on several measures at once, which would have been a requirement of compromise action. Instead, different reform camps were competing to see that their priorities were reflected in the handful of initiatives under consideration at any one time.

Clearly, there is no sense in which we can proclaim that either price or enterprise reformers were right or wrong. Both schools were analyzing important aspects of the transition to a market economy, and both made important contributions in their area of analysis. In some ways, the debate is reminiscent of the blind men touching the elephant, and describing the different parts in apparently contradictory fashion. Yet it is possible to point out some of the lacunae in the argument, and regret that the two sides did not come to a better understanding.

Enterprise reformers can be credited with an insightful analysis of the reality of Chinese economic reform. This was sometimes expressed as support for a uniquely Chinese strategy of reform. However, when their ideas are probed a little more deeply, they are really saying that the constraints on action in the Chinese case were particularly severe – a uniquely Chinese path to reform emerged basically because Chinese conditions made almost all other paths infeasible. Moreover, their analysis was informed by a nice recognition of political constraints. On the other side, price reformers can be credited with a clear recognition of the ultimate economic links between price and tax, and the ultimate need to create a system in which impartial price parameters actually guide enterprise activity. Moreover, price reformers saw more clearly – or at least stressed more actively – the fact that the continuing failure to adjust a few key prices, such as energy prices, was imposing continuing substantial costs on the economy during every minute of the reform transition. Distortions caused by failures to rationalize prices continuously created stumbling blocks and obstacles to a smoother reform process.

Conversely, we might point to some gaps in each side's arguments. Neither side succeeded in clarifying the debate about macroeconomic policy. The most striking fact about Chinese macroeconomic policy is its inconstancy. Yet price reformers concentrated on criticizing the excessively expansionary episodes, while enterprise reformers concentrated on criticizing the brief, perhaps excessively sharp, contractionary episodes. Since the argument focused on whether policy should be in general be expansionary or conservative, inadequate attention was focused on the technical issues needed to decide when policy should be adjusted, and when it was appropriate. It might have been feasible for the two sides to reach agreement on a stable, long-term rate of credit expansion, or on rules for adjusting macro policy. More discussion of the pattern of lags between policy adoption and enterprise response might also have created more common ground.

Enterprise reformers seem to have two blind spots. First, they seem to have willfully misinterpreted the argument of price reformers on macroeconomic policy. Price reformers did not contend that a slack macroeconomic environment should be maintained for many years, only that there would be a single, relatively short stage in the reform process – the price adjustment stage – that required a slack macro environment. Enterprise reformers never presented any reason to believe that this was not possible. Second, enterprise reformers have consistently neglected the importance of tax reform. By focusing on enterprise management, they were unable to concentrate on the difficulty of replacing the system of profit remittance with some other form of government tax revenue (Wood 1991). While their program for marketization was feasible, they had no clear program for assuring macroeconomic balance. Ultimately, since it was macroeconomic imbalance that terminated the creative phase of the dual track strategy, one must question whether enterprise reformers should have devoted more attention to this issue, and whether their opposition to conservative macro policies was wise.

The most difficult question for price reformers is whether their approach was feasible in the Chinese context. The repeated failure of rationalization schemes puts this in doubt. Moreover, price reformers, in stressing the interconnected nature of price and tax reforms, unintentionally made adoption of their program even more difficult, since they intensified the administrative difficulties associated with carrying it out. Ultimately, one most wonder whether it might have made more sense to advocate a few crucial price realignments, rather than a comprehensive price adjustment. A few crude and "dirty" price adjustments might finally have been more successful. Yet ultimately this question must remain unanswered. We cannot know whether, under different circumstances, agreement on necessary rationalization might have been achieved among China's economists and, more importantly, among the top leaders.

Ultimately, what remains most impressive is that the Chinese reform debate posed in acute form the questions that really were the most fundamental problems of the reform transition. In contrast to the earlier phase, where economic debates were often marginal and unrealistic, the post-1984 reform debate is rich in practical content and possesses broad applicability. The increasing sophistication of economic discussion mirrors the general growth of practical and intellectual capabilities in China in the course of the reform process.

Subsequent reform dynamics

Beginning in 1985, Chinese reform policy in practice turned away from its previous orientation toward rationalizing reforms, and followed a dual-track approach to reform. Thus, actual policymaking frequently accorded with the ideas of the enterprise reform group. Reforms focused on contractual relations with state enterprises and the consolidation of market price relationships outside the plan. These reforms are the subject of Chapter 6. Despite the clear shift to a new approach to reform after 1984, the contention between the two approaches continued throughout the 1985–88 period, and the issue was never really settled. Economists and political leaders never completely gave up on comprehensive reforms, but they continued to prove elusive in practice.[8]

One attempted comprehensive reform was particularly significant, although it ultimately miscarried. In the spring of 1986, after a brief austerity program had brought the overheated economy partially under control, Zhao Ziyang resumed the attempt to draw up a comprehensive reform program. Conditions seemed favorable. A sharp jump in urban living standards had followed the success of rural reforms. Policymakers continued to be cautious about the macroeconomy. They were not anxious to push for immediate new measures that might further decentralization and imbalances in the economy. The atmosphere was one of economic caution, but great enthusiasm for economic – and even political – reforms. The logical approach was to utilize the current slowdown in economic change to develop a more comprehensive program for the next phase of reforms. A group was established to develop a comprehensive economic reform package, which included six small groups to devise reforms in price, public finance, investment, banking, wages, and foreign trade. This group came to be known as the "program office."[9]

The approach of the "program office" represented one more attempt to introduce coordinated reforms. This time, however, advocates of comprehensive reforms had the benefit of extensive markets and the information they provided to assist in their task. Simplifying the reform strategy that emerged from the program office, we can say it included (a) continued macroeconomic slack; (b) simultaneous adjustment of prices and taxes, using market prices as an important reference point for adjustment of in-plan prices; and (c) full liberalization of prices within a year or two after implementation of the new price and tax system. High-level discussions on this proposal continued through the summer of 1986. Premier Zhao Ziyang, in charge of daily decision-making, reportedly met frequently with this group, and the program was close to being adopted. But by the fall of 1986, prospects for comprehensive reform began to fade again.

There were many reasons for the inability of the comprehensive reform program to compel acceptance. The problem of coordinated adjustment of prices and taxes once again seemed overwhelming. There were numerous competing estimates of what it would cost the budget in terms of foregone revenues from firms experiencing higher costs (it was taken for granted that there could not be full recovery from the higher profits of suppliers). The Ministry of Finance calculated that the cost of compensating enterprises for losses they would sustain from higher prices would greatly exceed the benefits of increased revenues from enterprises that gained. They estimated costs in the realm of many tens of billions of yuan. Furthermore, agreement on procedures to calculate prices was elusive. Finally, the political atmosphere began to change, and Zhao became worried about his ability to survive disruptive changes.

Faced with these problems, the scope of the proposed "comprehensive" reform began to shrink. First, it became a program to adjust the major producer goods prices, then a program to adjust steel prices. And finally that was abandoned. Zhao Ziyang instead opted for more focused sectoral reforms. He seized on foreign trade and banking as the crucial areas where significant reforms could be achieved, and he shifted his focus away from the comprehensive price-reform approach. By the fall of 1986, significant reforms were underway in foreign trade and, to a lesser extent, the banking system. Finally, in December 1986, Zhao abandoned the approach of the program office, and shifted to adopt a policy closely related to the ideas of the enterprise reform group. This was the policy of long-term contracting for enterprises, which Zhao accepted and formally put forward on December 26, 1986 (this is discussed in Chapter 6).

The failure of comprehensive reform did not mean that no reforms took place. Quite the contrary. A powerful and consistent process of economic change was set in motion during this period that markedly altered the operation of the Chinese economy. However, the failure of comprehensive reforms meant that the trajectory of change, by default, took on the pattern of the dual-track, enterprise reform strategy. Not that the attempt to carry out price reform was ever completely abandoned. In 1988, both Zhao Ziyang and Deng Xiaoping again pushed for the rapid implementation of price reform, although it is unclear exactly what form this would have taken. On that occasion, the plan again fell victim to macroeconomic problems, and its collapse corresponded with Zhao Ziyang's loss of political power. Those events are described in Chapters 7 and 8. The recurrence of attempts at comprehensive price reform should remind us that throughout the development of China's reform strategy, Zhao Ziyang kept trying to supplement the actual pattern of reform with elements of an alternative approach that was sometimes seen as contending, sometimes as complementary. Subsequently, beginning in 1992, reform policy returned to a focus on price reform and rationalization of financial parameters.

Conclusion

By 1985, Zhao Ziyang had completely broken out of the constraints that marked reform policy-making up through 1983. He had achieved a political victory that allowed him to push ahead with reforms, and combined with favorable economic conditions, this provided him a relatively large amount of leeway to develop successful reform programs. His actual policymaking had achieved both a major success and a significant failure. The successful compromise over the role of the plan provided the basis for the dual-track, growing out of the plan strategy. The failure to draw up a coherent tax for profit program, and the difficulty experienced in implementing even the program that was created, showed up the extreme weakness of all Chinese government attempts at rationalizing reform. In spite of the contrasting nature of these initiatives, they all opened up the way to further development of the dual-track strategy. Although debate continued to rage over the desirability of the dual-track, actual reform implementation primarily conformed to that strategy during the years 1985–88. It is therefore to the actual experience of reform during the 1984–88 period that we must now turn.

6

The second phase of reform, 1984–1988

The previous chapter described the acceleration of China's industrial reforms during 1984 and the new turn taken in reform policy. Although there were continuities with the first period of reform, the basic thrust of what reformers were trying to accomplish changed. Reformers, led by Zhao Ziyang, now had an idea of what they were attempting to accomplish as well as a general approach to the process of reform that informed specific policy measures. This approach never added up to a comprehensive strategy of reform, but it had an internal logic and consistency of application that justifies our labeling it a reform strategy. The essence of that strategy was to expand market forces by limiting the scope of planning, fostering entry, and improving incentives and autonomy for state-run enterprises to operate on the market. The strategy combined a dual-track (plan and market) economy with the attempt to introduce high-powered incentive for entrepreneurs even within the state sector. Successive reform measures had a cumulative impact that went a great distance toward converting China's economy to a market economy by the end of the 1980s.

In essence, Chinese leaders decided during 1984 that the buildup of government capabilities and the improvement of economic conditions that had occurred since 1978 would be used in the service of substantial economic reforms, rather than in the strengthening of the administrative economy. What is most impressive about this period beginning in 1984 was precisely that reform measures were adopted across a broad spectrum. There were failures of coherency, and implementation was uneven, but a defining characteristic of the second period was that numerous incremental measures in many areas combined to push the economy in the direction of marketization. Caution had been the hallmark of much of the earlier phase, but the second phase of reform was marked by a determination to accelerate the pace of economic change across the board. As in other socialist countries, this approach had a negative side. Almost simultaneous with the beginning of the second phase came a sharp shift to an expansionary macroeconomic policy. This led to a substantial acceleration in economic growth, but also to an increase in inflationary pressures and a reinstatement of the shortage economy (discussed further in Chapter 7). Thus, a second characteristic of the second phase was that it took place in an expansionary, and increasingly inflationary, environment.

This chapter examines the process of reform at the microeconomic level, with the focus on state-run enterprises. The different strands of reform policy are traced in the realm of finances, manpower and authority relations, and growth of markets. It is stressed throughout that a steady stream of reform measures were implemented between 1984 and 1988 that had a gradual and cumulative impact. An assessment of the impact of reforms in the state sector is then attempted. This combines a discussion of state enterprises with the developing non-state sector, which was described in Chapter 4. The conclusion is that reforms led to marketization combined with rapid output growth and improved productivity. On balance, then, they must be considered successful.

The reform package

The conditions for reform acceleration were created by the decision to limit the scope of the central plan, discussed in the previous chapter. Concrete reform measures can be grouped into two areas. First are enterprise reform measures. Here we discover a renewal and radicalization of each of the initiatives to expand enterprise autonomy that marked the early period of reform. Second are measures taken to consolidate and expand the dual-track plan and market system. After limiting the scope of planning, reformers had to ensure that outside-plan transactions were guided by market prices, and that the scope of markets would progressively expand. Together, these measures made up a highly coherent whole, but there was no attempt to integrate them into an explicit package. There was no programmatic document that can serve as a guide to reforms in this period. In a sense, then, reform continued to develop in an evolutionary manner, without a single blueprint. Reformers continued to "cross the river by groping for stepping stones." But this similarity of approach should not mask the difference between policy in the first and second reform periods. During the first period, reforms were scattershot and based on vaguely digested notions of reform in other socialist countries. Moreover, as stressed earlier, it was often the unintended consequences of reforms that were most significant and successful. During the second period, reforms were consistent in their objective of expanding the scope of market operation and simultaneously freeing state enterprises to respond to market incentives with increasing effectiveness. In general, reforms achieved their intended result: The scope of the market increased, and the behavior of state owned enterprises changed substantially. The different measures added up to a distinctive Chinese approach to economic reform. The absence of a programmatic statement of reform may be the result of political constraints as much as of any lack of coherence.

The October 1984 Communist Party "Decision on Reform of the Economic System" that was discussed in the previous chapter is generally taken as the beginning of the period of stepped-up reform. In fact, a series of meetings and proclamations marked a gradual acceleration of reform. An enterprise "Bill of Rights" in May 1984 was the first in this series. This document, sometimes called the "Ten Articles," reasserted the autonomy provisions first put forward in 1979 but never fully implemented. It also declared for the first time that certain types of activity in which enterprises had long engaged were to be recognized and protected. This included the right for all enterprises to sell output produced above or outside the state plan, and the right to freely select suppliers and customers. But the document did not give enterprises the right to price above-plan output at market prices: Prices could float a maximum of 20% above or below plan prices. The document also gave factory managers the right to name their own management team, subject to upper level approval, to hire technical personnel from outside the factory, and to promote 3% of their workers annually without external review. Expanded authority over enterprise finances and assets was granted, including the right to invest in other firms (*Economic* 1985: X-21-22).

The October 1984 plenum of the Communist Party Central Committee displayed for the first time a public consensus among top leaders that reforms could go forward. Yet, as described earlier, the actual resolution on economic reform was a vague and at times intentionally elliptical document, designed to elicit consensus, rather than to serve as a blueprint for reform (*Economic* 1985: I-1-11). The crucial liberalization of outside-plan prices in the first months of 1985 came without fanfare, and almost without publicity. Several months later, in September 1985, a specially summoned Communist Party Congress sketched in some of the details of the reform program. The "Suggestions of the Party Center on Drawing up the Seventh Five Year Plan" were described by Zhao Ziyang (CCP 1985: 28) as "the concretization of the resolution on economic reform of the [October 1984] Central Committee meeting." This is a good characterization. The "Suggestions" are about as close as we can come to an official program for China's reform strategy. They declared:

State management of enterprises should be gradually converted from direct control to indirect control as the main form, primarily employing economic and legal measures – while retaining necessary administrative measures – to control and regulate economic activity . . . As for the price of consumer goods, except for an extremely small minority of crucial products that will remain under state price controls, the price of ordinary products will be gradually decontrolled as market conditions permit. The proportion of producers goods for which the central government determines the price will progressively shrink, and the proportion determined by the market will increase. At the same time, we will gradually adjust planned prices, in order to shrink the gap between plan and market prices (CCP 1985: 22–23).

Here, in severely compressed form, is a description of the Chinese economic reform strategy. The rhetoric on shifting from direct to indirect control measures has been retained, but the focus of immediate policy prescriptions has shifted to expansion of the scope of the market, and within-plan rationalization of prices is slated to follow only gradually. This statement had the authoritative imprimatur of a full Communist Party Congress. For the first time, the official description was reasonably concrete and realistic, and this passage generally describes what the government actually accomplished.

   The most explicit and fully developed commitment to economic reform during this period came at the Thirteenth Party Congress in October 1987. The political atmosphere had swung sharply away from political liberalization at the beginning of 1987, with the ouster of Hu Yaobang and the accompanying campaign against "bourgeois liberalization." By late 1987, Zhao Ziyang, now first Party Secretary, felt confident enough to push the theoretical underpinnings of reform forward another step. In his report to the Congress he advanced the following model:

Planning work must be based on commodity exchange and the law of value. The direct management method that relies primarily on compulsory plans does not correspond to the development of the socialist commodity economy. . . . We must gradually shrink the scope of compulsory plans and gradually transform to a management system of primarily indirect management . . . Overall, the new system must be one in which 'the state adjusts the market, and the market guides the enterprise.' (*Economic* 1988: I-9)

Zhao here renounced compulsory planning, and recognized that enterprises must respond directly to market conditions. He retained the rhetoric of rationalizing reform, both in the slogan of the "socialist commodity economy" and in the stress he gave to indirect management. Yet even here, Zhao's indirect management has been reformulated and narrowed: The state no longer adjusts prices to steer individual enterprises, but rather adjusts the market as a whole, perhaps through macroeconomic policies of the kind that characterize all market economies. Later he declares:

The socialist market system not only includes a market for consumption goods and means of production, it must also include a market for factors of production such as capital, labor, technology, information, and real estate. If there is only a commodity market, it is impossible to give play to market forces. Moreover, the socialist market system must be competitive and open.

In practice, this seems to rule out any lingering adherence to the rationalizing reform ideal planners' optimal steerage of the economy. The distinguishing characteristic of socialism is the predominance of public ownership, Zhao declared, not the economic instruments used to allocate resources. Though Zhao stopped short of full advocacy of a market economy, presumably because of political constraints, it seems clear that he had by this time accepted the necessity of a complete transition to a market economy.

A renewed commitment to reform came in 1984, and 1984–85 was the period of maximum reorientation of policy at the top of the political system. Thus, it is tempting to see 1984–85 as a "wave" of reform (Harding 1987: 70–74). However, in most parts of the economy, 1984–85 was merely the beginning of a period of accelerated change. Throughout the entire 1985–88 period, policies initially set forth in general terms during the 1984–85 watershed were progressively implemented at the enterprise level, and liberalization measures gradually worked their way through the economy. Insofar as the actual operation of the economy is concerned, reform-inspired marketization gathered strength steadily after 1985. In all this period, there was no significant retreat from reforms; as a result, the 1984 to 1988 period stands out as one of the most remarkable periods of economic and social transformation in modern Chinese history.

Enterprise reforms

Enterprise reforms focused on giving enterprises sufficient autonomy and sufficiently powerful incentives to allow them to respond to market forces. Whereas in the early phase of reforms, expanded enterprise autonomy was seen as a provision to allow planners to steer enterprises through indirect levers, in the second phase of reforms autonomy was increasingly seen as fostering an entrepreneurial response to market-determined price signals. The Enterprise Bill of Rights of May 1984 was essentially an expression of good intentions. After all, similar enterprise autonomy provisions had been promulgated in the past without much effect. In order for enterprise autonomy to realistically increase, a series of concrete measures had to be taken as well. Those measures came more slowly, but they did come. Figure 6.1 shows the implementation of four important measures that increased enterprise auton-

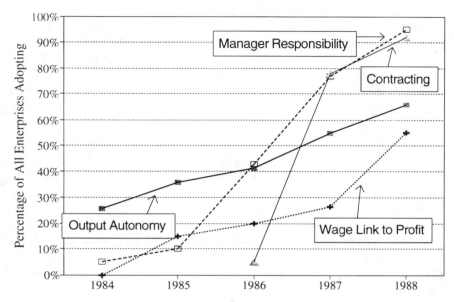

Figure 6.1. Enterprise reform implementation. Source: *Economic* 1986: IV-18; 1988, III-2; 1989: III-4-5; SRC/ER 1990: 234–36; CASS/UCSD.

omy. The four are (1) the factory manager responsibility system; (2) the authority to draw up the overall production plan inside the enterprise; (3) the system that linked total wage bill to profit, increasing enterprise control over wage distribution; and (4) long-term contracting over profit remittances between factories and their superiors. We discuss each of these measures, but it is important to note initially the pattern of their gradual spread. Only a small minority of enterprises enjoyed most of these privileges at the end of 1985. But steadily during 1986, 1987, and 1988, a large majority of state-run enterprises were granted these various expanded autonomy provisions.

Managerial reform

As a new group of enterprise managers gradually took over positions of authority in the wake of enterprise rectification, Deng Xiaoping revived the push for the factory manager responsibility system that had been halted abruptly after 1980. Factory manager responsibility gave the manager clear authority as director of the enterprise, and removed the Party secretary from his position of authority in the enterprise. As discussed in Chapter 3, without the explicit provisions of the factory manager responsibility system, the political role of the Party Committee and its control over the personnel system (*nomenklatura*) put the Party secretary in a structurally superior position to the manager, regardless of who was nominally in charge of production decisions. The job of the Party secretary under factory manager responsibility was explicitly restricted to ideological matters and the supervision of overall policy; even the Party's control of *nomenklatura* was severly restricted by provisions that gave the manager the right to select his own management. Indeed, in many factories, following the adoption of the factory manager system, Party secretaries lost their permanent offices and staff. Deprived of an organizational base within the enterprise, Party secretaries were transformed into ideological mentors, while the factory manager became the acknowledged boss.

One striking difference between factory manager responsibility after 1984 and what had been attempted in 1980 was the absence of any other factory-level organization to serve as a check on the manager's authority. Reformers had become less concerned about abuse of personal power and more convinced that only a strong authority figure at the factory level could effectively move the enterprise forward. From this time onward, factory managers began to emerge as extremely powerful individuals. To some extent this was intentional: Managers were increasingly seen as an autonomous interest that could be counterposed to that of the workers. Managers might contain pressures for wage increases and bonuses, because their own professional interest would encourage them to maximize profit. This change was extremely controversial. Not only did Party conservatives resist the change, but one group of reformers who had favored expanded worker control opposed the change as well. They worried that increasingly authoritarian and market-oriented managers would ride rough-shod over the interests of workers. This was not only bad in itself, it would also erode support for reforms among the urban working class (Jiang Yiwei 1988, 1989).

Selective implementation of factory manager responsibility began during 1984, and the October Reform Declaration called for nationwide adoption. Even so, reformers had to fight a political battle on the issue. In late 1985, during an episode of political infighting over corruption, conservatives attempted to reestablish the principle that "collective discussions" (by the Party Committee) were required to ratify all managerial appointments, and temporarily brought implementation to a halt.

Reformers were eventually able to overcome this obstacle, and during 1986 managed to write factory manager responsibility into a revision of the regulations defining authority within enterprises (one regulation each covered the factory manager, the Party Committee, and the Workers' Congress).

With the principle reestablished, implementation continued, and during 1987 and 1988 the factory manager responsibility system became nearly universal. In April 1988, a basic law on state industrial enterprises incorporated factory manager responsibility as one of its fundamental tenets (Clarke 1991: 46; *Economic* 1989: VIII–16; SRC/ER 1990: 458–59; Zhang Zhanbin 1988; Chamberlain 1987).

By the end of 1986 reformers began to move beyond factory manager responsibility to take additional steps to remove party groups from ministries and other central government bodies. This had occurred in a quarter of government ministries by the spring of 1989. Under the slogan of "separating political and economic tasks," the Party's role was deemphasized throughout the bureaucracy (except, of course, at the very top). At the Thirteenth Party Congress in the fall of 1987, a Civil Service System, designed to cover 4.2 million government cadres was announced. These measures made slow but steady progress until the catastrophe at Tiananmen Square in June 1989 (Burns 1989).

Besides removing the Party from control over enterprise management, factory manager responsibility had to give the manager effective control over the crucial economic decisions of the enterprise. The manager had to be freed not only of the Party, but also of the bureaucracy. A useful index of the manager's growing authority was his ability to draw up the enterprise production plan without interference from superior organs. According to the 1984 Enterprise Bill of Rights, all managers should have the authority to establish their own production plans, on condition they fulfilled mandatory state plans. In fact, a survey conducted in 1990 found that the proportion of managers actually having such authority increased gradually from only about a quarter of total enterprises in 1984 to two-thirds by 1988 and almost 90% by 1990 (CASS-UCSD 1990; Figure 6.1).

Labor reforms

Wages and bonuses: The link to profit

Beginning in 1984, reformers made a determined effort to overcome the limitations imposed by the rigid employment and wage system. Even after the initial phase of reform, wages were determined by a uniform national wage scale plus a bonus that was drawn from enterprise profits, and there was virtually no labor mobility. Reformers chipped away at this edifice through various partial reforms. The first was the elimination of bonus ceilings. During 1984, absolute ceilings on bonus payments were eliminated, and replaced by a progressive bonus tax. If aggregate bonuses were less than 2.5 months standard wage, there was no tax. Between 2.5 and 4 months, a 30% tax was imposed, and this increased to 100% between 4 and 6 months and 300% above 6 months. Tinkering with these parameters in subsequent years led to raising the starting point for taxation to 4 months worth of bonus in 1985, and tax rates were lowered further at the end of 1986 (*Economic* 1985: X-61-62; Jie and Chen 1989; SRC 1988b: 547). Enterprises were also given the freedom, in principle, to determine how the bonus fund would be combined with wages within the enterprise in 1984. Rather than simply deciding which workers would get bonuses, enterprises were permitted to experiment with different compensation systems, including floating wages, piece rates, and combined systems where the actual job performed would influence compensation.

A new system of wage determination was gradually implemented. This system dissolved the distinction between base wage and bonus, and instead established a link between enterprise productivity and the total wage bill. The most common indicators were total tax and profit remitted to the government, but some enterprises were permitted to designate total profit, output or sales revenue as the productivity indicator. The system established for each enterprise a value of the elasticity of the linkage between the productivity indicator and the total wage bill, with the elasticity generally set around 0.7. Thus, if an enterprise's remitted tax and profit increased by 1 percent compared with the previous year, its total wage bill was permitted to increase by 0.7%. If profitability decreased by 1 percent, the wage bill was expected to decrease by 0.7 percent as well.

In fact, the system was somewhat more complicated than would appear. The productivity link established the total amount of wages the enterprise was permitted to draw, but did not obligate the enterprise to actually pay out the full amount in wages. At the same time, instead of a bonus tax, a wage tax was levied based on the percentage increase in the entire actual wage bill, compared with the previous year. Thus, a factory might choose to draw a sum of money authorized for wages, but put it in the bank rather than actually paying it out, thereby avoiding taxes. This would be a kind of enterprise saving, available to be tapped for wages in a later year of slower growth. Although this allowed enterprises to shelter themselves from some risk by saving, the productivity link system, to the extent that it was fully implemented, subjected enterprises to substantially greater risk than had previous systems.

This system effectively ended the distinction between base wages and bonuses. Most enterprises therefore adjusted their accounting systems, so that bonuses were reclassified as wages and as part of enterprise costs. Total profits were accordingly reduced and such enterprises no longer drew bonus funds from retained profits. Following this change, the central government relaxed its traditional system of setting quotas for total provincial and ministerial wage bills. Beginning in 1986, similar productivity linkages were established between central planners and the various provinces and ministries, for a three to five-year period. The provinces and ministries were then responsible for establishing concrete mechanisms with their subordinate enterprises. Moreover, the central government no longer established separate targets for the total number of workers and the wage bill. Provinces and ministries could add workers if they did not increase the wage bill, and release workers without having wage bills reduced.

By 1988, about 60% of industrial workers were in some kind of program that linked wages to profitability or some other indicator. Detailed aggregate statistics are available for 1988 that permit us to trace the operation of the system (*Labor* 1990: 352–53). It seems to have worked very imperfectly in this inflationary year. In the aggregate, increased profits at participating enterprises would have permitted a healthy 22% wage increase. In fact, government officials intervened to make sure that *all* workers received wage increases to partially protect them against inflation (primarily by authorizing food price subsidies), and then deducted these increases from the permitted increase of those under the productivity link. In the end, the actual wage increased 21% – almost exactly what was permitted by the system – but only after extensive intervention and redistribution by government officials. At least in the inflationary year of 1988, the system lost its automaticity and become enmeshed in bargaining with government officials.

Wage determination within the factory

The system of linking total wage bill to profitability included the freedom for factories to determine the distribution of the wage bill within the factory. As this and related systems spread, the central government in theory ceased adjusting wages in business units nationwide. No longer were national quotas for promotions distributed periodically, nor did all members of a given category of worker receive raises. The government was willing to accept gradually increasing inter-enterprise differentials in wages. This also signaled enterprises that the only route to increased wages was through successful enterprise activity. In late 1986, it was decreed that all enterprise had the right to determine the inside factory distribution of wages as they chose, so long as they conformed to limits on the total wage bill and general distribution policies (SRC 1988b: 238). Enterprises were under pressure to adopt systems of floating wages and other types of compensation pay because the 1985 wage reform had reclassified some former bonuses as part of the base wage. In order to again increase the share of income linked to incentives, managers were forced to reclassify some part of the base wage as incentive pay. Various composite wage systems were broadly adopted in which worker compensation was determined by some combination of basic wage, seniority and task-specific supplements, and incentive payments.

The contract labor system

The next component of labor reform was the gradual shift to a system of contract employment. The vast majority of China's state labor force has traditionally enjoyed lifetime employment. Although there has always been a group of casual laborers without complete employment security, the approximately 85% of state workers classified as "permanent" had guaranteed lifetime jobs.[1] Beginning in 1983, the government began to promote a program under which some newly hired "permanent" workers would in fact be signed to five-year employment contracts. This program was not intended to demote permanent workers to casual worker status, nor did it apply in any way to the existing casual workers. Rather, the new contract labor represented an attempt to change the nature of the relationship linking state firms and workers in the category that had previously been labeled "permanent." The new contract system was designed to add some flexibility to the employment relation, because contracts would not necessarily be renewed after five years. Although contract workers experienced some reduction in job security, they were in all other respects to continue to enjoy the benefits and protections accorded to permanent workers.

During 1986, a major effort was launched to restructure the employment system, based on the adoption of contract employment for all new state sector employees (Howard 1991; Kozrec 1988). The reform resembled other aspects of Chinese reform in that it did not attempt to change the status of existing permanent workers. Instead, it created a system that would apply to all new workers. A two-track employment system was created as well. Four labor reform documents were promulgated during 1986. Beginning immediately, all new workers were to be employed on five-year contracts that would be renewed only by mutual consent. Recruitment was to be open: Enterprises would have the right, within their hiring quota, to hire whomever they wanted. Social security and unemployment funds were established. The social security fund was established initially only for contract workers, and received contributions both from the enterprise and from the individual worker. The enterprise was to deposit a sum from pre-tax profits equal to 15% of the contract labor wage bill, while the individual worker would have 3% of his wage withheld for the same purpose. Individual cities were encouraged to spread systems such as these that pooled social security contributions from workers in different factories. Many cities began to implement such systems to cover some or all of permanent workers, and they spread steadily in subsequent years. The unemployment fund covered all workers. Pre-tax profits equal to one percent of the wage bill were to be contributed to local unemployment and retraining funds, to which workers would have access in the event of unemployment. Unemployment compensation was closely linked to the contract labor system because it was anticipated that permanent workers would be unemployed primarily due to firm bankruptcy – which would remain rare – while contract workers would become unemployed much more frequently due to non-renewal of contracts. Finally, one document specified the terms under which workers could be fired. A 1982 regulation had permitted firms to fire workers guilty of gross malfeasance, but the new regulation made it clear that consistent minor misconduct and slacking could also be grounds for dismissal (Ling Hu'an and Sun Zhen 1992: 163–84). Gradually the proportion of contract workers in the total work force has increased, as more new workers come on board. By 1990, 18% of state industrial workers were contract workers of this type.

Cutting redundant workers

In attempt to deal with widespread overmanning, enterprises were encouraged, beginning in 1988, to carry out "reoptimization" of the labor force. In labor reoptimization, a major effort was made to cut down on redundant workers. Municipalities established labor retraining and unemployment funds to provide factories with the resources needed to transfer workers to new occupations. Factories would reassess labor needs in each workshop and auxiliary activity and send workers off for retraining, or declare them "in-house unemployed." Some workers would be put on reduced wages, but it seems that virtually no workers were truly fired. Nevertheless, labor reoptimization programs gave those managers who were interested in reducing labor costs an avenue to approach the problem. Moreover, enterprises in which one or another forms of labor reoptimization were carried out employed 20% of the total state industry labor force in 1988 and 27% in 1989, so the effort was reasonably broad in scope. Of covered workers, 6% were declared redundant. New jobs were found for 82% of redundant workers – either in the original or other enterprises, or in subsidiary occupations (35% of the total) organized by the original enterprise. 8% of redundant workers were still listed as in-house unemployed at year-end 1989, while 3% were still undergoing training (*Economic* 1989: III-5; *Labor* 1990: 354.).

A modest amount of flexibility was introduced into labor markets as well. The annual total quits and fires of state employees (permanent and contract, excluding casual) climbed steadily through the 1980s, reaching 219,000 in 1989. This is still tiny compared with the total number of such employees – only 0.25%. However, in addition, a similar number (204,000) of contract workers were released at the end of their contracts, and this amounted to 2% of the total number of contract workers. Thus, in 1989, 423,000 permanent and contract state workers (0.5% of the total) were laid off, quit, or were on contracts that were not renewed (*Labor* 1990: 58, 218, 222, 346). These are still very low rates of labor turnover, but significantly greater than the rates prevailing in the 1970s.

None of the labor and wage reforms adopted during the 1980s was revolutionary. The implementation of each of them was slowed by the extreme sensitivity of the regime to issues of unemployment. But cumulatively these measures began to chip away at the edifice of control. By 1988, China's labor system had modest amounts of flexibility. It was no longer the extraordinary rigid system of the 1970s. Indeed, an institutional framework had been put in place that was adequate to support significant change, but government officials still had not allowed those institutions to operate freely. Labor reform still lagged other aspects of reform, but was not so far behind as it had been in the past.

Financial reforms

The adoption of long-term profit contracting

In the previous chapter, we saw that the initial profit retention experiments had been succeeded by a bewildering variety of enterprise responsibility systems that set profit and other targets for the enterprise. The primary characteristics of these responsibility systems were that profit targets and the choice of financial systems were negotiated individually for each enterprise, while the rewards for fulfillment or over-fulfillment of targets were increased. The short-run compensation functions that faced managers were made steeper, as enterprises retained a larger percentage of marginal revenues. However, with only a few exceptions, profit targets were negotiated annually. Thus, managers had to be concerned with ratchet effects – the increase in the subsequent year's targets imposed on successful performers – and the continuing involvement of superiors in determining every aspect of the firm's compensation schedule. The failure of the tax-for-profit rationalization meant that, in practice, these responsibility systems were still in place for most state-run firms.

At the end of 1986, Premier Zhao Ziyang began to urge the adoption of enterprise systems of long-term contracting (*chengbao*). The basic idea of long-term contracting was to replace annual negotiated targets with a multi-year contract, signed between the enterprise and his superiors, that would specify profit deliveries and other targets. In most cases the enterprise was contracted by a single individual – 70% of contracts were held by individuals in a large sample of enterprises surveyed in 1989, while 26% were held by management groups, and 3% were contracted by the factory work force "as a whole" (CASS/UCSD 1990). Long-term contracts would reduce the importance of ratchet effects and continuous renegotiation of targets and would establish a quasi-legal guarantee for the enterprise manager's autonomy over a somewhat longer period. Manager's compensation functions would become steeper, both because of the reduction in ratchet effects and because the specific provisions of long-term contracts often allowed enterprises and managers to keep a larger portion of above-target revenues (sometimes 100%). In exchange for higher compensation and stabilization of authority, managers were expected to bear much higher levels of risk. Some long-term contracts required a personal security deposit from the manager, and in all cases enterprises were supposed to fulfill their profit delivery obligations regardless of total profit earned. Thus, steeper compensation functions would also apply to managers that failed to meet their targets, resulting in larger penalties in those cases. Finally, the signing of long-term contracts was intended to open up the selection of managers, with some degree of competition introduced between various aspirants to managerial jobs.

It is obvious that long-term contracting represented a retreat from the objective of financial rationalization, and an attempt to substitute an alternative approach to the problem of enterprise finances. The immediate cost was obvious: Financial obligations would continue to be established individually for each enterprise and be the outcome of a process of negotiation between managers and superiors. Advocates of long-term contracting argued, however, that this could be a desirable approach to financial reform. If the negotiation of long-term contracts could be converted into a competitive process of open bidding, it could become part of the revaluation of state capital. In such a system, the state, instead of earning revenues from its assets as a collector of capital fees and taxes, would instead earn a quasi-market return on assets in its role as the owner of those assets. A market for entrepreneurial managers would develop, as the best managers would make higher bids for available long-term contracts. The state's return on its assets would be converted into something like equity – the potential return determined by competition for the right to manage – instead of accruing as fixed interest payments as would be the case if capital fees were charged. Simultaneously, the development of a new stratum of entrepreneurial managers would be fostered.

Opponents of long-term contracting argued that such objectives were unrealistic. They felt that long-term contracting would simply introduce a new form of the bargaining relationship long pervasive between enterprise managers and their bureaucratic superiors. The problem with bargaining relations in the bureaucratic economy is not that they exist, but rather that the bargaining typically takes place in a one-on-one situation. The manager is fairly well entrenched in his enterprise, with extensive local knowledge not available to superiors; he has significant local human capital, and is not easily replaced. The superiors possess formal authority, and also dispose of numerous instruments that can be used to influence the success of the manager, including access to low-priced inputs and manipulation of tax and price levers. In such a situation, a bilateral monopoly tends to exist between manager and superior body. It is well known that in such situations, there are no competitive forces to drive the bargain toward equilibrium, and bargaining is indeterminate. The bargain merely serves to divide the available benefits between the two parties in proportion to the strength of their bargaining positions. This is particularly a problem when the two sides are bargaining over a huge volume of revenues, some of which are actually the tax revenues that should belong to all of society.

The greatest shortcoming of long-term contracting was the likelihood that it would simply codify this bilateral monopoly bargain. Existing factory managers are obviously in a highly favorable position at the outset of the bargaining. They have detailed knowledge of the inner workings of the firm not available to outsiders, and they have long-standing close relationships with the superior organs with whom they are negotiating. Moreover, when superiors are under pressure to adopt long-term contracts rapidly – because this approach was being stressed by the government as the proper reform mechanism – they would be especially willing to strike generous bargains with existing factory managers in order to achieve rapid agreement with minimum disruption. Outsiders would be under a double disadvantage in such situations. Not only would they labor under the inevitable handicap of possessing less local knowledge about the enterprise than the existing manager, but they would also face the danger that superiors could ensure their failure by manipulating the economic environment against them if they won the contract. Under such circumstances, some observers doubted that long-term contracting could be a practicable solution to the problem of enterprise autonomy.

Proponents of long-term contracting were well aware of this problem, but proposed to solve it by introducing open auctions and other institutions to bring competition and transparency into the process. A description of long-term contracting in Handan, Hebei Province, includes a remarkably apt description of the problem: "The main obstacle to further implementation of long-term contracting is the tendency toward one-on-one bargaining that pushes down contract targets. There are many reasons for this, but the most fundamental reason is that the original manager is given a seat at the bargaining counter first, and he makes this into his bargaining capital. The way to break down this ossified situation is to bring competition into the long-term contracting process by conducting open bidding" (Zhang Jiuda 1987: 36). A number of interesting attempts were made to institute various forms of open competition for long-term contracts, and during 1988 in particular, government policy stressed the need to open up the bidding process. But what was the reality of long-term contracting? Did it open up a managerial labor market, or was it just one more permutation of the bargaining economy?

Perhaps the most interesting attempt to carry out competitive auctions for long-term contracts occurred in Hebei province. Officials there made a major effort to publicize and carry out open competitive bidding for firms, establishing minimum bids and regularized procedures. The main elements were as follows:

1. Evaluation commissions were established to assess bidders. The evaluation commission was composed of four groups: government officials, experts, entrepreneurs, and workers' representatives. "Outstanding entrepreneurs" made up about one-third of the commission members, and workers were included primarily to ease the introduction of a new manager into the factory.

2. Minimum bids were established by examining the enterprise's performance in the three previous years, assessing development prospects for that sector, and comparing that enterprise with the best enterprise in the same sector and locality. An effort was made to assemble multiple bidders for each auction. Bidding opportunities were advertised in print and on television. Ultimately, 7,459 bids were received for 2,412 enterprises – an average of three bids per firm.

3. Evaluation commissions developed a point system to assess the charac-

teristics of bidders. Bidders were assessed on "political" and professional characteristics. Political characteristics included sense of responsibility, consciousness of reform and legal norms, as well as political awareness. Professional characteristics included technical skill, managerial experience, past accomplishments, ability to motivate, and physical health. There was no discussion in the source of how evaluation commissions handled the trade-off between qualifications of the bidder and the size of the bid.

Subsequently, officials surveyed the outcome in 590 of auctioned enterprises. The winning bidders were:

Original factory manager	47%
Middle management or workers from original factory	10%
Staff of government or party organizations	5%
All others	38%

It would be safe to say that about half of the enterprises maintained their original managerial personnel more or less intact and the other half experienced varying degrees of personnel change (SRC/ER 1990: 385–89).

This was probably the most thorough attempt in China to carry open auctions. Handan District in Hebei Province also carried out competitive auctions, but only two-thirds of the auctions were open to the public. Of 339 contracts surveyed, only 10% of successful bidders came from outside the original factory. The author of the study stresses that original managers were not necessarily the successful in-house bidders, and points out that 20% of successful bidders had formerly been workers, not managers at all. One striking example of competition within the factory is given.

After an open auction process, there were two groups still bidding for the district fertilizer plant. One was led by the 52-year old manager, who was simultaneously party secretary, and had 30 years seniority. The other was led by a 26-year old section head with four years seniority. They each explained their competing proposals and there was a poll of workers: the original manager got 194 votes, and the young man 296. This then assured the successful bidder broad support among the workers (Zhang Jiuda 1987: 36).

One can imagine the social tensions that had to be handled in this factory – especially given China's permanent employment system – and the temptation to avoid such open competition. It is clear that in a few cases, long-term contracting was carried out in an impressively open and competitive fashion.

However, when we shift from best to average practice, a more mixed picture emerges. An early nationwide study of 2,000 enterprises was carried out in 1987 jointly by groups from the System Reform Institute and the State Statistical Bureau. Separate reports were published. That of the Institute reproduces substantial aggregate data as well as detailed case studies (ESRG 1988), while the Statistical Bureau provides a brief analytical discussion of some of the results (Zhao Minshan 1987). There were two basic methods of setting profit delivery targets in long-term contracts. The first was merely a variant on traditional bureaucratic decision-making. Aggregate profit targets were first assigned to the industrial bureaus by the city government, which then disaggregated them to their subordinate enterprises and signed contracts. The second method involved establishing a committee to contract out factories, and then signing contracts individually or batch by batch with enterprises. (Zhao Minshan: 443). The second method was more of a genuine recontracting, but even then was not necessarily carried out through open bidding. Less than 5% of the enterprises studied had really gone through a competitive process to award the contract. (Zhao Minshan: 446). Of the successful contractors, 85% were the incumbent managers, 4.8% had been mid-level managerial personnel of the original firm, and 3.5% party or union leaders. When managers were asked why they signed long-term contracts, 55% said the primary reason was "because our superiors wanted us to."

Long-term contracting also reflected a change in the type of demands superiors made on enterprises. While there were many types of contracts, the overwhelming stress was on delivery of profit and tax to superiors. Compulsory deliveries were almost always set as a small increase from 1986 deliveries, and calculation was relatively straightforward. "The benefits come from the fact that objectives are clear, and the transparency of policy is high" (Zhao Minshan: 444). Managers expressed discomfort with the level of risk they were forced to bear in contracting for stable or increased profit deliveries. In particular, they felt vulnerable to increasing raw material costs that would cut into profitability. In compensation, managers may have experienced less intervention in firm business by bureaucratic superiors. Before contracts were signed, 24% of managers in the sample chose "directives from superiors" when asked to identify the greatest source of pressure they faced; after contracts were signed this response was chosen by only 5% of respondents[2] (ERSG: 194–220).

Overall performance of contracting firms was indistinguishable from national averages. Differences in output growth, profitability, and tax payments between the sample and national averages were insignificant. However, contracted enterprises increased their profit remittances substantially less than other enterprises, and their retained profits grew faster. While this may at first seem surprising given the stress on revenue delivery within contracts, it is in fact readily explicable. Managers were being called upon to guarantee revenue delivery, not necessarily to maximize it. Since managers were now bearing much greater risk, they were compensated by lower average delivery targets. Governments had to offer managers relatively moderate revenue delivery targets in order to induce them to accept the binding obligation to fulfill those targets. Thus, on average, revenue deliveries grew more slowly from enterprises that practiced long-term contracting (ERSG: 194–220; see also Fujian Statistical Office 1989).

In a later 1990 study of 769 firms, 14% of managers were selected by competitive auction, and incumbent managers won 55% of those auctions (CASS/UCSD). Comparison of the two studies shows that long-term contracting tended to evolve toward a greater reliance on open and competitive auction. Indeed, during 1988, official policy strongly stressed the need to move in this direction. According to one source, 35% of the long-term contracts signed in 1988 were let through competitive bids (*Economic 1989: III-4; Industry 1991: 201*. However, by 1988, most state enterprises were already operating under long-term contracts signed in 1987 or earlier, so the number of new contracts signed must have been small. Although the system was evolving towards a more competitive process, the new procedures could only be incorporated gradually upon the expiration of the first round of contracts, many of which had been signed in haste. In fact, in 1990, when a large number of the initial contracts did come up for renewal for the first time, political and economic conditions were quite different (see Chapter 8).

Other ownership reforms: Leasing and stock systems

Although long-term contracting became the predominant form of financial relations within the state sector, a number of other systems were tried on an experimental basis. During the period through 1988, none of these was developed enough to be considered major components of reform, but the institutional experimentation involved created some useful experience for the future. Experimentation was most widespread in the small enterprise sector. In fact, because experimentation was carried out primarily by local governments, and each firm involved was small, it is difficult to determine how widespread these measures were.

We discussed the fact that the small state industrial sector declined dramatically in relative terms during the 1980s, despite periods in which many new firms were created. It is possible that this shrinkage reflects some conversion of state firms into non-state ownership. Although "privatization" was not generally permitted, local governments were able to sell enterprises, and at least eleven (out of thirty) provinces did so. As early as 1985, examples are reported from Guangdong and Hebei in which state firms were sold to collectives, thereby becoming collectively owned. By 1988, there was a clear push to make such sales part of national policy (Tang Fengyi 1988; DRC 1988). One form or another of experimentation was fairly widespread in the small enterprise sector. One source claims that 40,000 small industrial enterprises, 46% of the total, went through some kind of transformation, either conversion to collective in management form (though not technically in ownership), leasing, or contracting to an individual (SRC 1988b: 797). But another source suggests that the more radical versions of experimentation were fairly limited in the industrial sector, saying that by the end of 1986, only 3,069 small state industrial enterprises were leased or converted to collective management (Liu Liang and Gong Zong 1987: 39). Leasing certainly increased during 1987 and 1988, in part because of its similarity to long-term contracting. But probably it remained a minority option in most localities. Change was far more common in the state commercial sector. Most small state commercial outlets – 82% of the total by one accounting – were leased or converted to collective-style management. And in the countryside, more than 90% of the often-tiny outlets of the Supply and Marketing Cooperatives were leased to individuals (SRC 1988b: 797).

The option of converting state enterprises to some kind of stock system was much discussed in China during the late 1980s. In fact, by the end of 1988, some 3,800 enterprises had issued stocks in one form or another. But in very few cases, if ever, was the issuance of stocks accompanied by a true conversion of the nature of enterprise ownership, shifting ownership to the stockholders. It was rare for stock to be issued for the entire value of the enterprise; indeed, there was no agreement as to how enterprise value should be assessed. Of the firms that issued stock by 1988, 85% had issued stock only to their own workers, 13.5% had sold stock only to another enterprise, and only 1.5% had openly sold stock (this would amount to less than 60 enterprises, *Economic* 1989: III-5, 8). In almost all cases, stocks actually issued fit into one of two categories. Most stock was simply a means for borrowing funds. Indeed, many certificates labeled equity actually carried a guaranteed return, and were thus more like bonds than stocks. There were extremely few cases in the state sector where stockholders were given any management or ownership privileges. The other major category was the issuance of stock to workers in the firm. In this case, the main motivation may have been the evasion of limitations on the wage bill. By reclassifying some worker earnings as stock dividends, firms sought to increase worker compensation without paying wage taxes.

At the end of 1987, there was additional movement in favor of enterprise stock systems. A number of conferences on stock systems were held during 1987, and Zhao Ziyang indicated general approval of the idea of stock systems. As a result, there was increased experimentation and discussion during 1988. However, concrete actions were not very advanced, and the idea became a casualty of the increased hardline influence after 1989.

The dual-track system in practice

The preceding chapter described the decision to freeze the scope of the traditional mandatory material balance plan. Fixing the plan in absolute terms immediately changed the significance of the plan. In the first place, a plan fixed in absolute size implied that the economy would gradually grow out of the plan, as incremental economic activity took place on a market basis. Moreover, the plan increasingly acted as a fixed tax on the enterprise. The size of the implicit tax on the enterprise could be calculated by taking the size of the plan and the differential between compulsory plan prices and market prices (Byrd 1991). Enterprise behavior would then be guided by market prices. Yet for this system to work, it must be accompanied by a clear authority to the enterprise to transact outside plan commodities at market prices. Curiously, this does not seem to have been explicitly recognized in the initial program to reduce the size of the plan, probably because reformers were still intending to carry out a broad price realignment. But the scope of outside-plan transactions had been increasing steadily through 1984, and planners were having increasing difficulty in enforcing price controls. By late 1984, officials in Beijing were openly recognizing that they could not control outside-plan prices, and were preparing to accept a transition to full market pricing outside the plan that seemed to them inevitable (Naughton 1986a). Market price quotations began to appear in official journals. In January and February 1985, official recognition caught up with concrete reality, and enterprises were formally given the right to transact outside plan goods at market determined prices (Tong Wansheng and Zou Xiangqun 1992: 163; Chen Fubao 1989; Wu and Zhao 1987: 312). With this decision, the dual-track system was fully in place and given clear legitimacy for the first time.

In so doing, the government gave explicit definition to two separate spheres of economic activity, each marked by its own characteristic means of regulation. The planned sector, with compulsory deliveries at state fixed prices, was to persist but its scope was clearly delineated and fixed in absolute terms (in subsequent years, it was to be shrunk in absolute terms). The market sector, with freely determined prices, was to cover the remainder of the economy, and was to grow steadily as the economy grew. Non-state firms made up an important component of the market sector – virtually all of their transactions were at market-determined prices. But the crucial innovation was that virtually all state firms also began to operate with markets – and market prices – on the margin. The general fixity of the state plan was translated into the fixity of delivery plans for individual enterprises as well. Marginal incentives for state-run firms were henceforth determined by market prices of inputs and output. The dual-track plan and market system should not be equated with the state and non-state sectors, for the scope of market operation was considerably bigger than the non-state sector. Participation in the market by state firms was, from 1985, a crucial component of the growth of market forces overall.

The fact that the absolute size of the plan overall was frozen beginning in 1984 generally implied that compulsory plans were frozen at the enterprise level as well. Individual state-owned enterprises in nearly all cases operated after 1985 with compulsory delivery targets and guaranteed supplies, but these were both substantially less than total output and total supplies required. Enterprise supply plans became inframarginal: Enterprises faced market prices on the margin for inputs and output. Since enterprise plans were generally fixed in scope and set well below total output, they began to function as a kind of lump sum tax on the enterprise. The enterprise was obligated to fulfill its plan as a precondition of operating on the market. But the fact that this obligation was fixed meant that it had no direct impact on enterprise decision-making. Enterprise behavior was determined by marginal incentives, and these were, in virtually all cases, determined by market prices. Like other lump-sum taxes, the enterprise plan could now be considered (as a first approximation) a non-distortionary tax on enterprise activity. In this sense, the impact of the plan on the enterprise was analogous to the impact of long-term contracting: In both cases, a fixed burden was imposed on the enterprise, which was then freed to face relatively high-powered, market-determined incentives on the margin.

In practice, the environment for the enterprise was complicated by the persistence of local government plans. During the 1984 shift of policy, there was a tendency in Beijing to treat all local plans as "guidance plans"–that is, as noncompulsory targets. In practice, local guidance plans often felt compulsory to the enterprise that received them. Typically, the firm was allocated inputs by local government, but was in turn expected to fulfill the guidance plan assigned to it by that government (Naughton 1986a; 1990). Conceivably, the relative shrinkage of the central plan could simply reflect a greater role for local plans, with little change for the enterprise. In practice, though, local plans were cut even more sharply than central government plans, beginning in 1985. The pace of change varied from region to region, but virtually all regions shrunk the local plan significantly (Ge Peng 1988; Tianjin 1988; Tian Jianghai 1985). Local government interference in enterprises did not cease, but the change in the balance between plan and market at the local level was consistent with the changes at the center.

The development of the dual-track system was particularly apparent with respect to raw materials and intermediate goods. It was in these areas that the traditional planning system was most firmly entrenched. Many final manufactured goods had already escaped from the traditional planning system in the wake of changing macroeconomic conditions during the first half of the 1980s. However, shortages of energy and raw materials were sufficiently severe that state controls had been maintained over these commodities even as shortages were ameliorated for most final goods. These relations are clearly reflected in the proportions of goods sold independently by enterprises as recorded in the 1985 industrial census. Enterprise self-sales accounted for the bulk of light industrial goods (61%) and heavy manufactures (68%), but only 33% of industrial materials and 24% of mining products (Industrial Census 1988: 122–25). Thus, the process of "growing out of the plan" after 1985 is most evident for industrial materials and mining products.

The evolution of the dual-track system is easiest to track in the case of relatively homogeneous producers goods, where there is data about the proportion of goods covered by central government allocation and by market processes. The data in Figures 6.2 and 6.3 compares actual deliveries to the planning authorities with domestic output. It may understate planner control somewhat because planners also allocate a portion of imports. Nevertheless, when we assemble all the available data, the picture that emerges is unequivocal. The dual-track system was actually brought into play and the economy was growing out of the plan.

The steel industry can serve as an example of the development of the dual-track system. Figure 6.2 shows the comparison between central government allocations and total output, both measured in million tons. The declining share of government allocation is the result of the almost unchanged quantity of steel entering government channels until 1987. Beginning in 1987, absolute reductions in the volume of commodities allocated began to be important in a number of sectors. For steel, the quantity of finished steel fed into the allocation process decreased by 11.7%, even as allocations for keypoint construction increased 6% (*Economic* 1988: IV-26-27). Thus the allocation process for steel was moving toward a closer link to the priority investment program, with ordinary uses of steel heading toward the market.

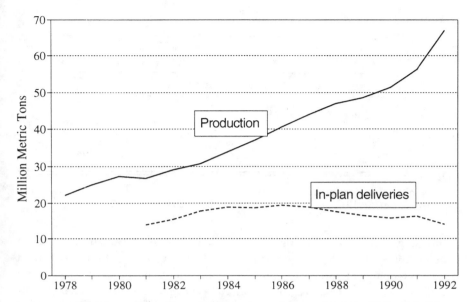

Figure 6.2. Steel output and in-plan deliveries. Source: *Statistic* 1993: 502–503; *Economic* 1983: III-77; 1985: IV-32.

One of the striking characteristics of the development of the dual track in the steel industry was that outside-plan transactions involved investment as well as product sales. Central government steel investment was almost entirely committed to the Baoshan project (Xue Muqiao 1981; see Chapter 2). Yet local governments and enterprises continued to demand steel beyond what existing mills could provide. From the mid-1980s, local governments began to invest in steel mills outside their own territory in return for a claim on the output stream that resulted from the investment. One calculation was that about 3 billion yuan was committed to steel mills in the 1986–90 period in return for a claim on 6.5 MMT of output, at "negotiated" prices. Steel mills, in turn, invested funds and equipment in distant iron and coal mines, in order to ensure access to raw materials (SRC 1988b: 338). Here we see a side benefit of the development of share systems during the 1980s. Although they were not important as a form of privatization, they were important in providing an institutional form through which enterprises and governments could take stakes in other enterprises, increasing the forms of economic cooperation and exchange.

Following the development of these mechanisms, exchanges of steel outside planned channels escalated rapidly. "Cooperation" in steel supplies –

Table 6.1. *Steel allocation and sales*

	Central government allocation	Local government allocation	Enterprise direct sales
	(percentage of total domestic output)		
1987	45	33	22
1988	39	32	29
1989	36	32	32
1990	32	30	37
1991	30	23	46

Local allocation derived as a residual.
Source: Statistic 1988: 461; 1989: 379; 1990: 498; 1991: 478; 1992: 494.

meaning barter trade among regions – had been significant under the old economic system. Now it grew rapidly. About 10% of output was traded interregionally in the early 1980s, and this increased rapidly, reaching 23 million tons, about half of output, in 1988 (*Economic* 1987: V-26; 1989: IV-28). Local governments continued to play a major role in controlling local steel supplies, as well as in interregional trade. It is theoretically possible that the reduction in central allocation shown graphically in Figure 6.2 merely implied an increase in local government control of materials. In fact, as Table 6.1 shows, local allocation is significant and has not declined as rapidly as central allocation. But the calculations reported there also show that the growth in true market transactions – direct enterprise sales – has been rapid, and that such transaction surpassed local allocations in importance in 1989.

The dual-track system was also applied to coal, China's primary energy source (Figure 6.3). But whereas in many sectors the main story was the introduction of above-plan marketing in state enterprises, the main story in the coal sector was the growth of an entirely new non-state sector – rural collective and individual coal mines. During the early 1980s, state-run coal mines were undergoing a difficult period of retrenchment, repairing dangerous mine tunnels and constructing new mine shafts. Between 1979 and 1983, central government production was basically stagnant – output grew by only 5 MMT. State mines run by local governments accounted for an additional 10 MMT increment. With critical energy shortages and no possibility of significant increases in state output, the government began to encourage rural collectives and individuals to operate small-scale mines. The response was remarkable: Output of that sector jumped from 106 MMT to 170 MMT

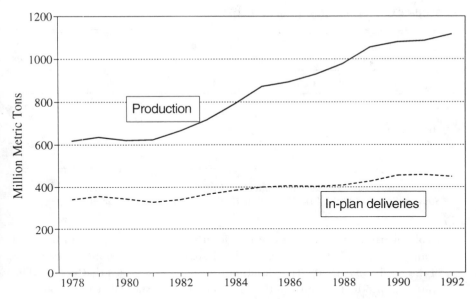

Figure 6.3. Coal output and in-plan deliveries. Source: *Statistic* 1993; 502–503; *Coal*, various years, Table 27.

during the same period. Non-state production accounted for more than 80% of the total increment.

Even more remarkable was what happened after 1983, as central government production again began to grow. Between 1983 and 1987, central government output grew by 57 MMT, or 16%. But rural collective and private output grew by 155 MMT, or 90%. Of the total increment between 1983 and 1987, the rural collective and private sector accounted for 72% and central government mines only 27% (locally run state mines contributed only 1% of the increment). Over the entire 1979–87 period, rural collective and private mines accounted for three-quarters of the total growth of coal output.

As a result of the importance of small-scale producers in the coal sector, the overall market breaks down into four segments (a similar pattern is evident for cement). The largest single segment is still central government allocated coal from the largest mines, accounting for just under half of total output in 1987–89. The second largest segment is the output from small mines under township, village, and private ownership, accounting for a little over a third of total output in 1987–89. The third segment consists of independent sales from large mines "owned" either by the center or by

Table 6.2. *Cement allocation and sales*

	Central government allocation	Local government allocation	Large enterprise direct sales	TVP sales
	(percentage of total domestic output)			
1987	13	22	38	28
1988	11	16	44	29
1989	10	15	44	31
1990	10	14	48	28
1991	8	10	51	32

Large enterprises are state and collective firms at county level or above.
Source: Statistic 1988: 461; 1989: 379; 1990: 498; 1991: 478; 1992: 494.

local governments, which accounted for 13–14% of the total. And the final component is direct allocations by local governments accounting for 6–9% of the total (*Coal* 1990). The situation in cement resembles that in coal: The sphere of production outside the plan is shared by state allocation and state enterprise sales, as well as a significant participation of non-state producers (Table 6.2).

Further marketization via entry

We have stressed that the dual-track system was operational within the sphere of the state-run economy. State-run firms widely faced "markets on the margin," and it is therefore important not to identify the division of the economy into plan and market spheres with the division of ownership into state and non-state producers. While non-state output was preponderantly traded on the market, a substantial portion of state output was also traded on the market. The proportion of industrial production regulated by the market was thus substantially larger than the proportion of industrial activity accounted for by non-state producers.

Nevertheless, the entry of non-state producers was a crucial part of the overall process of marketization. In many sectors, non-state producers accounted for the bulk of market activity. More fundamentally, the entry of non-state producers was critical in ensuring the healthy development of the market sphere. Non-state, particularly rural, enterprises provided competition for state firms. Vigorous growth of the non-state sector, described in Chapter 4, was crucial in converting the market fringe into a viable part of the economy as a whole. Drawn disproportionately into high-profit sectors, new entrants were crucial in driving market prices toward a pattern more consistent with scarcity costs.

Growth of the market was also fostered by a gradual reduction of the barriers that separated China's domestic economy from the world economy. China's foreign trade grew rapidly through the 1980s, and at the same time planners reduced traditional forms of intervention that had insulated the domestic price system from world prices. By 1986, 80% of China's imports was priced according to the agency system, in which the domestic price equals the world price multiplied by the exchange rate plus taxes and handling fees for the agent. Since imports were equal to 15% of China's GNP in that year, world prices were directly reflected in 12% of the value of domestic final sales. Both the share of imports in GNP and the proportion of imports priced according to the agency system continued to climb in subsequent years. Although export pricing was not liberalized to the same degree, the demonopolization of most export trade meant that producers increasingly had some bargaining power with exporters. The ability to choose among exporters allowed firms to maneuver for a bigger share of the world market value of their product. This undoubtedly meant that world prices played an increasingly direct role in influencing producer decisions (Lardy 1992: 74–79).

Marketization was thus being driven simultaneously by three forces: the new freedom given to state firms to operate on markets at the margin, rapid entry of start-up firms, and increased transmission of world prices to the domestic economy. Each of these factors gained force as the decade proceeded. China was indeed growing out of the plan.

Evaluation of second-stage reforms

Coherence of reforms

The reform measures described in this chapter shared certain common characteristics. In each case, attempts to fine-tune administrative relations were abandoned in favor of bold measures to improve incentives. Attempts at price adjustment were replaced with rapid movement to market prices at the margin. Attempts to reform tax and financial systems were replaced by long-term profit contracting with enterprises retaining a large share of residual income. In both cases, lump-sum, inframarginal obligations were imposed on the enterprises in exchange for the grant of substantial autonomy and better incentives. Factory manager responsibility systems clarified authority relations and put managers in a position where they were much more likely to respond to, and profit from, new incentives. From the enterprise perspective, these were an internally consistent set of reform measures.

From the point of view of central planners and fiscal authorities, reforms sought above all to stabilize the contribution enterprises made to central authorities. While stability implied that the relative importance of central planning would decline over the long term, it also reduced uncertainty for central planners and provided them with a stable basis for their own plans and activities. Enterprises were intended to bear greater risk, but in return were granted greater autonomy and a steadily increasing share of resources. Even the labor reforms were designed in such a way that changes for existing permanent workers were extremely modest. Rather, change was to come gradually as the share of contract workers increased and new social security institutions were built up gradually. Thus, the package of reforms adopted after 1984 were consistent. They provided for a radical break with the old system, but were designed in such a way that the actual process of marketization would occur gradually. The Chinese reform strategy was successful because it actually led somewhere – it was a feasible, if imperfect, transition path to a market economy. Moreover, that transition occurred along with, and as an inseparable result of, economic growth.

Problems with the dual-track system

The dual-track system had important problems and shortcomings – specifically, (a) forgoing tax and price reform, (b) corruption, and (c) local government intervention and protectionism.

Forgoing tax and price reform. Perhaps the most important shortcoming of the dual-track strategy is that it foreclosed immediate progress in enterprise tax reform. Instead of developing a system of non-negotiable taxes at uniform rates, China's limited administrative resources were concentrated on elaborating a system of negotiating enterprise-specific contributions to the public treasury (Wood 1991). In a sense, long-term contracting dealt with state-enterprise financial relations as if they were *only* ownership relations. In its capacity as owner of the enterprise, the state adopted a system something like leasing to induce managers to operate state assests more effectively. But the government also stands in relation to the enterprise as taxation authority and as regulator of economic activity. As progress to a market economy proceeds, these functions must become increasingly distinct.

The dual-track system may actually obstruct this progressive differentiation of function. Under long-term contracting there are no clear taxes on income (turnover taxes remain) and they are simply lumped into profit remittances as under the traditional system. Moreover, introduction of a tax system is impeded by the fact that the state has already signed a long-term contract with the enterprise promising to exact no more that a stipulated total revenue. Under these conditions, to adopt new taxes would clearly be a violation of the government's commitment: Long-term contracts would have to be renegotiated for each enterprise in order to adopt new taxes. Moreover, the dual-price system makes it nearly impossible to assess the future profitability of enterprises. Each enterprise faces different proportions of its output under state fixed prices, and the degree of distortion implied by state fixed prices is different for different products. Thus, the distortions of the unreformed price system affect each enterprise individually. This is clearly true for long-term profit contracting as well.

Difficulties in assessing future profitability make ownership reform more difficult. How is the value of the enterprise to be established? It also makes it difficult to make progress in hardening budget constraints and introducing effective bankruptcy provisions. Since enterprise losses continue to be largely a function of externally imposed price controls and other distortions, it is not possible to allow creditors to force firms into bankruptcy. In short, under the dual-track strategy very little progress was made in establishing a level playing field for different firms. An impartial and universal tax system was not developed. Comprehensive price liberalization – which could be carried out overnight – was extended over many years. Separation of government functions as owner, taxation authority, and regulator was impeded. As a result, little progress was made in establishing conditions for more thorough ownership reform. This is a version of the criticism that profit contracting merely institutionalizes the particularized bargaining relationship that had always characterized the bureaucratic economy.

The importance of these objections is somewhat ameliorated by some of the side benefits of the dual-track strategy. If marketization occurs sufficiently rapidly, a vastly improved price system will come into play quickly, and this will provide much better signals for both price rationalization and for ownership reform than if this had not been the case. Moreover, if privatization is to be carried out gradually – as seems to be the case in most socialist economies in transition – it will require an enterprise-specific process of revaluation, restructuring of enterprise balance sheets, and clarification of enterprise obligations to the government. In this kind of gradual, enterprise-specific process, the additional impediments imposed by the dual-track strategy are unlikely to add significantly to the difficulties of privatization. Finally, since most enterprise long-term contracts are synchronized, new tax measures could be designed to take effect upon the expiration of the majority of contracts. Taxation reform and creation of uniform and impartial regulations have repeatedly proven difficult for Chinese reformers. They will undoubtedly continue to be difficult, regardless of the complications introduced by the dual-track strategy.

Corruption. Corruption is a problem in any gradual reform process. Marketization gives power-holders the ability to monetize the rents created by price and other distortions, while new and often unclear regulations are subject to selective enforcement. The dual-track strategy, however, presents a particularly rich menu of temptations to corruption. Because nearly every good has more than one price, illicit income can be made merely by transforming the status of a good. Anyone who can purchase a good at the low, state-set price and then sell at the higher market price derives substantial profit. For example, duting the mid-1980s, a standard medium-weight truck sold for a plan price of 20,000 yuan, and a market price around 35,000 yuan. Illicit sale of a single truck in high demand by emerging peasant entrepreneurs would yield a profit of 15,000 yuan, about fifteen times the average *annual* urban wage. Distortions are large relative to money incomes, so temptations are great. Spread of the factory manager responsibility system, by reducing oversight of day-to-day managerial activities, probably increased opportunities for dishonest behavior as well. The dual-track system tends to generate corruption.

Corruption takes a wide variety of forms in practice. Simple resale of allocated materials at market prices may be relatively rare, since this activity is clearly illegal and relatively easy to detect (a clear paper trail follows state allocations). More common, perhaps, is the proliferation of middlemen. Enterprises sell materials to intermediaries for a modest markup over plan price, disguising the nature of the transaction. These intermediaries mark the price up further and sell to other intermediaries. Chains of paper transactions are created; each link in the chain owes an obligation to the preceding link that provided access to goods at below market prices. These obligations can be repaid when the next chain is formed, simply by reversing the direction of transactions. In the final transaction, the good is sold at the market price. Instead of two prices (plan and market), the good is sold at a spectrum of prices between the extremes of plan and market.

Enterprises have other reasons to sell outside-plan products at less than market prices. Enterprises face taxes on bonuses and enterprise investment. To the extent that these types of activity are evaluated at lower prices, the enterprise tax burden will be lower. Thus, the enterprise may sell its own output at the plan price in exchange for the ability to purchase commodities at the low plan price. For example, the firm may purchase televisions (and distribute them to their workers at low prices) or cement (for use in an investment project that will thereby seem less expensive). Sales at low plan prices thus becomes a form of tax evasion. Yet such enterprises might be praised by the local price bureaus for aiding in the fight against inflation!

Clearly, there is an enormous range of behavior associated with attempts to operate in the dual price environment. Some behavior is entirely innocent. Much behavior represents a kind of mild corruption in which benefits are distributed to the enterprise as a whole. And some is simple profiteering by individuals. There is no doubt that corruption is a serious problem under this system. Such corruption might be seen as a process of buying out power-holders (Winiecki 1989). In an undemocratic system, corruption is the compensation the ruling class exacts in exchange for giving up its direct control over the allocation of goods. It is not accidental that the most egregious cases of corruption involve the children of very high officials in Beijing. If economic reform is successful, the gains to the economy would be large enough to buy out the existing ruling stratum and still make the remainder of the population substantially better off.

Local government intervention and protectionism. Reform in the absence of clarification of ownership rights has tended to strengthen the position of local governments. Local govenments, which "own" and oversee the bulk of state-run industrial enterprises, have substantial incentives to interfere in enterprise management; they also generally have power to do so.

1. Local governments rely on enterprises as a source of informal tax revenues. "Exactions" (*tanpai*) on the enterprise by various local quasi-governmental organizations are common. For instance, charges may be levied on the enterprise to fund local schools, municipal facilities, and other less worthy causes. In one survey of 168 enterprises, such charges equaled 9.5% of enterprise retained profit ("Exactions" 1985). These exactions have been repeatedly forbidden by the central government, and since 1988 enterprises have had the legal right to refuse them. But they remain common in practice (Clarke 1991: 37–43).

2. Local governments may formally implement reforms without making any real changes. For example, in a large-scale survey conducted in mid-1987, the factory manager responsibility system was reported to have resulted in no changes at all in 10% of the factories surveyed, and to have been only partially implemented in another half (SRC/ER 1990: 459). This may reflect only the early stages of gradual implementation, or it may reflect a pattern of merely nominal implementation.

3. Local governments may engage in protectionist policies with respect to interregional trade. Local governments may be eager to protect producers of high markup items from "outside" competition; correspondingly, they may restrict the export to other regions of low-price raw materials that support production of high profit items. Since local governments are so dependent on "their" enterprises for revenues, they have strong incentives to engage in protectionist policies. Such policies have also been repeatedly condemned and forbidden by central government policy; the very need to repeat the condemnations shows, of course, that the practice continues.

Yet how important are such practices? No systematic study of interregional trade in China has ever been performed for any commodity except for grain. The very fact that barriers to interregional trade can be an issue at all indirectly highlights one of the crucial features of the Chinese economy. Control of industrial production is exerted by a very large number of geographically separated government entities: 30 provinces, a large number of cities, and more than 2,000 counties. No government, therefore, has a monopoly on production. Even the most monopolistically minded local government must face substantial competition from other jurisdictions; while it may resort to trade barriers it must be careful to disguise those barriers so as not to provoke central government intervention. Moreover, the pattern of exports to the domestic Chinese market from Guangdong has been studied (World Bank 1992). This study found that the high-profit manufactured goods produced in Guangzhou have been exported to the remainder of China in increasing volume over the 1980s, growing about twice as rapidly as GNP. Such a pattern is hardly consistent with the presence of pervasive barriers to inter-regional trade.

4. Finally, local governments imposed varying degrees of price controls even on outside-plan transactions. We have already seen that enterprises had a variety of motives for transacting at below market prices. As inflationary pressures accumulated during 1987 and 1988 (see next chapter), local governments became increasingly concerned about price stability. As a result, they tended to encourage, and even compel, enterprises under their authority to "hold the line" on price increases and limit market prices, thus giving enterprises another motive for below-market price transactions. Such local government actions even received central government encouragement during 1987 and 1988, as directives encouraging anti-inflation efforts proliferated. Local governments were permitted to establish price ceilings for market prices (Tian Yuan and Qiao Gang 1991: 105–6). These regulations were not success-

ful in reining in market prices, but they further distorted market signals and encouraged the proliferation of prices between plan and market levels (Chen Fubao 1989).

Achievements of the second-stage reforms

Were second-stage reforms successful in actually increasing the market-ization of the economy? We have already seen that by a mechanical defini-tion the answer is yes, because the scope of outside-plan, market-like trans-actions increased steadily. However, ultimately we can only answer this question by examining economy-wide changes in industrial behavior and performance. Did the growth of the market sector actually change the behavior of state-run enterprises? I argue in this section that there is sub-stantial evidence that it did.

To understand the marketization of the economy, we must begin by recog-nizing the pressures created by large monopoly profits in industry. Drawn by the presence of unexploited niches in the economy and the lure of monopoly profits, widespread entry dramatically increased competition. New entrants competed away much of the preexisting monopoly profits in industry. Thus, increased product market competition is an essential part of whatever changes in behavior we can identify. If this interpretation is correct, we would expect to see a reduction in the dispersion of profit rates among industrial sectors. In the extreme, complete marketization should result in the equalization of marginal rates of return to factors of production in differ-ent sectors. With a few exceptions, data are not yet sufficient to estimate marginal returns, but data on average rates of profit strongly support the hypothesis of a tendency toward convergence. There is evidence that state-run enterprises have found themselves under increasing pressure due to these trends, and that this pressure is effectively manifested at the enter-prise level. Enterprise closures are significant. Finally, there is substantial evidence of improving total factor productivity in state-run industry. Such evidence cannot be considered totally conclusive. However, it provides very strong evidence that supports the proposition that reforms have created significant changes in behavior in state-run firms, and significant gains in economic efficiency.

1. Entry and increased product market competition. It is unlikely that any of the reform policies adopted after 1984 would have a substantial impact on state-run enterprises unless they were faced with substantially greater compe-tition in product markets than had been the case in the past. Yet there is substantial evidence of just such an increase in competition. Interviews in

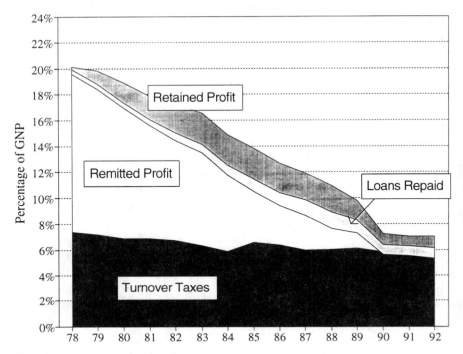

Figure 6.4. Disposition of profit and tax: in-budget state industry. Source: SRC/ER 1990: 645; *Abstract* 1993: 82.

factories during the latter part of the 1980s revealed an increasing concern with competition from other producers, and particularly from rural township and village enterprises. A critical feature of this period is that state-run enterprises were under increasing *pressure.* One indicator of the magnitude of the pressures faced by industrial firms is the dramatic decline in the total volume of profits reaped by the large-scale industrial sector. As Figure 6.4 shows, profit of in-budget firms (the large state-owned factories) has declined steadily as a share of GNP. Notwithstanding industry's growth – substantially more rapid than GNP overall – the share of industrial profits has been declining rapidly. The most plausible explanation for this pattern is rapid entry that has eroded profitability. (We will demonstrate that the obvious alternative explanation, decreasing efficiency, is not supported by available evidence.) Moreover, the trend to declining profitability is manifest not only in the large-scale industrial sector. As shown in Chapter 4, rural industries – despite their rapid growth and appparently robust competitiveness – have experienced nearly identical reductions in profitability.

These trends are essential in understanding the impact of expanded enterprise autonomy. As increased entry eroded the formerly comfortable profit margins of state firms, managers came under increasing pressure to fulfill their long-term contracts, and indeed to survive as independent firms. Moreover, these macroeconomic trends are essential to understanding the changing role of the bureaucratic organizations that oversee enterprises. Most Chinese discussions of long-term contracting focus on its function of inducing enterprise managers to commit to specific actions (particular productivity-enhancing investment). However, Littwack (1991) argues that a fundamental problem in socialist reform is the inability of *bureaucrats* to credibly commit to a policy of non-interference in enterprise operations. In his view, bureaucrats are unable to adopt a "hands off" management style, preferring instead to reintervene in enterprise operations whenever important objectives are concerned. An obvious characteristic of long-term contracting is that it involved commitments from both of the contracting parties. Bureaucrats committed themselves, in writing, to a simple and easily monitored pledge of non-interference. To be sure, non-interference was never absolute: Bureaucrats could and did intervene in a range of specific enterprise actions. But it appears that long-term contracting did limit the ability of bureaucrats to impose ex post changes on tax rates and other key financial variables.

Why would bureaucrats commit themselves to non-interference in this fashion? One plausible explanation is that bureaucrats found themselves under increasing fiscal pressure. The erosion of monopoly profits in industry cut deeply into budgetary revenues (discussed in more detail in the next chapter). Bureaucratic interest in the enterprise increasingly became focused on halting the decline in budgetary revenues. As a result, bureaucrats focused their monitoring of enterprise behavior on the single variable of enterprise profit remittances. Driven by fiscal necessity, bureaucrats no longer had the luxury of constant intervention and redistribution between enterprises, and were forced instead to rely on incentive mechanisms favoring unrestricted profit maximization at the enterprise level. An unexpected side benefit of these macroeconomic trends was that the informational problems involved in setting profit remittance targets under long-term contracting were ameliorated. If the objective was to arrest the decline in remittances, the obvious remittance target was the remittance of the previous year. In fact, large-scale surveys frequently stress that the central requirement of supervisory bodies was that remittance targets should be set no lower than the previous year's remittances, with some increase if possible (Zhao Minshan 1987).

2. Evidence of convergence of returns. The changes that were sweeping through the economy had a major impact on relations among industrial sectors as well. Under the old system, not only was industrial profitability on average extremely high, variation in profit rates among sectors was also large. This was part of the redistributional character of the system. The government would, in any case, collect all industrial surpluses and redistribute them in accordance with its own priorities; profit rates played no role in allocation of capital. Therefore, it was unimportant that profit rates varied greatly among sectors. Good data on profit rates by industrial sectors are available beginning in 1980, at which time there would already have been some substantial movement toward equalization of profit.[3]

In the following analysis, the rate of profit refers to total profit and tax divided by the total value of capital, defined as depreciated fixed capital plus working capital. The justification for including tax is that continued failure of tax reform has meant that revenues classified as tax are in fact available to local governments and other sponsors of industrialization. Tax is part of the total return that local governments realize from their investments.[4] The universe is all independent accounting enterprises at the township level and above. Thus, only the small-scale rural sector, composed of village and private industries, is excluded. In 1980, there were enormous differences in sectoral profitability. The profit rate on textiles was 69%, and on petroleum refining, 98%; profits rates on iron mining and transportation machinery were 7% and 11%, respectively. In general, profit rates on light consumer goods industry were substantially higher than those on heavy industry. Light industry based on processing agricultural goods had an average profit rate of 55% in 1980, light industry processing industrial materials had a 39% profit rate, and heavy industry had an 18% profit rate. Thus, in spite of enormous variation, profit rates generally reflected the determination to maintain high mark-ups on consumer goods, ensuring ample revenues to the government.

In the years between 1980 and 1989 the dispersion of profit rates declined dramatically. Table 6.3 shows the simple standard deviation and coefficient of variation of 38 industrial sectors. The standard deviation of profit rates declined by more than half; since mean profitability also declined, the coefficient of variation declined by 44%. Additional insight into this process can be gained by examining Figure 6.5. It is possible to read from this figure both the sources of equalization of profit rates and the limits to this process. Sectors are arranged from left to right according to their profitability in 1989, which is shown by the front row of columns. The rear columns show the profitability of the same sectors in 1980. Of the 37 sectors shown, 31 had profit rates in 1989 between 8% and 23%. (Table 6.4 provides a key to the

Table 6.3. *Dispersion of industrial sectoral profit rates*

	1980	1985	1986	1987	1988	1989
Standard deviation	19.7	14.9	15.2	13.1	9.4	7.4
Coefficient of variation	0.78	0.63	0.74	0.65	0.46	0.44

Source: Industrial Statistics 1990: 153–59.

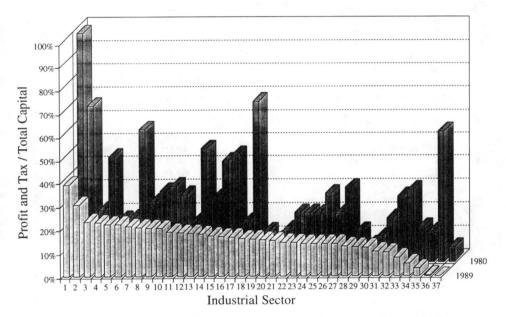

Figure 6.5. Industrial sector profit rates. Source: *Industrial Statistics* 1990: 151–59.

sectors.) The four sectors with lower profitability were coal mining, coking, petroleum and gas extraction, and public water supplies. By contrast, the only sectors with profit rates above 23% were petroleum refining and rubber processing.

With the exception only of petroleum refining and rubber processing, profit rates declined sharply in *all* of the sectors that had high profitability in 1980. This was most striking for light industry, the profitability of which overall declined from 49% to 21%, while heavy industrial profit declined only from 18% to 14%. The most obvious explanation for this phenomenon is

Table 6.4. *Key to industrial sectors*

| | | Sectoral profit rates (profit + tax total capital) | |
		1980	1989
(0)	tobacco	326.9	152.3
1	refining	98.3	38.7
2	rubber	67.2	30.5
3	chemicals	22.0	23.1
4	medicine	45.0	22.8
5	ferrous metals	18.3	22.1
6	salt	19.0	22.1
7	culture/sports items	56.7	21.0
8	electric machinery	25.7	20.6
9	paper	30.0	20.4
10	chemical fibers	32.1	20.2
11	printing	28.6	18.8
12	nonferrous metals	17.2	18.4
13	drink	48.5	18.0
14	metalworking	27.0	17.8
15	handicrafts	43.0	17.0
16	garments	46.0	16.6
17	nonmetal mines	17.0	16.5
18	textiles	69.0	15.8
19	timber	13.0	15.7
20	nonferrous mines	9.7	15.3
21	electronics	14.0	14.9
22	fodder	20.8	14.3
23	building materials	20.8	14.2
24	power	20.6	13.8
25	food	28.9	13.7
26	instruments	20.5	13.6
27	plastic	31.6	13.6
28	machinery	13.1	12.7
29	iron mines	7.3	12.1
30	transport machinery	10.5	12.0
31	furniture	18.4	10.3
32	wood products	27.6	10.0
33	leather	30.3	7.9
34	water	14.7	5.4
35	coking & town gas	12.7	3.2
36	oil & gas	55.8	0.2
37	coal mines	6.0	−1.8
	Average	25.2	16.8

increasing entry and competition. It is precisely in the light industrial sectors where technological barriers to entry are low and where substantial entry by rural factories and small-scale urban enterprises has occurred. Moreover, the process of equalization of profit failed to occur only in those sectors that are strongly shaped by the continuing influence of state price controls. We saw in the previous chapter that state control of energy supplies has remained tight. Although markets on the margin have been important in coal supplies, the bulk of coal continues to be supplied by state mines subject to strict price controls. Petroleum extraction is subject to an even higher degree of state monopoly. In the basic coal and petroleum industries, the state has been unwilling to raise prices, because it fears the ripple effects on the overall price level of higher energy prices. It is precisely in these sectors where we would expect the heavy hand of state control to continue to obstruct the process of profit equalization. Conversely, the two remaining sectors with above-normal profits are obvious beneficiaries of this state price policy. This is obvious in the case of petroleum refining, and in rubber processing presumably reflects state price policy on crude rubber combined with a continuing high degree of monopolization of supplies. Ironically, by keeping prices low in primary energy sectors where it has a large stake, the central government essentially taxes itself and subsidizes the economy as a whole. This, of course, contributes greatly to continuing fiscal difficulties.

Indeed, in order to test the degree to which marketization has led to convergence of profit rates in industry, it would make sense to exclude the coal, coke, and petroleum extraction sectors from the analysis. When this is done, the coefficient of variation of profit rates for all other sectors – the bulk of the industrial economy potentially subject to competitive pressures – declines from .77 in 1980 to .37 in 1989, a reduction of 52%. This is not, in itself, proof that the convergence of profit rates comes from increased competition and mobility of factors. It must be acknowledged that the shift in state pricing policy, beginning in 1979, was also a significant causative factor. Since industry that processed agricultural materials had the highest profit rate initially, the policy of raising agricultural prices would, by itself, tend to reduce the dispersion of profit rates. But the changes noted are far too broad to be explained by this single factor. In particular, note that the profit rate of consumer goods produced from processed industrial materials has also declined dramatically – from 39% to 18% over the 1980–1989 period.

Moreover, if the true explanation for converging profit rates lies with increased entry and competition, we would expect other procedures to find similar evidence of convergence. Jefferson, Rawski and Zheng (1992) estimate production functions for state and collectively run industry using a cross section of Chinese cities. They find a tendency toward convergence of marginal returns to both capital and labor between the two types of ownership. Thus, all the available evidence is consistent with the hypothesis that increased entry and competition has been the primary cause of equalization of profit among China's industrial sectors. This also makes it more plausible that the steady decline in industrial profitability in the aggregate is also the result of the same forces.

3. Pressure is passed through to the enterprise level. We have already seen that during 1988, managers began to carry out programs of labor reoptimization in a substantial minority of enterprises. Similarly, the rate of enterprise failure increased. Although China passed a bankruptcy law in 1988, it quickly became a dead letter. Through February 1991, only a single report exists of a state enterprise closed down through court action under the Bankruptcy Law (Clarke 1991: 52), along with a handful of collectives. But during 1988, as a substitute for bankruptcy, reformers promoted enterprise reorganization or "consolidation" (*jianbing*). Enterprise consolidation relied on other enterprises to take over the operation of loss-making enterprises. Enterprises that were taking over would receive a number of benefits: control of the land that the loss-making enterprise occupied, expansion of their labor and wage-bill quotas, and the opportunity to integrate the existing firm into their own operations. Such transactions increased sharply during 1987 and 1988. Enterprise failures were thus handled as the failure of one division of "China Incorporated": Failure was not to be followed by unemployment of the divisions' workers, who would instead be transferred to other divisions.

According to one survey of the practice, from 1987 through mid-1989, 3,424 enterprises were taken over by a total of 2,856 other enterprises in 27 provinces. Three-quarters of the enterprises taken over were loss-makers, and only 4% were "relatively profitable." It is clear from the accompanying discussion that most, but not all, of the enterprises taken over were state-owned. The number of taken-over firms given above equals 3.5% of state-run enterprises. This is not a trivial rate of failure, compared with market economies such as the United States or Japan. Indeed, the means of arranging takeovers of failing firms is quite reminiscent of the practice used within large Japanese enterprise groups when their subordinate firms are failing.

Firms also reacted to economic pressure by furloughing workers, providing them with some fraction of their base pay – typically 60% – as a subsistence wage. Such actions were not commonly observed in the big cities such as Beijing and Shanghai, but in smaller cities enterprises in trouble frequently found that fiscal authorities were in no position to bail them out. In Sichuan province, it was reported that in 1987, thousands of state-run and collective enterprises had furloughed workers, who had become peddlers in the free markets to support themselves ("Peddlars" 1988). Such responses accelerated during the contractionary policies of 1989, and there were many examples of enterprises putting their workers on short time, or sending them home on a stipend equal to 50–60% of their ordinary wage. Moreover, individuals on short time or otherwise drawing wages are not counted in the unemployment statistics. Thus, the individuals described here are separate from, and in addition, the approximately 0.5% of the labor force that was discharged during 1989 and described in the section on labor reforms.

Thus, there seems to be some evidence that as reform accelerated during 1987–88, enterprises felt under sufficient pressure that they began to respond in fairly fundamental ways to the dictates of market pressure. Along with Adam Smith's invisible hand, at work to equalize rates of return on capital, we find some evidence of Joseph Berliner's "invisible foot," which administers a sharp rebuke to the backside of unsuccessful firms. Managers of such firms stood to be penalized by forfeiture of deposits, reduction of income and, most importantly, loss of their jobs (Groves et al. 1993). Firms themselves failed in substantial numbers, although workers were generally protected from the worst consequences of failure. In many instances, economic pressures on firms were passed through to workers in the form of reduced incomes and, on relatively rare occasions, in open unemployment. Such mechanisms were far from perfect. There is no doubt that numerous inefficient firms continued to be propped up and sheltered from the impact of market competition. But such protection was nowhere near as complete as it had been several years previously.

4. Productivity improved. The previous sections may seem to argue that declining profitability and enterprise failure are evidence of reform success; this would be quite ironic if, as in a market economy, profitability and success reflected real productivity trends. This position can legitimately be taken, however, for there is substantial evidence that productivity increased during this period, even in the state-owned sector. Once it is recognized that state industrial profitability was initially high primarily because of large monopoly profits, it is not difficult to reconcile the evidence of declining profitability with that of increasing productivity. To be sure, erosion of monopoly profits does not necessarily lead to increasing productivity: new entrants might expend real resources simply to gain a share of a

Table 6.5 *Growth of sectoral total factor productivity*

	annual percentage grwoth 1980–1989
Food Products	2.3%
Textiles	2.5%
Chemicals	2.7%
Building materials	3.4%
Machinery	6.1%
Electronics	7.9%

Source: Groves et al. 1995.

fixed volume of monopoly rents. In this type of rent-dissipation scenario, real productivity would decline.

In fact, there is substantial evidence of improving total factor productivity. Indeed, every study that has adjusted the data to account for inflation in the price of inputs (particularly buildings) has found evidence of significant productivity improvement. Chen et al. (1988) found moderate total factor productivity improvement in state industry through 1985. Jefferson, Rawski, and Zheng (1992) found evidence of continuing productivity improvement through 1987 in both the state and urban collective industrial sectors. Jefferson (1990) reports significant productivity gain in ferrous metallurgy.

Recent work with enterprise data also supports the hypothesis of increasing total factor productivity. Table 6.5 shows estimated results for six industrial sectors (Groves et al 1995). Productivity trends differ substantially between sectors. Textiles show particularly slow growth in productivity. Overall, however, productivity improvement is strong. Indeed, productivity improvement in machinery and electronics may seem implausibly high. However, it may in fact be reasonable. Productivity improvement is being measured with reference to 1980, a difficult year for machinery producers. Moreover, the electronics industry has been converted from a military to a civilian industry in the course of the 1980s. Product mix has changed dramatically and capacity utilization has increased (Folta 1992). The poor results for textiles are compatible with the picture that emerged in Chapter 4, in which changes in the textile industry are primarily driven by attempts to capture rents maintained by tight state price controls on textile raw materials. There is substantial evidence that China's second-stage reformers have been successful, even within state industry. Thus far, available evidence strongly supports the hypothesis of changed behavior and improved performance.

Conclusion

During the second reform period, reformist leaders consciously adopted as elements of a reform strategy the characteristics that had been emerging in an unintentional manner from the first phase. The dual-track economic system, which had been born as a response to specific economic problems and situations, was embraced as a reform strategy. The defining characteristic of the dual-track approach was the coexistence of planned and market sectors that operated under different principles. It represented the abandonment – or at least deferral – of attempts to subject the entire economy to an integrated and consistent set of rules. In this context, progress in reform was identified with expansion of the area subject to market regulation, and no longer with the attempt to rationalize the control mechanisms that shaped the economy as a whole. This shift in emphasis gave the Chinese reform its distinctive character.

Second-stage reforms were internally consistent, and achieved substantial success. To some degree the coherence of the post-1984 reforms reflects a consistent approach to the reform policymaking process on the part of the key policy-maker, Premier Zhao Ziyang. Zhao approached the problem of reform in an eclectic and flexible manner. Perhaps guided by a consistent feel for the benefits of marketization and the dangers of bureaucracy, perhaps constrained by political considerations that limited his ability to impose comprehensive reform packages, Zhao tended toward a piecemeal approach to reform. In each particular issue area, Zhao pushed for adoption of quite radical reforms. But he never developed a comprehensive or integrated approach to the reform transition as a whole. Nevertheless, as reforms evolved, consistency of purpose and general approach ultimately yielded a coherent and robust program of reform.

7

Rapid growth and macroeconomic imbalance

Along with the shift in reform strategy, China's macroeconomic policy regime also shifted sharply during 1984. Credit policy became much more
expansionary – the rate of credit creation doubled – and monetary instability also increased. Expansionary monetary policy let to rapid growth of demand and an acceleration in economic growth. An extended economic boom,
particularly in industry, unfolded through the mid and late 1980s. Economic
growth interacted with reforms to create rapid structural change, and the
Chinese economy became more diverse, more open, and much bigger. But
sustained expansionary policy gradually but inexorably led to inflation. Accumulating inflationary pressures erupted during 1988 in a burst of high open
inflation. Austerity policies adopted at the end of 1988 were effective in
containing the incipient inflationary dangers, but at the same time tougher
economic policies – reinforced by renewed political conservatism – brought
an abrupt end to this period of dynamic change and growth.

The preceding chapter argued that China was successful in carrying out
reforms at the microeconomic level. Why did problems develop at the
macroeconomic level? This chapter first reviews the macroeconomic characteristics of the 1984–88 period, laying out the main patterns of growth and
inflation. Macroeconomic policy-making is then examined in greater depth.
The proximate cause of inflation is, not surprisingly, identifiable with the
overly rapid pace of credit creation. However, rapid credit creation itself
needs to be explained. I argue that the very success of microeconomic reform
undermined the traditional basis for macroeconomic policy. As the state
relaxed its monopoly control over industry, the traditional means for accumulating investment funds eroded. Government and enterprises found themselves in a financial squeeze that could only be eased by recourse to bank
credit. Unwilling to exclude any major group from the ongoing investment
boom, the government left the credit spigot open, allowing inflationary pressures to build steadily. Such failures were not inevitable, but neither were

policymakers merely foolish. Rather, the very difficult task of guiding the economy through the transition period posed major challenges to policy makers as they struggled to strengthen inadequate institutions and cope with unprecedented situations.

Rapid growth and structural change

The period 1984–88 was marked by a sharp acceleration in economic growth, particularly in industry. Between 1978 and 1983, China's GNP had grown briskly, at 7.8% annually according to official statistics (see Statistical Appendix). That growth was fairly balanced: GNP produced in agriculture grew 6.2% annually, while industrial GNP grew 7.6% annually (construction and services grew more rapidly). Between 1983 and 1988, GNP growth accelerated to a remarkable 11.5% annual rate.[1] Moreover, while agricultural growth actually decelerated slightly – to 5% annually – industrial GNP growth nearly doubled to 14.2% annually. Service sector growth also accelerated to 14% annually during this second period.

Rapid growth led to an accelerated pace of structural change. Although the agricultural labor force continued to grow throughout the 1980s, during the 1983–88 period this growth slowed to a crawl, and agriculture's share of the total labor force dropped rapidly. In the five years of rural reform between 1978 and 1983, the proportion of the total national labor force in agriculture began to decline, inching down from 71% to 67%. In the following five years, between 1983 and 1988, after the success of agricultural reforms and during a period when national policies facilitated industrial growth, the agricultural share of total labor dropped from 67% to 59%. Most of the increase in non-agricultural workers occurred in the countryside: the number of rural workers in industry, transport, construction and commerce more than doubled, from just under 30 million to 62 million, while agricultural workers increased a meagre 3.5% (*Statistics* 1991: 96,113). Indeed, while total agricultural output grew through this period, crop output barely grew at all after the bumper harvest of 1984. Total grain output reached a peak of 407 MMT in 1984 that was not reached again until 1989. Thus, most of the agricultural growth was due to rapid expansion of animal husbandry and aquaculture.

The acceleration in industrial growth was widely spread. Industrial growth rates increased for both state and collective firms. Growth of gross output doubled, from 8.3% annually in the 1978–83 period, to 17.6% in the 1983–88 period. The acceleration in state industrial growth was more modest, but still substantial: State output growth increased from 6.7% annually to 10.4% annually. For every year since 1979, collective industry growth has been more rapid than state industry growth, and the state industrial share declined from 78% in 1978 to 54% in 1990. Indeed, the most rapidly growing ownership forms were private industry and various kinds of joint ventures. These forms were non-existent in the 1970s, but have speedily become significant contributors to total industrial output. Purely private firms contributed 4.4% of industrial output in 1988. Joint ventures between different ownership types contributed 2.7% of industrial output in 1988. More than half of this was from foreign-invested enterprises.

Although state industrial growth rates have been below those of other ownership forms, they have nonetheless been substantial. A sustained annual growth rate of 10% must be considered rapid. Moreover, because the state sector accounted for such a large share of industry at the outset, state sector growth has continued to be the primary component of industrial growth overall. Between 1978 and 1983, 65% of incremental industrial output was contributed by the state sector; during 1983–88 this dropped, but only to 48%. Even in this period of extraordinary rapid growth of collective and private industries, state sector growth was contributing half of incremental output. Indeed, probably more than half if we take into consideration the state stake in various joint ventures. Moreover, as discussed in the Statistical Appendix, growth rates of collective industry are somewhat overstated due to inadequate deflation procedures. Thus, it is inappropriate to conclude that China's economy is growing only because of the vigor of the non-state sector, and in spite of the sluggishness of the state sector. Quite the contrary. China's vigorous growth performance would not have been conceivable without sustained output expansion from the state sector.

Industrial growth also comprised a broad range of sectors. Electricity output grew 9.2% annually between 1983 and 1988, and coal production at 6.5% annually. Fueled by vigorous demand from urban households, consumer goods production grew rapidly. Particularly striking is the emergence of a significant consumer durables industry. From negligible output levels in 1978, China consumer durables production in 1988 included 25 million television sets, 45 million electric fans, 7.6 million refrigerators, and 10.5 million washing machines (*Statistic* 1991: 424). A consumption revolution was taking place, particularly for urban dwellers. At the same time, the dollar value of manufactured exports grew 21% annually in current prices between 1983 and 1988 (*Statistic* 1991: 616).

Growth was fueled by a sustained investment boom. Fixed investment had been held to about 25% of GNP through 1983, but jumped to 30% by 1985, and remained over 30% through 1988 (see Figure 2.2). All sectors increased their investment. Central government investment maintained its share; rural

Table 7.1. *Inflation and change in relative prices*

	Increase in overall urban CPI	Increase in price of slowest growing CPI component	Increase in nonstaple food prices
	(annual percentage change)		
1978	0.7	0.0	2.2
1979	1.9	−0.6	3.5
1980	7.5	−4.5	14.1
1981	2.5	−2.0	3.2
1982	2.0	−2.9	−0.2
1983	2.0	−2.2	4.6
1984	2.7	−0.1	6.0
1985	11.9	1.2	23.0
1986	7.0	0.7	8.3
1987	8.8	3.2	14.9
1988	20.7	12.9	31.1
1989	16.3	13.8	13.8
1990	1.3	−4.8	−0.3
1991	5.1	−4.5	2.9
1992	8.6	−4.5	7.0

Source: Statistic 1989: 691; 1993: 243–45; 258.

and collective investment grew particularly rapidly. A substantial share of investment went to housing, and both rural and urban dwellers approximately doubled their per capita housing stock in the ten years between 1978 and 1988. Urban residents covered by the household survey increased their per capita living space from 4.2 square meters per capita in 1978 to 8.8 square meters in 1988. Rural residents live in lower quality housing, but enjoy more abundant space. This increased from 8.1 square meters in 1978 to 16.6 in 1988. (*Statistic* 1990: 719).

Inflation

Rapid growth was accompanied by a substantial increase in the rate of inflation. Consumer price inflation had been moderate through 1984, notwithstanding the brief spurt of prices during 1979–80. Beginning in 1985, inflation was consistently high, and it accelerated sharply during 1988 (Table 7.1). Inflation was accompanied by a significant realignment of consumer prices. The most important part of consumer price inflation was the increasing cost of food. Although urban food grains continued to be subsidized and supplied by the government at a controlled price, the cost of other food items skyrocketed. Immediately following the October 1984 Reform declaration, an effort was made to decontrol the price of "non-staple" foods. The most important of these non-staple foods are vegetables, poultry, eggs, and meat. Urban wage-earners were compensated with wage increases, and price restrictions were lifted at the beginning of 1985. This price reform was not entirely successful: The government became alarmed at the acceleration of inflation during 1985, and some price ceilings were reestablished by year-end. Nevertheless, the proportion of food sold at market prices increased significantly, and government subsidies for non-staple foods declined. This incident was only one episode in the long-term increase in the relative price of food. Over the entire 1978–1989 period, the price of non-staple food items more than tripled, driving a doubling of the overall urban price level. Food prices grew more rapidly than the overall price level during both post-1978 periods. Between 1978 and 1984, the urban consumer price index (CPI) increased by a cumulative 20%, while urban non-staple food prices increased by 35%. From 1984 through 1989 inflation accelerated, but the relationship between increases in the overall price level and in food prices stayed roughly constant. The 1989 urban CPI was 83% higher than in 1984, but urban non-staple food prices were 128% higher.

There were three bursts of inflation during the 1980s, and each was marked by a rapid growth in non-staple food prices. In 1980, 1985, and 1988, large increases in non-staple food prices led increases in the overall price level. During the entire period, a steadily increasing proportion of nonstaple foods has been provided through the free market. As a result, the overall increase in nonstaple food prices is composed of both the increase in the price charged by state commercial outlets and the increase in the proportion of food purchased at higher priced free markets. During each burst of food inflation, the government increased the price of food at state commercial outlets and simultaneously compensated state employees by increasing their wages. In 1979–80 and 1985, those wage increases permitted most urban employees to stay ahead of inflation, but in 1988 the modest wage adjustments were soon swamped by accelerating inflation.

If only food prices were increasing, then all of the inflation would be the result of changes in relative prices. Since it is generally recognized that the relative price of food must be raised, this would indicate that the inflation, although painful, was serving a useful economic purpose. Table 7.1 shows the increase in non-staple food prices alongside the increase in price of the component of consumer prices with the lowest inflation rate (durables or daily-use items). It can be seen that through 1986, prices were generally stable for the items with the minimum inflation rate. Indeed, through 1984, prices of these items were actually declining slightly, usually because of government-mandated reductions in controlled prices. This indicates that through 1986, nearly all the inflation experienced was an inescapable cost of the necessary realignment of relative prices. Indeed, throughout this early period, the Chinese government devoted substantial effort to matching price increases with offsetting price reductions. This effort succeeded in maintaining a low inflation rate, but at the cost of an overall slow pace of economic change. Even the simplest realignment of prices strained Chinese administrative capabilities and required elaborate political compromises before adoption.

From 1987, the relative price stability of non-food items began to change. In 1988–89, even the slowest growing component of the consumer price index increased by 13–14%. This can be taken as a rough measurement of the amount of "excess inflation" during those years. This is the amount of inflation that did not contribute anything to realignment of relative prices. The same rationalization of prices could in theory have occurred with an overall inflation rate that was thirteen or fourteen percentage points lower.

The increasing price of non-staple food in relation to manufactured goods such as textiles and consumer durables has significantly altered Chinese price relationships, bringing them more in line with world prices, and reducing the degree of discrimination against agriculture. But during this period, the government also failed to adjust some of the most important state-controlled prices. The prices of staple grains, housing, and social services all remained practically constant, despite the fact that all of these had long been controlled at extremely low levels. In the context of the overall increase in the price level, the relative price of these goods and services became even more distorted: The relative price should have been increased, but actually decreased. A kind of "reverse price reform" occurred with respect to these items. An additional result of the failure to adjust or liberalize the price of these items was that government subsidies remained large despite the reduction in subsidies for non-staple foods. This unresolved problem remained to confront policy-makers during the post-1990 period of renewed reform.

Inflation seemed to stabilize during 1986-87, and a certain amount of complacency about inflation was evident among government policy-makers during those years. However, inflationary pressures were building slowly, and a tendency toward gradually accelerating inflation (particularly in farmers' markets for food) was evident by the end of 1987 and through the first part of 1988. In the spring of 1988, state prices for several non-staple foods were increased again, and Deng Xiaoping announced that comprehensive price reform would be attempted soon. In the context of growing inflationary pressures, this announcement proved to be exceptionally ill-timed. Inflationary expectations among the population were dramatically confirmed, with serious consequences. Individuals began to engage in speculative buying, purchasing whatever they could before prices increased, while enterprises abandoned whatever price restraint they had been exercising in order to position themselves for the coming price reform. As a result, prices exploded during the summer of 1988. For three months, prices were increasing at more than a 50% annual rate. The eruption of inflation alarmed China's conservatives and unsettled the urban population, and led directly to the abrupt suspension of China's second phase of economic reforms and indirectly to the political crisis at Tiananmen square.

Overall changes in prices of producer goods followed similar trends to changes in consumer prices. In the case of producer goods, however, the situation is complicated by the coexistance of plan and market prices for most goods. China only began to compute price indices for industrial commodities in 1985, and the procedures for compiling the indices have not been studied. The available summary indices are shown in Table 7.2. They show that, like the CPI, producer goods prices surged in 1985 and then moderated in 1986–87, before increasing very rapidly during 1988–89. Subsequently, price increases slowed markedly during the 1990–91 period (see Chapter 8). The indices also show that prices of raw materials purchased by factories increased more rapidly than prices received by factories for their output in every year. This relationship reflects the impact of the dual-price system as well as changes in relative prices.

The increase in raw material prices to factories primarily reflects the growth of the dual-track system, which was most broadly applied to industrial producer goods. Unfortunately, systematic price indices for in-plan and outside-plan producer good prices are not currently available. However, some generalizations can be made on the basis of price trends for individual commodities. During 1985, the vestiges of price controls were removed from outside-plan commodities and prices rose rapidly. By the end of 1985, market prices for most standardized producer goods were typically two to three times those of the plan. From 1985 through 1987, though, many market prices stabilized. The overall price level continued to increase, but

Table 7.2. *Price indices of industrial products and raw materials*

	Raw materials purchased by factories	Ex-factory product price
	(annual percentage increase)	
1985	18.0	8.7
1986	9.5	3.8
1987	11.0	7.9
1988	20.2	15.0
1989	26.5	18.6
1990	5.6	4.1
1991	9.1	6.2
1992	11.0	6.8

Source: Price 1991: 449, 538–39; *Zhongguo Wujia* [China Price] 1992:4, p. 56; 1993:4, p. 58.

the primary cause seems to have been that an increasing share of goods were transacted at the higher market prices. The fact that market prices stabilized during this period may result from the more abundant supplies reaching the marketplace, or it may reflect some initial overshooting in market prices immediately after liberalization (Byrd 1991: 171–77). By the end of 1987, market prices for industrial raw materials were beginning to increase again, and throughout 1988, rapid increases in market prices contributed to more rapid inflation in industrial material prices overall (Li Lei *et al.* 1988; Xie and Ding 1990). Thus, market prices for industrial commodities displayed many of the same characteristics as food prices on farmers markets: They both grew more rapidly than the overall price level and they both provided sensitive indicators of the onsets of inflationary pressures. Indeed, as inflation accelerated during 1988, the same panic buying phenomena that appeared on consumer markets also appeared for some producer goods: Prices of some non-ferrous metals and light steel products doubled within a few months.

The inflation rate for industrial products at the factory gate (ex-factory prices) rose and fell in line with inflationary pressures overall, but remained lower than that of raw materials. In part, this reflects differences in sectoral composition. Raw materials include some non-industrial commodities (especially inputs into the food processing and textiles industries) for which price increases were rapid. Industrial products include a large proportion of manufactured finished goods for which price increases were quite modest, because technological progress and productivity improvement was rapid (compare column 2 of Table 7.1, composed of consumer prices of various types of manufactured goods). In this sense, the differential rate of price increases reflects the desirable realignment of prices in the economy as a whole, and indirectly the erosion of monopoly barriers that had kept the price of manufactured goods high relative to other commodities.

The higher inflation rate for purchased raw materials also reflects the increased expenditure going to commercial enterprises. In turn, part of this represents an entirely desirable reallocation of society's resources. As the clumsy material allocation system was gradually replaced by a much more responsive network of markets and middlemen, the real resources devoted to distribution of goods increased, and so did the monetary outlays made for distribution purposes. Obviously, this is reflected in the prices paid by factories for delivered goods.[2] Yet not all this differential is economically rational. Part of the differential may be due to factories selling their output at below market-clearing prices. As discussed in the previous chapter, factories may sell at lower prices in order to curry favor with bureaucrats or to generate additional profits for middlemen with whom they have links. This part of the lower rate of price increases for industrial products would simply reflect continuing distortions of the system imposed by the incomplete nature of reform.

Detailed examination of consumer and producer price trends thus produces a consistent story. In both cases, we see evidence of substantial price realignment, combined with an accelerating inflationary crisis in 1988. During that crisis, inflation became a generalized problem for the economy, and forceful stabilization measures were called for.

Income distribution

Inflationary growth reversed some of the achievements of economic reorientation in the early 1980s. Much of GNP growth was channelled into investment, the share of which in total national income increased sharply. A significant share of increased income also must have gone to an entrepreneurial minority, comprised both of independent business people and government officials who did not scruple to profit from the new opportunities present in a distorted market economy. The result was surprisingly slow growth of household income for large groups of the population. Both urban and rural households experienced a sharp slowdown in income growth during the latter part of the 1980s.

Rural incomes, according to household surveys, grew exceptionally rapidly between 1978 and 1985, increasing about 150% in real terms. But after 1985, stagnation set in, and real per capita rural incomes did not increase at all between 1985 and 1988–89. This stagnation was caused both by the slowdown in agricultural production growth after 1984 and by government price policy, which became much less solicitous of rural residents after the successes of 1983–84 seemed to promise the end of chronic agricultural problems (Sicular 1991). Overall stagnation seems to imply that increasing non-staple food prices benefited only a relatively small section of the rural population, predominantly suburban farmers who directly supplied urban markets. Conversely, farmers in more remote areas probably experienced some deterioration in incomes, and inter-regional income disparities may have increased.

Income trends for urban wage-earners were similar, but with somewhat different timing. Real urban wages grew very rapidly between 1983 and 1986, increasing a total of 33% (see Figure 3.1). This reflects both the effort to compensate urban workers for the food price increases at the beginning of 1985 and the effect of relaxing controls over bonuses and other incentive payments during that period. But after 1986, urban wage growth ceased, and real wages even dropped 5% in 1989. In essence, urban wage increases were simply swamped by accelerating inflation. This process was inevitably unfair: Workers with access to bonus income were able to protect their living standards and even achieve some real gains. Government workers, teachers, and others in not-for-profit undertakings experienced significant erosion. There is some evidence that the share of urban residents experiencing reductions in real incomes increased from 1987 through 1989. Thus, inflation was accompanied by real economic hardship for some, and by perceptions of increased unfairness.

Monetary and credit policy

It is not surprising to find that monetary policy became substantially more expansionary during the second half of the 1980s. The change is particularly evident in credit policy: Between year-end 1977 and year-end 1983, total credit had grown at 13.5% annually. Over the next four years, the pace of credit creation exactly doubled, rising to 27% annually. The growth of real GNP also accelerated (by about 50%), but considerably less than the acceleration in credit creation. This shift to an expansionary credit policy occurred quite abruptly at the end of 1984. Credit creation jumped from 13.7% in 1983 to 36.4% in 1984. This obviously excessive growth of credit was alarm-

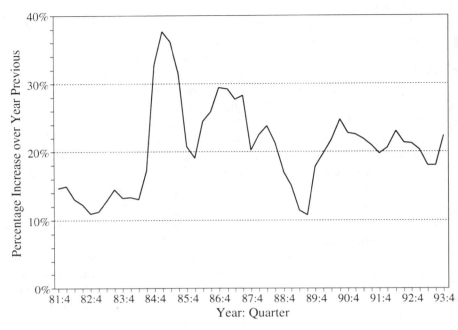

Figure 7.1. Growth of total domestic credit. Source: see Statistical Appendix.

ing to planners, and they made substantial efforts to slow the pace of credit creation over the following year. Nevertheless, they were never really successful in this effort. Between September 1984 and September 1988, the rate of credit growth never fell below 20%, and was often substantially higher (Figure 7.1 and Table 7.3).

There is little doubt that the acceleration in the rate of credit creation was the proximate cause of China's inflationary crisis of 1988. But what caused the acceleration in credit creation? Even after Chinese budgetary data are converted to conform to international conventions, budgetary deficits remained moderate throughout this period. In most years, deficits were less than 2% of GNP. The largest deficit was recorded in 1988, amounting to 2.5% of GNP. These were well below the 1979 and 1980 deficits and are quite modest by international standards. The need to cover such a deficit cannot explain the sustained rapid growth of credit. In order to explain credit policy, we first examine factors internal to the banking system, reflecting the adequacy of new institutions. Subsequently, factors external to the banking system, reflecting pressures put on the banks by economic and political conditions, are addressed.

Table 7.3. *Growth of total credit*

	September 30	Year-end
	(Percentage increase over year-previous period)	
65–78 average	–	8.4%
1979	–	10.1%
1980	–	19.6%
1981	–	14.6%
1982	13.1%	11.7%
1983	14.9%	13.7%
1984	20.9%	36.4%
1985	33.9%	23.1%
1986	26.0%	29.4%
1987	28.3%	20.2%
1988	21.3%	16.9%
1989	10.7%	17.8%
1990	24.8%	22.8%
1991	21.0%	19.7%
1992	21.3%	21.2%
1993	18.0%	22.4%

Source: Statistical Appendix.

Banking institutions

Expansionary macroeconomic policy between 1984 and 1988 occurred simultaneously with substantial reforms in the banking system. The framework for a two-tier central/commercial banking network was created in 1983 (Chapter 3). The Industrial and Commercial Bank (ICB) was created to take over the commercial bank functions of the People's Bank of China (PBC), and the PBC was to function as a central bank thereafter. It was necessary, however, to breath life into this skeletal framework, and the first steps in the change-over to a true central bank system began at the end of 1984, to take effect in 1985. To understand the change-over, we must briefly review the mechanisms through which the central bank exerted control over credit creation.

Under the old "monobank" system, lending was controlled through a system of credit quotas that were established in Beijing, and then disaggregated to local banks. Separately, targets for attracting saving deposits were also assigned to local banks. This separation was convenient for planners, who simply assigned credit quotas to accommodate planned production and investment. Local banks were little more than cashiers, channeling funds from depositors to the government and government credit allocations to specific firms and projects. Incentives were weak throughout the system. The objective of bank reform was to eliminate compulsory allocation of saving and credit resources among bank divisions of this type. Instead, each local bank was to be gradually converted into an independent commercial entity. Loanable funds would be determined by the bank's own deposits, minus some required reserves deposited with central bank authorities, plus funds loaned to the local bank by superior levels (including the central bank). As a transitional reform measure, bankers in 1983 adopted a system known as "gap" control. Under gap control, the difference (or gap) between the balance of deposits and loans outstanding in a given branch was calculated, and the branch was given the authority to make additional loans as deposits increased, so long as the gap remained unchanged.[3] This method gave branches an incentive to raise savings deposits, but was otherwise a modest step in the process of transition toward a commercial bank system.

The most important step in the change-over to a central bank/commercial bank system was set for 1985. The capital position of each of the specialized banks with the PBC was defined, and reserve ratios established for deposits in the specialized banks. Initial reserve ratios had been set at relatively high rates, but for the formal creation of the two tier banking system in 1985, reserve ratios were lowered to a uniform 10%. Interest charges were instituted on deposits and loans of specialized banks with the PBC. Thus, for the first time, local bank branches were to have assets at the PBC and liabilities to the PBC. In theory, this institutional structure would allow the PBC to conduct monetary policy with the standard tools of central banks in market economies. Credit quotas and gap control would no longer be required (although quotas were retained as an insurance policy). Central bank lending and loan rediscounting, along with manipulation of reserve ratios, could be used to determine aggregate credit supply. However, during the initial change-over at the end of 1984, mistakes were made in the design of policy that led to the collapse of control over credit at the end of 1984.

During 1984, the central bank announced that the pending definition of local bank assets and liabilities would be based on the loans and deposits that each branch bank had at the end of 1984. This created a very large incentive for local branches to expand lending as much as possible, since loans outstanding at the end of 1984 would become the assets of that particular branch. The unprecedented nature of the incentives uncovered a flaw in the method of gap control that had remained implicit under the old system. Under gap control local banks had the authority to expand lending without limit, so long as they could ensure that the receipts from the loans were deposited in the local branch (since both deposits and loans would increase by the same amount, the gap would not change). The money multiplier was not defined. Under normal conditions, the perverse incentives to lend were not too serious, because banks would realize that the loans made would eventually be paid out (so the increase in deposits would be only temporary). But at the end of 1984, banks had a one-time only opportunity to expand lending on the basis of a merely temporary increase in deposits. Thereafter, the loans created would be their assets, and the subsequent reduction in deposits would force them to recall loans only to the extent that required reserves fell below statutory minimums.

Local banks responded with a flood of credit, clearly visible in Figure 7.1. Local bank officials were drawn by the one-time opportunity to expand bank assets, and encouraged by local government officials eager to show that the new reform policies were accelerating economic growth. In the countryside, the Rural Credit Cooperatives (RCCs) normally reduced lending at year-end as farmers repaid loans at the end of the agricultural production cycle. In 1984, RCCs rushed to reloan those funds to rural enterprises. RCC loans outstanding doubled compared with year-end 1983, and the proportion of RCC deposits reloaned locally jumped from 34% to 57% in a single year. State banks and RCCs together increased total credit by a whopping 35% during 1984.

Policymakers knew that this was a dangerously rapid rate of credit creation, and they worked hard to reduce credit growth in subsequent years. Credit quotas were reimposed, and an uneasy compromise was worked out in which local banks were subject to a dual constraint: Their lending was to be controlled within the quotas, and they could also only loan funds they had available. From a macroeconomic standpoint, one of these control mechanisms would be redundant; individual banks, however, might be restrained by either one. As a transitional device, a dual system of controls might be considered a reasonable compromise.

Setting a reasonable growth rate of credit was difficult under any circumstances. It was particularly difficult for macroeconomic planners to know which indicators they should monitor in assessing credit policy. The economy was changing rapidly, and progressive monetization (particularly in rural areas) was raising demand for money. Socialist economists had been accustomed to a few simple "rules of thumb" to determine money demand. The most common one had been the ratio of money supply to total retail sales. But rapid growth of money demand since the beginning of reform had con-

founded analysts in the banking system. During the early 1980s, bank economists had repeatedly warned that overly rapid increase of the money supply
was leading to an inflationary disaster, but their warnings had repeatedly
been proven unfounded (Liu Hongru 1982). Thus, by the mid-1980s, with
the economy growing rapidly and inflation seemingly under control, it was
difficult for advocates of more cautious policies to gain a hearing. Moreover,
other technical problems – such as changing seasonality of credit in an industrializing economy – challenged bank planners.

Despite these problems, banking reform continued to make progress.
Local banks in the aggregate possessed substantial excess reserves with the
central bank. That is, they formally had sufficient capital available to make
additional loans. Some portion of excess reserves were held so that local
banks would have funds available when payments became due: Given the
traditional slowness and inefficiency of the banking system, these were
initally large and could be expected to decline. Some local banks could not
locate good lending opportunities or were constrained by lending quotas.
While required reserves were 10% of total deposits, the specialized banks at
the end of 1985 had more than twice that much on deposit at the central
bank, so that excess reserves were 11.56% of deposits. However, excess
reserves declined steadily, and amounted to only 6.4% of deposits in October
1987 (Zhu Pingxiang 1988). The rapid draw-down of reserves contributed to
rapid credit growth. The interbank lending market expanded quickly between 1986 and 1988, providing new lending opportunities. It is possible
that local banks improved efficiency more quickly than macroeconomic planners expected, and drew down excess reserves at the PBC more quickly than
anticipated. This would have raised the money multiplier and contributed to
an excess rate of credit creation.

Progress in banking reform has also been limited by the dependence of
local bank branches on local political leaders. Provincial bank branches are
strongly influenced by the wishes of party leaders and planners at the
provincial level. This influence has many sources. Occasionally it stems
from the extra-legal authority enjoyed by local power-holders, and frequently from the authority over personnel decisions and infrastructure development that local leaders enjoy. Of even greater importance than these
semi-coercive relations, however, is the simple fact that local banks are
involved in a long-term collaboration with local planners, the ultimate intention of which is to accelerate economic development in that locality. Continued price distortions make it impossible for banks to base lending purely on
profitability considerations, and they naturally look to local planning com-

missions for guidance on the priority sectors for development. It is thus inconceivable that local banks could be truly independent of local authorities under present conditions.[4] Local authorities naturally push for more lending, especially since the benefits of the loans accrue entirely to their locality, while the associated costs – excess demand and inflation – spill over to other localities. Thus, to overcome this built-in tendency at the local level to expand lending, central leaders must be willing to hold the line with tough restrictive credit policies. In practice, however, they have rarely been able to do so.

The state budget and the investment plan

In earlier sections of this book, macroeconomic policy – on both the supply and demand sides – was treated as an exogenous force that shaped the environment in which reform unfolded. Shifts in macro policy were themselves frequently compelled by challenges to the economy over which policymakers had little control, but reform in the system did not in itself cause substantial changes in the overall macroeconomy. Causation ran from macro policy to reform policy, rather than the reverse. During the second period of reform, the situation changed radically. Increasingly, changes in the economy that were themselves the result of economic reforms shaped macroeconomic conditions. Both the successes and the shortcomings of the reform process fundamentally altered macroeconomic balances in the economy, creating new stresses and opportunities. The cumulative impact of these large-scale changes was such that the banking system was under substantial external pressure to increase credit. The most important external factor was the steady erosion of government financial resources, which forced authorities to have recourse to the banking system.

The changing role of the state budget

The weight of budgetary revenue in GNP has declined rapidly and steadily since 1978.[5] In that year, budgetary revenues amounted to 35% of GNP, a level far above that of other low-income countries, but below that of the European centrally planned economies, which typically have budgetary shares of national income above 50%. The share of budgetary revenue declined to about 20% of GNP by 1988, a level only slightly above the average 19% recorded both for other low-income countries and lower middle-income countries in 1987. The expenditure comparison is even more striking:

Table 7.4. *Evolution of budgetary revenues (percentage of GNP)*

	1978	1988
Total revenues	35.4	19.8
of which (subsidies)	(4.2)	(5.4)
Extra-budgetary revenues	9.7	16.8
Budgetary plus extra-budgetary revenues	46.1	36.6

Source: Statistic 1989: 28, 657, 672, 674; Wang Chaocai and Luo Wenguang 1989.

China's total fiscal outlays in 1988 amounted to 21.7% of GNP, compared to 21.6% for low-income and 25.5% for lower middle income countries. China's budget deficit – 1.9% of GNP – is therefore considerably smaller than the average of lower and lower-middle income countries, which are 2.7% and 6.4% of GNP, respectively (World Bank 1989: 184). It must be considered peculiar, at the very least, that China's socialist economy is characterized by a smaller government budget than most developing countries, nearly all of which are market economies. China's budgetary authorities undeniably play a more important role in the economy than the direct comparison indicates, since they establish the rules for many categories of expenditure which are not funded by fiscal outlays. One of the largest of these is social security expenditures. In contrast to the practice in most countries, the bulk of these outlays are not included in the Chinese budget. The comparison with other developing countries is designed to show that the changes in the size of China's government budget are comparable in size to the difference that separates the qualitatively different economic systems of centrally planned and market economies.

Overall trends in fiscal revenue have been quite consistent since 1978, and therefore a simple comparison of 1978 and 1988 displays the main features of change (Table 7.4). Total revenues declined by 15.6% of GNP if subsidies are included, or 16.8% if subsidy outlays are netted out. At the same time, extra-budgetary revenues, primarily controlled by enterprises, increased by about 7% of GNP. These dramatic changes in fiscal revenues are closely linked to the sectoral incidence of taxation in China. As described earlier, in 1978, before the initiation of reform, industrial revenues accounted for 75% of budgetary revenues. We have also described the dramatic decline in industrial profits that occurred due to the impact of increased entry and competition in the industrial sector. Indeed, Figure 6.4 showed graphically the

Table 7.5. *Evolution of budgetary expenditures (percentage of GNP)*

	1978	1988
Fixed Capital	14.4	5.4
Working capital	1.9	0.1
Military	4.7	1.6
Civilian current	10.4	9.2
Subsidies	4.2	5.4
Total outlays	35.4	22.1
Deficit	0	1.9

Source: Statistic 1989: 28, 657, 672, 674; Wang Chaocai and Luo Wenguang 1989.

reduction in profit remitted to the budget by modern industry. The total reduction through 1988 amounted to 14% of GNP – the bulk of the reduction in total budgetary revenues. Moreover, most of this reduction (9% of GNP) was due to the overall reduction in industrial profits. Profit retention by the enterprises accounted for a maximum of 3% of GNP, and was thus a secondary factor in the overall decline of budgetary revenues.

Budgetary expenditures

The decline in revenues has been matched by a decline in three types of budgetary expenditures: fixed capital investment, allocations for working capital, and military spending. These three components together accounted for 21% of GNP in 1978 and only 7.1% of GNP in 1988, for a net reduction of 12.9 percentage points. Current civilian outlays, net of subsidies, declined quite modestly from 10.4% to 9.3% of GNP. Among current expenses, outlays for health and education grew from 3.1% of GNP to 3.4% of GNP. These changes are summarized in Table 7.5.

The sharp reduction in budgetary outlays for investment kept the overt fiscal deficit under control. Yet the central government was not actually willing to abandon its investment plan. Quite the contrary, as we saw in Chapter 5, consensus on the need for a continued investment plan was part of the package that allowed second-stage reforms to go ahead. In fact, central government investment actually grew as a share of GNP between 1981 and 1987, while budgetary financing declined. The inevitable result was a resort to the banking system to provide credit for the investment program. These trends are summarized in Figure 7.2. The line marked budgetary shows

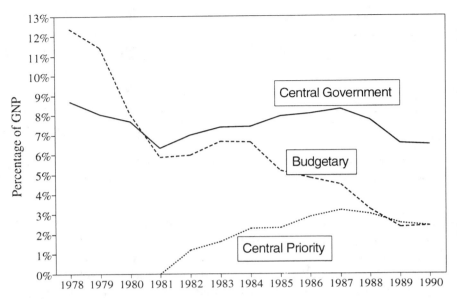

Figure 7.2. Central government investment. Source: *Fixed Investment* 1949–1985: 64, 219; 1986–1987: 68, 172, 255; 1988–1989: 60, 162, 242. *Zhongguo Jiben Jianshe* 1983:3, pp. 21–22; *Zhongguo Touzi yu Jianshe* 1991:4, p. 18.

completed investment funded by the government budget, or by foreign capital borrowed by the national government (*tongjie tonghuan*). Investment funded by the budget plunged between 1979 and 1981, dropping from 11% to 6% of GNP. Thereafter it remained at a plateau for four years, actually increasing slightly through 1984. From 1985, it resumed a steady decline, dropping to under 3% of GNP by 1989. Only one-quarter as much investment (scaled to GNP) was funded by fiscal authorities in 1989 as in 1978. This includes both central and local budgets, but traditionally most budgetary investment was carried out by the central government: 68% in 1987 and as much as 80% in earlier years (Lardy 1978: 72). Thus, most of the decline in budgetary investment was in fact a decline in central government budgetary investment.

In spite of this, actual investment included in the central government plan did not display the same pattern. The line labeled "central government" shows the sum of completed investment in capital construction and technical renovation investment projects that are included in the central government plan.[6] While the central plan did decline by more than two percentage points of GNP between 1978 and 1981, it subsequently began to increase again, and increased to above 8% of GNP in 1986 and 1987. While centrally planned investment overall was increasing by not quite two percentage points, the priority investment plan increased from nothing to over 3% of GNP in 1987. Thus, all of the increase in the size of the central investment plan was accounted for by the initiation of the priority investment plan described in Chapter 3 (pp. 133–135).

Putting these two trends together, we can see that throughout the 1980s, the central government had direct control over a shrinking proportion of the economy's resources. However, the government was not doing less. Quite the contrary, the government was doing more. Resources were mobilized into the priority investment program, and this swelled the proportion of actual resources under the control of planners. Alternately stated, in 1978–79 the central investment plan was fully funded from the budget. During 1981–84, around 60% of the plan was funded. Beginning in 1985, a renewed steady erosion took place, and the share funded declined from 46% to 22%. The share of GNP going to the central investment plan increased, but the share of this that the government could actually pay for declined sharply. Inevitably, in order to fund this deficit, the government turned to the banking system for additional credit supplies.

If we think of the central plan as a mandated use of resources, it is clear that its implementation without budgetary funding involves some kind of borrowing of funds. Funding is either provided directly by the banking system, or the government taps the total pool of saving in some other way. A rough measure of government borrowing for the central investment plan can be taken by subtracting funded investment from completed investment in the plan. That sum grows from zero in 1978 to 5.2% of GNP in 1988 (see Statistical Appendix). The actual funding requirements are somewhat larger than this, because funding is needed for expenses that do not end up as completed investment, and investment is growing steadily so that funding in a given year is always larger than investment completed in that year. Historically, it appears that funding requirements run at about 140% of the value of completed investment, so actual funding requirements in 1988 might be about 7% of GNP. Total credit creation jumped about 8% of GNP to around 15% annually after 1984. Thus, nearly all the increase in the pace of credit creation was required to accommodate the increased demands of the central investment plan. The increased burden of the unfunded central investment plan would have crowded out decentralized borrowing and spending if the pace of credit creation had remained unchanged. In order to accommodate the growth of the central plan, total credit creation had to accelerate.

Deficit

It is in this context that we should examine the Chinese budget deficit. Computed according to internationally comparable procedures, the deficit hovered around 2% of GNP during the late 1980s, which is not particularly large. However, a broader definition of central government borrowing requirements provides more information about the underlying fiscal stance of the central government. In this broad definition, central government borrowing requirements in 1988 are defined as the sum of the budget deficit (1.9% of GNP) and the additional funding requirements of the central government investment plan (5.2% of GNP at a minimum). Total central government borrowing requirements in 1988 thus amounted to 7.1% of GNP, and this relatively large figure begins to explain some of the inflationary pressures that have been evident in China in recent years. It should be stressed that there should be no presumption that these borrowing requirements are best set at zero. Quite the contrary, given China's high household saving rate, there are substantial resources available for the government to tap. The crucial task is to devise appropriate financial mechanisms to allow the government access to a sufficient amount of voluntarily supplied national saving, while still leaving enough saving in the pool to be tapped by other investors. Sustained growth requires uninterrupted access to China's abundant pool of national saving both by the central government and by local and private investors.

Expanded credit to state enterprises

At the beginning of the reform process, state firms had very few external liabilities. As might be expected, given their roles as "cash cows," state industrial firms relied primarily on the government for investment funds, which were granted costlessly. State industrial enterprises owed banks a sum of money equal to only about 11% of their book value (depreciated fixed capital plus the value of all inventories). During the reform years, the enterprises have become increasingly dependent upon bank funds for investment of all kinds. Counting inventory as well as fixed capital investment, the banking system has provided the large majority of new investments. By 1988, external liabilities were about 45% of the book value of state industrial enterprises. These firms are becoming increasingly "leveraged."

In itself, there is nothing alarming about this process. Indeed, it is a necessary and positive concomitant of the increase in household saving. As households deposit more money in the bank, and the bank loans those funds to state firms, financial development, or intermediation, proceeds. Households become, through the banks, the ultimate owners of a large piece of "state-owned" industry. The degree of leverage of Chinese firms is about the same as that for U.S. manufacturing corporations, and substantially below that in Japan, Korea, or Taiwan. However, lending to state firms remained high despite the steady erosion of state firm profitability. The proportion of total investment going to state firms remains stubbornly high, much higher than their share in industrial output. Moreover, we simply do not know how much bank lending is going to prop up the least efficient state firms, and how much is being made as a legitimate investment in the future. The banking system has not achieved commercial independence, so their loan decisions must reflect political pressures to subsidize inefficient producers. The pressure to loan to state firms must be added to the pressure to loan to the government investment program. The banking system is under constant external pressure to provide a steady stream of credit to the state sector. The inability to maintain control over the pace of credit creation between 1984 and 1988 must be seen in the light of this external pressure.

The difficulty of contractionary policies

The difficulty in developing a stable macroeconomic policy became apparent during two attempts to reign in credit growth and implement a period of macroeconomic austerity. The first of these attempts came in late 1985-early 1986 and the second at the end of 1987. In both cases, macroeconomic indicators were sufficient to convince China's leaders that austerity policies were needed; yet in both cases, those policies were abandoned when they began to bite into economic growth. In this section we examine why it was so difficult for planners to develop credible contractionary policies.

The first episode of contractionary policy was begun in mid-1985 and ratified by the Party Congress in October 1985. The loss of control over credit at the end of 1984 was obvious and the leadership was quite concerned. At first, this policy simply served to sop up excess liquidity: Enterprise bank balances were at record highs, and through most of 1985 the new contractionary policy had relatively little impact on production, because enterprises were simply drawing down excess bank balances. By the end of 1985, however, enterprises were beginning to be squeezed by a difficulty in obtaining access to bank credits. Difficulties in funding purchases of needed inputs surfaced, and industrial growth rates slowed drastically, becoming slightly negative in the first months of 1986. During April 1986, Premier Zhao Ziyang intervened to reverse the contractionary policy. Since he did not have the authority to unilaterally reverse party policy, he adopted a circumlocution: The policy would continue to be contractionary, but would be modified to allow "flexibility within contraction" (*jinzhong youhuo*). In practice, bank credits once again increased rapidly. (Figure 7.1).

The second episode of contractionary policies was initiated in the fourth quarter of 1987. Rather than simply reducing credit quotas, banking officials announced ten coordinated policy measures designed to reduce the overall growth of money and credit. Reserve requirements were raised from 10% to 12%, thus shrinking the money multiplier; the interest rate the PBC charged the specialized banks was raised to 7.2% from a previous range of 4.68% to 6.84%; and 5 billion *yuan* in excess reserves maintained at the PBC by the Rural Credit Cooperatives were temporarily converted into required reserves. At the same time, some credit quotas were tightened, specifically through the requirement that lending to rural enterprises be frozen at the levels prevailing at the end of the third quarter of 1987. Overall, the policy displayed a new sophistication in the implementation of monetary policy (Zhou Zhengqing 1987). However, once again, the policy was short-lived. In February 1988, Premier Zhao Ziyang once again intervened to relax credit policy. The timing was particularly ominous, since in the same month the annual increase in the CPI poked above 10% for the first time since 1985, and the conditions were thus created for the inflationary crisis of 1988.

Why were these two attempts at monetary austerity abandoned? The short-run problem was not that monetary policy was ineffective. Rather it was that severe short-run austerity policies caused contractions in output that were more severe than the leadership was willing to countenance. In part, this was because the economic cost of contractionary policies was increased because of the limited role played by interest rates (credit quotas played the most important role). When interest rates fluctuate, the market automatically discriminates between producers on the basis of their ability to pay higher prices for capital, which ensures that within any given sector, less productive enterprises are most likely to reduce production. Without the automatic discrimination of high interest rates, even efficient producers are likely to be hurt by credit cutbacks. Agriculture and rural enterprises are both highly influenced by credit policy, since both have hard budget constraints. Agriculture, handicapped by the continuing influence of low state-set prices, particularly for grain, is highly dependent on provision of subsidized credit for the purchase of agricultural inputs. State efforts to shield agriculture from the impact of contractionary policies by setting separate quotas for agriculture lending are rarely entirely successful.

In 1985, the imposition of a tight credit policy caused a dramatic decline in demand for fertilizer, a decline that was in turn implicated in the poor showing of agriculture in that year. More than a third of fertilizer production in 1985 – some 22 million tons – piled up in warehouses because the credit crunch prevented farmers from making purchases (Zhang Yu'an 1988). Similarly, demand for trucks, simple machinery, and some consumer durables is quite sensitive to credit availability (*Economic* 1987: V-36).

The bulk of credit is extended to state-run enterprises, which are highly "leveraged" – that is, they are highly dependent on bank credit for their working capital needs. This implies that they should be very responsive to changes in the availability of such credit, and this is in fact the case. However, the nature of their response is not necessarily what is desired by macroeconomic planners. While highly dependent on bank credit for working capital, Chinese enterprises, as we have seen, also retain substantial funds for their own use. These funds are primarily used either for fixed investment in the enterprise itself, or for provision of bonuses and benefits to workers. Enterprises almost never use their own retained funds to finance working capital, preferring to rely on the banks for these funds. Needless to say, enterprises have a strong interest in maximizing internal investment to ensure long-run growth and in keeping bonuses and benefits high to keep workers happy. (Indeed, these goals are the basis of the interest in profit that is in turn the main accomplishment of enterprise reform.)

By contrast, working capital (financing of inventories) is a requirement of current production activity. Without major improvements in enterprise efficiency – unlikely in the short run – a certain normal level of inventories is necessary to ensure regular production. In the short run, a reduction in bank credit would require enterprises to shift funds away from their investment and bonus funds in order to maintain current levels of production. However, enterprises resist this transfer of funds, and with good reason. Bank credits to fund inventories are relatively cheap, because real interest rates are low. But if enterprise funds are used to finance inventories, those funds will in all likelihood be permanently lost to the enterprise. Once they are tied up in financing inventories, the enterprise is unlikely to gain access to them again. As a result, the enterprise has an interest in defending its retained funds, while allowing production to suffer as a result of input shortages. The decline in production can be blamed on adverse national credit policy. That allows enterprises to maintain control over their existing retained funds, and even appeal for more lenient financial treatment since their difficulties are created by national policy, not by their own mistakes in production.

Such behavior reflects a short time horizon. If enterprises face "hard" budget constraints, and can draw retained funds only according to some fixed proportion to actual profitability, current production reductions will translate into future reductions in retained funds. But in order for enterprises to adopt a longer-run perspective, they must believe that their future retained funds will actually be affected by a slower growth (or decline) of output. That is, both contractionary credit policies and enterprise incentive rules must be credible in order for contractionary policies to have the desired effect. If enterprises believe either that contractionary policies are likely to be short-lived, or that they can revise incentive provisions ex post to compensate for short-term reductions in profitability, they will have a strong incentive to attempt to wait out contractionary policies. It is in the interest of enterprises to wait and see, keeping their own funds in reserve, and hoping they can ride out the short-term disturbances to business as usual.

If contractionary monetary policy is to alleviate inflationary pressures, it must reduce aggregate demand more than it reduces supply. But if enterprises behave in the short-sighted way described in the last paragraph, the opposite will be the case in the short run. Demand for investment and consumption goods emanating from the enterprise will be unchanged even as production declines. According to some Chinese economists, this is precisely what happened in the early months of 1986. Even as industrial output declined, and a widespread credit crunch proclaimed, total bonus payments continued to expand (Song Guoqing and Zhang Weiying 1986). If monetary policy is not credible in the long run, it will not work in the short run. In the Chinese case, in which contractionary policies were twice abandoned in mid-course, establishing that credibility would be an extremely difficult task. In fact, in both the 1985–86 and the 1987–88 episode, credit restraint caused surprisingly rapid slowdowns in industrial growth. Interpretation of the episodes was therefore controversial among Chinese economists. One school focused on the short-run costs and argued that credit was excessively tight; another group focused on the short duration of credit restraint and argued that it had not been given sufficient time to have effect. In a sense, both were right. The fundamental problem was that in the semi-reformed economy, the short-run costs of credit restraint were exceptionally high. As a result, credit restraint was not sustained, and the lack of credibility raised the short-run costs for the next episode.

The crisis of 1988

Accelerating inflation through the early months of 1988 led to widespread incidents of panic buying during the summer of 1988. Ironically, panic buying was stimulated by statements by Deng Xiaoping and Zhao Ziyang indicating that rapid price reform would be attempted. The Chinese people interpreted these statements to mean that prices would be sharply increased. Residents drew down savings accounts and began stockpiling goods, further contributing to inflationary pressures. For a few months in the summer of 1988, inflation spiraled up to annual rates approaching 50%. With confidence in economic policy crumbling, Zhao Ziyang was pushed aside and hardliners led by Li Peng and Yao Yilin assumed direct management of the economy. They initiatied tough economic austerity measures designed to control inflation: This marked the beginning of hard-line dominance of economic policy.[7]

Zhao was vulnerable because of the breakdown of a tacit political consensus that had marked Deng Xiaoping's policies through the 1980s. Deng had always promised economic reform and improved living standards, with modest liberalization but without democratization. Through most of the 1980s, the bulk of China's urban dwellers, including most intellectuals, accepted this implicit bargain, in part because their options were so much worse. But the implicit promise of steady economic improvement broke down in 1988. Accelerating inflation in 1988 cast into doubt for the first time the likelihood that most urban dwellers would experience steady increases in real incomes. Indeed, after increasing almost a third between 1983 and 1986, real wages stagnated through 1988. With the onset of economic austerity policies, real incomes began to decline at the beginning of 1989. At the same time, urban residents saw the reforms stalling, an unpopular new leadership, and pervasive corruption. Meanwhile, the political liberalization that had occurred simultaneously with the economic boom was changing the rules that governed Chinese society. In this context, the political protests by Beijing students in Tiananmen Square, beginning in April 1989, met with enthusiastic support from a broad range of urban residents. It was not only that economic pain intensified political discontent, but also that with economic benefits uncertain, the sense of an implicit bargain was undermined and there was no longer any reason to restrain political demands.

Conversely, China's hardliners had been willing to acquiesce in economic reform if it didn't create economic disorder or threaten Communist Party political control. Since 1984 the hardliners had stayed on the sidelines, occasionally sniping at reformist economic policies but not presenting determined opposition. But hardliners now found that their fundamental doubts about radical reform were converted into actual opposition. The inflationary episode was seen by the Communist Party oligarchs as the outcome of serious policy errors by Zhao Ziyang, and his power was sharply curtailed. For the Party elders, inflation was also a metaphor for the chaos they saw growing in China, as new groups were establishing claims on economic resources and voicing new political opinions. To these elders, Zhao Ziyang had permitted an unacceptable escalation in both political and economic demands. When students went out on the streets, the stage was set for a bitter conflict between these two sides.

From a comparative perspective, China's performance with respect to inflation has not been bad. By international standards, China's inflation rate has been low to moderate over the whole period of reform, and there has been nothing in China like the uncontrolled inflations that gripped Poland and other eastern European countries, including the Soviet Union. Nevertheless, the bout of inflation led to a profound crisis for the Chinese regime and for the entire reform program. A new hardline leadership was given effective control over economic policy, and they quickly introduced an austerity program of remarkable strictness. Thus political pressures from the top not only downgraded the primary architect of the Chinese reform strategy, they also forced a turn away from the market growth-oriented reform strategy that had prevailed up to that time. Inflation brought China's first decade of reform to an end, and ushered in a hiatus in the progress of reform overall. Nevertheless, when one examines the inflation in the context of the progress in economic reform and the economic growth that occurred between 1984 and 1988, it is clear that the achievements far outweigh the failures. That one of those failures, the inflationary outbreak, was sufficient to bring down Zhao Ziyang only shows how narrow his margin of error had been all along.

Phase three

To a market economy

8

The post-Tiananmen cycle of retrenchment and renewed reform

The events at Tiananmen Square in June 1989 marked a watershed in China's political evolution and in the world's perception of China. Ending a period of gradual liberalization and inaugurating one of renewed political repression, Tiananmen shattered the benevolent image of steady progress that the Chinese government had presented to the world. The hardliners who consolidated their power around the Tiananmen incident initially attempted to roll back both economic reforms and political liberalization. During 1989, they began to carry out a program of recontrol of the economy that would have reversed many of the achievements of the previous decade of economic reform. But this program failed. As failure became evident, the hardline leadership backed away from the main elements of the program of recontrol and then gradually discarded it. By late 1990, a renewed search for practical reform measures was evident, and the momentum of reform accelerated through 1992. The years 1992–93 emerged as a new period of significant reform, and the achievement was punctuated by the implementation of important reforms on January 1, 1994. In the economic arena, then, Tiananmen did not mark a sustained shift to more conservative policies. Instead, it merely touched off one more cycle of retrenchment followed by renewed growth and reform. By the end of 1993, dramatic advances in reform had occurred, and economic growth had accelerated to new peaks. Indeed, a number of the politically most difficult reforms that had been stumbling blocks in the past were successfully adopted during this period. The dramatic successes were clouded only by the revival of inflation, which made the prospects for rapid implementation of further reforms uncertain.

The post-Tiananmen cycle was probably the last of this specific type of policy cycle. After Tiananmen and the purge of many leading reformers, the economic conservatives at last had a free hand to impose their policies, and it turned out that they had no real solutions to offer. The 1989–90 period was the last time that a significant group in the Chinese leadership could plausibly argue that China needed a strengthening of the traditional planning apparatus, the last time that a necessary program of macroeconomic austerity was systematically packaged with measures to restrict marketization. After the hardline program failed, it was abandoned with remarkable thoroughness. The failure of the hardline program made it clear that there was no alternative to a market economy, and no coherent way to combine the market with remnants of the old planning system over the long run. In October 1992, the Fourteenth Party Congress declared that the objective of reform was a "socialist market economy." It was the first time that the leadership had committed itself unambiguously to transition to a market economy. At the same time, China began to dismantle the old planning system, systematically cutting back on compulsory allocation and price controls. The strategy of "growing out of the plan" had reached its logical conclusion, and the objective of reform was shifting to dismantling the plan and creating a well-functioning market economy. In that respect, the post-Tiananmen period was another familiar policy cycle, but also the beginning of an entirely new period.

The last stand of the economic conservatives

Rise of the hardline faction

After the Tiananmen crisis was settled by military force, the hardliners were in a position to impose their policies across the board. With Zhao Ziyang out of the way, the most important economic policymaker was the Premier Li Peng. An engineer by training, Li approached economic problems with conservative instincts, but without any discernable ideological position or vision. After Tiananmen, Li made common cause with the more ideologically committed conservatives such as Yao Yilin, and attempted to reimpose strict controls on the economy. This meant an attempt to intensify the macroeconomic austerity policies already adopted, but also to go beyond the austerity policies to an explicit attempt to recentralize the economic system. A special Party meeting in November 1989 produced a manifesto for these policies, the "Thirty-Nine Points." This manifesto called for a period of economic rectification lasting at least three years, from 1989 through 1991. For the rectification period, conservatives put forward an internally consistent program to recontrol the economy. This program had three main goals: macroeconomic austerity, recentralization and strengthened planning, and preferential policies for state-owned industry. Together, these programs implied a significant rollback of economic reform.

The hardliners had interpreted the inflationary outbreak as a symptom of more fundamental problems. According to the Thirty-Nine Points: "Our present economic difficulties are conspicuously evident in worsening inflation, overall imblances, irrational economic structure and chaotic economic procedures. These difficulties did not just emerge suddenly in the last year or two; they are a concentrated reflection of deep-rooted problems that have accumulated over many years" (CCP 1990: 25). Conservatives proclaimed a profound economic crisis, a crisis that served to justify their proposed resumption of central control. They saw deep-rooted structural imbalances: bottlenecks in the supply of energy, transport, and basic raw materials created by overly rapid growth of manufacturing; an agricultural sector seen as weakened by the outflow of labor to rural industry. To the conservatives, both the macroeconomic and the structural imbalances were caused by a loss of control over the economy. In other words, conservatives saw in 1988–89 many of the same problems that had been evident at the beginning of reform in 1978. Seeing the same problems, they pulled out the same solutions, and proclaimed a three-year rectification of the economy, similar to the reorientation of 1979–81. But if the conservatives had forgotten nothing about the economic crises of the past, it soon became apparent that they had also learned nothing from the economic successes of the 1980s. For the hardline analysis was fundamentally mistaken. While macroeconomic restraint was necessary to control inflation, the Chinese economy was much healthier overall than they supposed, and it was capable of recovery and vigorous growth without a prolonged rectification program. Instead of being the beginning of a new era, the Thirty-Nine Points turned out in retrospect to be only the furthest swing of the pendulum, and the retreat from the hardline agenda began soon after the November 1989 meeting.

Macroeconomic austerity

Macroeconomic austerity was given the highest priority, not only because of the need to control inflation but also because of concern over China's foreign economic relations. China had run a large trade deficit at the end of 1988 – roughly $1 billion a month – as imports were stepped up to tame inflationary pressures. But after June 4, an international credit embargo was slapped on China, and leaders wary of appearing vulnerable to credit sanctions were anxious to eliminate trade deficits by reducing domestic demand. Tight quotas were placed on fixed investment and credit growth. Wage increases were held down substantially below the rate of inflation. Some macroeconomic levers were employed – interest rates on loans and savings deposits were raised – but planners did not hesitate to use any weapon in their arsenal. Price controls were reestablished and strengthened on a range of consumer and producer goods, and further price liberalization was put on hold.

A sharp deceleration in the growth of bank credit was caused by the imposition of strict quantitative quotas on credit. Between the end of September 1988 and the end of September 1989, total credit grew only 10.6%, down from a 27% average increase in the preceding four years. Because the overall price level at year-end 1988 was already 30% above that of a year previously, this was a very sharp contraction in real credit availability. Interest rates were pushed up sharply. Indexed savings deposits were introduced, in which the interest rate equaled the inflation rate of the preceding year. Interest rates on ordinary loans were increased in two stages from 7.9% to 11.3%, while the highest interest rate, that on multi-year fixed investment loans, reached 19%. While such rates were initially below the inflation rate, real interest rates became positive as inflation subsided. The growth of worker wages was held down substantially below the rate of inflation. Real state wages in 1989 were 4.6% below those in 1988 (Figure 3.1). Thus, standard macroeconomic policy instruments were used to cool off the economy.

Price controls were reimposed on some consumer goods. Table A.1 showed that the proportion of total retail sales transacted at state fixed and guidance prices declined steadily through 1988, but that this trend was halted and slightly reversed in 1989–90. After increasing to almost 50% of retail sales, market price transactions fell back to about 45% in 1990. Informal controls were intensified as well. In many cities, producers were required to report increases in market prices to local price bureaus, which could refuse to approve them. The local rate of inflation was made an important performance indicator for local officials, so price increases were often rejected. One city, Harbin, received favorable national publicity for controlling 383 categories of consumer goods prices (Interview 89p84; 89p47).

Tight controls were put on fixed investment. The total value of fixed investment spending in 1989 was supposed to remain constant at the 1988 level, but controls were imposed so strictly that the nominal value of fixed investment actually declined 8% in 1989, and even in 1990 remained slightly below the level of 1988. Total fixed investment plummeted from 32% of GDP in 1988 to 25% in 1990. Investment quotas were established for each province, and provincial leaders were made personally responsible for seeing that they were respected. All investment projects were required to have approval at either the provincial or national level. With these controls in place, demand for both investment and consumption dropped, and inflationary pressures eased.

Strengthening planning

Conservatives reemphasized the 1984 slogan that China was a "socialist planned commodity economy," but the stress was now on the word "planned" and the fact that China was not an unfettered market economy. Conservatives began to see merit in the idea of a state-controlled market, though they had never actually endorsed the idea in the past. They pushed for the adoption of an "industrial policy" as the specific charter for state steerage of the market, in an attempt to modernize planning and focus government resources on priority sectors (State Council 1989). The industrial policy stressed energy and transportation, but also materials industries such as steel and chemicals, as well as agriculture. It was thus strikingly similar to the priorities of the old command economy development strategy. Conservatives argued that sectoral policies were both more rational and more fair than the regional policies associated with Zhao Ziyang (the coastal development strategy). Investment quotas established for macroeconomic purposes were used to channel investment to the state sector and to the priority sectors under government industrial policy. The state share of fixed investment increased from 61% to 66% between 1988 and 1990. Particular priority was given to energy investment, which increased 31% over 1988. As a result, energy investment accounted for an unprecedented 47% of state industrial investment in 1990. Fueled by this increase in energy investment, the proportion of state investment going into heavy industry reached its highest level since 1978. Preferential interest rate policies were adopted to channel resources to priority sectors. In addition, central government resources were to be dramatically enhanced by fiscal recentralization: The ratio of total fiscal revenue to national income was to be raised, while the share of total fiscal revenues going to the central government was also to increase.

Conservatives wanted to build a more powerful government apparatus that could carry out its priorities by manipulating the market economy. But they were not willing to limit themselves to the rationalizing reform ideal of an activist state steering the market. Conservatives also wanted to strengthen the traditional material balance planning system. Increased planning was specifically designed to limit the dual-price system, toward which conservatives were particularly hostile. Conservatives wanted to increase the proportion of the economy covered by material balances and compulsory output plans, while simultaneously increasing indirect government control over the remainder of the economy. The number of commodities subject to compulsory plans was to increase, and the planned "track" of dual-track commodities was to grow. The provisions that were permitting the economy to "grow out of the plan" were to be cancelled. Plan deliveries would no longer be fixed: Built-in escalators would ensure that planned deliveries increased as output grew and new firms were created. Simultaneously, planners established upper limits for market prices under the dual-price system. As macroeconomic conditions stabilized, planners hoped to adjust planned prices upward (to account for past inflation) while screwing market price limits down toward plan prices. The ultimate objective was a single price system, but one subject to planners' control.

Since planners recognized they did not have the administrative capability to enact such a system immediately, they proposed to do it in stages, with coal selected as the first target (CCP 1990: 32, 35). Government allocations of coal actually increased 12% between 1988 and 1990, about the rate at which output increased, so that the share of coal allocated increased a fraction of a percentage point. But allocations of other key commodities, such as steel or cement, did not increase (*Statistic* 1992: 498). Renewed state monopolies were declared over agricultural inputs and four varieties of finished steel that were in short supply. Private companies engaged in trading in producer goods were audited, and many were closed down. Central planners added six commodities to their allocation schedule in 1990, and increased the number of central production plans for industry to 65 from a low of 45 in 1988 (Wei Liqun 1990; Ma Hong 1991; "China's Capital Goods" 1989). In all these measures, planners saw themselves as struggling to gradually exert control over a chaotic market, which they recognized could not be recontrolled simply by decree.

Preferential policies for state-owned industry

Finally, the government adopted across-the-board policies that gave preference to state-owned firms and discriminated against non-state firms, particularly rural industries. State firms were to be shielded as much as possible from the impact of the credit crunch, while credit to rural enterprises would be tightly restricted. Strengthened material balance planning would be used to channel scarce materials to the large state firms, seen as the backbone of the industrial sector. But though state firms were to benefit from preferential policies, they were also to be subject to increased government interference. Financial contributions to the government from state enterprises were to be ratcheted upward (CCP 1990: 34), and oversight of managers by Communist Party officials was to be intensified. Thus, the increased preference to state firms was an attempt to improve their relative position in the economy in order to permit the government to extract more resources from them.

Initially, policies that discriminated in favor of state firms were primarily intended to insulate them from the costs of contractionary policies. Rural enterprises were singled out to bear the burden of credit restraints, as they were targeted for zero credit growth in 1989. By contrast, large state firms were to enjoy preferential access to credit. State firms were also protected by policies that guaranteed them access to inputs at low state-set prices. Beginning in 1990, 234 of the largest state firms were designated "double guarantee" enterprises: The state guaranteed supplies in return for enterprise guarantees of delivery of output to the planning system. These firms accounted for 46% of large enterprise output and 35% of remitted profit and tax of all in-budget firms (Liu Suinian and Cai Ninglin 1991: 39). Heightened political control amounted to direct intrusion into state enterprise management. As we have seen, the gradual spread of the factory manager responsibility system, capped by its incorporation into the Enterprise Law of 1988, had finally removed the Communist Party from direct participation in enterprise management. Hardliners now violated the Enterprise Law by insisting once again that Party Committees had a role in enterprise management. They put forward an absurd slogan: "The manager is the center, and the Party committee is the core, of enterprise management." Central Document Number 9 of 1990 set specific guidelines for rebuilding the party apparatus in the enterprise, as well as specific issues the Party secretary should examine. "Excess" income differentials were to be corrected, and enterprise practices incompatible with national principles were to be changed. Ultimate Party authority over personnel issues, particularly junior managers, was reasserted (Interviews 90c71–72; 90c80–81; 90c108–109). Factory managers were losing hard-won autonomy.

Outcome of the conservative policies

It should be clear that conservatives were pushing an extremely broad array of policies that were intended to roll back reforms and lead the economy to renewed central control. But conservative policies affected the economy in ways that conservatives did not at all anticipate. The conservative reaction to the problems of 1988–89 was panicky, and macroeconomic austerity was overly strict. The rapid decline in aggregate demand reduced shortages but also pushed the economy into recession. With shortages eliminated, markets functioned very effectively, and the demand for planning dropped off rapidly. Moreover, conservative plans for recentralization were politically unrealistic, and policies toward state enterprises were disastrous. The specific plans the conservatives put forward to guide their program were practically worthless. Within a short time, the conservatives had used up their stock of slogans, and had nothing left to contribute.

The austerity program was intended to be rigorous, but its effect on the macroeconomy was amplified by a number of factors which were not foreseen by policymakers. These factors operated as austerity accelerators, and made the ultimate impact of the policies more contractionary than policymakers had foreseen. In the first place, planners miscalculated the impact of past inflation on their policies. Planners decreed that 1989 investment should be held at the 1988 level, implicitly decreeing that *nominal* investment expenditures would be unchanged. However, prices of investment goods increased more than 20% in 1989, so that with nominal investment decreasing 8%, the real volume of resources going into investment declined by about 30%.[1] Conservative policies were inconsistent: While cutting investment sharply, they were channeling resources to the heavy industry sectors whose demand depended primarily on investment (the opposite of the 1979–81 reorientation of the economy). Demand for energy and other "bottleneck" commodities dropped.

Chinese households responded to austerity by cutting back on consumption purchases dramatically. Household psychology changed significantly in 1989. In previous years, Chinese households had faced a booming but inflationary economy – prices were going up and uncertainty was increasing. Households stocked up on consumer durables and other non-perishable items as a way of hedging against the future. The austerity policies, combined with remnant inflation, cut into real incomes. Interest rates on bank deposits were increased sharply as part of the austerity policies, drawing money into bank accounts and away from consumer goods. Moreover, expectations of the future changed drastically. As inflation began to fade, households began to postpone purchases. Fears about the future probably increased, but it began to seem wiser to stockpile money rather than goods as a defense against future adversity. Household saving skyrocketed and consumption purchases declined. Savings deposits increased at a 40% annual rate during 1989–90 (Figure 8.1). This remarkable rate partially reflected the return of "hot" money, withdrawn during the panic buying of 1988, and now attracted by high interest rates. But the total saving rate increased as well: From 16–17% of household money income in 1987–88, saving rates ratcheted upward to 22–23% of income in 1990–91 (calculated from *Statistic* 1988: 681–83; 1992: 596–97; 605).

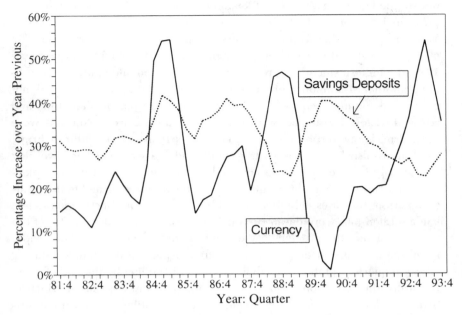

Figure 8.1. Growth of currency and savings deposits. Source: see Statistical Appendix.

Demand for both consumption and investment goods fell sharply during 1989. Markets reflected the change in demand conditions promptly, and inflation came down quickly. Free market prices of farm produce responded most quickly: By December 1989, those prices were 7% below that of a year previous. Outside-plan prices of producer goods began to fall by the end of 1989 as well. From September 1989, the overall consumer price index, recalculated on a month-to-month basis, was falling.[2] Just as market prices responded quickly to demand conditions, firms responded quickly to market prices. Inventories of some unsold commodities increased – including "priority" items like coal – and factories and mines reduced output. Planners prepared allocation plans for some commodities in 1990, only to find that enterprises were not interested in receiving allocations, since they knew that market supplies were abundant. Market-linked responses also reduced problems in the externally oriented sectors. A 10% decline in Chinese imports in 1990 was combined with a boom in Chinese exports, both developments fed by the change in domestic market conditions. Foreign markets remained open to Chinese goods, and, led by a surge in Taiwan investment into the mainland, foreign investment into China remained strong.

More ominously, production and employment were falling. Industrial output stopped growing after June 1989, and by October dipped below the year previous level for the first time. As factories struggled to cope with falling sales and prices, they laid off workers and put workers on short time. The officially registered urban unemployment rate crept up to 2.6% at year-end 1989, the highest since 1982, representing 3.8 million unemployed. In addition, another 4 million were temporarily laid-off in the cities (and not counted as unemployed), while millions more were put on short-time and reduced wages. The impact was even greater in rural areas. Not only were rural firms more responsive to market forces than urban state-run firms, rural areas also had to absorb the rural residents who had been working temporarily in cities and were now laid off (but not counted in unemployment statistics). In hard-hit Sichuan, a million laborers returned to the countryside from the cities, where most had been engaged in construction, while half a million jobs were cut in rural private businesses, and a quarter of the workers outside the province came home (*Reform* 1991: 382). Nationwide, rural non-agricultural employment fell from a peak of 95.5 million during 1988 – a quarter of total rural labor force – to 92 million by the end of 1989. Ironically, this reduction in rural non-farm employment was caused primarily by market forces, and not by government discrimination against rural industry. Only about 100,000 rural enterprises were closed down during 1989–90, one half of one percent of all rural enterprises. While there are no exact figures, this is far less than the number of rural enterprises that fail for economic reasons during even a good year (RMRB 30 March 1991; Huang Juefei 1989).

In contrast with the rapid changes in market conditions, planners labored long and hard to produce plans that turned out to be clumsy, flawed and outdated by the time they were produced. The Eighth Five Year Plan, produced by the State Planning Commission, was nearly worthless. It contained inconsistencies among targets, and failed to systematically integrate the targets for nominal income growth, real growth, and inflation. It was obvious that the plan was cobbled together from individual sectoral projections prepared by production ministries, without any clear coordinating methodology. The industrial policy promulgated by the government had far too many "priorities" to provide any kind of realistic guide to decision-makers. The list of priority sectors and products covers some 200 items, including "export products," high-grade cigarettes, and cotton textiles (State Council 1989). It was not merely that the plans fell behind the rapidly changing economic reality – they were unreliable to begin with. Ultimately, the weak economy completely undermined the conservatives' claim that the planning system desperately needed to be strengthened. The urgency of recontrol of materials faded as those materials shifted into relative surplus, and market prices began to fall.

Other conservative policies failed because of political opposition. During September 1990, a central government work conference was convened to design measures of fiscal recentralization. The Ministry of Finance proposed measures to strengthen central revenues at the expense of localities. Excise taxes would be reclassified as central revenues, and many local factories would be organized into centrally sponsored "enterprise groups," remitting profits directly to the central government. Representatives of local governments – particularly Ye Xuanping from Guangdong and Zhu Rongji from Shanghai – vigorously opposed these measures. Local government representatives pointed to their extensive expenditure obligations – many mandated by central government policies – and the reduction in their revenues that was occurring due to the central government's austerity policies. Without any broadening of the total revenue base, and in the midst of recession, the entire cost of centralization would have been borne by local governments. Local governments, speaking in unison, were able to block the proposal, and it was killed off at a December Central Committee meeting. Similarly, local governments did not allow TVEs to be seriously harmed by discriminatory policies. In coastal provinces like Zhejiang, Jiangsu, and Shandong, TVEs contributed a quarter or more of total budgetary revenues. Thus, although the growth of credit to rural enterprises slowed down sharply during 1989, it soon resumed. In 1990, lending to rural enterprises resumed growth rates in excess of 20% (*Rural Finance* 1992: 31, 78, 120). It was no longer possible to discriminate against an economic sector that had become such a large part of China's total economy.

Under these conditions, the objectives and plans of the leadership changed steadily. In overall economic policy, the main problem facing the leadership had changed from controlling inflation to reigniting growth. The collapse of communism in Eastern Europe made Chinese conservatives nervous, particularly after Romanian President Ceaucesceau was executed on Christmas Day, 1989. China's leaders began to worry that large-scale unemployment and underemployment might lead to unrest among urban workers. At the very end of 1989, planners began to shift gears and pump credit into the economy. Li Peng began to distance himself from the conservative agenda of recontrol. In early 1990, Li announced his support for the coastal development strategy (developed by Zhao Ziyang) and moderated his opposition to rural enterprises. From this point on, the leadership moved steadily away from the conservative program, and began to search for workable measures to reform the economy and improve its operation.

284   *To a market economy*

The problem of state enterprises

As macroeconomic policy shifted, the preferential policies for state firms were reinterpreted. Originally intended to shield state firms from the credit crunch, they quickly became conduits to channel large amounts of credit to state firms. In order to keep workers occupied, state factories were ordered to recall furloughed workers and keep them busy, regardless of whether or not they were needed. Factories were commanded to keep producing regardless of market conditions. Unsold inventories of completed industrial products, financed by state credits, increased rapidly. In short, factories were being commanded *not* to be profit-maximizers, but rather to give primary importance to governmental social and political objectives.

These policies cut deeply into state-owned enterprise profitability. State factories experienced a double blow – income was reduced because of the sharp decline in demand caused by recession, while costs increased because of government mandated actions designed to blunt the political impact of recession. Wage costs grew, and interest payments, needed to finance accumulating unsold output, increased rapidly. For years, profits had been growing slowly because of the impact of increased competition. Now they declined sharply. Table 8.1 shows the pattern of adjustment to the recession of different industrial ownership types. The in-budget state firms, which are the largest firms, and account for the majority of state output, experienced the largest reduction in profit in each year. In the initial 1989 recession, profit declined by a similar order of magnitude in all ownership forms, except for the smallest rural firms. In 1990, the economic situation stabilized, and smaller state and rural firms experienced only moderate changes in profits. But the profitability of large state firms collapsed. In the following year, all smaller firms began to recover, and their profit grew significantly. But large state-firm profit continued to erode. Only in 1992 did profits in large state firms begin to grow again, fed by rapid overall economic growth (see Appendix Table S.3).

Why this dramatic collapse of state-sector profitability? The most immediate cause was the squeeze between stagnant sales and increased state-mandated costs. But other factors were also at work. For most state firms, long-term contracts expired at the end of 1990. Profit targets for the next round of contracting had to be negotiated. Conservatives had emphasized the need for state firms to increase their contributions to the government. To defend themselves against increased revenue demands in the next contracting cycle, firms would find it advantageous to experience a drop in profits in 1990. Conveniently, a recession that provided ample justification was at

Table 8.1. *Change in profit by ownership type*

	1989	1990	1991
	Annual percentage change in profit net of losses		
In-budget state	−18	−57	−7
Non-budget state	−11	−16	+23
Township and village	−7	−3	+22
Other rural	+13	+8	+13

Sources: Abstract 1990: 65; 1993: 67, 82; *Industry* 1991, 65–66; *Statistic* 1992: 424.

hand. As one manager put it: "Since everyone else's profits are falling, shouldn't ours fall as well?" (Interview 90c88) Long-term contracting had eliminated ratchet effects from the annual plan, but they returned with a vengeance at the end of the contracting cycle.

Moreover, managerial morale had clearly declined. The bureaucracy had grabbed back much operational autonomy. Both mandated state policies and Communist Party interference had eroded the managers' position. For a prolonged period during the 1980s, state enterprise managers had experienced a steady increase in autonomy, authority, and incentives. Within a few years, conservatives had seriously undermined all three. The result was both a sharp decline in profitability, and also confusion and uncertainty about what kind of incentive system should now apply to enterprise managers. The government had already abrogated many of its past promises to managers, and it was now unclear whether the government could credibly commit itself to any set of enterprise arrangements. In this environment, the government had to decide how to proceed after the expiration of the first round of long-term contracts.

Initially hostile to long-term contracting, the Li Peng government eventually agreed to go ahead with a second round. But this was not easy. Managers were having difficulty meeting their contractual obligations already, and were reluctant to commit themselves to a second round of contracts. In 1987 and 1988, most of the annual targets in long-term contracts had been fulfilled. Most surveys found fulfillment rates were around or above 90%. The onset of recession changed this picture. It was official policy that contract targets could be adjusted downward to reflect the impact of events that were external to the enterprise, including macroeconomic policy. But even with this generous policy, contract fulfillment fell to around 80% in 1989 and between 70% and 75% in 1990. Through 1989, firms were generally held to the terms of their (adjusted) contracts, and significant penalties were imposed for non-fulfillment. But such efforts disappeared in 1990. With economic conditions making it impossible for them to fulfill their side of the bargain, and with the government having abrogated its promise of operational autonomy, many contractors were reluctant to begin the process over again. A survey in Yunnan province found that 80% of state factory managers in that province were unwilling to recontract. Given the reluctance of individuals to commit themselves to new contracts, most second-round contracts were assumed by the "collective management" of the enterprise, with an obvious weakening of incentives. In different provinces, the share of contracts going to groups ranged from 65% to 100%, in contrast to the 70% of contracts assumed by individuals in the first round. Auctioning of enterprises became rare to non-existent in the second round. Moreover, between 80% and 90% of second-round contracts signed in 1990 were taken by the incumbent managerial groups, so turnover declined significantly from the first round. Finally, long-run contracts were made more "flexible," subject to mutually agreed annual revisions (Industry 1991:201, 203; Du 1992; *Reform* 1991: 163–65). In short, long-term contracts were renewed, but they became much more like the standard short-run bargaining relations between enterprises and their superiors. The provisions that had made long-term contracts attractive transitional devices for clarifying autonomy and increasing incentives were largely discarded. The renewal of the contracts was a mere figleaf, covering up the government's failure to find an adequate contractual form.

The deteriorating financial position of state-owned enterprises significantly changed their role in the economy. After 1989, losses in the state industrial sector became significant for the first time since China's reform process began. Loss-making firms had always existed, but their total losses had always been substantially less than 1% of GDP. During 1989 and 1990, total losses doubled two years in a row, and surpassed 2% of GDP in 1990. The main source of industrial losses were coal and petroleum extraction, still hampered by price controls, which together contributed one-third of total losses. But losses in previously profitable sectors – especially textiles – became significant too (*Statistic* 1992: 421). After subtracting losses, repayments to banks, and retained profits, the in-budget state factories contributed no profit to the state budget after 1990. The large state firms were no longer cash cows, and were increasingly seen as financial liabilities. Ironically, the conservative program to "support state firms" ended up undermining them. The financial support given to state firms was really a form of compensation. Firms were paid to carry out the conservative political agenda at the expense of their own economic interests. After the conservative political agenda evaporated, the problem of how to manage a financially weakened state sector remained.

Achievements and limitations

The conservative period had some significant achievements. Conservative policies quickly succeeded in controlling inflation. Markets were in balance and supplies abundant. Moreover, macroeconomic restraint permitted the economy to build up a cushion of reserves, including energy supplies and foreign exchange. Additional investment in energy production ensured that new energy supplies would come on stream in the future. Thus, ironically, conditions were propitious for a renewal of reform. The economy had the necessary slack to support the disruption, uncertainty, and rapid expansion of demand that would accompany a renewed push for reform.

Yet, fundamentally, conservatives had created slack not by improving planning or better coordinating economic decision-making, but simply by cutting back growth. GDP grew only 4.4% and 3.9% respectively in 1989 and 1990, by far the slowest in the reform era. Moreover, the annual figures conceal four quarters of zero or slightly negative industrial growth, from mid-1989 to mid-1990. Conservatives had hoped to smooth economic performance by adjusting state-set prices, an activity congenial to conservative approaches to reform. The inflationary surge of 1988–89 had left some price relationships seriously out of balance, and subsidies were a significant burden to the government. In fact, a number of the most sensitive prices were increased, beginning with energy and raw materials, and then expanding to grain, edible oils, and housing rentals. The increase in plan prices, coming as market prices were falling, shrunk the gap between plan and market prices (*Price* 1991: 449; *Banking* 1992: 297.) Nevertheless, these price adjustments were modest compared to the steady changes in costs and prices ceaselessly registered in a market economy. The increase of the grain selling price, for example, came after several years of steady inflation, in which the overall urban price level had more than doubled. Thus, while the relative price of grain was increased compared with the previous year, it was still lower than it was in 1980, relative to the overall price level. Similarly, while the price of petroleum was raised, extraction costs grew even more rapidly, so that the deficit in that sector continued to grow. Across the board, outside-plan, market prices were adjusting far more rapidly to changing economic conditions that the government could ever change planned prices. The government was running faster and falling ever further behind.

Finally, state enterprise management had been seriously damaged by the government's inability to credibly commit itself to a new system, combined with the effects of increased administrative and political interference. Attempts to harden enterprise budget constraints had been seriously set back, and it was obvious that continual government tinkering with the economic system was unlikely to produce qualitative improvements in economic performance. Ultimately, the most important achievement of the conservative interlude was to finally demonstrate that there was no going back. A credible commitment to renewed radical reform was desperately called for, and was not long in coming.

The pendulum swings: New reform momentum

As economic conditions began to improve in the fourth quarter of 1990, renewed movement in reform became evident. An official Communist Party document at year end echoed the Thirty-Nine Points in calling for the elimination of the dual-track system, but managed to suggest that the way to do so was by a gradual shift to a market price system (CCP 1991). By February 1991, the conservative Zou Jiahua (head of the State Planning Commission) had rediscovered the market and added marketization to the bundle of measures necessary to "revitalize" state enterprises. Zou called for reduction in the enterprise's compulsory plan in order to "push the enterprise towards the market" (*Reform* 1992: 248). Zou was here calling for a policy in some sense more radical than advocated by Zhao Ziyang. Under Zhao, the plan had only been "frozen," whereas Zou was advocating cutting back the plan. Zou seems to have been motivated largely by the problem of plummeting profits in state-run firms. Since compulsory plans and remaining price controls were most significant for large state-owned factories, removing those controls would improve state-sector profitability and reduce government financial burdens. Concerted efforts to restart the enterprise reform process also began in 1991.

At the beginning of 1992, Deng Xiaoping gave the renewed reform momentum a decisive push by making an "imperial tour" of South China, in which he endorsed reform-created institutions and attacked conservative opposition. In October 1992, the new reform agenda was ratified by the 14th Party Congress, which proclaimed that China would adopt a "socialist market economy" (Lam 1993). This was one of the few official formulations that actually had a significant impact on the evolution of subsequent events.

Outside China, the juxtaposition of the two words socialist and market can seem confusing or unclear, but within China the meaning is unambiguous. China has been socialist for forty years, and during that time the word socialist has been drained of all concrete meaning. By contrast, the market economy is new and the meaning of the term is straightforward, so all the stress of the formulation falls on the word "market." This was the first unambiguous official declaration that the ultimate objective of reform was transition to a market economy. Reform acceleration continued in 1993, and at an important Party meeting in November, a programmatic document was ratified that outlined the broad areas where reform was needed (CCP 1993). This was intended to serve as the basis for comprehensive reforms at the end of the year, and in fact, January 1, 1994 saw the adoption of an entirely new tax and fiscal system, as well as the unification of China's exchange rate.

Substantial achievements were made during 1992–93. In most sectors, the remaining plan was cut back substantially, and market pricing was spread through the bulk of the economy. A level playing field was largely created, in which all ownership systems were treated equally. A key milestone in the creation of the level playing field was the adoption of the new tax system on the first day of 1994. State enterprise reform perhaps proceeded less successfully during this period, but two key breakthroughs were nonetheless achieved. In the area of labor, state firms began to acquire the ability to hire and fire labor more freely. The slow maturation of the social security reforms begun in the 1980s was a key feature in allowing firms this freedom. Moreover, the ownership form of state firms began to reflect accounting and ownership forms appropriate to a market economy. Not coincidentally, those forms would also be convenient to subsequent privatization of state firms, although privatization itself has remained limited up through the end of 1993.

Marketization

The most fundamental achievement of the renewal of reform in 1992–93 was rapid progress toward market prices. For the first time, the scope of planned prices for the most important commodities was reduced. The government began to dismantle price controls on those commodities where they had been most deeply entrenched. This included both key producer goods such as coal, oil, and steel, as well as sensitive consumer goods, particularly grain. For the first time, the government moved decisively beyond "growing out of the plan," and started to cut back the plan in order to move toward full market pricing. This transition was remarkably smooth, even for the most sensitive commodities. Supplies of most goods were fairly abundant, so there were few extreme surges of price after decontrol. But even more important was the fact that a functioning market had already been created around the remaining plan sectors, and most producers and consumers had become accustomed to that market. The plan had already become an island surrounded by an ocean of market price transactions, so the final liquidation of the plan was not difficult.

For crucial producer goods, beginning in 1992, production and allocation plans were reduced in quantity and coverage. Only eighteen industrial commodities were covered by state allocation or compulsory contracts in 1993, and compulsory output plans assigned for only thirty-six industrial commodities (*Reform* 1993: 254). Of course, such plans had long ago ceased to cover the bulk of output, and much "in-plan" production and delivery was being transacted at market prices (Ma Hong 1991). During 1992–93, the expansion of market prices occurred both because plans were sharply cut back, and because a larger share of in-plan production and transactions was shifted to a market price basis. For example, at the Anshan Iron and Steel Company, China's largest steel producer, 80% of output was subject to price controls in 1992, but only 20% in 1993 (Interview, 93-a-Q4). The prices of all petroleum products were decontrolled at the end of 1993. Numerous other products were released to the markets.

The most sensitive industrial area was energy pricing. The primary energy sector had the highest level of price control and compulsory allocation, and the gap between plan and market prices was large. As a result, planners were very concerned about the effect on inflation of decontrolling energy prices. The decision was made in 1992 to decontrol energy prices in stages over three to five years. Coal was most important, supplying about 70% of China's energy needs. China produced a staggering 1.14 *billion* tons of coal in 1993, with not quite 500 million tons coming from the large, state-controlled mines that fed into the state's allocation system. Through the "growing out of the plan" stage, this coal had been sold at low planned prices. The basic state price had been raised several times, but remained far below market clearing prices. A portion of this state coal had been allowed to be sold at prices intermediate between plan and market levels, but basically this sector had remained outside the progressive marketization transforming the economy. Beginning in 1992, this core allocation system was shifted toward a market price system. Coal from eastern China's Anhui province and all coal sold at intermediate prices were fully released to the market in 1992 (over 200 million tons). During 1993, additional central mines were shifted onto the market. An acceleration was contemplated that would eliminate all coal price controls on January 1, 1994, but faced with fears of inflation, planners returned to the original scheme of removing controls in stages through the end of 1995. At China's three biggest oilfields, a fifth of the output was to be released from price controls annually between 1991 and 1995 (Huang Langhui 1992; *Reform* 1993: 296; Chang Weimin 1993, 1994).

Another important milepost was passed with the gradual decontrol of state grain prices in the cities. For years, this had been the most important and most persistent symbol of the state's supply system, costing billions of yuan in subsidies per year. Reformers in the 1980s had been unwilling to tamper with the supply of cheap grain to the cities, for fear that this would unsettle the urban population. Decontrol was carried out in a curious way. Pricing authority was decentralized to the individual provinces, along with the subsidy burden. Then individual provinces, beginning with Guangdong, carried out decontrol when they thought conditions were ripe. By mid-1993, "all but one or two" of China's provinces had removed grain price controls (NCNA 1993; "Steady vow" 1993). Similar decontrol of edible oil and other staple foods occurred as well. In 1993, according to one account, only 5% of retail sales and 15% of industrial producer good sales were subject to price controls (Niu Genying 1994).

Government willingness to slash the scope of planning and price control in the energy sector was greatly influenced by declining profitability and increased subsidies to these sectors. Continued budget difficulties and increasing production costs (particularly in petroleum) forced the government to recognize that maintaining price controls in those areas amounted to subsidizing the economy as a whole by penalizing the largely government-owned energy sector. Similarly, budgetary difficulties encouraged the government to finally address the issue of subsidies going primarily to urban consumers. The overall subsidy burden (including "price subsidies" and enterprise losses) had been over 5% of GNP since 1979, when the government raised farm prices for the first time. The large majority of these subsidies have gone to commercial organs to keep the urban food price down. Decontrol of grain and oil prices paid a rapid dividend as the government subsidy burden declined from 5.4% of GDP in 1990 to only 2.3% of GDP in 1993 (Liu Zhongli 1994).

Tax reform and the level playing field

Along with the consolidation of market prices, the government moved decisively to eliminate restrictions on private ownership and steadily create the conditions for a level playing field for all ownership forms. A number of restrictions and discriminatory provisions had hobbled private businesses at times during the 1980s, and discriminatory treatment had intensified during the conservative period of 1989–90. During 1993, most remaining restrictions on private businesses were dropped. The State Administration of Industry and Commerce (SAIC) specified that private businesses were allowed to perform virtually all types of industry and commerce, except for a few specifically prohibited items. Moreover, private businesses were allowed to conduct business outside China, and to engage in joint ventures with foreign businesses within China, as indeed some 200 firms had already been doing. An important part of establishing a level playing field was that barriers that inhibited *state* firms from changing product lines or engaging in diversified business were falling away as well. In early 1993, the SAIC published regulations allowing most state firms to engage in most types of business, regardless of their original activity (*Liaoning Jingji* 1993:4, p. 48; 1993:6, p. 48.)

Encouragement for private entrepreneurship was reflected in a program adopted by the city of Shenyang, in Liaoning, in order to reduce municipal administrative personnel. City workers who voluntarily quit were given a personal stake of 15,000 yuan (about five years wages) plus 1,000 yuan for every year of seniority. This large severance payment would serve as their initial capital for a private business. Moreover, they were allowed to maintain their formal employment at the city government for one year, to serve as insurance in case their attempt to go into business failed (*Liaoning Jingji* 1993:5, p. 48.) Indeed, "taking the plunge" into private business became widespread in China during 1993. Many state employees held onto their jobs, but began working a second job on private account, thus retaining medical benefits and social security. The number of registered private businesses soared, and total employment of individual and private businesses leaped from 24 million at the end of 1991 to 33 million at the end of 1993 (*Reform 1993: 347;* Li Rongxia 1994).

An important stage in the creation of a level playing field was the promulgation of a new enterprise accounting system that went into effect on July 1, 1993. The previous accounting system had been based on Marxist economic categories and had all kinds of defects. It reflected production costs very inaccurately; did not clearly account for all flows of funds during the accounting period; and did not have clear provisions for expressing ownership and net worth. Moreover, the accounting categories and reporting requirements differed among state, collective and private firms (and even among different categories of state firms). The new accounting standards reflect costs much more accurately, and are also uniform across ownership systems. They will make it possible to proceed with further development of the share system in state ownership, and further the conversion of state control into a true owner-ship concept that can be shared with other stake-holders (Lu Dong 1993).

By far the most important step was the adoption of a new tax system, which went into effect on January 1, 1994. With state enterprise reform in disarray after repeated changes in long-term contracts and a cycle of interfer-ence and retreat in enterprise management, even conservatives began look-ing for a new way to address state enterprise financial relations. Through the early 1990s, a trend gradually emerged to reduce enterprise income tax rates in order to eventually achieve convergence with tax rates of other ownership forms. This made sense since it had become increasingly clear to government leaders that they had no special program of financial relations to implement in state-owned enterprises. Yet, as we have seen, government officials had been unable to carry out comprehensive tax reform in the past, most notably during the failed "tax for profit" experiment in 1984–85. The crucial stum-bling block had been the difficulty of devising impartial rules that would affect state firms with widely varying levels of profitability equally, but with-out giving away too much of government revenuess. By 1993, this was much less of a problem since most state firms no longer had a great deal of profit after tax had been paid and bank loans returned. Moreover, state firms no longer dominated the economy. The share of industrial output produced by state firms fell below half in 1992, and was about 42% in 1993. It began to seem increasingly attractive to submit state enterprises to the same basic tax regime as other ownership forms, and by the end of 1993, the government was ready to move forward with the most thorough overhauling of the tax system ever attempted in the People's Republic of China.

The tax reform of 1993/94 represents a dramatic effort to restructure the overall tax system. It marks the abandonment of the old socialist system of relying on state industrial enterprises as revenue sources, and instead shifts to a modern tax system that falls more equally on all sectors and ownership forms. The main revenue source became the value-added tax (VAT), which applied to nearly all commodities at the rate of 17%. A handful of basic foods and agricultural inputs were taxed at 13%, while 11 goods were subject to additional excise taxes (cigarettes, liquor, some luxury items, gasoline, and so on). Enterprise income (profit) taxes were also unified at 33% for all owner-ship forms above a moderate size (smaller firms fell into 18% or 27% brack-ets). Personal income taxes were standardized and unified with taxes on individual proprietorships. A number of other taxes were adjusted and stan-dardized, with resource taxes and urban land taxes perhaps the most impor-tant among them. The tax system applies equally to all ownership systems (except that tax concessions given to foreign-invested firms were grandfathered in). Clearly the new tax system is a major step in the creation of a "level playing field" and a fully functioning market economy (Yunnan Tax Bureau 1994).

Strikingly, the tax reform was accompanied by a major restructuring of the fiscal relations between central and local governments. Overall, the reform substantially recentralized tax collection power. The central government would be responsible for collecting all of the VAT and about 70% of total tax. The center will then rebate tax to the local governments according to formulas based on total local revenue in 1993. The center guarantees that local revenues will not fall below 1993 revenue for the next three years, but expects to take a larger share of increased revenues, so that the central share of total tax revenues will gradually increase. Since the center now collects the bulk of the tax, it should be in a position to carry out this plan. In the old system, most taxes were initially collected by local governments, and the center was dependent on local remittances for its own revenues. The adoption of this recentralization stands in sharp contrast to the failure to recentralize fiscal revenue in 1990, or indeed throughout the 1980s. An important difference is that this tax reform had something to offer the local governments in exchange for their surrender of taxation authority: They should experience less central government interference and growing tax revenues with a more efficient tax system. Moreover, the most dynamic and wealthy provinces could see the benefits from a market-conforming tax system, including the fact that exports would be encouraged by the expanded rebate of VAT on exported products. Their confidence was enhanced by visits from the patron of the tax reform, Vice-Premier Zhu Rongji, who had good reformist credentials.

Enterprise reform

Late 1991 saw the revival of many of the enterprise reform measures originally introduced during the latter half of the 1980s. In September 1991, policymakers began drawing up still another "bill of rights" for state-run enterprises. Drafting began under Zhu Rongji, who had been brought back to Beijing after a successful stint managing Shanghai's economy. The drafting process culminated in the "Regulations on Transforming the Management Mechanism of State-Run Industrial Enterprises" issued by the State Council on July 23, 1992. These regulations featured fourteen areas in which state-run enterprises were legally entitled to autonomy, including setting their own output prices, using and firing labor, and allocating investment finances and fixed capital. The "Regulations" were a sharp repudiation of conservative enterprise policy of the previous years, and accompanied a reassertion of the Enterprise Law of 1988, which should be interpreted as a renewed commitment to remove Communist Party officials from enterprise management. However, the mere statement of enterprise "rights" is, in the Chinese context, no proof that they will be realized. At each previous reformist phase, an enterprise rights document has been issued, and in each previous case the document has often been breached in practice but has nonetheless served to nudge the reform process forward a step. The new Regulations follow a unique strategy: They are extremely specific. For example, they describe exact situations under which enterprises may refuse plans (if there are no implementing contracts, if necessary supplies are not available, and if the plans are not from the legal planning authorities). By being as precise as possible, the Regulations attempt to provide enterprises with increased bargaining power and better arguments that will allow them to resist interference from governments at all levels (Sun Yanhu 1992).

Labor

Striking progress was made in 1992–93 in making the labor system more flexible for the 76 million state enterprise workers (45 million in industry) and the 35 million urban collective workers. These policies were in stark opposition to the guaranteed employment policy of the year 1990. By 1992, official publications were hammering away at the "iron rice bowl" (the permanent employment system), as if they had forgotten that two years ago government had itself been demanding precisely that enterprises provide an iron rice bowl. Hardliners were newly confident of their ability to maintain control over the urban population. Living standards had risen substantially since mid-1990, and the Eastern European example no longer seemed so appealing to the populace, nor so threatening to the leaders. With fears easing, policymakers could contemplate allowing some unemployment to emerge, and also returned to the package of labor reform measures originally introduced in 1986.

The first step was to return to the relatively flexible methods of wage bill determination that had spread during the 1980s. The system of linking wage bill to profit was revived and extended to cover a majority of state enterprise workers (41 million), while most other workers were covered by one of a variety of experimental systems. Some enterprises eliminated the permanent worker system altogether, shifting all of their workers onto a contract basis, so that some flexibility in quits and fires would be achieved as contracts expired. By the end of 1992, these fully contractual systems covered nearly

14,000 enterprises and 8.8 million workers. The number of contract workers also grew because new employees continued to be hired on a contract basis, and the total number of these contract workers reached 20 million. Over a third of industrial workers were on the contract system (*Reform* 1992: 228, 273; 1993: 325; *Industry* 1993: 106–107).

Gradual institutional reforms over a number of years had begun to reduce the bonds that tied workers to a single enterprise for life. Social Security and housing, in particular, were areas in which the prereform system of distributing benefits through the enterprise had tied workers to the factory, making it impossible for workers to quit, and difficult for factories to fire workers or go bankrupt. Reform of the pension system had been particularly pressing, since the number of retirees increased sharply after 1978. Widespread creation of local pension funds began after the 1986 labor reforms (discussed in Chapter 6). Those reforms created pooled local pension funds for contract workers, and regions gradually began to extend coverage to permanent workers. Oddly, pooled pension funds were created first at the level of the individual county or city, and only subsequently pooled into province-level funds. It was not until 1992 that all counties or municipalities had set up pooled pension funds, and by that time, eleven provinces were in the process of creating province-wide funds. By the end of 1992, 85 million workers were covered by these funds: all state permanent and contract workers, and most urban collective workers (*Reform* 1993: 338–39). Moreover, the system is being converted into one with contributions from the government, enterprises, and individual workers, and steps were taken in that direction. Individual contributions were set initially at the relatively low rate of 3% of standard wages. By the end of 1991, there were already 11.6 billion yuan in assets of the pension and unemployment funds, all of which are now deposited in the bank or invested in government bonds (*Reform* 1992: 491–92). The pension system as of 1993 had many peculiarities, and was far from perfect. Wealthy enterprises still felt obligated to supplement the pensions of their retirees, so the link between individual enterprise profitability and pension burden had not been severed. But despite the flaws, a Chinese worker could by then be reasonably confident of receiving a minimum pension, even if his former employer went bankrupt.

A similar effort has been launched with regard to unemployment insurance. Unemployment insurance itself is rare in a country at China's level of income, but most Chinese workers have been nominally covered since 1986. By the end of 1991, 95% of state enterprise workers were covered. However, the fund was basically moribund until the end of 1991. Only 200,000 unemployed workers received benefits in the five years after 1986. The fund had been taking in over 600 million yuan annually, but paying out only 170 million yuan a year. Of expenditures from the fund, the bulk went to subsidize retraining or reallocation of labor within existing enterprises, and only 5% of the total was paid directly to the unemployed. It appears to have been very difficult for unemployed workers to qualify for support before 1992 (*Reform* 1992: 228, 492). With the new willingness to contemplate unemployment, use of the fragile unemployment system suddenly took off. During the first nine months of 1992, 300,000 workers received unemployment benefits and, according to one account, this surged to 655,000 in the first six months of 1993 (*Reform* 1993: 157; Yeung 1993). Despite their flaws, the social security and unemployment compensation systems at least provided some minimum security to workers facing unemployment.

Under these circumstances, labor optimization programs were revived. In 1991, they covered 10.8 million workers, of whom 980,000 were declared redundant, and 880,000 of these were reassigned. In 1992 as well, "almost a million" workers were declared redundant and more than 800,000 were reassigned to jobs located for them (*Reform* 1992: 273; *Industry* 1993: 106). These controlled unemployment programs affected a large number of state workers, but they are certainly not the whole story. It is certain that large numbers of redundant workers were simply laid off during 1992 and 1993, but the government-controlled press did not provide much information about this. A handful of firms were described as laying off workers "into society." In these model cases, the total number of layoffs was not supposed to exceed 1% of the enterprise workforce (*Reform* 1992: 275). But firms that were poorly managed and losing money were not in a position to follow these careful rationalization measures, and they simply discharged their workers. Although the total number of discharged workers is not known, the number must be significant, since the number receiving unemployment compensation (to qualify for which one must have been previously employed) increased so rapidly. Moreover, in 1993, a year in which GNP grew 13.4% and industry at over 20%, urban unemployment actually *increased*, growing from 2.3% to 2.6% (Chen Jinhua 1994). Significant numbers of firms are undergoing restructuring and shedding workers.

Controlled rationalization was also apparent in the approach to enterprise failure followed through 1991. A significant number of state firms were shut down during 1991: 1,097 of the 37,488 in-budget industrial enterprises were closed or taken over by other firms, a non-trivial 3% rate of failure. However, only two of these firms declared bankruptcy, the remainder were shut down or taken over in carefully managed proceedings (*Reform* 1992: 228). Here, too, there is reason to believe that the pace of change accelerated during 1992–93. The number of bankruptcies reported in the official press certainly increased markedly during 1993.

Ownership reform

Despite the revival of reform, China has still not undertaken a large-scale privatization of state assets. The bulk of the change in ownership structure in the Chinese economy has occurred through the growth of non-state producers – collective, private, and foreign invested firms – rather than through transformation of the state sector. Nevertheless, important changes have taken place at both ends of the spectrum of state ownership. The larger, more modern and more profitable state firms are increasingly being "commercialized," converted into modern corporate forms of various types, including limited liability joint stock companies. At the same time, local governments have been given greater freedom to deal with the smaller and less profitable state firms, and one of the methods they have adopted is to sell them off. Thus, the traditional state-owned sector is being nibbled away at both ends. Moreover, many of the financial and other preconditions for ownership reform and privatization are being created.

During 1992, China's two stock exchanges in Shanghai and Shenzhen received an enormous amount of attention from the world's news media. The stock exchange is such a potent symbol of the capitalist economy that the establishment of stock exchanges in what was formerly a command economy is inevitably viewed as a indication of fundamental change, and this is not inappropriate in the Chinese case. Nevertheless, it is also important to recognize that this has been a tightly controlled experiment, and substantial limitations have been imposed on the development of the stock exchange in China. The number of companies listed on the two exchanges has been tightly controlled by administrative decision (there is no presumption that any firm satifying certain criteria could be listed) such that, after rapid expansion in 1992, there were only 70 stocks (including the "B" shares sold to foreigners) listed on the two exchanges. Moreover, ownership of joint stock companies continued to be held overwhelmingly by government bodies. Of all Shanghai joint stock corporations at the end of 1992, 62% of the share value was held by the government, 24% was held by "legal persons" (predominantly other state enterprises), 7% by domestic individuals, and 7% by foreign capital (Li Zhangzhe 1993). Virtually every individual corporation is securely controlled by the government or by trustworthy agents of the government. Thus, the share system has not been the vehicle for a significant divestment of state-owned companies.

It is important to put the stock market into the context of the much larger and much less regularized process of financial market development. First, the listed firms are a tiny proportion of the total number of nominal "joint stock" corporations in China. Most of these are not really joint-stock companies at all, but rather are companies that have issued "shares" to their own workers as a means to raise capital. These shares do not bear any of the rights of ownership, and sometimes payment of a fixed dividend is specified (like a bond). In any case, ownership of the firm remains murky, since such firms on average only issued shares equal to about 20% of the total value of the firm. Of the 3,320 registered joint stock firms at the end of 1991, 86% were of this form, in which only workers of the firm hold shares. Only 2% of joint stock companies (89 firms) sold shares to the general public – though these firms were much larger than the others and formed the pool from which firms listed on the stock exchange were drawn (*Reform* 1992: 322). Overall, the share system has been a secondary part of the development of capital markets in China. Progressive liberalization of the economy has led to a steady growth in capital markets outside the banking system, growth that accelerated markedly in 1992. Direct finance of various kinds has become increasingly important in China, but company stocks have remained a modest part of this overall growth. By far the most important form of direct financing has been the issuance of bonds, with Treasury bonds leading the way. During 1992, a total of 127.4 billion yuan worth of securities were issued, but of this, 116 billion were bonds and 11.4 billion stocks (Li Zhangzhe 1993; Bei, Koontz and Lu 1992).

But if stock exchanges were not of huge importance in themselves, they were an important constituent part of a broader process of ownership change. The growth of the stock exchanges was an important impetus for the new accounting standards described earlier, since it was recognized that the existing accounting standards were not adequate to support public trade shares. At the end of 1993, a decision was made to select a batch of 100 large state enterprises and convert them to "modern market-oriented firms." In practice, this means setting up limited liability joint stock companies, with primary ownership remaining with the state, but with corporate organization otherwise completely restructured (Sun Shangwu 1993). The government is clearly moving in the direction of a policy of batch-by-batch commercialization of firms, which could be followed by privatization if and when political constraints ease. This appears to be a resumption of the idea first intensively discussed around the time of the Thirteenth Party Congress in November

1987. Firms were then to have been restructured and converted rapidly to joint-stock corporations on a batch-by-batch basis, with subsequent privatization as an option.

The ability of state firms to take stakes in other firms, or create new subsidiaries, became an important part in the process by which state-owned enterprises struggle to free themselves from bureaucratic control. Taking a stake in a foreign-invested joint venture is particularly beneficial, since any firm with 25% foreign equity participation qualifies as a foreign-invested firm far less subject to bureaucratic intervention (and sometimes subject to lower tax rates). Several hundred "enterprise groups" were formed in the early 1990s, and a review concluded that 431 of these qualified as genuine enterprise groups, with effective control exerted directly over branch plants by a large core firm, thus breaking down the bureaucratic and administrative barriers that had made enterprises appendages of the bureaucratic apparatus. Many of these groups have diversified interests, and often hold foreign trade rights (*Reform* 1992: 306–10). Indeed, the Chinese government designated 100 of these enterprise groups to receive government support. The stated objective is to create a nucleus of large corporate groups like the Japanese *keiretsu* or Korean *chaebol*. These groups will have diversified production interests and substantial financial depth, and will be encouraged to operate internationally. Some, like Capital Iron and Steel (*Shougang*) already have a significant presence in Hong Kong. These firms operate with substantial autonomy, sometimes aided by political and patronage ties with top politicians and military figures. Whether these "favorites" ultimately emerge from China's market ferment as large internationally competitive firms remains to be seen, but in the interim they have certainly developed substantial room for maneuver. They can be clearly distinguished from limited experiments with enterprise groups and "horizontal linkages" in the 1980s. The new enterprise groups of the 1990s seem to be genuine corporations with substantial autonomy and international reach.

At the other end of the spectrum, local governments were given renewed authority to experiment with their own firms after 1991. Under the renewed pressure of enterprise losses, there was a sense that local governments should be freed to do whatever they could to deal with loss-making enterprises (*Reform* 1992: 167). One result of this enhanced local autonomy was that the sale of small state-run factories, which had occurred on a very limited scale during the 1980s, picked up speed in 1992–93. The city of Wuhan announced a program to sell off small state firms to any buyers, including private enterprises or groups of investors. Designed to unload loss-making enterprises, the scheme included substantial tax breaks for buyers who took over firms making large losses or with debts greater than assets (*Liaoning Jingji* 1993:2, p. 48.) Even the relatively conservative province of Liaoning tacked "sell off" onto the end of a list of measures for dealing with unsuccessful firms (Wen Shizhen 1993). By 1994, Sichuan was preparing to sell off 33 factories and stressing that most were profitable ("Sichuan to Sell" 1994). In a sense, the bureaucratic state industrial apparatus is being nibbled away from both ends. Many of the smallest firms are being sold or leased off, while some of the largest firms are being commercialized or transformed into relatively autonomous enterprise groups.

The reform package of late 1993

The preceding discussion has referred to a number of important reform initiatives taken at the end of 1993. In fact, in November 1993, a Communist Party plenum passed an important resolution on the "Establishment of a Socialist Market Economic System" (CCP 1993). Subsequent work groups translated the rather vague principles of the resolution into a package of reform measures. This package reflected the fact that with the basic success of marketization, the subsequent need was to push ahead with reforms that created a more sound fiscal, monetary, and legal system within which the market could operate. Thus, reforms were directed at the creation or improvement of new systems of taxation and fiscal management, banking, investment, foreign exchange, and property rights. The most important of these was the tax reform, which was adopted beginning January 1, 1994, discussed earlier. The commercialization of state firms was also an important element.

The reform package includes a broad range of additional measures, which should be mentioned here. The banking system is to be transformed through a continued separation of functions. Government-influenced lending will be concentrated in "policy banks," including a National Development Bank, an Import-Export Credit Bank, and an Agricultural Development Bank. This will allow the People's Bank of China (PBC) to divest itself of policy-lending decisions and concentrate on its central bank functions. A Monetary Policy Commission will be established to direct PBC policy, and implementation will depend on standard central bank tools such as reserve ratios, open market operations, and central bank lending. The existing specialized banks (such as the Industry and Commerce Bank) will also be freed of policy considerations and allowed to operate as independent commercial banks. Thus, the objective of bank reform is to resume and extend the progress made in the 1980s, and convert the banking system into an independent market system. Banking reforms were to be phased in gradually during 1994 (Sun Shangwu 1993; Li Ning 1994).

Dramatic progress was made on January 1, 1994 with the foreign payments system. The dual exchange rate that had been in effect since the mid-1980s was abolished and the exchange rate was unified at the market rate. The existing currency swap centers were to be abolished, and the partial convertibility to be established through the banking system. With a unified national exchange rate, set daily by the national authorities in response to market forces, authorized individuals would be able to convert foreign exchange at any authorized exchange bank. Although still somewhat short of a fully convertible currency, even for trade purposes, the reform marks a dramatic step forward.

A range of additional reforms were also laid out, including ownership reforms discussed before. Certainly, the implementation of these reforms will not be smooth. These are precisely the type of reforms that have been most difficult for China to implement in the past. They aim to create new institutions that limit the discretionary power of individuals. Precisely because the application of these institutions is expected to be impartial, there is little scope for bargaining and compromise in the implementation process. In some important cases, including the tax system, implementation requires a significant recentralization of power that harms certain local interests. The legal foundations for such institutions are weak, and the continuing arbitrary power of the Communist Party clashes with the principle of equal treatment under law. Moreover, short-run implementation of further reform is threatened by increased inflation and macroeconomic pressures, described in the next section. Clearly, implementation of these measures will be uneven and sometimes disappointing. That does not take away from their profound importance. In essence, these measures represent the near completion of the process of gradual marketization that China began in 1979. The economy has grown out of the plan. As a result, the necessity has shifted to building the new set of institutions that are necessary to operate a well-functioning market economy.

Key role of foreign sector

A distinctive feature of the most recent wave of reform has been the active role played by the foreign sector. In previous reform phases, the foreign sector, though important and successful, played a secondary role in the process of domestic reform. In contrast, in 1992–93 the possibility of progressive trade liberalization is being used to drive forward domestic marketization. There are a number of reasons why the foreign sector came to play an enhanced role. First, after 1991, foreign investment into China became so large that its overall role in the economy was altered. Through 1990, direct foreign investment had never amounted to 6% of total domestic fixed investment. Moreover, being regionally concentrated in Guangdong province, the impact of foreign investment on the national economy as a whole was rather limited. But foreign investment surged into China after 1991, doubling annually until it reached the rather staggering figure of $25 billion in 1993. This figure amounts to almost 20% of total domestic fixed investment, a far from negligible proportion. The surge in foreign investment reflects not only the success of China's reforms to date, but also the fact that foreign investors have since 1992 increasingly been offered access to the Chinese domestic market in return for investment. Moreover, the share of domestic industrial production from foreign-invested firms has been increasing steadily, and may have surpassed 10% in 1993. Thus, from the sheer force of numbers, foreign businesses are becoming important actors in the Chinese economy.

Moreover, China's success with export promotion after 1989 has been striking indeed. The severe macroeconomic contraction program drastically curtailed demand for Chinese imports. This combined with some additional administrative restrictions on imports in 1989–90, and the robust growth of exports, to produce China's largest-ever trade surpluses. By the end of 1991, China's gross foreign exchange reserves had grown to U.S. $44 billion, equivalent to 8.3 months of imports (World Bank 1992: 29). With an export surplus of U.S. $8–9 billion in both 1990 and 1991, and an even larger current account surplus, China's traditional fear of running trade deficits and encountering payments difficulties to foreign creditors finally started to dissipate. Under these circumstances, it began to seem realistic to contemplate a further opening to international competition. It was fairly apparent that the reforms of the 1980s would not have been successful were it not for the market pressure of new firms competing with the established state-run enterprises. Competition from new entrants had driven forward the market development process, and this was most apparent in sectors where small firms could compete effectively. Sectors in which economies of scale and technological entry barriers were significant had, however, remained protected. In the 1990s, it began to seem possible to use import liberalization to foster competition with the larger state firms. Thus, trade liberalization was to some extent seen as an alternative to the difficult and frequently unsuccessful attempts to restructure the state economy through the redesign of administrative and incentive mechanisms.

This approach had additional political advantages, since China continued to experience significant political difficulties with the United States, its largest export market. Annual renewal of China's Most Favored Nation status became increasingly contentious, with China's large trade surpluses with the U.S. reinforcing discontent over China's human rights record. The feeling grew in the Chinese government that the only way to overcome this perennial problem was through a fundamental liberalization of China's trade regime, and in particular through China's re-accession to GATT, the General Agreement on Tariffs and Trade. This, it was felt, would defuse the bilateral issues between the U.S. and China by providing a broader framework for liberalization. Clearly, though, entry into GATT would require a substantial liberalization of China's import regulations, even under special provisions within GATT for developing countries. Thus, import liberalization under the aegis of GATT became both an effective foreign policy initiative, and a potent domestic economic initiative. By 1992–93, entry into GATT was becoming something for which Chinese enterprises were increasingly being urged to prepare, a symbol of the maturity of market relations (Zhao Xiaodi 1992; Wu Yue 1992). By making the public commitment to GATT membership, the government was preparing enterprises for increased competition, and from potentially formidable foreign firms. This locks in the government's commitment to marketization, and helps solidify expectations that the marketplace will grow increasingly competitive.

The end of an era of economic reform

The wave of reform in 1992–93 was accompanied by a remarkable surge of economic growth. Official GDP growth was 13.2% in 1992 and 13.4% in 1993. Real industrial growth was 27.5% in 1992 and well over 20% in 1993 as well. The Chinese press picked up a phrase from Deng Xiaoping, and began to speak of "reaching a new level" every few years. Moreover, the rapid growth was accompanied by a qualitatively new market environment, particularly for industry. In the coastal provinces, the economic environment was substantially altered by an emerging alliance between foreign invested firms (in practice, mainly Hong Kong and Taiwan invested) and township and village enterprises. Capital, labor, and land markets developed rapidly under the impetus of the demand created by these marketized forms. With the newly emerging private sector beginning to play a significant role as well, the overall economic environment was changing significantly.

At the same time, it was also apparent that China had not merely embarked on a phase of stepped-up reform and growth, it had also touched off a period of potentially dangerous inflation. Signs of intensifying macroeconomic imbalances and building inflationary pressures were all too obvious by late 1992. Market prices of investment goods started to climb, the market value of the renminbi tumbled, and signs of financial disorder multiplied (Figure 8.1). During early 1993, these intensifying pressures finally began to push consumer prices up at a fairly rapid rate, and in June 1993 the inflation rate in large cities surged up to 22% on an annual basis. Under these circumstances, it was inevitable that a renewed phase of macroeconomic austerity would begin, and at the beginning of July 1993, just such a program was announced.

Austerity was signaled by the takeover of the Central Bank by the Vice-Premier Zhu Rongji. Zhu immediately announced a 16-point program to restore order to the economy, not least through the rectification of the financial system. Austerity always causes some hardship to new market-oriented actors, but there appeared to be some desire this time to make clear that this was a program of macroeconomic austerity, not an attempt to subject the economy to administrative recontrol. There is reason to fear that macroeconomic disorder and the subsequent austerity program may have some adverse impact on the program of economic reform. This is so for two reasons: First, the increase in inflationary pressures has made the program of price decontrol and subsidy elimination more difficult to sustain. Already in 1993, there were some calls to delay further price decontrol because of accelerating inflation. In this sense, an opportunity has been missed. The struggle to contain inflation during the austerity phase will naturally tempt policymakers to delay price liberalization. Second, the rapid increase in domestic demand (combined with foreign trade liberalization) led to a rapid increase in imports and a dramatic slowing in the growth of exports. By 1993, China's trade surplus had disappeared, and a trade deficit of $12.2 billion emerged for the year as a whole. Such a deficit is sustainable, and indeed healthy, as long as China is able to continue to attract large inflows of foreign investment. The danger is that the threat of a deficit may cause a loss of nerve among China's leaders. If it appears that domestic firms will be swamped by a flood of imports, and that foreign exchange reserves will evaporate quickly, then trade liberalization will be slowed. Since this liberalization, as described here, has an important force driving domestic marketization forward, this would have significantly harmful effects on the progress of reform as a whole.

Nevertheless, one is driven to the unavoidable conclusion that what is in sight here is not the end of a phase of accelerated reform, but rather the end of a whole era of economic reform. For the prolonged process of economic reform gradually created a consensus, even among China's leaders, that the creation of a market economy was the only feasible approach to successful economic growth. Although an austerity program emerged in 1993–94, support had evaporated for across-the-board policies of economic re-control. There was no longer a constituency for the kind of hardline economic policies that were followed in 1989. It was clear within China that those policies failed, and failed spectacularly. Thus, policy-makers in 1993–94 were attempting to implement an austerity policy within the framework of a market-oriented economic policy.

To an important extent, the leadership had committed itself, publically and unambiguously, to the goal of a market economy. This objective was adopted at a full Communist Party Congress, and one can see in China today that even the most hidebound conservatives have accepted the inevitability that they must prepare for a fully market economy within the next few years. It would be immensely costly to reverse that commitment and upset those expectations; and there is no compelling reason to do so, and no significant constituency pushing to do so. Thus, an era of economic reform is over, the era in which China cast about for an acceptable transition strategy in a context in which there was no agreement among the top leaders about the ultimate objective of the transition.

Second, the coming of the 1993 macroeconomic austerity program marked the first time that conservatives have had *no* constructive role to play. Since 1978, and even before, conservatives have played a sometimes vital role by insisting that the economy be subject to macroeconomic controls, and that macroeconomic imbalances not be allowed to get permanently out of control. To be sure, this constructive role has been inextricably bound up with the obstructionist side of the conservative policy. Their cautious macroeconomic policy advocacy has been tangled up with their unwillingness to countenance real systemic change. But the converse could also be said of the reformers. Their willingness to carry out real systemic change has consistently been compromised by their readiness to plunge the economy into unsustainably rapid growth spurts that end up costing the economy dearly. Throughout the period under review in this book, these two groups checked and balanced each other, with excess caution and excess daring constantly complementing each other. This is not to say that it was the best of all possible worlds – only to say that given this rough division of opinions between competing advocacy groups, one must concede that both groups made some constructive contributions. Moreover, as described here, the periods of slack macroeconomic policy engineered by the conservatives often ended up contributing to real marketization in ways just as profound as the bold initiatives of the reformers.

This peculiar configuration of opinions had come to an end by 1993. Vice-

Premier Zhu Rongji, who took over the austerity policies, is not an economic conservative, but rather a pragmatist with a commitment to economic reform. He clearly would be put in the reform camp, yet he seeks to shed the baggage of excessively expansionary macro policy that has hobbled the reformist camp (Lam 1993). The former conservatives seem to have no role to play any longer. Indeed, hardline Premier Li Peng was rather closely linked to the former central bank head, who was implicated in serious financial mismanagement. Thus, the basic pattern of reformist-conservative oscillation, so prominent throughout the entire 1978–1992 period, seems to be shifting to a new political dynamic.

Third, the end of the dual-track system was in sight. To be sure, the system still existed, and was likely to hang on for a couple of years. But the end was in sight, because the compulsory plan was being sharply cut back, and because the principle of moving to market prices had been widely accepted. In a fundamental sense, the economy had successfully grown out of the plan, and the government was in the process of cutting away the vestigial plan remnants. Even in industry, once the bastion of the state-run economy, pure state ownership was in the minority. In the rural sector, household farms and businesses had long been dominant. China had a market economy with a mixed ownership base. Within its large state sector, a traditional command economy plan still existed, but its importance to the economy as a whole was minimal, and its future likely to be short. Thus, the period when the plan was used to provide stability while market institutions were created was over; the market had matured sufficiently to create its own stability, and the plan was no longer needed.

Finally, it is striking that in the 1992–93 reform period, China was able to carry out precisely the reforms that had proven most difficult during the 1980s. Rationalizing reforms had consistently failed during the 1980s. In particular, tax reform – or even regularization of fiscal relations between the center and the localities – had particularly frustrated reformers. Moreover, the government had been unable to muster the political will to cut subsidies to urban residents or the core state-run energy sector. But in the new market context of 1992–93, all those measures had been carried through relatively smoothly. In that sense, Chinese policymakers had shown that they could circumvent some of the most difficult stumbling blocks that had obstructed progress in the 1980s. China has managed to demonstrate that it will not be perpetually stuck in a phase of half-reformed institutions and coexisting incompatible instruments of plan and market.

China's economy today faces fundamentally new and different problems. Those problems, to be sure, are formidable. China has created a rudimentary market economy. It now needs to create a well-functioning market economy, and it still has a long way to go. Implementation of the ambitious reform package laid out at the end of 1993 will undoubtedly be disappointing in some respects. But in any case, those challenges will define the second era of economic reform. The challenges of the first era have mostly been overcome. This marks a new phase of economic reform, and is an appropriate point to break off the story.

9

Conclusion: Lessons and limitations of the Chinese experience

After fifteen years, it is clear that there is substantial ex-post coherence to the Chinese reform process. It should also be clear that this coherence is not the result of a carefully plotted reform strategy. Indeed, during some crucial periods, the coherence of the reform process emerged in spite of, not because of, the policies of Chinese leaders. Coherence was a characteristic of the economic environment in which the transition path unfolded, rather than of the explicit choices of policymakers. Just as planned economies have an internal consistency, so also is there a generally consistent logic to the way such systems dissolve. The interrelatedness of command economies – which is usually seen as an obstacle to reform – may also become an advantage in the transformation process. There are certain critical, or core, features of the command economy, and once those are eliminated or weakened, the system has a tendency to devolve into a different type of system. Provided there is some political will to move the system in the direction of a market economy during this dissolution process, a positive process of transformation may be set in motion even without a clear or comprehensive commitment to a reformed market economy at the outset.

The Chinese transition process has also been robust. Clearly, many of the initiatives advanced by the Chinese government failed, and many of the most successful reform measures were introduced with little forethought or awareness of the consequences. That the process overall could move forward despite the failure of many individual initiatives was an advantage to the overall transition "strategy." Failure did not abort the process of change, which reasserted itself with extraordinary resilience. There was nothing special about the particular sequence of reform measures that characterized the Chinese transition. Following a Chinese-style approach to economic reform would not mean replicating the individual steps in the Chinese path. Rather, it would imply a general commitment to opening markets as rapidly as possible, while using the traditional coordination mechanisms (the plan) to resolve immediate economic problems. By maintaining administrative coordination while allowing market coordination, the economy faces less risk of catastrophic failure. Chinese reforms did not – contrary to the claims of some Chinese publicists – proceed through step-by-step empiricism. But they did proceed by diversifying options – not putting all their eggs in one basket – and that diversification led to a robust transition, one that survived under a wide variety of economic and political circumstances.

The Chinese reform process took place in the midst of a broadly based and extremely rapid process of development. Looking back to China in 1978, at the onset of reforms, one is struck by the recognition of how far China has come in fifteen years. It is not just that China has experienced quantitatively rapid economic growth. More important is that China has experienced qualitatively significant development. Human resources have been strengthened; communication, information, and awareness of the outside world are much greater; living standards are higher, not merely in that a greater volume of goods is available, but rather that the entire spectrum of personal choice has expanded. For all its problems, China is a much "richer" place than it was fifteen years ago. After centuries of poverty, China is now on the verge of achieving a decent life for the majority of its people.

This achievement is both obscured and rendered fragile by China's failure to achieve political reform. China lacks not only democracy, but also minimum levels of accountability and legitimacy. The political system is simply not adequate to cope with the challenges that confront it. The dysfunctional political system might prevent the Chinese people from quickly building the kind of future economic system they would prefer; it might even jeopardize the achievements of recent decades. However, the inadequacy of China's political system is chronic and longstanding. In spite of its inadequacies, that political system did manage to promote a large number of competent managers and leaders during the 1980s, which contributed significantly to economic success. Furthermore, China's poverty as of 1978 was partially self-imposed. Maoist policies strengthened some parts of China's economy, but systematically depleted other parts. Underdevelopment limited China's options at the end of the 1970s, and the capabilities that have been built since then have expanded China's options. A gradual process of reform at least provided time for enhancing human capabilities and building institutions. In that sense, the processes of reform and development have been braided together into a single process of change.

Main lessons of the Chinese experience

Gradual reform is feasible

The Chinese experience shows that gradual change of a command economy is feasible. The institutions of the command economy are sufficiently closely knit together that unhooking a single key connection can cause the entire fabric to unravel. The argument that one must engineer a "big bang" transition because that is the only way to ensure the destruction of the old system simply does not stand up to scrutiny. Indeed, the tentative commitment of the Chinese leadership to reform in the early period and the many false leads pursued show that gradual reform is not merely feasible, it is also a resilient, "natural" way to transform an economic system.

Relaxation of the state monopoly over industry is crucial

Given the central position of state-run industry in the command economic system (described in Chapter 1), it is not surprising to find that the crucial link in the reform process has been the relaxation of the state monopoly over industry. Once that monopoly is relaxed, the powerful attraction of temporarily large monopoly profits in the industrial sector induces entry on a large scale – entry that in turn puts great pressure on the state sector and gradually drives a realignment of prices. Because of the central importance of industry to development strategy and macroeconomic balance, transformation in that sector has a significance even greater than that of successful transformation of the rural sector.

An important question is how Chinese reformers were able to credibly commit to a relaxation of the state industrial monopoly despite the obvious disadvantages (to the government) of doing so. As we have seen, there was a backlash among conservatives in 1981–83 against this process, and one would have expected planners in China – like those in Eastern Europe – to have fought harder to maintain their monopoly position. It appears that the relaxation of the state monopoly over industry was definitive in China because of two supporting conditions. First, as discussed in Chapter 1, China had never possessed detailed central government control over industry. The fundamental characteristics of the industrial monopoly, to be sure, had been maintained by government control over agricultural and other raw materials, and by limitations on the types of activity local communities could initiate, restrictions that in tandem were sufficient to maintain the profitability of state industry. But the principle of locally operated industrial systems independent of the central plan had been firmly established. Thereafter, once entry barriers were lowered, there was no ideological precedent for a reestablishment of across-the-board monopoly. The second supporting condition was simply China's huge size. At the outset, China's vast rural hinterland contained thousands of local communities empowered to initiate community-sponsored industries. As reform deepened, China's cities also became increasingly independent sponsors of local industrialization programs. Though these municipal factories were nominally state-run, they in fact responded to local incentives and local interests. Soon hundreds of urban areas were engaged in competition with other areas. Even though municipal governments initially attempted to maintain monopolies over industrial production in their jurisdiction, they found that their producers were subject to competition from producers outside their boundaries – initially from rural enterprises, but increasingly from other cities, and even from foreign-invested firms in China's coastal regions. Such a dynamic probably could not have been established in a small Eastern European country without rapid liberalization of foreign trade at an early stage.[1]

Entry is rapid in response to opportunity

Once the state monopoly was relaxed, entry of new firms proceeded at a remarkable pace. The Chinese experience shows that even in the absence of legal protection for independent businesses, entry can be *a more* powerful force in socialist economies than in comparable market economies. This is so because the very distortions in the price and output structure that are such distinctive characteristics of the socialist system make entry more attractive. First, as stressed throughout this book, the socialist price system skews profitability toward the manufacturing sector. The opportunity to share in monopoly profits thus induces rapid entry. Second, the size distribution of industrial enterprises is highly skewed toward large firms. While China was known for the large number of "small" firms in its pre-reform system, even these were relatively large, typically having over 50 employees. By contrast, the size distribution of industrial firms in market economies, both developed and developing, consistently shows small firms (less than 50 employees) accounting for at least 25% of industrial employment. There are numerous niches in both modern and developing economies that are best filled by small firms. This is undoubtedly the case in China and other socialist countries as well. Since those niches were initially empty, the potential rewards to entrepreneurs who arrived first were large. Rapid entry ensured high returns and, at the same, promised significant gains for the economy as a whole. In essence, socialist economies create the conditions for the "unbalanced growth strategy" advocated by Hirschman (1958). Unbalanced state investment raised returns to independent entrepreneurs in associated sectors.

The ECEs have also experienced rapid entry, sometimes called "privatization from below." In Poland, for example, extremely rapid increases in small-scale private activity have been one of the few really positive short-range outcomes of the transition program. It should be clear, even after only a few years experience, that the forces that propel rapid entry are not unique to China, but can be expected in most transitioning economies. However, the role that entry plays differs as transition strategies differ. In a big bang transition, large-scale entry begins at virtually the same moment as other programs of major systematic change, so that rather than driving the realignment of prices, entry takes place in the wake of a big bang deregulation of prices. Arguably, this may slow entry, since the lure of monopoly profits is reduced, and high levels of uncertainty will discourage some potential entrants. But conversely, the big bang deregulation of prices should drastically reduce opportunities for corruption, and allow the transition to occur with less injustice.

Entry of new firms is a powerful force for systemic transformation

1. Output grows rapidly. As newcomers fill empty niches, total output grows rapidly. With existing firms maintaining output of essential raw materials and heavy industrial products, newcomers are free to concentrate on high-profit and scarce items. Many new products come onto the market, reversing the impoverished consumer markets so characteristic of the planned economy, and creating a kind of consumer revolution. Since unmet consumer demands were pervasive under the old system, it is easy to respond to those demands during reform, and a "golden age" of improved living standards ensues (Wang Xiaoqiang 1993). Increased output and availability of consumer goods builds support for reform during the initial reform period.[2]

2. Competition grows, putting pressure on the state sector. As demonstrated in Chapter 6, entry increases competitive pressures and drives down super-normal profits. This strips state enterprises of the comfortable cushion of high prices that previously protected their managers and disguised their inefficiencies. State firms face competitive pressures as well as the enhanced incentives that are an intended outcome of the reform process. State firms do not simply operate in the "simulated market" that was the goal of the rationalizing reform process. They face real market pressures and real costs when they fail to perform adequately.

3. Entry and increased competition drive a realignment of the price system. Price changes in response to profit-seeking entry throughout the economic system. One of the most striking aspects of the Chinese experience is that the government failed repeatedly over a period of more than a decade to reform prices. But by the end of that period substantial price rationalization had in fact taken place. As evidenced by equalization of profit rates among industrial sectors, the fact of entry is sufficient to force a substantial realignment of prices.

4. A slow-motion fiscal crisis develops. The decline in state sector profitability erodes government revenues. In a big bang transition, this happens quickly, creating immediate fiscal crisis; in a Chinese-style transition, the same thing happens, but it develops gradually. This unraveling of state budget resources can cause a backlash among central planners, who may seek to smother the infant reform in its crib, and reconstitute the seamless web of the command economy. But in the Chinese case, top governmental leaders, led by Zhao Ziyang, tended to respond to the pressures created in ways that enhanced the marketization process. They looked for ways to make credible the government commitment to a hands-off management process, while seeking to improve monitoring and profit orientation of state-run factories. These were the freezing of the central government plan, and the move to long-term contracting for state enterprises.

From the standpoint of state bureaucrats, this interaction does not appear to be so virtuous, and they are typically not sanguine about the process. The planning apparatus must be willing to acquiesce in a relative decline in the importance of traditional state planning. In China, this was easier for bureaucrats to accept because they had been forced to confront the haphazard and wasteful nature of past planning, and the limitations on their ability to impose a meaningful plan on the economy. Focusing on profitability, they see the erosion in state sector profits as a profound crisis of the state sector. Without good measures of total factor productivity, they conclude that state sector performance is deteriorating. Foreign observers, hearing the cries of alarm from state planners, shake their heads knowingly as they perceive still further evidence that state ownership is intrinsically inefficient. Neither party sees that the difficulties are the result of an ultimately beneficial transition to a different type of economy, and are entirely compatible with gradually improving efficiency.

The fact that the transition is gradual is crucial in mediating the paradoxical situation that confronts planners. Although planners are confronted with sustained fiscal crisis based on what appears to be a sustained crisis of the state-run industrial system, they also perceive vigorous growth in the economy as a whole, combined with improving living standards. From time to time, they are tempted to solve the twin crises by reimposing state controls on the economy, but they quickly find that these efforts are futile and interfere with the positive trends in the economy long before they arrest the decline in state monopoly profits. Learning proceeds, and many of the planners conclude that only an ultimate evolution to a market economy can resolve the dilemmas.

Big bang deregulation amounts to the rapid abandonment of the traditional fiscal system. This imposes severe strains on reformers, who are therefore required to build a new fiscal system immediately, or suffer prolonged macroeconomic instability. The ECEs, with their higher levels of administrative and institutional skills, may well be capable of this difficult task. It certainly was beyond the reach of China in the early stages of its reform. Creation of a new fiscal system will take the place of intensified government monitoring of state firms. Indeed, government monitoring is typically weakened during big bang transitions. In part, this may be due to large-scale replacement of bureaucrats following democratic transition, leaving weaker monitoring capabilities. In part, it is due to the expectations – now rapidly receding – of rapid privatization of large state firms. Finally, it is also due to the changed fiscal system. Since government officials tend not to see state enterprises as their primary revenue sources in the future, they are unlikely to focus as single-mindedly on profit delivery incentives as the Chinese did in their transition.

State-firm performance can be improved

The combined effects of fiscal crisis and intensified competition bring pressure to bear on the state-owned industrial sector. The sheltered position of state firms is eliminated, while the state's demands on that sector for revenue are intensified and take on a different character. As state bureaucracies increasingly subordinate other objectives to the need to maintain a steady flow of revenues, they intensify their profit-oriented monitoring of firms. Bureaucrats begin to demand that state firms become revenue maximizers. Since the demand for revenue takes place in a context of steady erosion of those revenues – absolutely and as a share of GNP – state bureaucracies attempt to maintain roughly constant revenue deliveries. In China, this led them to adopt long-term profit contracting which sought to stabilize revenues by fixing deliveries; in turn, this gave state firms high powered incentives on the margin. This interaction created a virtuous cycle of heightened profit orientation of state firms. From this interaction came a steady improvement in the productivity of state firms.

Although much work remains to be done on Chinese enterprises, the preliminary evidence summarized in Chapter 6 thus far has provided strong and consistent evidence of changed behavior and improved productivity. Why was the Chinese experience different? The initial reason seems to be that the interests and incentives of bureaucrats superior to the enterprise were changed in two important ways. First, for reasons discussed earlier, Chinese bureaucrats were able to credibly commit to at least partial non-interference with enterprise operation. Long-term contracting represented a commitment to the firms not to change tax rates ex post, while the basic fixity of the plan represented a commitment not to increase other kinds of obligations arbitrarily. Second, relatedly, bureaucratic superiors themselves had become if not exactly profit maximizers, at least revenue-seeking agents. The subordination of most state-run industry to local industrial officials, combined with the general erosion of state industrial revenues, placed officials in a severe fiscal squeeze, which has been amply documented here. Bureaucrats were dependent on "their" enterprises for revenues. This had a negative side, as bureaucrats were tempted to intervene to help out local enterprises, but it also implied that bureaucrats were less interested in ensuring that enterprises remained cemented into an edifice of direct control, and more interested in stabilizing the flow of revenue from the enterprise to the local government. Bureaucrats did not merely play with compensation schedules that would reward profitability. They genuinely sought managers who could provide profits.

It is of crucial importance that this change was occurring within the context of a sustained erosion in state industrial profitability. Indeed, the whole program of long-term contracting only makes sense in this context. Blejer and Szapary (1990) describe long-term contracting from the fiscal standpoint, stressing the low buoyancy of fiscal revenues implied. They find the system to be perverse, since as revenues increase, the state share will decline. But from the standpoint of bureaucratic superiors, long-term contracting was a desperate attempt to stabilize revenues at their existing level. Bureaucrats were not behaving irrationally. They were willing to cede control over uncertain marginal revenues if they could thereby stabilize their existing revenues.

In a fine coincidence, the general erosion of revenues helped solve one of the crucial informational problems bureaucrats face in trying to monitor enterprises. In general, it is rather easy for bureaucrats to measure changes in profit from existing levels, but difficult for them to assess the unrealized potential profit and productivity gains. Enterprises thus possess private information about possible improvements in efficiency that they can use to purchase easy targets and a quiet life. This problem leads in all the socialist countries to persistent suboptimal behavior, as enterprises "conceal reserves" from superiors, and produce well inside their efficiency frontiers. Erosion of profit gives bureaucrats an easy second-best solution to this dilemma. By simply insisting that enterprises deliver approximately constant revenues to the government, bureaucrats can devolve to the enterprise the problem of handling cost increases, linking it directly to productivity improvements. Bureaucrats sacrifice potential revenue gains, but purchase secure revenues. Thus, ironically the erosion in profitability both made bureaucratic superiors more interested in profits, and made it easier for them to establish a crude but effective incentive device to monitor firms' profitability performance.

In this environment, long-term contracting could be a part of an effective strategy to change enterprise incentives. Clearly long-term contracting by itself could not be an adequate reform strategy. It would certainly be ineffective in a business as usual environment. But long-term contracting from the enterprise perspective imposed steep compensation functions on firms in the context of intensifying competition that was driving a fundamental realignment of prices and eroding profitability. Firms were simultaneously under great pressure from increasing costs and facing high-powered incentives from high marginal profit-retention rates. Firms were not operating in a simulated market environment – they were operating in a true market environment in which unsuccessful firms would become impoverished, unable to provide managerial bonuses or benefits to workers. Moreover, superiors were unlikely to promote managerial careers in cases where those managers failed to meet this fundamental challenge. Enterprise incentives really did change, and enterprise behavior changed as a result.

Liberalization of production and consumption induces an increase in household saving

As one might suppose, the promise of supernormal returns on investment increases the supply of investible funds. Household saving in pre-reform China, like other socialist countries, had been minimal. Accumulation of financial assets was only 3% of household income on average before 1978.

During the 1980s, this increased to 15%. Total household saving was even higher, since a substantial volume of saving took place directly as household construction of housing and creation of real assets in the household business sector. The supply of saving turned out to be highly elastic.

The attraction of lucrative investment possibilities in increasing saving was enhanced by the greater need of funds for transactions purposes, and the need to accumulate monetary balances preparatory to the purchase of newly available consumer goods. After the agricultural collectives were disbanded, individual households needed to carry larger monetary balances throughout the agricultural production cycle. Previously, the collectives had centralized transactions and relied primarily on agricultural credit for purchase of inputs, with money entering the picture only when net income was distributed to households. Upon the dissolution of the collectives, economies of scale in monetary transactions were forfeited, and households increasingly received gross income in money terms, using money to purchase inputs during the agricultural cycle.

Similarly, in the absence of consumer credit, the purchase of consumer durables or other lumpy expenditures required preparatory saving. Newly available televisions and washing machines induced new saving, while relaxation of ideological restrictions on weddings and funerals increasingly made those life cycle ceremonies what they had been under the old society – expensive productions that require substantial precautionary accumulation of funds. Driven by increased investment, transactions, and consumption demands, households saving skyrocketed. Increased accumulation not only moderated incipient macroeconomic imbalances, it also provided essential funds for the use of new enterpreneurs. Of course, this depended on the ability of the banking system to recycle those funds to independent entrepreneurs. In general, this was accomplished, particularly through the mechanism of the rural credit cooperatives.

The increase in household saving was a fundamental constituent element of Chinese economic success. Increased saving allowed continuing high levels of investment, giving the economy the resources necessary to build infrastructure and break recurring bottlenecks. Moreover, it was never necessary for the economy to adjust to a fundamentally different set of macroeconomic realities. Structural adjustment could occur much more gradually, and without the sudden collapse of entire sectors producing investment goods. The fundamental reason China was able to avoid profound macroeconomic crisis was the rapid increase in household saving. Perhaps some portion of this increase was due to innate, but latent, characteristics of Chinese households – perhaps, like other East Asian households, they had a high propensity to save that was merely obstructed by the disadvantageous position of households in the old command economy. But the nature of the Chinese transition process would also be expected to encourage and reward high household saving, and must be given at least a portion of the credit for the creation of this beneficial condition.

Changing macroeconomic policies lead to deepening of reform

Despite the long-run stability of China's transition from a macroeconomic standpoint, there were certainly significant short-run episodes of overly expansionary and overly contractionary macroeconomic policy. Ironically, the transition process seems to have thrived on *both* phases of the macroeconomic cycle. The contractionary phases were essential to create buyers markets, and reduce the demand for planning and rationing. Yet expansionary phases also seemed to contribute because they fostered the rapid growth of new producers, created favorable conditions created for entry, and propelled the growth process that allowed restructuring to take place relatively smoothly. A moderate amount of macroeconomic instability seems to have contributed to the overcoming of the traditional economic system. That system might be likened to an initially fragile structure that was pushed and pulled in different directions as macroeconomic conditions changed. Each change in direction widened the cracks in the initial structure, and revealed the inadequacy of that structure to deal with rapidly changing economic life. Eventually, pushed and pulled in many directions, the old cage simply collapsed.

Coherence

Thus, China's jumble of ad hoc reforms can be seen, ex post, to have added up to a coherent package. State control of the price system ensured high profitability of manufacturing at the start of the reforms. High profitability induced rapid entry of new firms once restrictions on nonstate firms were removed. The profits earned elicited high levels of household saving, generating still more investment by nonstate firms. Entry in turn subjected state enterprises to market discipline and reduced state-sector profitability. As a result, the government faced gradual erosion of its revenue base. In an attempt to slow this erosion, the state intensified its monitoring of state firms, and increasingly provided them with incentive systems based on profitability. State firms responded by increasing their efficiency (which was abysmal to begin with), providing the economy with enough stability to encourage further growth, both inside and outside the state sector, and providing essential producer goods. Faced with the erosion of its traditional sources of revenue, the state also sought to strengthen newly developing financial systems – the banking system and embryonic capital markets – in order to transfer private saving to productive uses.

Reform proceeds by a series of feedback loops – reform begets further reform. A microeconomic reform (resulting in competition for state firms) creates a macroeconomic problem (a squeeze on government revenue), which impels further microeconomic reforms (more profit-oriented regulation of state firms). This positive feedback presupposes a series of constructive policy responses from government leaders. Reform will not proceed without appropriate state action, but the dynamics of the process create opportunities for pro-reform leaders to push the reforms forward.

Big bang transitions thus sacrifice most aspects of the virtuous cycle that characterized the Chinese reforms. In place of the gradual virtuous cycle is a difficult and often painful period of accelerated change, during which institutional reconstruction is carried out in the midst of substantial economic disruption. Yet clearly economies in transition reap benefits from rapid transitions as well. The pace of change is accelerated, and there are fewer opportunities for the former nomenklatura to benefit personally from the opportunities of the transition. Ten years after the Eastern European countries begin their transitions, they will undoubtedly have made a far more thorough transition to a market economy than the Chinese have made after a decade of reforms. Whether the thoroughness of that transition will have been worth the economic dislocation experienced will have to be determined in the future.

Ambiguities and shortcomings

Because the Chinese reform process has been gradual and piecemeal, it is sometimes difficult to assess the extent and nature of change. In 1993, as in 1978, the Chinese central government intervened actively in the economy, but did not control anything like the totality of economic interactions. In 1993, as in 1978, state firms engaged in pervasive bargaining relations with bureaucratic superiors over targets and rewards. But over the course of more than a decade, the balance between bureaucratic and market coordination has gradually shifted. As the proportion of goods transacted at market or near-market prices has increased, those prices have increasingly come to express the relevant information about relative scarcities that face decision-makers at all levels. By the end of the 1980s, fixed prices were increasingly perceived by economic agents as providing information on exactions or implicit taxes on enterprises, rather than on the value of goods themselves. Market prices were the real prices for most commodities, and plan prices merely a legacy of the past. During the 1990s, most of those fixed prices were finally being swept away.

There are even ambiguities in the Chinese growth achievement. Chinese GNP growth is almost certainly overstated somewhat, due to inadequate deflation techniques, particularly in the rural industrial sector. There is no doubt that real growth remains impressive, though, even if we could carry out all the necessary statistical corrections. And yet bureaucratic economies are capable of superficially impressive growth that actually represents a much less estimable contribution to improved welfare. This is so basically for two reasons. First is accounting reasons. Collection of price data is faulty and tends to overstate growth. Moreover, the prices by which output is measured are distorted in ways that give too much importance to rapidly growing sectors. In particular, because the price of manufactured goods is high in socialist countries, and manufacturing is typically the fastest growing sector in any developing country, growth is overstated. Moreover, quantitative limitations mean that consumers cannot even optimize their selection of goods at given prices. As important as these considerations are, they probably became less significant in China during the course of reforms and therefore the growth contribution might actually have been larger than indicated.

The second reason is more important, particularly for a country in the midst of reform. This is that the bureaucratic economy creates the wrong kind of wealth. That is, the bureaucratic economy builds factories and other facilities that appear viable and productive in the context of the bureaucratic economy, but turn out to have little value once real marketization is completed. This has been strikingly demonstrated by the case of East Germany, in case anyone doubted it. For the past ten years, in spite of the overall improvement in the incentive environment, China has been building and expanding factories that will ultimately turn out to be unviable and will have to be closed. That is, the very gradualness of the transition path on which China has embarked has implied the maintenance for many years of the set of incentives that lead to wrong and wasteful investment choices. How much of the economic growth of the last decade will turn out to be useless, with conversion costs merely deferred until a later date?

This point was most strikingly demonstrated to me during a visit to a light truck assembly plant in Chengdu in 1988. Somehow, this factory had obtained precious cold-rolled steel sheet from the Wuhan Steel mill. The factory pressed the sheet steel into body parts and assembled light trucks, including assembly of the motors. Assembly was done by hand, and output was 3–4 vehicles per day. This factory was new, and was being expanded, slowly, workshop by workshop, and machine tool by machine tool. Its output showed up as an increase in production, purchased at the cost of substantial effort, material, and technical ingenuity. Yet this factory will have no future in a fully reformed economy. Only larger, more efficient auto assembly plants will survive, and only those possessing some kind of integrated and partially automated assembly lines. Moreover, the investments made to that time will do virtually nothing to prepare this small factory to make the leap into production at a competitive scale. Yet all this investment – surely destined to be wasted ultimately – has been made since the beginning of China's second phase of reforms in 1984.

In a broader sense, China's reforms have failed to establish clearly demarcated property rights, both in the state sector and in the rural enterprise sector. Ownership remains extraordinarily vague for a surprising number of Chinese firms. Privatization of existing firms has contributed almost nothing to Chinese performance, and even entry of new strictly private firms has been of distinctly secondary importance. According to currently prevailing economic orthodoxy, failure to properly specify property rights should be a critical shortcoming to any reform process. Yet this failure seems to have had surprisingly little harmful impact in the Chinese case. Does China, as it appears, present a challenge to prevailing economic theory? Why don't the vaguely specified Chinese property rights present a larger obstacle to robust economic growth? These questions remain to be addressed.

Shortcomings

The most obvious shortcoming of the Chinese reform process has been the continuing failure to develop institutions and impartial rules that apply to all economic organizations. The failure to specify property rights is simply one aspect – though an important one – of this general failing. Institutional development has consistently lagged behind the changes that were taking place in the economy, but we might nevertheless characterize those changes as "barely adequate." As the main process of reform was protracted over several years, incremental institutional development occurred in fits and starts. These failures of legality are in turn implicated in the continuing serious problems of corruption. There are a lot of new institutions in place, but in general they don't work very well.

The failure to build institutions is particularly evident is the investment system. State firms, in particular, continue to have access to large amounts of capital under conditions in which their liability and ability to repay are unclear. The increasingly leveraged financial position of China's state enterprises was discussed in Chapter 7. Although most increased enterprise indebtedness is probably benign, there are undoubtedly a significant number of state firms that continue to pile up debt as an alternative to simply going out of business. Estimates of the proportion of loans from the state banks that are non-performing or in arrears differ significantly, and it is probably fair to say only that in an environment of rapid economic change, we simply do not know what proportion of state loans will ultimately not be returned. Although the government has made some initial progress in placing government-influenced loans into separate policy banks, there is clearly a long way to go to make the banks really independent. Moreover, there will be an unavoidable "shakeout." Bank balance sheets will need to be restructured as significant amounts of loans are written down to reflect effectively bankrupt state firms. This is a difficult, though by no means impossible, process.

Certainly, a close look at a related program suggests that there are serious problems. The program to convert fiscal investment grants to repayable loans was described above. It has never worked well, and after the recession of 1989–90, it was in an utter shambles. By 1990, of the total funds disbursed, only 70% was covered by explicit repayment contracts, with the remainder either retroactively exempted from repayment, or else loaned under short-term "use of funds" agreements. Of the amount covered by explicit contracts, some 14 billion yuan was due for repayment by the end of 1990, but only 68% of the amount due was actually paid (8.7% of the total amount lent). Repayment rates increased to 78% in 1991, but the lending organization, the Bank of Construction, was predicting reductions in repayment rates in subsequent years (*Banking* 1992: 296). If this picture is at all applicable to lending from commercial banks, the picture is troubling indeed. It is difficult to escape the conclusion that development of capital markets has remained woefully deficient. Small-scale capital markets work reasonably well in rural areas, but large-scale capital markets remain highly distorted. Government control of the banking system is as strong as ever, and this has meant that the entire investment finance mechanism has remained remarkably resistant to reform. Enterprises still bargain over access to capital, budget constraints remain soft, and interest rates play little role in rationing scarce investment funds. As the system becomes more open to market forces, this may create serious problems both for the state enterprise sector and for the banking system as a whole.

Uncompleted tasks

It is easy to compile a short list of uncompleted tasks that confront Chinese reformers. Clearly, that includes provisions for the financing of public goods. It also includes restructuring the financial system, putting banks on an independent commercial basis, and cleaning up bank balance sheets to accurately reflect the value of current assets. One might add that privatization should begin to play a more important role in the Chinese transition. It certainly does not appear to be essential to rush into a mass privatization of Chinese state-run firms. But conversely, there is absolutely no reason to delay the beginning of a gradual privatization process. Even if the government decides to maintain predominant state ownership in certain heavy industrial and infrastructure sectors for a prolonged period, there is no reason to hold off the privatization of moderate sized or small firms in competitive markets. It is hard to see what benefit the Chinese people gain from state ownership of, say, a textile firm in Wuhan. Moreover, significant de facto privatization is occurring anyway, and it would be better to bring the whole process out in the open. An improved tax system and steady privatization of such firms would make the economy as a whole work much better.

The economy does face a clear additional challenge. Thus far, the Chinese government has been able to restrict the transition process to protect inefficient firms and also to protect the position of state urban workers as well. To be sure, such protection has not been absolute. Failing firms are pushed to merge with other firms, and some tiny fraction has been pushed into formal or informal bankrupcty. Yet there seems little doubt that there are many Chinese firms that will simply not survive the unfettered play of market competition. Thus far, the government has been unwilling to allow them to close down in really large numbers. Relatedly, the urban working class continues to be shielded from labor market competition by restriction on rural to urban migration, and by its privileged bargaining position as individuals already inside the state system. A qualitative increase in market competition might threaten the position of some of these workers by exposing them more directly to the force of competition from lower-wage rural and suburban workers. Real urban wages might be pushed down, or open urban unemployment might increase. Indeed, as we have seen, there are signs of this occurring in 1993.

In short, although the Chinese economy has undergone a real and profound process of restructuring since 1978, that process is not yet complete. Many of the painful aspects of restructuring have been postponed, and as a result remain as challenges to face Chinese policymakers. The economy is much larger than it was, and the ability to provide alternative occupations for displaced workers is much larger. Arguably, China could undertake something like a big bang now, without anything like the disruptions experienced in Eastern Europe. But even if this is true, it should not obscure the fact that there are still painful adjustments that remain to be made as the Chinese economy completes its transition to a market economy.

The two biggest dangers that confront the Chinese economy are therefore the specter of macroeconomic instability, fundamentally due to the unreconstructed nature of government finance and banking institutions, and public discontent caused by a further round of restructuring. Neither of these dangers is trivial, yet neither will necessarily derail the process of change. If China enters GATT, both these challenges will face China on an accelerated timetable, but the basic nature of the challenges will be unchanged.

The future of Chinese economic reforms

While Chinese reforms have been generally successful, they are certainly far from complete. Arguably, the dual-track strategy of Zhao Ziyang has now succeeded, and a new set of challenges face the economy today. We can expect to see Chinese economic reforms continue with an attempt to construct institutions that will be effective in dealing with what is generally a market economy. The pace and effectiveness of those reforms will certainly depend on the nature of the Chinese leadership. Prolonged political uncertainty may yet disrupt the ongoing reform process. But both conservatives and reformers will face a similar set of economic demands and constraints. We can expect conservatives to be overly cautious; and the return of a committed reformist leadership is much to be desired. But even continued conservative dominance is unlikely to block continued progress in economic reform.

Nevertheless, institutional development will probably continue to lag behind the demands of the economy. As in the earlier periods, new institutions will be "barely adequate" to deal with the accelerating demands of a growing and increasingly complex economy. China is still a poor country with a dysfunctional political system. That will make the creation of even the most straightforward institutions a difficult and prolonged process.

Future reforms will continue to be driven by the chronic problems with which government officials have to cope: fiscal shortfalls, investment inefficiency, and excess subsidy burdens. But reforms will also be driven by the vast potential of the Chinese economy. The current Chinese economy is still extremely inefficient. Bottlenecks and environmental crises will repeatedly threaten to disrupt development. But, conversely, very large efficiency gains can be anticipated from future reforms. An accelerated period of industrial restructuring can raise efficiency and prolong very rapid growth well into the next century. Moreover, investment remains robust. Such a process would lead to the emergence of dynamic city-centered growth poles along the

Chinese coast. The first such modern metropolis may already be taking shape, under the influence of Hong Kong, in Guangdong province. With accelerated reform, similar dynamic regions would emerge along the length of the Chinese coast, and vigorous growth would ultimately move inland as well. Future reforms will be pushed ahead by necessity and pulled forward by opportunity.

Statistical appendix

China's economic statistics are now abundant and fairly reliable by developing country standards. However, there are still a number of pitfalls that can make it difficult to use Chinese data. Chinese data are often presented in categories that are idiosyncratic or misleadingly labeled. Even worse is that categories are sometimes revised, and data series are published without adequate warning that coverage has changed. Under these conditions, straightforward use of the data can sometimes be misleading. An even more common experience is to find that abundant data are available, but that they are organized into categories that are not very informative. This appendix is provided to highlight some of the limitations to the data, and to explain to the reader the adjustments to the data which have been made in order to achieve consistency and make the data more informative. In general, the quality of data is improving, but sometimes rapid growth and economic change overwhelms the statisticians at the State Statistical Bureau (SSB). More recently, the SSB has had to cope with significant competition from the private sector for their most competent statisticians, and this may have on occasion affected the quality of statistics.

National income

Chinese statisticians organized national income data into the socialist system of "net material product" (NMP) until the mid-1980s. As is well known, NMP calculations are less desirable than GNP because they do not account for all current income streams. They are limited to "productive" activities, and thus exclude many types of services. Moreover, much of the data used in computing NMP is reported to statisticians in constant prices of a given base year, rather than in current prices. For the years since 1978, China has published both NMP – which they call *guomin shouru*, or national income – and estimates of GNP, which is about 20% larger than NMP.

Despite their shortcomings, NMP figures are calculated according to well-established rules, and can be useful. They have been used in Chapter 1 to make comparisons between China and the Soviet Union before reform, when both used NMP.

The remainder of this book uses data on gross national product (GNP) that are drawn from the most recent edition of the Statistical Yearbook. There are a number of shortcomings to the GNP data, but their use is essential anyway. The shortcomings spring from the fact that the series was created by the SSB by drawing on but revising its existing system for collecting NMP data. The shortcomings of the GNP data derive directly from their adaptation from NMP data. Two problems are most important. First, overall GNP is understated because the prices used to value in-kind consumption and subsidized goods and services (especially housing) are too low. Second, price indexes used to deflate GNP components are extremely weak. The implicit GNP deflator yields lower rates of inflation than most other available price indexes, and almost certainly understates the true rate of inflation. Deflation of rapidly growing rural industrial output is especially problematic. As a result, the growth rate of real GNP is probably overstated. The first GNP figures were not published in the Statistical Yearbooks until 1988, at which time a series from 1978 was provided, based on retrospective estimates. These figures are given in Table S.1.

Despite these shortcomings, the GNP data are still an essential part of our picture of the Chinese economy. In general, the end of price stability in China caught the Chinese statistical system singularly unprepared to deal with problems of deflation. This has made intertemporal comparison difficult, but it has made it even more essential to compare various nominal magnitudes with GNP in the year in which they occur. The degree of understatement of GNP does not appear to vary substantially over time, so changes in relative shares of GNP can still be tracked. Since 1985, output data has been collected in current as well as constant prices, improving the reliability of comparisons of contemporaneous data sources. Although the real growth rate of the economy is somewhat overstated, plausible adjustments would likely reduce the growth rate by 1–2% at a most. China's GNP is still growing rapidly.

The calculations of distribution of national income and national saving used in Chapters 2 and 4 and Figure 4.1 come from ESRRI Macro (1987) and Cheng Xiaonong (1991). They define national disposable income as GNP minus capital consumption plus net transfer from abroad. In-kind incomes have been included in both calculations.

Table S.1. *Gross National Product*

	Nominal GNP (billion yuan)	Real GNP growth rate	Implicit GNP deflator
1978	358.8	na	na
1979	399.8	7.6%	3.6%
1980	447.0	7.8%	3.7%
1981	477.3	4.5%	2.2%
1982	519.3	8.7%	0.0%
1983	580.9	10.4%	1.3%
1984	696.2	14.7%	4.5%
1985	855.8	12.8%	9.0%
1986	969.6	8.1%	4.8%
1987	1130.1	10.9%	5.1%
1988	1406.8	11.3%	11.8%
1989	1599.3	4.3%	9.0%
1990	1769.5	4.0%	6.3%
1991	2019.3	7.7%	5.9%
1992	2398.8	12.8%	5.3%
1993	3138.0	13.4%	15.4%

na = figures not available.

Industrial output data

The evolution of the statistical system for industrial output data parallels that for national income. Through 1984, output data were collected in constant prices and only from factories and mines subordinate to government administrations at the level of the township (then called the commune) and higher. Small-scale activity at the level of the village (then called the brigade) and by rural households was classified as household sideline activities carried out subsidiary to agriculture. Those small-scale activities were only a little over 4% of total output in 1978, but they were poised to grow rapidly. The rapid growth of all kinds of small-scale industrial activity severely strained the existing statistical system, both because many small producers were outside the system to begin with, and because small producers did not have ready access to the lists of constant prices that the statisticians would have preferred they use to value their output. In 1985, following a major industrial census, the statistical system was overhauled to collect primarily current price output data from all producers, regardless of size or administrative subordination. Although work also began simultaneously on preparing input and output deflators for each sector, this work proceeded slowly, and for a transition period the SSB both collected constant price data and compiled deflators. Neither system was entirely adequate, and the SSB did not feel sufficient confidence in their industrial deflators to publish them in the Statistical Yearbooks until 1993 (p. 268). The result is that deflation of the value of output is weak even after 1985, and very weak before 1985, particularly with respect to rural industry.

Industrial output value is commonly broken down into four ownership categories: state, collective, private, and other. Beginning in 1985, the collective category is regularly broken down into four main components: urban, township, village, and cooperative (urban and rural). These data are shown in Table S.2. (For 1978, production at the below-village, or "team," level has been estimated as 10% of village production, and assimilated into the co-operative category.) As discussed in the text, different types of collectives can be quite different, and have had very different growth experiences in the 1980s. Private output includes both very-small-scale household producers (*getihu*) and larger private firms.

The "other" category was the fastest growing in the late 1980s, but is also the least informative category. Originally, in the early 1980s, the other category was created primarily to describe joint ventures between domestic firms of different ownership types. Joint ventures between state firms and domestic collectives produced more than 80% of "other" output in the early 1980s (*Industry* 1949–1984: 47). However, foreign-invested firms have become an increasingly more important part of other ownership, and dominate the category by the 1990s. Data are available on formally registered foreign-invested firms: foreign joint ventures and wholly-owned subsidiaries of foreign companies and companies registered in Hong Kong and Taiwan. However, these data understate the total output from foreign-invested firms. There is also a category of informal foreign-invested firms in which individual residents of Hong Kong or Taiwan are listed as joint-venture partners with state or collective firms. Output data for such firms have not been published, but employment data are available.

Employment data for the "other" ownership form reveal some interesting patterns. Unfortunately, the data are for all types of enterprises, although industry accounts for about 85% of employment, with most of the rest in real estate development. The data reveal that in 1985, 70% of other employment was in joint ventures between state firms and domestic collectives, and almost 15% was in formal foreign-invested firms. By 1991, however, employment in state-collective joint ventures accounted for only 21% of the total, and formal foreign-invested firms accounted for 51%. Another 21% of employment was accounted for by joint ventures between individuals and state or collective firms, but it turned out that 94% of this employment was in firms in which the individuals were from Hong Kong or Taiwan (19% of the

Table S.2. *Industrial output by ownership and size*

	1978	1985	1991
	(billion yuan)		
Total	442.2	971.7	2824.8
State	341.6	630.2	1495.5
Collective	100.5	311.7	1008.5
[Urban]	[60.3]	[154.2]	[358.0]
[Township]	[21.2]	[76.1]	[300.1]
[Village]	[17.3]	[66.3]	[293.4]
[Rural cooperatives]	[1.7]	[15.2]	[50.0]
[Urban cooperatives]	[0.0]	[0.0]	[6.9]
Private	0.0	18.0	160.9
[Rural private]	[0.0]	[14.6]	[148.0]
[Urban private]	[0.0]	[3.3]	[12.9]
Other	0.0	11.7	160.0
[Foreign-invested]	[0.0]	[3.7]	[70.2]
[Domestic joint ventures and other]	[0.0]	[8.1]	[88.8]
Township level and above	423.1	872.2	2312.1
["Big"]	183.4	245.8	792.0
["Medium"]		165.2	438.6
["Small"]	239.7	461.2	1081.5
	(percentage of total)		
Total	100.0	100.0	100.0
State	77.3	64.9	52.9
Collective	22.7	32.1	35.7
[Urban]	[13.6]	[15.9]	[12.7]
[Township]	[4.8]	[7.8]	[10.6]
[Village]	[3.9]	[6.8]	[10.4]
[Rural cooperatives]	[0.4]	[1.6]	[1.8]
[Urban cooperatives]	[0.0]	[0.0]	[0.2]
Private	0.0	1.9	5.7
[Rural private]	[0.0]	[1.5]	[5.2]
[Urban private]	[0.0]	[0.3]	[0.5]
Other	0.0	1.2	5.7
[Foreign-Invested]	[0.0]	[0.4]	[2.5]
[Domestic Joint Ventures and Other]	[0.0]	[0.8]	[3.1]
Township level and above	95.7	89.8	81.9
["Big"]	41.5	25.3	28.0
["Medium"]		17.0	15.5
["Small"]	54.2	47.5	38.3

total), while another 5% was in cooperative (short-term) ventures between foreign and domestic partners. Fully 76% of other employment was in formal or informal foreign-invested firms (*Statistic* 1993: 109). Thus, the output data on foreign-invested firms seriously understate their total contribution. Indeed, they probably even understate the contribution of formal foreign-invested firms, since these larger, more modern firms are likely to contribute more than the 44% of other output shown, given that they account for 51% of other employment. It would be reasonable to estimate that foreign-invested firms of all types, formal and informal, accounted for 80% of other output in 1991. That would total 128 billion yuan, or not quite 4% of total output. Indeed, using, without comment, an alternative classification of foreign invested output, *Industry* 1993: 1049 reported that 1992 foreign-invested output was 206.6 billion yuan, or 5.6% of total output, which would be consistent with the larger figure and reported growth rates. The larger estimate is used in Table A.1 to show change in the ownership structure of industry.

Data is also available on the structure of industrial output by size of producer. All factories at the township level or above are classified as large, medium, or small. Ironically, by limiting the classification to township level or above, nearly all the very small producers are excluded from the classification! Indeed, the "small" firms by Chinese definition are not that small, often consisting of over 50 employees. In fact, Chinese definitions of these size categories are a heterogeneous mixture of sector-specific definitions (for example, a large steel mill is one that produces over 1 million tons annually). The 1985 industrial census includes a list of the 7,588 non-military large and medium sized industrial enterprises, with a few summary statistics for each enterprise, including labor force. Only a little more than 2% of of the enterprises had a work force of less than 500 employees (Industrial Census 1987: Volume 2). Thus, the Chinese category of large and medium sized enterprises can be roughly equated to the category of enterprises employing over 500 workers. This is the most common international standard for the dividing line between "very large" factories and all other size categories. Thus, while Chinese size data suffer from a misleading terminology and sector-specific definitions, they are nonetheless usable: the division between "medium" and "small" in China corresponds roughly to the division between "very large" and everything else in international practice. I label this category "large-scale."

The state sector accounted for 97% of large-scale output in 1985 (Industrial Census: I:63), and only a trivial share of collective output (2.3%) was from large-scale firms. However, some 30% of other output was produced by large-scale firms in 1985, and, while very small in 1985, that sector was poised for rapid growth, as described earlier. This is primarily because of the importance of foreign-invested firms, which tend to be large. As the share of foreign-invested firms in other (and in total) industrial output value has grown, the share of foreign-invested firms in large-scale output will also have grown. Table S.2 shows that formal foreign-invested firms produced 2.5% of industrial output in 1991, and the preceding discussion has estimated that all formal and informal foreign-invested firms produced just under 4% of output. It is reasonable to estimate that 3% of total output comes from large-scale firms with foreign investment. However, as discussed earlier, alternative estimates of the share of foreign-invested firms are also plausible.

This information is used to derive text Table 4.2 from Appendix Table S.2. First the large-scale sector is computed by summing total large-scale output (i.e., Chinese "big" and "medium" enterprises). The sector is then divided into state and other components by subtracting the data or estimates on other large-scale output (predominantly foreign invested). The urban medium/small sector is then constructed by combining urban collectives with small state firms (derived by substracting large-scale state from total state output). The rural medium/small sector simply consists of township and village level collective firms, while the very small scale sector consists of private and cooperative firms in urban and rural areas. The final other category is simply the residual of the original other category after large-scale firm output has been subtracted. Unlike the large-scale other sector, at least half of other medium/small output consists of joint ventures between domestic ownership forms, espeically state and collective.

Industrial financial data

In addition to the categories described in the last section, two additional categories are used to aggregate industrial financial data. The first corresponds to firms at the administrative level of the township or higher, including all ownership forms. However, for financial reporting (and some other) purposes, only those firms that practice "independent accounting" are included. That excludes industrial workshops subsidiary to other operations, such as railroads or schools, if they do not calculate their own profit and loss accounts. This category thus excludes village industry and rural private and cooperative firms. However, it corresponds roughly to the category of modern manufacturing and mining firms, except for the very-small sector. This is the category of industry for which the sectoral profit rates are reported in Figure 6.5 and Tables 6.3 and 6.4.

Table S.3. *Financial data for in-budget state-run industrial enterprises*

	Sales revenue	Tax and profit	Sales taxes (billion yuan)	Profit	Loan repayments	Retained profit
1978	271.70	72.62	26.60	46.04	1.09	0.78
1979	298.70	79.94	28.63	51.30	1.45	4.06
1980	319.70	85.83	30.70	55.13	1.70	6.92
1981	326.30	84.96	32.84	52.12	2.03	8.49
1982	352.00	87.03	35.10	51.93	2.94	11.20
1983	383.90	93.89	36.76	57.13	3.85	13.89
1984	416.30	102.50	41.09	61.46	5.23	16.01
1985	493.20	118.30	56.10	62.20	7.78	20.44
1986	554.10	118.90	61.73	57.15	9.70	21.43
1987	654.70	128.30	67.46	60.89	13.40	23.37
1988	809.60	151.70	81.47	70.21	18.35	28.59
1989	902.73	155.89	98.54	67.35	16.19	23.70
1990	944.52	127.08	102.47	24.60	12.85	15.14
1991	1121.86	141.96	119.16	22.80	14.93	15.80
1992	1330.38	167.22	133.05	34.17	18.71	21.56

Source: 1978–88: SRC/ER 1991: 646; 1989–92: *Abstract* 1993:82.

A further category is that of "in-budget" state enterprises. This refers to the larger state firms that report their financial results directly to the Ministry of Finance on a regular basis (accounting for over 80% of state firm output and revenues). The aggregate financial data from these firms are relatively detailed and timely. Since this is a good representation of the large-scale state sector, I have frequently used these data. There may be some bias in the selection of this category of enterprises. As a share of total state enterprises, in-budget enterprises have been declining over time, and they have lower profits and a higher proportion of loss-making factories than all independent accounting enterprises (Naughton 1992: 38).

Principal financial data for in-budget state enterprises is given in Table S.3. Tax refers to indirect taxes only, including turnover and sales taxes, as well as value-added taxes. It does not include profit tax. Two different series are spliced together at 1988, and there are some slight differences. Retained profit refers to net retained profit, after additional levies on "extra-budgetary funds" have been paid. This is explicit in the earlier source, which also gives profit handed over to the government. Profit remitted includes profit taxes, adjustment taxes and traditional remittances of profit. In most years, the sum of profit retained, remitted, and repaid to the bank slightly exceeds the total amount of profit realized. The later source does not provide a separate figure on remitted profit. After 1990 the total of profit retained and repaid to the bank exceeded the total amount of profit realized by a similar margin. After 1990, in-budget firms in the aggregate remit no profit to the government.

Investment data

Chinese investment data are partitioned into series on "capital construction" (*jiben jianshe*), "technical renovation" (*gengxin gaizao*), and "other." Technical renovation is sometimes translated as replacement and renewal, upgrading, or technical transformation. Originally, capital construction was to refer to state investments in new facilities, while technical renovation referred to incremental investment in existing facilities. Other investment refers primarily to investment in oilfields, with a few additional miscellaneous categories. However, this distinction is by no means absolute. During the 1970s, the distinction between capital construction and technical renovation became one of funding source (technical renovation was funded primarily from retained depreciation funds, while capital construction was funded through the government budget). Subsequently, during the course of the 1980s, technical renovation continued to be funded primarily by retained funds (including profit as well as depreciation), but both capital construction and technical renovation relied increasingly on bank loans and other external sources of capital. Thus, throughout the 1980s, this distinction became less clear-cut. For our purposes, it is important to recognize that while there is no precise dividing line between the categories of capital construction and technical renovation, there is a general distinction between the two. Capital construction generally consists of large projects with a substantial construction component. Technical renovation refers to projects that are smaller on average, more likely to be in existing firms, and with a smaller construction component. Thus, the relative increase in technical renovation does correspond to a proportionate reduction in large-scale projects and an increase in investment in existing firms. Table S.4 provides the basic investment data, drawn from the Statistical Yearbook, various years.

Figure 2.2 uses these basic investment categories. Investment in housing and other "non-productive" services is first subtracted (separately) from capital construction and technical transformation, then aggregated into new categories. The remaining "productive" investment within capital construction is labeled "new productive" in Figure 2.2, while the remaining productive investment within technical enovation is labeled "renovation" in the graph.

Table S.4. *State fixed investment*

	State fixed investment	Capital construction	Technical transformation	Other
	(billion yuan)			
1977	54.83	38.24	16.59	na
1978	66.87	50.10	16.77	na
1979	69.94	52.35	17.59	na
1980	74.59	55.89	18.70	na
1981	66.75	44.29	19.53	2.93
1982	84.53	55.55	25.04	3.94
1983	95.20	59.41	29.11	6.67
1984	118.52	74.32	30.93	13.28
1985	168.05	107.44	44.91	15.70
1986	197.85	117.61	61.92	18.32
1987	229.80	134.31	75.86	19.63
1988	276.28	157.43	98.06	20.79
1989	253.55	155.17	78.88	19.50
1990	291.86	170.38	83.02	38.46

na = figures not available.

Full breakdowns of the composition of technical renovation investment before 1981 are not available and have been estimated. Non-productive investment was estimated at 20% of the total, and the proportion of non-productive going to housing was assumed to be the same as for capital construction, or 37%, 49% and 56% respectively in the years 1978 through 1980. These numbers are quite small relative to total investment.

Figure 7.2 shows various categories of central government investment. The budgetary data are straightforward, and taken from the Statistical Yearbook, various years. Central government investment is determined by aggregating the capital construction and technical renovation investment that is considered to be subordinate to central government ministries and commissions. A breakdown of this data is provided in Table S.5. This information is available in *Fixed Investment*, various years, and in *Abstract*, various years. Priority investment refers to those projects entered into the central government keypoint construction program, sometimes referred to as "projects on an accelerated construction timetable." Although information on this program is scattered in various sources, much of the information has been collected in SSB (1991). The 1989 and 1990 data are from *Zhongguo Touzi yu Jianshe* [China Investment and Construction] 1991:4, p. 18.

Table S.5. *Funding and central government direction of fixed investment*

	Budgetary capital construction	Budgetary technical transformation and other	Central government capital construction	Central technical transformation and other	Priority investment plan
	(billion yuan)				
1977	31.24	1.84	na	na	na
1978	38.92	2.65	26.64	4.53	na
1979	39.69	4.36	27.32	4.75	na
1980	30.01	3.30	29.26	5.05	na
1981	22.26	3.49	24.10	6.09	na
1982	23.25	3.30	29.66	6.54	6.30
1983	29.60	4.08	35.50	7.49	9.41
1984	35.99	5.81	44.12	7.58	15.90
1985	38.12	2.18	57.52	10.48	19.83
1986	41.74	2.11	63.25	21.93	27.99
1987	43.85	3.36	76.17	25.61	36.19
1988	36.99	2.83	87.37	30.98	42.10
1989	32.32	1.54	83.77	33.04	40.89
1990	36.36	1.86	91.92	34.65	42.69

na = figures not available.

Fiscal and financial data

Fiscal data in broad categories are readily available in the Statistical Year-books. However, that data must be adjusted to correct for idiosyncratic reporting practices. The Chinese report borrowed funds as revenue. Those funds must be subtracted from total revenues to derive actual budgetary revenues. An additional correction is necessary to handle subsidies consistently. Data are published on two types of subsidy, "price subsidy" and "enterprise losses." There is, however, no consistent definitional difference between the two. Most price subsidies went to support low-price sales of food to urban residents. However, a large part of enterprise losses went for the same purpose, at least through the 1980s. The Chinese distinction between these two categories largely reflects an attempt by the central government to limit its price subsidy burden by placing a cap on certain categories of price subsidy (in 1985). However, since the underlying cost trends were outside the government's control, continued low fixed prices led to increases in commercial enterprise losses. The only consistent way to handle subsidies

Table S.6. *Total subsidies*

	Price subsidies	Enterprise losses	Industrial losses
	(billion yuan)		
1978	9.39	6.01	4.21
1979	18.07	6.73	3.64
1980	24.21	5.11	3.43
1981	32.77	6.43	4.60
1982	31.84	5.29	4.76
1983	34.17	10.27	3.21
1984	37.00	6.79	2.66
1985	29.95	12.08	3.24
1986	25.75	32.48	5.45
1987	29.46	37.64	6.10
1988	31.70	44.65	8.19
1989	37.03	59.89	18.02
1990	38.08	57.89	34.88
1991	37.38	51.02	36.70
1992	32.15	44.50	36.93
1993	29.62	41.26	–

is to aggregate price subsidies and enterprise losses into a single category. This includes some subsidies to foreign trade (both import and export) and some industrial losses, but, at least until 1993, most subsidies went to state commercial enterprises.

Until 1985, both price subsidies and compensation for enterprise losses were deducted from budgetary revenues. Beginning in 1986, price subsidies were included as both a revenue and expenditure item. In this book, both price subsidies and enterprise losses have been added back into revenues and expenditures for all years. The series on price subsidies and enterprise losses for the first half of the 1980s comes from Wang Chaocai and Luo Wenguang (1989). Additional details are available in Qiao Rongzhang (1990). Since 1985, the figures have been readily available in the annual budget reports by the Minister of Finance, and have been updated from *Statistic* 1993: 216, 219, 231, and Liu Zhongli 1994. For comparison, total industrial losses in all independent accounting units (township and above) are shown from *Statistic* 1993: 430. Through 1989, industry was a small part of total subsidies, but since 1990, industry has accounted for almost half of total subsidies. These data are shown in Table S.6.

Despite major improvements, availability of credit data is still sketchy and inconsistent. Quarterly data are available only beginning in 1981, in successive issues of *Banking* (Annual), *Economic* (Annual) or the monthly *Zhongguo Jinrong* [China Finance]. Moreover, there are some inconsistencies in data classification. Retrospective annual data to 1952 are available in PBC (1989). The major problem is the tendency of the Chinese government to create new institutions under state sponsorship that extend credit to the economy, but only later integrate those institutions into the statistical base. The creation of the Construction Bank, and its entry into large-scale lending during the early 1980s was the first example of this. In the data presented in Figures 7.1 and 8.1 and Table 7.3, growth rates are calculated with the Construction Bank and the Rural Credit Cooperatives included in all cases. During 1992, significant sums of money from the banking system escaped from the statistical system (and probably from the oversight of banking officials) through on-lending to non-bank financial institutions. The real rate of credit creation in that year was probably significantly higher than indicated by official statistics. The series are updated through 1993 from *Zhongguo Jinrong*, 1993:10, pp. 55–57 and SSB 1994. 1993 figures should be considered preliminary.

Notes

Introduction

1. The most important advocate of emulating the Chinese approach was Academician Oleg Bogomolov, head of the Institute of the Economy of the World Socialist System (Aslund 1991: 7, 103, 137, 144–45, 227). Alexander Yakovlev, the "father of perestroika," claimed, "More than once I said that perestroika should have first been launched in agriculture." His suggestion, as of 1985–86, was to begin private farming immediately on uncultivated land (Parks 1991). See also Bunich 1991: 250.

2. General works on agriculture include Kueh and Ash (1993); Lardy (1983); Putterman (1993); Sicular (1991); on trade see Hsu (1991); Lardy (1992); Shan (1989) and World Bank (1988).

3. "European command economies" means the Soviet Union, Poland, Czechoslovakia, East Germany, Hungary, Romania and Bulgaria, but not Yugoslavia or Albania.

4. Lange (1972) explicitly argued that computers could replace the market. The pioneers of reform design in the Soviet Union were engineers, mathematicians, and mathematical economists. The advocacy of optimal prices also attracted support from economists who believed in a greater role for market determination of prices and who saw price adjustment as an intermediate step in the revival of market forces.

5. It is probably more appropriate to evaluate rationalizing reforms in the ECEs as a set of measures adopted under the tight political constraints to ameliorate some of the worst defects of the traditional command economy than as a comprehensive reform program. From this perspective, the reforms had some success, at least in Hungary. Hungarian consumers were much better off than their counterparts in other ECEs, and Hungary entered the era of radical reform after 1989 with substantial advantages created by its twenty-year experience with limited reforms. Even in Hungary, progress was limited by the severe political constraints under which reformers labored (Berend 1990), constraints that were far more serious in the other ECEs. From the 1980s, Hungarian reforms began to diversify, and took on some of the characteristics of the Chinese reforms, experimenting more boldly with new incentive mechanisms and liberalizing some small-scale sectors. But government controls remained pervasive, and the government budget remained a very large share of GNP (Newbery 1993).

Chapter 1

1. GNP is approximated by multiplying net material product (NMP) produced by 1.15. NMP measures national income but is less inclusive than GNP (see Statistical Appendix). There are no reliable GNP figures before 1978.

2. Granick (1990) describes divided control but stresses local government property rights created by investment. This is an important factor in the 1980s and with respect to smaller enterprises. However, examination of the history of large enterprises reveals that the majority were originally created by the central government and then delegated to local governments in the early 1970s (People's University 1979: 230; Gong Guanshi 1984).

3. To facilitate comparison, I have scaled magnitudes to net material product, the statistical category used to calculate national income in both China and the Soviet Union.

Chapter 2

1. Contrast Harding's argument with K. T. Li's observations about economic policy-making in Taiwan. "To attribute the cause of a policy change entirely to ideology only begs the question of what caused the ideological position. . . . Policy is more likely to be a handmaiden of [ideology and economic conditions] than in the driver's seat. This is not to say that policy is unimportant, only that the more important issues are the economic environment in which the policy is made and the limits ideology places on policies considered acceptable to deal with that environment" (K. T. Li 1988: 145–56).

2. Soviet military intervention in Ethiopia in September 1977 was followed during 1978 by Vietnam's invasion of Kampuchea, expulsion of ethnic Chinese businessmen, and signing of a treaty of friendship with the Soviet Union. These actions intensified China's fear of strategic encirclement by the Soviet Union.

3. Except for the artificially inflated and unsustainable revenues recorded during the Great Leap Forward.

4. This plan is linked to the original two-stage development strategy put forward by Zhou Enlai in 1964. Zhou envisaged creating a basically complete and self-sufficient industrial economy by 1980. The agricultural mechanization plan was part of that first stage. Beginning in 1980, policy was to shift outward and toward a comprehensive modernization of agriculture, industry, science and technology, and national defense – the "Four Modernizations."

5. As a result of this personality characteristic, Chen Yun managed to avoid the brunt of Mao Zedong's mercurial temperament. Whereas Deng Xiaoping was twice purged by Mao, Chen was never publicly purged, and played an important role throughout virtually the entire history of the PRC.

6. This was a slightly revised version of a slogan that had been used in the early 1960s during the rehabilitation of the economy after the catastrophic Great Leap Forward (when Chen Yun had been the guiding force in economic policy).

7. A handful of projects, including the Baoshan Steel Mill, were carried through, largely because the agreements with foreign suppliers had already been signed. Most of the projects just disappeared.

8. See Statistical Appendix for discussion of investment categories. Capital construction consists of the large, new plants that are the core of traditional development strategy, mostly controlled by the central government.

9. The reduction was distributed roughly as a 2% reduction in total investment; a slightly more than 1% increase in renovation and replacement investment in existing firms; and an income of slightly less than 2% of GNP in investment in housing and services.

10. Chinese unemployment rates express registered urban job-seekers as a proportion of the official urban labor force. Unemployed or underemployed individuals with rural household registrations are uncounted, even if they are resident in urban areas and seeking work.

11. Among the capitalists, in the Chinese account of the process, 160,000 had "really been" capitalists, and over 700,000 petty merchants had been inappropriately classified as capitalists.

12. Rong Yiren's family alone was paid more than 5 million yuan, as were three other Shanghai capitalist families (Ceng Bijun 1990: 317; Li Wenjie 1993: 139).

Chapter 3

1. For example, Deng Xiaoping: "We began with the countryside, applying the open policy there, and we achieved results very quickly. In some places it took only one or two years to get rid of poverty. After accumulating the necessary experience in the countryside, we shifted the focus of reform to the cities." (Deng Xiaoping 1987: 176).

2. The reform group was formally headed by the Finance Minister, Zhang Jingfu, and evolved through a number of stages into the Economic Reform Commission, a source of reform proposals throughout the 1980s. The reform programs it produced over the years are collected in SRC 1988. The economic structure group, headed by Ma Hong, produced an influential report (Ma Hong and Sun Shangqing 1981), and evolved through merger and acquisition into the Development Research Center, which, among other things, built some sophisticated economic forecasting models during the 1980s (Ma Hong 1980: 2; Halpern 1985: 375–80; Hamrin 1990; Li Xiannian in CCP 1982: 140–43).

3. Piece-rates played a minor role in employee compensation (in contrast to the ECEs). Although reinstated in 1978, piece-rates grew slowly to make up 6% of total state worker compensation in 1981, and still only 10% in 1985. Separate breakdowns for industrial wages became available only in 1985. These show the share of industrial wages paid as piece-rates are only slightly higher, at 11% of wages (*Statistic* 1986: 664, 666). Piece-rates became significant primarily in mining and construction work.

4. One factory manager interviewed in 1984 described a dispute in which a group of disgruntled workers showed up at his home every evening at dinner time for several weeks. They would discuss grievances while first delaying, and then ultimately sharing in, the family dinner. Eventually the manager capitulated to their demands.

5. Chen Yun sometimes uses the word "plan" to refer to any kind of careful forward-looking behavior, and especially to moderate balanced growth. For example, in a January 1982 discussion of planning, Chen said, "In our enterprises, we need to have a plan. Do products have a market? What is the source of raw materials? All this must be planned. . . . As far as this point goes, capitalist firms definitely have plans – if they didn't, they wouldn't succeed at all. . . . In the past, if you wanted the Planning Commission to set a 10% growth rate, they'd set a 10% growth rate; if you wanted 20%, they'd set 20%. This is no good. . . ." (CCP 1982: 1133–34) Here the insistence on planning is not in opposition to the market, but rather in opposition to reckless administrative commands. Sometimes Chen even comes close to equating good planning with good macroeconomic policy (Li Zhining 1987: 494; Bachman 1985; Lardy and Lieberthal 1983).

6. Some reformist economists, however, stressed that organized consultation and information sharing between institutions would be part of state guidance – rather like French indicative planning in the 1950s (Liu Guoguang 1980).

7. It is a concept with a long pedigree in the socialist world, dating back to Oskar Lange in the 1930s. Chinese economists in the early 1980s were not simply adapting foreign ideas. During the 1950s, the older generation of Chinese economists, such as Sun Yefang, had participated in the elaboration of some of these ideas. They were therefore engaged in rehabilitating ideas that had been rejected in Maoist China (Naughton 1986a).

8. A group within the State Planning Commission continued to advocate a moderate increase in material balance planning. They argued for allocation of 110 commodities, with an additional 90 to be allocated by the Ministry of Commerce (SRC 1988: 113). But this seems to have remained a minority opinion.

9. These loans were to be made by the budgetary authorities; a separate program of bank loans for investment is described elsewhere.

10. One last attempt to implement capital charges was made in 1984 as part of the tax-for-profit scheme. The failure of that attempt is discussed in Chapter 5.

11. All surplus value could be assigned to labor, as in the orthodox view. Alternatively, surplus value could be classified as profit and assigned to capital, producing Marx's "production prices," an outcome of the market economy. Finally, a two-channel assignment can be made as a compromise between these extreme views. The two-channel approach had been adopted in Czechoslovakia in the 1960s.

12. Similar proportions prevailed during the 1986–89 period: 45% of total outlays went to energy; 32% to raw material industry (steel industry investment fell by five percentage points); and 18% to transportation and communications, for a total of 94% to these three sectors.

Chapter 4

1. See the two documents on agriculture: "Draft Regulations Governing Rural Commune Work," (SRC 1984: 83–94) and "Draft Resolution on Certain Problems in the Acceleration of Agricultural Development" (SRC 1984: 109–19).

2. This was also net in the sense that local tax-like set-asides for accumulation and community welfare were deducted before distribution.

3. Thus, Deng Xiaoping was quite unfair to his own agricultural planners when he subsequently said, "Our greatest success – and it is one we had by no means anticipated – has been the emergence of a large number of enterprises run by villages and townships. . . . They were like a new force that just came into being spontaneously. . . . The Central Committee takes no credit for this" (Deng Xiaoping 1987: 89). Deng is here eager to put his own "spin" on the reform process.

4. Whether rural industries are responding to state-induced price distortions or to previously unmet needs, they are likely to trace the same path of high initial and then declining profitability. However, the implications for total social welfare of the two cases could be quite different. Entry in response to price distortions may simply result in the diversion of production away from state firms to rural enterprises without any net gain to society. Entry in response to unmet needs immediately increases social welfare by the full amount of the increased production.

5. In 1978, RCCs were only allowed to lend out a little over a quarter of their deposits (the remainder were deposited in the state banking system), and a little over a quarter of their loans went to TVEs, so that 7% of deposits was loaned out to TVEs. By 1988, RCC deposits had increased dramatically. Moreover, RCCs were allowed to loan out almost two-thirds of their deposits, and half of those loans went to TVEs, so that over 30% of RCC deposits was loaned to TVEs (*Rural Finance* 1992: 77–78).

6. This calculation depends on our ability to measure fixed capital accurately, which might not be the case. Township producers probably pay higher prices for the capital they purchase; on the other hand, this calculation is based on undepreciated values, and the state capital stock is considerably older. Moreover, township producers may be able to sell lower quality goods at higher prices (due to lingering price rigidities in the state sector), which would bias the comparison in favor of township producers. The point is not to condemn township level textile firms, but simply to point out the importance of distortions in the economic environment in rural development patterns.

Chapter 5

1. The origins of this effort can be traced back to 1980, when Deng Xiaoping suggested a target of $1,000 GNP per capita by the year 2000 (Zheng Derong 1987: 68). In November 1982, Hu Yaobang called for a "strategic objective" of quadrupling of output by the year 2000, which was roughly equivalent. These slogans did not reflect genuine optimism about the economy at that time. On the contrary, they were essentially attempts to rally the faithful to look beyond contemporary difficulties to a bright future. They were in sharp contrast to the targets of the Sixth Plan, which was drawn up at the same time. Ironically, these quintessentially political gestures had a positive economic impact by stimulating realistic growth projections which informed planning during the subsequent decade.

2. The senior leaders "signed off" on the letter in a literal sense, using an ink brush to draw a circle in the margin, thus signifying their assent. The letter is sufficiently important that it has been published openly, an unusual step for letters among the top leadership (CCP 1986: 533–38).

3. Indeed, Chen's formulations (*tifa*) on plan and market, pervasive in the early 1980s, disappeared from the press in May 1984. In September 1985, Chen grumbled that his formulations "really are not outmoded." (Li Zhining 1988: 494).

4. One of the costs of Zhao's obfuscation has been continuing misunderstanding of the Chinese reform path. An amusing example of this is revealed in a retrospective account of China's early negotiations to re-enter the GATT: "Although the Chinese delegation repeatedly and specifically explained that China was practicing a 'planned commodity economy' and pointed out that that was a great breakthrough in economic theory for China. . . . foreign representatives in the China Working Party could not understand what 'planned commodity economy' meant at all, and so the two sides could not go on with the talks." Chen Jianping, "China's Reentry into GATT is Likely to Be Delayed," Wen Wei Po (Hong Kong), May 6, 1993, p. 2, translated in FBIS-CHI, May 11, 1993, p. 17. Misunderstanding has been particularly significant among those most familiar with Eastern European reforms. Although Hewett (1985) already recognized that Chinese reality was diverging significantly from that of Hungary post-1968, even an astute and experienced East European economist like Csikos-Nagy could subsequently state that in China "only the reform of socialist economic planning is on the agenda. . . . what actually is happening in China is similar to the Hungarian economic reform of the early 1980s" (Csikos-Nagy 1991).

5. Keypoint tasks appear to be primarily related to military industry, either for military tasks or for the conversion of military industry to civilian production (Chen Xian 1984).

6. See Shirk 1992: 245–79 for a detailed description and analysis of this process. The following draws heavily from Shirk's account.

7. This view of stabilization is often held by advocates of "big bang" transitions to the market economy as well. See, for example, the views of the Czech economist, later Prime Minister, Vaclav Klaus (1990).

8. To a certain extent, the fortunes of the price/comprehensive group rose and fell with changes in the macroeconomic situation. During favorable macroeconomic periods, the leadership was disposed to listen to comprehensive reform proposals. But before comprehensive plans could be drafted – much less implemented – the resumption of rapid economic growth would begin to create problems for policymakers, distracting their attention from comprehensive reform packages, and delaying implementation of already prepared measures. This dynamic characterizes much of the period from 1984 onwards.

9. In Chinese, the *fang'an ban*, short for the office of the State Council Leadership Small Group for the Study of an Economic Reform Program (SRC 1988: 164–85). A number of the proposals are collected in Wu Jinglian and Zhou Xiaochuan 1988.

Chapter 6

1. Casual workers have consistently accounted for around 15% of the total state work force (*Labor 1978–87: 67*. They are used most frequently in county-level firms – that is, the state firms that are the most like rural enterprises and have the greatest need for seasonal and short-term employment. These workers are now usually called temporary or extra-plan workers, but until recently these casual laborers were often referred to as contract workers. This creates a linguistic tangle, since the post-1983 contract worker reform does not apply to these workers at all. Here we use the term "contract worker" exclusively to refer to those workers with privileges similar to permanent workers, but on five-year employment contracts.

2. In both periods, shortage of raw materials was most often chosen as the greatest source of pressure.

3. Profit rates are available before this time, but only according to a much cruder breakdown of industry into only ten sectors.

4. Throughout, the rate of return on cigarette production is extremely high: 327% in 1980 and 152% in 1989. As a result, in the analysis following, the cigarette industry is omitted. The analysis was also carried out *including* the cigarette industry, with the same results.

Chapter 7

1. This torrid growth was unsustainably high, and GNP growth dropped to 4.6% between 1988 and 1990.

2. By contrast, the costs of the previous system were disguised by the artificially low prices paid. Costs showed up in lower industrial productivity caused by goods that did not meet factory specifications, or which were delivered at the wrong time. In this sense, improvement of the distribution network would be expected to show up as measured improvement of industrial productivity.

3. In addition, credit planners could allocate additional "gap" to bank branches when they wished to support particular projects.

4. An example of coercive relations is given in the journal of the banking system (ZGJR 1985: 7), which describes how a vice-mayor in Xi'an locked the bank leaders in a room until they agreed to make a loan to his favorite project. See also Zhou and Zhu (1987); White and Bowles (1987: 26, 42, 46, 53, 64).

5. Chinese budgetary data are converted into internationally comparable statistics. Government borrowing and principal repayments are subtracted from revenues and expenditures respectively. Price subsidies and subsidies to loss-making enterprises are included in both revenues and expenditures for all years.

6. These are estimates since there are no breakdowns on funding of investment inside the central investment plan. The numbers given are based on the assumption that the central government share of budgetary investment was constant throughout this period (at 68%), and compare central government budgetary investment directly with the central government investment plan. Figures from the banking system show bank credit going almost entirely to enterprises, but this is because once an investment project is begun it is set up as an independent accounting unit – that is, an enterprise. The figures presented here actually understate the real resources flowing into the priority investment program, because materials are acquired by the state at low state-set prices, while most of the resources being acquired by outside-plan investors are purchased at higher market prices. Since the differential between the prices is often 100% or more, the real difference can be substantial.

7. The initial shift of policy occurred during the final weeks of August 1988. During August 15–17, the Communist Party Politburo, under Zhao Ziyang, declared its intention of persisting with the policy of rapid decontrol of most prices (advocated by Deng Xiaoping). But on August 30, the government State Council under Li Peng issued an urgent circular freezing prices for the remainder of the year, and postponing price decontrol back to a five-year time horizon (*Prices* 1989: 13–15). The hardliners had effectively gained control. This created an impossible situation: Zhao Ziyang formally outranked Li Peng (since the Communist Party outranks the government), and was known for his expertise in economics. Yet his nominal subordinate, holding opposite views, had with the support of Communist elders usurped his authority in the realm of economic policy.

Chapter 8

1. The Chinese have not published a price index for investment goods. However, in 1989, ex-factory prices of heavy industrial manufactured goods increased 21.8%, and factory purchase price of building materials increased 22.7%, providing an approximate value for an investment goods deflator (*Price* 1991: 538–39).

2. Remarkably, the Party leaders drawing up the 39 points were unaware that consumer prices were actually declining at the time they met. They looked only at price indices calculated in relation to the year previous period, which aggregates over the past twelve months of price changes, and thus contains a large element of past inflation. They vowed to hold price increases under 10%, but prices were already falling.

Chapter 9

1. For example, in Hungary – much smaller than a single one of China's thirty provinces – planners were able to maintain their monopoly through informal pressures and influence. With only a single major metropolitan region, and in the absence of a firm commitment to marketization by the political leadership, there was no force to prevent planners from maintaining their monopoly.

2. Competition for monopoly rents, to be sure, does not necessarily increase output, and some gains are dispersed in rent-seeking activity.

Bibliography

Abstract (Annual). *Zhongguo Tongji Zhaiyao [Statistical Abstract of China]*. Beijing: Zhongguo Tongji.

Aganbegyan, Abel (1988). "Economic Reforms." in A. Aganbegyan, ed. *Perestroika 1989*. New York: Scribners. pp. 73–108.

Agriculture (Annual). *Zhongguo Nongye Nianjian [China Agriculture Yearbook]*. Beijing: Nongye.

Anderson, Dennis (1982). "Small Industry in Developing Countries: A Discussion of Issues." *World Development*. 10(11): 913–48.

Aslund, Anders (1991). *Gorbachev's Struggle for Economic Reform*. Ithaca: Cornell University Press.

Augustinovics, Maria (1975). "Integration of Mathematical and Traditional Methods of Planning." in M. Bornstein, ed. *Economic Planning, East and West*. Cambridge, Mass.: Ballinger. pp. 127–48.

Bachman, David (1985). *Chen Yun and the Chinese Political System*. China Research Monograph. Berkeley: Center for Chinese Studies, University of California, Berkeley.

  (1986). "Differing Views of China's Post-Mao Economy." *Asian Survey*. 26(3): 292–321.

Banking (Annual). *Zhongguo Jinrong Nianjian [China Banking Annual]*. Beijing: Zhongguo Jinrong.

Bei Duoguang, Arden Koontz, and Lewis Lu (1992). "Emerging Securities Market in the PRC," *China Economic Review* 3:2 (Fall), pp. 149–72.

Berend, T. Ivan (1990). *The Hungarian Economic Reforms, 1953–1988*. New York: Cambridge University Press.

Bialer, Seweryn (1980). *Stalin's Successors: Leadership, Stability, and Change in the Soviet Union*. Cambridge: Cambridge University Press.

Blank, Grant and William Parish (1990). "Rural Industry and Nonfarm Employment: Comparative Perspectives." in R. Kwok, W. Parish, A. Yeh and Xu Xueqiang, ed. *Chinese Urban Reform: What Model Now?*. Armonk: M. E. Sharpe. pp. 109–39.

Blejer, Mario and Gyorgy Szapary (1990). "The Evolving Role of Tax Policy in China." *Journal of Comparative Economics*. 14(3): 452–72.

Brown, William (1986). "China: Energy and Economic Growth." in U.S.C. Joint Economic Committee, ed. *China's Economy Looks Toward the Year 2000*. Washington, D.C.: U.S. Government Printing Office. pp. 22–59.

Brus, Wlodzimierz and Kazimierz Laski (1989). *From Marx to the Market: Socialism in Search of an Economic System*. Oxford: Oxford University Press.

Budget (Annual). *Zhongguo Caizheng Tongji*. Beijing: Zhongguo Caizheng Jingji.

Bunich, Pavel (1991). "The Remonstrations of Pavel Bunich." in E. Hewett and V. Winston, ed.. *Milestones in Glasnost and Perestroyka*. Washington, D.C.: Brookings. pp. 249–52.

Burns, John (1989). "China's Civil Service Reform." *China Quarterly* 120. (December): 739–70.

Byrd, William (1983). *China's Financial System: The Changing Role of Banks*. Boulder, Colorado: Westview.

(1987). "The Role and Impact of Markets." in G. Tidrick and Chen Jiyuan, ed.. *China's Industrial Reform*. New York: Oxford University Press. pp. 237–75.

(1987). "The Impact of the Two-Tier Plan and Market System in Chinese Industry." *Journal of Comparative Economics*. 11(September): 295–308.

(1989). "Plan and Market in the Chinese Economy: A Simple General Equilibrium Model." *Journal of Comparative Economics*. 13(June): 177–204.

and Lin Qingsong (1990). *China's Rural Industry: Structure, Development, and Reform*. New York: Oxford University Press.

(1991). *The Market Mechanism and Economic Reforms in China*. Armonk, N.Y.: M.E. Sharpe.

Cai Donghan (1988). "Rural Industry Development Paths." *Gongye Jingji Guanli Congkan*. 1988(2): 61–65.

Campbell, Robert (1958). "A Comparison of Soviet and American Inventory-Output Ratios." *American Economic Review*. 48(4): 549–65.

Cao Chengneng (1981). "Recognize the Important Role of Commune and Brigade Enterprises." *Caizheng Yanjiu Ziliao*. 1981(65): 24–26.

Capital Construction (1989). *Dangdai Zhongguo de Jiben Jianshe (Capital Construction in Contemporary China)*. Beijing: Zhongguo Shehui Kexue.

CASS/UCSD (1990). *Survey of 769 State-Owned Industrial Firms*. University of California, San Diego, Graduate School of International Relations and Pacific Studies.

CCP, Documents Research Office (1982). *San Zhong Quanhui Yilai [Since the Third Plenum]*. Beijing: Renmin.

(1985). "Party Center Suggestions on Drafting the Seventh Five Year Plan for Economic and Social Development (September 23, 1985)." *Hong Qi*. 1985(19): 10–27.

(1986). *Shierda Yilai [Since the Twelfth Party Congress]*. Beijing: Renmin.

(1990). "CPC Decision on Improving Economy." *FBIS China Report*. (January 18, 1990): 24–37.

(1991). "CPC Proposals to Seventh Central Committee Plenum." *FBIS China Report*. (January 29, 1991): 14–34.

(1993). "Establishment of a Socialist Market Economic System." Translated in FBIS China Report, November 17, 1993, pp. 22–35.

CCPW ("Contemporary China Planning Work" Office) (1987). *Zhonghua Renmin Gongheguo Guomin Jingji he Shehui Fazhan Jihua Dashi Jiyao 1949–1985 [Chronology of Major Events on PRC Plans for the National Economy and Social Development 1949–1985]*. Beijing: Hongqi.

Ceng Bijun and Lin Muxi (1990). *Xin Zhongguo Jingji Shi, 1949–1989 (An Economic History of New China)*. Beijing: Jingji Ribao.

Chamberlain, Heath (1987). "Party-Manager Relations in Chinese Industries: Some Political Dimensions of Economic Reform." *China Quarterly*. (112 (December)): 631–61.

Chang Weimin (1993). "Oil Price Controls to be Lifted Gradually." China Daily. August 25.

(1994). "New Prices to Boost Coal Mining," *China Daily – Business Weekly.* January 9–15, p. 8.

Chen, Kuan, G. Jefferson, T. Rawski, H. Wang and Y. Zheng (1988). "Productivity Change in Chinese Industry: 1953–1985." *Journal of Comparative Economics.* 12: 570–591.

Chen Fubao (1989). "The Reform of Means of Production Prices." *Gongye Jingji Guanli Congkan.* 1989(7): 2–7.

Chen Huiqin (1981). "China's Experience with Technology Import." *Gongye Jingji Guanli Congkan.* 1981(5): 44–54.

Chen Jinhong (1990). "There is much to be accomplished with the return of capital construction loans." *Zhongguo Touzi yu Jianshe [China Investment and Construction].* 1990(10): 37–38.

Chen Jinhua (1994). "Report on the Implementation of the 1993 National Plan." *Jingji Ribao.* March 25. p. 2.

Chen Xian (1984). "Overall Material Balancing Is an Important Part of Overall National Planning." ed. *Guomin Jingji Jihua Gailun Cankao Ziliao [Reference Materials on Principles of National Economic Planning].* Wuhan: Zhongyang Guangbo Dianshi Daxue. pp. 209–20.

Chen Yizi (1990). *Zhongguo: Shinian Gaige yu Bajiu Minyun [China: Ten Years of Reform and the Popular Movement of 1989].* Taipei: Lien-ching.

Cheng Xiaonong (1991). "Distribution of National Income during Economic Reform." Processed. San Francisco: 1990 Institute. June.

"China's Capital Goods Market" (1989). *Beijing Review* 32:46 (November 13–19), pp. 30–31.

Chung, Jae Ho (1993). "The Politics of Agricultural Mechanization in the Post-Mao Era." *China Quarterly.* (134): 264–90.

Clarke, Donald C. (1991). "What's Law Got to Do With It? Legal Institutions and Economic Reform in China." *UCLA Pacific Basin Law Journal.* 10(1): 1–76.

CMEA [China Materials Economics Association] (1983). *Zhongguo Shehuizhuyi Wuzi Guanli Tizhi Shilue [An Outline History of China's Socialist Materials Management System].* Beijing: Wuzi.

Coal (Annual). *Zhongguo Meitan Gongye Nianjian [China Coal Industry Yearbook].* Beijing: Meitan Gongye.

Commentator (1977). *How the "Gang of Four" Used Shanghai as a Base to Usurp Party and State Power. Peking Review.*

(1981). "On Strengthening Party Leadership." *Hong Qi.* 1981:2, p. 2–8.

Commerce, Ministry of, Economic Research Institute (1984). *Xin Zhongguo Shangye Shigao [Draft History of Commerce in New China].* Beijing: Zhongguo Caizheng Jingji.

Crane, George T. (1990). *The Political Economy of China's Special Economic Zones.* Armonk, N.Y.: M. E. Sharpe.

Cumings, Bruce (1989). "The Political Economy of China's Turn Outward." in S. S. Kim, ed. *China and the World: New Directions in Chinese Foreign Relations.* Boulder: Westview. pp. 203–36.

Deng Liqun (1982). "Correctly Handle the Relation between the Planned Economy and Market Adjustment." in Editorial Board of Hongqi Magazine, ed.. *Jihua Jingji yu Shichang Tiaojie Wenji [Collected Essays on the Planned Economy and Market Adjustment].* Beijing: Hongqi. pp. 79–83.

Deng Xiaoping (1984). *Selected Works of Deng Xiaoping (1975–1982).* Beijing: Foreign Languages Press.

(1987). *Fundamental Issues in Present-Day China.* Beijing: Foreign Languages Press.

Denny, David (1991). "Regional Economic Differences During the Decade of Reform." in U.S. Congress Joint Economic Committee, ed.. *China's Economic Dilemmas in the 1990s.* Washington, D.C.: U.S. Government Printing Office. pp. 186–208.

Dernberger, Robert (1982). "The Chinese Search for the Path of Self-Sustained Growth in the 1980's: An Assessment." in U.S. Congress Joint Economic Committee, ed.. *China Under the Four Modernizations.* Washington, D.C.: U.S. Government Printing Office. pp. 19–76.

Dhanji, Farid (1991). "Transformation Programs: Content and Sequencing." *American Economic Review.* 81(2): 323–28.

Ding Changqing (1984). "Experience and Problems of Implementing the Three Types of Plan Management in the Machinery Industry." *Jingji Guanli.* 1984(4): 8–9.

Ding Jiatao (1983). "A Brief Discussion of the Problem of Transforming Military Factories." *People's University Reprints: Industrial Economics.* (10): 10–14.

Dong Furen (1979). "On the Forms of China's Socialist Ownership." *Jingji Yanjiu.* 1979(1): 21–28. Translated in *Chinese Economic Studies* 23:1 (Fall 1989). pp. 8–23.

DRC, (Development Research Center of the State Council) (1988). "A Discussion Report on Policies toward the Transferance of Enterprise Property Rights." Jingji Ribao. March 29, 1988.

Du Ang and Chen Qizhang (1981). "The Way to Reduce Costs in the Metallurgy Industry." *Gongy Jingji Guanli Congkan.* 1981(11): 30–36.

Du Haiyan (1992). "The Second Stage of Profit Contracting." Chinese Academy of Social Sciences, Institute of Economics.

Du Zhenbiao (1980). "Correctly Handle the Problem of Loss-Making Coal Mines in South China." *Jingji Guanli [Economic Management].* 1980(8): 11–13.

Eberstadt, Nicholas (1986). "Material Poverty in the Peoples Republic of China in International Perspective." in U.S. Congress Joint Economic Committee, ed.. *The Chinese Economy Looks to the Year 2000.* Washington, D.C.: U.S. Government Printing Office. pp. 263–322.

Economic (Annual). Zhongguo Jingji Nianjian *[Almanac of China's Economy].* Beijing: Jingji Guanli.

Economics Delegation (1979). "Report of a Trip to China." Yale University. November 1979.

Energy (Annual). Zhongguo Nongyuang Tongji Nianjian *[China Energy Statistics Yearbook].* Beijing: Nongyuan.

ERSG (Enterprise Reform Study Group) (1988). *Chengbaozhi Zai Shijian Zhong [The Chengbao System in Practice].* Beijing: Jingji Guanli.

ESRRI Macro (Economic System Reform Research Institute, Macroeconomic Research Office) (1987). "The Macroeconomy in the Process of Reform: Distribution and Use of National Income." *Jingji Yanjiu.* 1987(8): 22–28.

"Exactions" (1985). "Exactions demand payment which is hard to resist." Jingji Ribao. October 9.

Fang Sheng (1981). "Criticize the Opposition to Discussing the Goal of Socialist Production." *Xin Shiqi.* 1981(1): 7–10.

Fang Weizhong (1982). "A Basic Principle that Cannot be Altered." in Editorial Board of Hongqi Magazine, ed. *Jihua Jingji yu Shichang Tiaojie Wenji [Collected Essays on the Planned Economy and Market Adjustment].* Beijing: Hongqi. pp. 153–65.

(1984). *Zhonghua Renmin Gongheguo Jingji Dashiji [An Economic Chronology of the People's Republic of China].* Beijing: Zhongguo Shehui Kexue.

Fei Hsiao-t'ung (1989). *Rural Development in China: Prospect and Retrospect.* Chicago: University of Chicago Press.

Feng Lanrui and Zhao Lukuan (1982). *Zhongguo Chengzhen de Jiuye he Gongzi (Employment and Wages in Urban China).* Beijing: Renmin.

Ferris, Andrew (1984). *The Soviet Industrial Enterprise.* London: Croom Helm.

Field, Robert M. and Judith Flynn (1982). "China: An Energy-Constrained Model of Industrial Performance Through 1985." in U.S. Congress Joint Economic Committee, ed. *China Under the Four Modernizations.* Washington, D.C.: U.S. Government Printing Office. pp. 334–64.

Findlay, Christopher and Andrew Watson (1992). "Surrounding the Cities from the Countryside." in R. Garnaut and Liu Guoguang, eds. *Economic Reform and Internationalisation: China and the Pacific Region.* St. Leonards, N.S.W.: Allen & Unwin. pp. 49–78.

Fischer, Stanley and Alan Gelb (1991). "Issues in the Reform of Socialist Economies." in V. Corbo, F. Coricelli and J. Bossak, ed.. *Reforming Central and Eastern European Economies: Initial Results and Challenges.* Washington, D.C.: World Bank. pp. 67–82.

Fixed Investment (Biennial). *Zhongguo Guding Zichan Touzi Tongji Ziliao (China Fixed Investment Statistical Materials).* Beijing: Zhongguo Tongji.

Floyd, Robert H., Clive Gray and R. P. Short (1984). *Public Enterprise in Mixed Economies: Some Macroeconomic Aspects.* Washington, D.C.: International Monetary Fund.

Folta, Paul Humes (1992). *From Swords to Plowshares? Defense Industry Reform in the PRC.* Boulder: Westview.

Foreign Trade (Annual). *Zhongguo Duiwai Jingji Maoyi Nianjian [Yearbook of Chinese Foreign Economic Trade].* Beijing: Zhongguo Duiwai Jingji Maoyi.

Friss, Istvan (1969). *Reform of the Economic Mechanism in Hungary: Nine Studies.* Budapest: Academia Kiado.

Fujian Statistical Office, Industry Division (1989). "Tracing the Impact of Long-term Contracting on Fujian's Factories." *Gongye Jingji Guanli Congkan.* 1989(11): 63–71.

Garvy, George (1966). *Money, Banking, and Credit in Eastern Europe.* New York: Federal Reserve Bank of New York.

Ge Peng (1988). "Beijing's Industry Grows while Reforming." *Gongye Jingji Guanli Congkan.* 1988(2): 24–29.

Gold, Thomas (1991). "Urban Private Business and China's Reforms." in R. Baum, ed. *Reform and Reaction in Post-Mao China: The Road to Tiananmen.* New York: Routledge. pp. 84–103.

Gomulka, Stanislaw (1992). "Polish Economic Reform: Principles, Policies and Surprises." in M. Keren and G. Ofer, ed. *Trials of Transition: Economic Reform in the Former Communist Bloc.* Boulder: Westview. pp. 107–28.

Gong Guanshi (1984). "How to Solve the Problem of Multiple Leadership of Industrial Enterprises." *Jingji Guanli.* 1984(1): 6–10.

Granick, David (1987). "The Industrial Environment in China and the CMEA Countries." in G. Tidrick and Chen Jiyuan, ed. *China's Industrial Reform.* New York: Oxford University Press. pp. 103–31.

Granick, David (1990). *Chinese State Enterprises: A Regional Property Rights Analysis.* Chicago: University of Chicago Press.

Grossman, Gregory (1983). "Economics of Virtuous Haste: A View of Soviet Industrialization and Institutions." in P. Desai, ed. *Marxism, Central Planning, and the Soviet Economy.* Cambridge, Massachusetts: MIT Press. pp. 198–216.

Groves, Theodore, Hong Yongmiao, John McMillan and Barry Naughton (1993). "China's Managerial Labor Market." Processed. University of California, San Diego.
  (1994). "Autonomy and Incentives in Chinese State Enterprises." *Quarterly Journal of Economics*. 109:1 (February). pp. 185–209.
  (1995). "Productivity Growth in Chinese State-Run Industry." In Furen Dong, Cyril Lin, and Barry Naughton, eds. *Reform of China's State-owned Enterprises*. London: Macmillan.
Guan Xiarong (1981). "The Problem of Duplicate Construction in Liaoning." *Jingji Yanjiu Ziliao*. 1981(3): 17–20.
Gui Shiyong, Wang Renzhi and Xu Jing'an (1980). "Restructure the Economic Management System." *HongQi*. 1980(5): 12–15.
  (1984). Interview with American Economists Study Team. December 5, Beijing.
Halpern, Nina (1985). "Economic Specialists and the Making of Chinese Economic Policy, 1955–1983." University of Michigan Ph.D. Dissertation.
Hamrin, Carol Lee (1990). *China and the Challenge of the Future*. Boulder: Westview.
Han Xiugang (1981). "Raise the Effectiveness of Factory Manager Responsibility." *Gongye Jingji Guanli Congkan*. 1981(9): 4.
Harding, Harry (1987). *China's Second Revolution: Reform After Mao*. Washington, D.C.: Brookings.
Hare, Paul (1988). "What Can China Learn from the Hungarian Economic Reform?" in S. Feuchtwang, A. Hussain and T. Pairrault, ed. *Transforming China's Economy in the Eighties*. Boulder: Westview. pp. 51–66.
Hartford, Kathleen (1985). "Socialist Agriculture Is Dead; Long Live Socialist Agriculture! Organizational Transformations in Rural China." in E. Perry and C. Wong, ed.. *The Political Economy of Reform in Post-Mao China*. Cambridge, Massachusetts: Harvard University Press. pp. 31–62.
Hartland-Thunberg, Penelope (1989). *A Decade of China's Economic Reform*. Washington, D.C.: Center for Strategic and International Studies.
He Jianzhang (1979). "Some Existing Problems in the Management System of the State-Owned Planned Economy and Directions for Reform." *Jingji Yanjiu*. 1979(5): 35–45.
He Jianzhang and Zhang Zhuoyuan (1981). "Exert Efforts to Raise Economic Results." Renmin Ribao [People's Daily]. March 30.
Hewett, Ed (1985). "Reflections on a December, 1984, Trip to the PRC." in J. Cady, ed.. *Economic Reform in China: Report of the American Economists Study Team to the People's Republic of China*. New York: National Committee on U.S.-China Relations. pp. 33–38.
  (1988). *Reforming the Soviet Economy: Equality versus Efficiency*. Washington, D.C.: Brookings.
Hirschman, Albert O. (1958). *The Strategy of Economic Development*. New Haven: Yale University Press.
Ho, Samuel and Ralph Huenemann (1984). *China's Open Door Policy: The Quest for Foreign Technology and Capital*. Vancouver: University of British Columbia.
Hongqi, Editorial Board (1983). *Jihua Jingji yu Shichang Tiaojie Wenji [Collected Articles on the Planned Economy and Market Adjustment]*. Beokomg: Hongqi.
Howard, Pat (1991). "Rice Bowls and Job Security: The Urban Contract Labour System." *Australian Journal of Chinese Affairs*. 25(January 1991):
Hsu, John (1990). *China's Foreign Trade Reforms: Impact on Growth and Stability*. New York: Cambridge University Press.

Hu Qiaomu (1978). "Do Things According to Objective Economic Laws; Accelerate the Four Modernizations." Renmin Ribao [People's Daily]. October 6.

Hua Sheng, He Jiacheng, Jiang Yao, Gao Liang and Zhang Shaojie (1985). "On a Path Toward Price Reform with Chinese Characteristics." *Jingji Yanjiu*. 1985 (2): 27–32. Translated in *Chinese Economic Studies* 22:3 (Spring 1989). pp. 34–49.

Hua Sheng, Zhang Xuejun and Luo Xiaopeng (1988). "Ten Years of Chinese Economic Reform: Review, Reconsideration, and Prospects." *Jingji Yanjiu*. 1988(9): 13–37.

Huang Juefei (1989). "A Preliminary Exploration of the Economic Mechanism of Township and Village Enterprises." *Gongye Jingji Guanli Congkan*. 1989(8): 63.

Huang Langhui (1992). "Price Trends for Industrial Products During 1991." *Zhongguo Wujia*. 1992(4): 25–27.

Industrial Census Leading Group (1987). "Basic Conditions of Large and Medium State Enterprises." *Gongye Jingji Guanli Congkan*. 1987(7): 8–10.

(1988). *Summary Volume, 1985 Industrial Census*. Beijing: Zhongguo Tongji.

(1989). *Zhongguo Gongye Xianzhuang [The Current State of Chinese Industry]*. Beijing: Renmin.

Industrial Statistic (Annual). *Zhongguo Gongye Jingji Tongji Nianjian [Industrial Economic and Statistical Yearbook of China]*. Beijing: Zhongguo Tongji.

Industry (Annual). *Zhongguo Gongye Nianjian [Almanac of China's Industry]*. Beijing: Zhongguo Laodong.

Interview. Confidential Interviews are designated by a code. The first two digits are the year; remainder is an identification code.

Jefferson, Gary (1990). "China's iron and steel industry: source of enterprise efficiency and the impact of reform." *Journal of Development Economics*. 33(October): 329–55.

Jefferson, Gary, Thomas Rawski and Zheng Yuxin (1992). "Growth, Efficiency and Convergence in China's State and Collective Industry." *Economic Development and Cultural Change*. 40(2): 239–66.

Jiang Hongqi (1981). "Carry through readjustment, continue to enliven the market." *Jianghan Luntan*. 1981(4): 43–46.

Jiang Yiwei (1980). "The Theory of an Enterprise-based Economy." *Social Sciences in China*. 1(1): 48–70.

(1988). *From the Enterprise-Based Economy to Economic Democracy*. Beijing: Beijing Review Press.

(1989). "On Economic Reform." *Gongye Jingji Guanli Congkan*, 1989(12): 2–8.

Jie Shusen and Chen Bing (1989). "A Retrospective of Enterprise Wage Reform in the Past Ten Years and Prospects for the Future." *Gongye Jingji Guanli Congkan [Digest of Industrial Economic Management]*. (4): 38–47.

Jin Shuwang (1984). "The Evolution of the State Council's Functional Departments and Several Research Questions." in State Council Office, Investigation and Research Room, ed.. *Zhongguo Xingzheng Guanlixue Chutan [Preliminary Exploration of Administrative Management in China]*. Beijing: Jingji Kexue. pp. 45–54.

Kelliher, Daniel (1992). *Peasant Power in China: The Era of Rural Reform, 1979–1989*. New Haven: Yale University Press.

Kim, Hong Nack (1985). "Sino-Japanese Relations in the Post-Mao Era: The Peace Treaty and Beyond." in U.S. House of Representatives Committee on Energy and Commerce, ed.. *China's Trade with Other Pacific Rim Nations*. Washington, D.C.: U.S. Government Printing Office. pp. 65–104.

Klaus, Vaclav (1990). "Monetary Policy in Czechoslovakia in the 1970s and 1980s and the Nature and Problems of the Current Economic Reform." *Communist Economies*. 2(1): 61–71.

Kohn, Martin (1970). "The Stock of Unfinished Construction in the USSR." Yale University Ph. D. Dissertation.

Komiya, Ryutaro (1987). "Does China Have Industrial Enterprises?" *Journal of the Japanese and International Economy*. 1:1 (March). pp. 31–61.

Kornai, Janos (1980). *The Shortage Economy*. Amsterdam: North-Holland.

(1982). *Growth, Shortage and Efficiency: A Macrodynamic Model of the Socialist Economy*. Berkeley: University of California Press.

and Agnes Matits (1984). "Softness of the Budget Constraint – An Analysis Relying on Data of Firms." *Acta Oeconomica*. 32(3): 223–49.

(1986). "The Hungarian Reform Process: Visions, Hopes, and Reality." *Journal of Economic Literature*. XXIV(December): 1687–1737.

(1990). *The Road to a Free Economy*. New York: W. W. Norton.

Korzec, Michel (1988). "New Labour Laws in the People's Republic of China." *Comparative Economic Studies*. XXX2 (Summer): 117–49.

Kueh, Y. Y. and Robert Ash (1993). *Economic Trends in Chinese Agriculture: The Impact of Post-Mao Reforms*. Oxford: Oxford University Press.

Labor (Annual). *Zhongguo Laodong Gongzi Tongji Ziliao [Nianjian]* (*China Labor and Wage Statistical Materials [Yearbook]*). Beijing: Zhongguo Tongji.

Lam, Willy Wo-lap (1989). *The Era of Zhao Ziyang*. Hong Kong: A. B. Books and Stationery.

(1993). "Leadership Changes at the Fourteenth Party Congress." in J. Cheng and M. Brosseau, ed. *China Review 1993*. Hong Kong: Chinese University Press. pp. 2.1–2.50.

Lange, Oskar (1972). "The Computer and the Market." in A. Nove and D. M. Nuti, ed. *Socialist Economics*. Harmondsworth: Penguin. Pp. 401–5.

Lardy, Nicholas (1978). *Economic Growth and Distribution in China*. New York: Cambridge University Press.

and Kenneth Lieberthal (1983). *Chen Yun's Strategy for China's Development*. Armonk, N.Y.: M.E. Sharpe.

(1983). *Agriculture in China's Modern Economic Development*. New York: Cambridge University Press.

(1992). *Foreign Trade and Economic Reform in China, 1978–1990*. Cambridge: Cambridge University Press.

Lee, Hong Yong (1990). "China's New Bureaucracy." Processed, Claremont College.

Li, K. T. (1988). *The Evolution of Policy Behind Taiwan's Development Success*. New Haven: Yale University Press.

Li, Cheng and David Bachman (1989). "Localism, Elitism, and Immobilism." *World Politics*. October.

Li Chengrui and Zhang Zhuoyuan (1982). *Zhongguo de Jingji Fazhan 1977–1980 [Economic Growth in China 1977–1980]*. Beijing: Renmin.

Li Dazheng (1989a). "Adjusting the development strategy of our coal industry." *Gongye Jingji Guanli Congkan*. 1989(5): 20–26.

(1989b). "Analysis of the Appropriate Scale of Exploitation and the Development of the Coal Industry." *Gongye Jingji Guanli Congkan*. 1989(11): 17–23.

Li Fuchen (1981). "Control the Scale of Capital Construction." *Zhongguo Jinrong*. 1981(6): 25.

Li Juwen (1981). "Clearly Recognize the Situation With Respect to Energy Production." *Jingji Yanjiu Cankao Ziliao*. 1981: 52: 28.

Li Lei, Peng Zhaoping and Xue Peng (1988). "Change, Current Situation and Mechanism of Industrial Ex-Factory Prices." *Gongye Jingji Guanli Congkan.* 1988(2): 18–23.

Li Nanling and Cheng Jian (1990). "Third Front Enterprises are Growing Vigorously Amidst Readjustment." *Renmin Ribao (Overseas).* (December 8): 5

Li Ning (1994), "From State Treasury to Real Bank," *Beijing Review* 37:18 (May 2–8), pp. 8–12.

Li Ping'an (1987). *Shaanxi Jingj Dashiji 1949–1985 [An Economic Chronology of Shaanxi 1949–1985].* Xi'an: Sanqin.

Li Rongxia (1994), "China Expands Development of Private Economy," *Beijing Review* 37:25 (June 26), pp. 18–21.

Li Weiyi (1991). *Zhongguo Gongzi Zhidu [China's Wage System].* Beijing: Zhongguo Laodong.

Li Wenjie (1983). "The International Connections of Chinese National Merchants and Industrialists." *Gongshang Jingji Shiliao Congkan.* 1983(3): 74–92

Li Yun'an (1980). "Enterprise Planning Must Be Improved." *People's University Reprints: National Economic Planning and Management.* 1981(2): 32.

Li Zhangzhe (1993). "1992: An Account of Trends in the Chinese Share System." *Gaige.* 1993(3): 53–59.

Li Zhining (1987). *Zhonghua Renmin Gongheguo Jingji Dashidian 1949.10–1987.1 [A Dictionary of Major Economic Events in the PRC, October 1949–January 1987].* Changchun: Jilin Renmin.

Liaoning Statistical Bureau (1987). "Attitudes of Enterprise Leaders Toward Some Reform Problems." *Tongji.* 1987(3): 32–33.

Liaoning Jingji [Liaoning Economy]. Periodical. "News Window": Short features on current policy.

Lieberthal, Kenneth (1978). *Central Documents and Politburo Politics in China.* Ann Arbor: University of Michigan, Center for Chinese Studies.

Lin, Cyril (1981). "The Reinstatement of Economics in China Today." *China Quarterly.* (85): 1–48.

   (1989). "Open-Ended Economic Reform in China." in V. Nee and D. Stark, ed.. *Remaking the Economic Institutions of Socialism: China and Eastern Europe.* Stanford: Stanford University Press. Pp. 95–136.

Lin, Justin Yifu (1992). "Rural Reforms and Agricultural Growth in China." *American Economic Review.* 82:1 (March): 34–51.

Lin Fatang (1984). "Key Projects During Sixth Five Year Plan." *Beijing Review.* (January 9): 22–27.

Lin Ling (1981). "Questions in the Further Development of Enterprise Autonomy." *Jingji Yanjiu Ziliao.* 1981(1): 17–18.

Lin Senmu, Zhou Shulian and Qi Mengchen (1982). *Zhongguo de Gongye yu Jiaotong (Industry and Transportation in China).* Beijing: Renmin.

Lindblom, Charles (1959). "The Science of "Muddling Through." *Public Administration Review.* 19: 79–88.

Ling Hu'an and Sun Zhen (1992). *Laodong Gongzi Tizhi Gaige Zhuan [Volume on Reform of the Labor and Wage System].* Zhongguo Gaige Quanshu [Encyclopedia of Chinese Reform]. Dalian: Dalian.

Lipton, David and Jeffrey Sachs (1990). "Creating a Market Economy in Eastern Europe: The Case of Poland." *Brookings Papers on Economic Activity.* (1): 75–147.

Litwack, John (1991). "Legality and Market Reform in Soviet-Type Economies." *Journal of Economic Perspectives.* 5(4): 77–90.

Liu Guoguang (1980). "Several Questions Concerning Plan Adjustment and Market Adjustment." *Jingji Yanjiu.* 1980(10): 3–11.

Liu Hongru (1982). "Speech at the Annual Finance Meeting." *Jinrong Yanjiu.* 1982(3): 24.

Liu Jingtan and Hong Huiru (1981). "Investigative Report on the Baoshan Steel Mill." *Gongye Jingji Guangli Congkan.* 1981(2): 29–32.

Liu Junlian (1980). "Analysis of Changes in China's Energy Efficiency." *Gongye Jingji Guanli Congkan.* 1980(8): 1–7.

Liu Li and Lu Chunheng (1990). "What is the Way Out?" *Zhongguo Tongji.* 1990(4): 1–11.

Liu Liang and Gong Zong (1987). "Changes in the Ownership Structure in Industry." *Gongye Jingji Guanli Congkan.* 1987(8): 39–42.

Liu Suinian and Cai Ninglin (1991). *Zhongguo Wuzi Xitong Gaikuang* [*General Situation of China's Material Supply System*]. Beijing: Zhongguo Wuzi.

Liu Yi (1982). "Consolidate the Favorable New Situation." *Caimao Jingji.* 1982(10): 7–9.

Liu Yishun (1987). "Ceng Xisheng and the responsibility fields in Anhui." *Dangshi Yanjiu.* 1987(3): 26–17.

Liu Zhongli (1994). "Report on Implementation of the 1993 State Budget." *Zhongguo Caijing Bao.* March 26, p. 2.

Lu Chaorong (1981). "Reforms of the Commercial System over the last Two Years." *Caimao Jingji Congkan.* 1981(3): 10–13.

Lu Dong (1993). "Implementing the Two Sets of Standards Is an Important Part of Carrying out the Regulations [on Transforming Enterprise Management]." *Gaige.* 1993(3): 17–18.

Lu Nan (1983). "Principles to Follow in the Reform of the Price System and Management Methods." *Caimao Jingji.* 1983(1): 16–20.

Lu Nan and Li Mingzhe (1991). "Use of Input-Output Techniques for Planning the Price Reform." in K. Polenske and Chen Xikang, ed. *Chinese Economic Planning and Input-Output Analysis.* Hong Kong: Oxford University Press. pp. 81–92.

Ludlow, Nicholas (1981). "China's New Development Strategy." *China Business Review.* (May-June): p. 2.

Ma Hong (1980). "Chinese Style Socialist Modernization and Readjustment of the Economic Structure." *Gongye Jingji Guanli Congkan.* 1980(1): 2.

  and Sun Shangqing. (1981). *Zhongguo Jingji Jiegou Wenti Yanjiu* [*Studies of China's Economic Structure*]. Beijing: Renmin.

  (1982). *Xiandai Zhongguo Jingji Shidian* (*Encyclopedia of The Modern Chinese Economy*). Beijing: Zhongguo Shehui Kexue.

  (1989). *Erlinglinglingnian de Zhongguo* [*China in the Year 2000*]. Beijing: Zhongguo Shehui Kexue.

  (1991). "Preface." *Zhongguo Jingji Nianjian 1991.* Beijing: Jingji Guanli. pp. i–vii.

Ma Jisen (1988). "A General Survey of the Resurgence of the Private Sector of China's Economy." *Social Sciences in China.* 1988(3): 78–92.

Macroeconomic Research Office, Economic System Reform Research Institute (1987). "The Macroeconomic in the Process of Reform: Distribution and Use of National Income." *Jingji Yanjiu.* 1987(8): 16–28.

Maruyama, Nobuo (1990). *Industrialization and Technological Development in China.* Tokyo: Institute of Developing Economies.

McKinnon, Ronald (1973). *Money and Capital in Economic Development.* Washington, D.C.: The Brookings Institution.

McMillan, John, John Whalley and Zhu Lijing (1989). "The Impact of China's Economic Reforms on Agricultural Productivity Growth." *Journal of Political Economy*. 97: 781–807.

Metal Ministry (1984). "Rapid Development of Ferrous Metallurgy." in *Guanghui de Chengjiu [Glorious Achievement]*. Beijing: Renmin. pp. 246–54.

Naughton, Barry (1985). "False Starts and Second Wind: Financial Reforms in China's Industry." in E. Perry and C. Wong, ed.. *The Political Economy of Reform in Post-Mao China*. Cambridge, Mass: Harvard University Press. pp. 223–52.

(1986). "Sun Yefang: Toward a Reconstruction of Socialist Economics." in T. Cheek and C. Hamrin, ed.. *China's Establishment Intellectuals*. White Plains: M.E. Sharpe. pp. 124–54.

(1987). "The Decline of Central Control Over Investment in Post-Mao China." in M. D. Lampton, ed. *Policy Implementation in Post-Mao China*. Berkeley: University of California Press. pp. 51–80.

(1988). "The Third Front: Defense Industrialization in the Chinese Interior." *China Quarterly*. 115: 351–86.

(1989). "Incomplete Investment in China: With Comparisons to the USSR." University of California, San Diego. September 1989.

(1990). "China's Experience with Guidance Planning." *Journal of Comparative Economics*. 14(4): (743–67.

(1991). "The Pattern and Legacy of Economic Growth in the Mao Era." in J. Kallgren, K. Liberthal, R. MacFarquhar and F. Wakeman, ed.. *Perspectives on Modern China: Four Anniversaries*. Armonk, New York: M.E. Sharpe. pp. 226–54.

(1992). "Macroeconomic Obstacles to Reform in China: The Role of Fiscal and Monetary Policy." in Bih-Jaw Lin, ed. *The Aftermath of the 1989 Tiananmen Crisis for Mainland China*. Boulder: Westview. Pp. 231–55.

NCNA [New China New Agency] (1993). "Shanghai to Abolish Grain, Oil Coupons." Translated in Survey of World Broadcasts. March 22.

Nee, Victor (1992). "Organizational Dynamics of Market Transition: Hybrid Forms, Property Rights and Mixed Economy in China." *Administrative Sciences Quarterly*. 37: 1–27.

Newbery, David (1993). "Transformation in Mature Versus Emerging Economies: Why Has Hungary Been Less Successful Than China?". International Symposium on Theoretical and Practical Issues of the Transition towards the Market Economy in China, Haikou. July.

Niu Genying (1994). "China's Economic Reform in 1994." *Beijing Review* 37:2 (January 10–26), pp. 10–12.

Nolan, Peter and Dong Fureng (1989). *Market Forces in China: Competition and Small Business – The Wenzhou Debate*. London: Zed.

Nuti, Domenico Mario (1979). "The Contradictions of Socialist Economics." *Socialist Register*.

Oksenberg, Michel and James Tong (1991). "The Evolution of Central-Provincial Fiscal Relations in China, 1971–1984: The Formal System." *China Quarterly*. (125): 1–32.

Parks, Michael (1991). "Alexander Yakovlev: The Father of Perestroika Surveys Wreckage of Soviet Empire." *Los Angeles Times*.

"Party and government leaders in some regions compel banks to make loans." *Zhongguo Jinrong [China Finance]*. 1985(9): 7.

"Peddlars" (1988). "Peddlars Without Licenses Create Problems for Cities." *China Daily*. June 11, 1988.

People's University, Planning and Statistics Department (1979). *Guomin Jingji Jihuaxue [Planning of the National Economy]*. Beijing: Zhongguo Renmin Daxue.

Perkins, Dwight et al. (1977). *Rural Small-Scale Industry in the People's Republic of China*. Berkeley: University of California.

Perkins, Dwight (1986). *China, Asia's next economic giant?*. Seattle: University of Washington.

(1988). "Reforming China's Economic System." *Journal of Economic Literature*. XXVI((June)): 601–45.

(1990). "The Influence of Economic Reforms on China's Urbanization." in R. Y. Kwok, W. Parish, A. Yeh and Xu Xueqiang, ed.. *Chinese Urban Reform: What Model Now?*. Armonk, New York: M. E. Sharpe. pp. 78–106.

Portes, Richard and Anita Santorum (1987). "Money and the Consumption Goods Market in China." *Journal of Comparative Economics*. 11(3): 354–71.

Preobrazhenski, Evgeny (1965). *The New Economics*. Oxford: Oxford University Press.

Price (Annual). *Zhongguo Wujia Nianjian [China Price Yearbook]*. Beijing: Zhongguo Wujia.

Pryor, Fred (1985). *A Guidebook to the Comparative Study of Economic Systems*. Englewood Cliffs: Prentice-Hall.

Pu Shumian (1981). "Report on a Study of Bonus Payments in Shenyang." *Jinrong Yanjiu*. 1981(5): 60–63.

Putterman, Louis (1993). *Continuity and Change in China's Rural Development: Collective and Reform Eras in Perspective*. New York: Oxford University Press.

Qi Guan (1987). "Enliven State Enterprises." *Gongye Jingji Guanli Congkan*. 1987(8): 42–47.

Qi Guang (1984). "Separation of Powers in Materials Planning." ed.. *Guomin Jingji Jihua Gailun Cankao Ziliao [Reference Materials on Principles of National Economic Planning]*. Wuhan: Zhongyang Guangbo Dianshi Daxue. pp. 190–208.

Qian, Yingyi (1988). "Urban and Rural Household Saving in China." *IMF Staff Papers*. 35(4): 592–627.

Qian Jiemin and Ni Jiangsheng (1990). "Policies to Perfect the Rural Land Legal System." *Zhongguo Faxue*. 1990(6): 81–82.

Qiao Rongzhang (1988). *Zhonghua Renmin Gongheguo Wujia Dashiji [Chronology of Major Events in PRC Prices]*. Beijing: State Price Bureau Price Research Institute.

(1990). *Jiage Butie [Price Subsidies]*. Beijing: Zhongguo Wujia.

Rawski, Thomas (1989). *Economic Growth in Prewar China*. Berkeley: University of California Press.

RDSG (Rural Development Study Group). (1987). *Guomin Jingji Xin Cengzhang Jieduan he Nongcun Fashan (The new stage of growth of the national economy and rural development)*. Hangzhou: Zhejiang Renmin.

Reform (Annual). *Zhongguo Jingji Tizhi Gaige Nianjian [Yearbook of China's Economic System Reform]*. Beijing: Gaige.

Ren Tao (1982). "Expanded Autonomy is the Key to Enlivening Industry." *Caizheng Yanjiu*. 1982(2): 11–13.

Riskin, Carl (1971). "Small Industry and the Chinese Model of Development." *China Quarterly*. 46 (June): 245–73.

(1987). *China's Political Economy*. Oxford: Oxford University Press.

Rong Jingben, Wu Jinglian and Zhao Renwei (1981). "Opinions of Foreign Economists on China's Economic Reform." *Jingjixue Dongtai*. 1981(12): 35–37.

Rural (Annual). *Zhongguo Nongcun Tongji Nianjian* [*Rural Statistical Yearbook of China*]. Beijing: Zhongguo Tongji.

Rural Finance (Annual). *Zhongguo Nongcun Jinrong Tongji Nianjian* [*China Rural Financial Statistics Annual*]. Beijing: Zhongguo Tongji.

Schoenhals, Michael (1991). "The 1978 Truth Criterion Controversy." *China Quarterly*. (126): 243–68.

Schroeder, Gertrude (1972). "The "Reform" of the Supply System in Soviet Industry." *Soviet Studies*. (July):

   (1979). "The Soviet Economy on a Treadmill of Reforms."

SEC [State Economic Commission]. (1983). "An analysis of economic efficiency of local small-scale iron and steel mills." *Jingji Diaocha* [*Economic Investigations*]. (2): 15–21.

Seventh Plan (1986). *Zhonghu Renmin Gongheguo Diqige Guomin Jingji he Shehui Fazhan Wunian Jihua* [*The Seventh Five-Year Plan for Economic and Social Development of the PRC*]. Beijing: Renmin.

Shan, Weijian (1989). "Reforms of China's Foreign Trade System: Experiences and Prospects." *China Economic Review*. 1(1): 33–56.

Shen, Guanbao (1990). "Rural Enterprises and Urbanization: The Sunan Region." in R. Y.-w. Kwok, W. Parish, A. Yeh and Xu Xueqiang, ed. *Chinese Urban Reform: What Model Now?*. Armonk, New York: M. E. Sharpe. pp. 158–79.

Shen Yi (1979). "Materials Cooperation in Jiangsu." *Jingjixue Dongtai*. 1979(7): 32–35.

Shirk, Susan (1989). "The Political Economy of Chinese Industrial Reform." in V. Nee and D. Stark, ed. *Remarking the Economic Institutions of Socialism: China and Eastern Europe*. Stanford: Stanford University Press. pp. 328–62.

   (1993). *The Political Logic of Economic Reform in China*. Berkeley: University of California Press.

"Sichuan to Sell Enterprises" (1994). *Beijing Review* 37:22 (May 30), pp. 28–29.

Sicular, Terry (1991). "China's Agricultural Policy During the Reform Period." in U.S. Congress Joint Economic Committee, ed. *China's Economic Dilemmas in the 1990s*. Washington, D.C.: U.S. Government Printing Office. pp. 340–64.

Sixth Plan (1984). *Sixth Five-Year Plan of the People's Republic of China for Economic and Social Development*. Beijing: Foreign Languages Press.

Solinger, Dorothy J. (1991). *From Lathes to Looms: China's Industrial Policy in Comparative Perspective, 1979–1982*. Stanford: Stanford University Press.

Song Bai (1987). "The origin and implementation of the readjustment policy." *Dangshi Yanjiu* (*Studies in Party History*). (3): 16–23.

Song Guoqing and Zhang Weiying (1986). "Several Theoretical Problems of Macroeconomic Balance and Macroeconomic Control." *Jingji Yanjiu*. 1986(6): 23–35.

SRC [System Reform Commission] (1984). *Jingji Tizhi Gaige Wenjian Huibian 1977–1983* (*Collected Economic System Reform Documents*). Beijing: Zhongguo Caizheng Jingji.

   (1988a). *Zhongguo Jingji Tizhi Gaige Guihua Ji* [*Collection of Long-Run Plans for China's Economic System Reform*]. Zhangjiakou: Zhonggong Zhongyang Dangxiao.

   (1988b). *Zhongguo Jingji Tizhi Gaige Shinian* [*Ten Years of Economic System Reform in China*]. Beijing: Jingji Guanli.

SRC/Comp (1988). *Zhongguo Gaige Da Silu* [*Large-scale Deliberations on China's Reform*]. Shenyang: Shenyang.

SRC/ER (System Reform Commission, Enterprise Reform Section) (1990). *Zhongguo Qiye Gaige Shinian* [*Ten Years of Enterprise Reform in China*]. Beijing: Gaige.

SSB, Industry and Transportation Division (1989). "An Investigation of Chengbao Responsibility System Implementation in Twenty Cities." in SSB Industry
and Transportation Division, ed. *Gongye Tongji Fenxi Baogao Xuanbian [Se-
lected Industrial Statistical Analysis Reports].* Beijing: Zhongguo Tongji. pp.
11–16.

SSB, Investment Division (1991). *Zhongguo Zhongdian Jianshe [China's Keypoint
Construction].* Beijing: Falu.

State Council (1989). "Text of State Council's Industrial Policy." *Federal Broadcast
Information Service.* (March 31, 1989): 40–51.

Statistic (Annual). *Zhongguo Tongji Nianjian (China Statistics Yearbook).* Beijing:
Zhongguo Tongji.

"Steady Vow on Reform of Prices" (1993). China Daily. August 3.

Sun Dejun (1981). "An Exploration of Several Questions Related to Developing
Urban Collective Industry." ed. *Chengzhen Jiti Jingji Yanjiu (Studies in the
Urban Collective Economy).* Beijing: Renmin. pp. 236–37.

Sun Shangwu (1993). "Reform Package Flags New Era for Market Economy." *China
Daily.* (November 30), p. 1.

Sun Xiangyi (1993). "An Account of Price Reform in 1992." *Zhongguo Wujia.* 1993(1):
9–11.

Sun Yanhu (1992). *"Quanmin Suoyouzhi Gongye Qiye Zhuanhuan Jingying Jizhi
Tiaolie" Jianghua [Lectures on the Regulations for Transforming the State-
Owned Industrial Enterprise Management Mechanism].* Beijing: Gaige.

Tang Fengyi (1988). "Clarification of property rights and the change of the enterprise
system." *Gongye Jingji Guanli Congkan.* 1988(2): 10–17.

Tao Youzhi (1988). *Sunan Moshi yu Zhifu zhi Dao [The Southern Jiangsu model and
the Road to Prosperity].* Shanghai: Shanghai Shehui Kexue Yuan.

Taylor, Jeffrey (1986). "Labor Force Developments in the People's Republic of China,
1952–83." in U.S. Congress Joint Economic Committee, ed. *China's Economy
Looks Toward the Year 2000.* Washington, D.C.: U.S. Government Printing
Office. pp. 222–62.

Third Front Study Group, Sichuan Academy of Social Sciences (1989). "Adjusting the
Production Structure of Third Front Military Industry." *Gongye Jingji Guanli
Congkan.* 89(8): 6–13.

Tian Jianghai (1985). "Problems that Appear during the Crossover Between the Old
and New Systems." *Jingjixue Dongtai.* 1985(8): 26–29.

Tian Ying (1988). "Civilian Auto Drive in Ordnance Factories". China Daily. February 25, 1988.

Tian Yuan and Qiao Gang (1991). *Zhongguo Jiage Gaige Yanjiu 1984–1990 (Studies of
China's Price Reform).* Beijing: Dianzi Gongye.

Tianjin Social Scientists Association (1988). "The Recent Economic Changes in
Tianjin." *People's University Reprints: Urban Economics.* 1988(2): 60.

Tong Wansheng and Zuo Xiangqun (1992). *Jiage Tizhi Gaige Zhuan [Volume on
Reform of the Price System].* Zhongguo Gaige Quanshu [Encyclopedia of China's
Reform]. Dalian: Dalian.

Tong Zhimin (1979). "Planning Should be Comprehensive and All-Around." *Jingji
Yanjiu.* 1979(2):

UN [United Nations]. (1990). *National Accounts Statistics: Main Aggregates and
Detailed Tables, 1988.* New York: United Nations.

Unger, Jonathan (1985). "Remuneration, Ideology, and Personal Interests in a Chinese Village, 1960–1980." in W. Parish, ed.. *Chinese Rural Development: The
Great Transformation.* Armonk, N.Y.: M. E. Sharpe, pp. 117–40.

(1986). "The Decollectivization of the Chinese Countryside: A Survey of Twenty-eight Villages." *Pacific Affairs.* 58(4): 585–607.

Urban Household, Survey Section, State Statistical Bureau (1988). *'Liu Wu' Qijian Woguo Chengzhen Jumin Jiating Shouzhi Diaocha Ziliao [Urban Household Survey Materials, 1981–1985]*. Beijing: Zhongguo Tongji.

Van Ness, Peter (1989). *Market Reforms in Socialist Societies: Comparing China and Hungary.* Boulder: Lynne Rienner.

Various Views (1983). "Various Views on the Reform of the Planning System." *Jingjixue Dongtai.* 1983(7): 1–4.

Wallich, Christine I. (1990). "Recent Developments in China's Financial Sector: Financial Instruments and Markets." in J. Dorn and Wang Xi, ed.. *Economic Reform in China: Problems and Prospects.* Chicago: University of Chicago, pp. 133–48.

Wang Chaocai and Luo Wenguang (1989). "An examination of several fiscal problems from the standpoint of the changing structure of revenues and expenditures," *Jingji Yanjiu Cankao Ziliao* 191 (December 20), pp. 16–32.

Wang Chengyao (1983). "A General Account of the Reform of the Tax System Since 1949." *Caizheng Yanjiu.* 1983(2): 62–70, 77.

Wang Hongmo (1989). *Gaige Kaifang de Licheng [The Course of Reform and Opening]*. Volume Four of *1949–1989 Nian de Zhongguo [China from 1949 through 1989]*, Four Volumes. Zhengzhou: Henan Renmin.

Wang Mengkui (1991). "Study Chen Yun's Four Points about the New Economic Period." *Chen Yun yu Zhongguo Jingji Jianshe [Chen Yun and China's Economic Construction]*. Beijing: Zhongyang Wenxian, pp. 367–80.

Wang Qingyi (1988). *Zhongguo Nengyuan [Energy in China]*. Beijing: Yejin Gongye.

Wang Qiren (1981). "Assure a good turn in market conditions." *Jinrong Yanjiu.* 1981(Supplement No. 1): 32.

Wang Xiaoqiang (1987). "Transcending the Logic of Private Ownership." *Zhongguo: Fazhan yu Gaige.* (4): 27–31, 48. Translated in *Chinese Economic Studies* 23:1 (Fall 1989), pp. 43–56.

Wang Xiaoqiang (1993). " "Groping for Stones to Cross the River": Chinese Price Reform against "Big Bang" ". University of Cambridge, Department of Applied Economics.

Wang Yongjiang (1981). "What is the Aim of Socialist Production?" *Social Sciences in China.* 1981(1): 2–10.

Wang Zhong (1983). *Qinggongye Jingji de Zuzhi yu Guanli [Organization and Management of the Light Industry Economy]*. Beijing: Qinggongye.

Ward, Benjamin (1980). "The Chinese Approach to Economic Development." in R. Dernberger, ed. *China's Development Experience in Comparative Perspective.* Cambridge, Massachusetts: Harvard University Press. pp. 91–119.

Watson, Andrew (1983). "Agriculture Looks for 'Shoes that Fit': The Production Responsibility System and Its Implications." *World Development.* 11(8): 705–30.

Christopher Findlay and Du Yintang (1989). "Who Won the 'Wool War'?: A Case Study of Rural Product Marketing in China." *China Quarterly.* 118: 213–41.

Wei Liqun (1990). "Speech at Sino-U.S. Conference." State Planning Commission, Beijing. March 1990.

Weil, Martin (1982). "The Baoshan Steel Mill: A Symbol of Change in China's Industrial Development Strategy." in U.S. Congress Joint Economic Committee, ed. *China Under the Four Modernizations.* Washington, D.C.: U.S. Government Printing Office. pp. 365–93.

Weitzman, Martin and Xu Chenggang (1994). "Chinese Township-Village Enterprises as Vaguely Defined Cooperatives." *Journal of Comparative Economics*. 18:2 (April): 121–45.

Wen Shengmei, Lu Chaorong and Meng Zhenhu (1981). "Trial Reforms in Sichuan Commerce." *Caimao Jingji Congkan*. 1981(2): 35–40.

Wen Shizhen (1993). "Liaoning's Second Period of Ground-breaking Construction." Processed, Shenyang. June 25.

White, Gordon and Paul Bowles (1987). "Towards a Capital Market? Reforms in the Chinese Banking System: Transcript of a Research Trip." Institute of Development Studies, Sussex. 1987.

Whiting, Susan (1993). "Contract Incentives and Market Discipline in China's Rural Industrial Sector." University of California, San Diego, Conference on the Evolution of Market Institutions in Transitional Economies. July.

Wiens, Thomas (1982). "The Limits to Agricultural Intensification: The Suzhou Experience." in U.S. Congress Joint Economic Committee, ed.. *China Under the Four Modernizations*. Washington, D.C.: U.S. Government Printing Office, pp. 462–74.

Winiecki, Jan (1989). "Buying Out Property Rights to the Economy from the Ruling Stratum: The Case of Soviet-Type States." *International Review of Law and Economics*. 9: 79–85.

Wong, Christine (1982). "Rural Industrialization in the People's Republic of China: Lessons from the Cultural Revolution Decade." in U.S. Congress Joint Economic Committee, ed.. *China Under the Four Modernizations*. Washington, D.C.: U.S. Government Printing Office. pp. 394–417.

(1985). "Material Allocation and Decentralization: Impact of the Local Sector on Industrial Reform." in E. Perry and C. Wong, ed. *The Political Economy of Reform in Post-Mao China*. Cambridge, Mass.: Harvard University Press. pp. 253–78.

(1986). "Ownership and Control in Chinese Industry: The Maoist Legacy and Prospects for the 1980s." in U.S. Congress Joint Economic Committee, ed.. *China's Economy Looks Toward the Year 2000*. Washington, D.C.: U.S. Government Printing Office. pp. 571–603.

(1988). "Interpreting Rural Industrial Growth in the Post-Mao Period." *Modern China*. 14(1): 3–30.

Wood, Adrian (1991). "China's Economic System: A Brief Description, With Some Suggestions for Further Reform". London School of Economics, Development Economics Research Programme. April 1991.

World Bank (1986). *China: Long Term Development, Issues and Options*. Washington, D.C.: World Bank.

(1988). *China: External Trade and Capital*. Washington, D.C.: World Bank.

(1989). *World Development Report*. Washington, D.C.: World Bank.

(1990). *China: Reforming Social Security in a Socialist Economy*. World Bank.

(1992a). *China Country Economic Memorandum: Reform and the Role of the Plan in the 1990s*. World Bank.

(1992b). *China: Urban Land Management in an Emerging Market Economy*. Washington, D.C.: World Bank.

Wu Dongyan (1981). "Collective Ownership is an Important Component of the Socialist System." *Jingji Yanjiu Cankao Ziliao*. 1981(56): 77.

Wu Jinglian (1987). *Jingji Gaige Wenti Tansuo [Explorations of Economic Reform Problems]*. Beijing: Zhanwang.

Wu Jinglian (1987). "On Differences Concerning Macroeconomic Problems: A Reply to Comrade Zhang Xuejun." *Jingji Yanjiu*. 1987(11): 48–52. Translated in *Chinese Economic Studies* 23:3 (Spring 1990), pp. 91–101.

and Zhao Renwei (1987). "The Dual Pricing System in China's Industry." *Journal of Comparative Economics.* 11(3): 309–18.

and Zhou Xiaochuan (1988). *Zhongguo Jingji Gaige de Zhengti Sheji (The Integrated Design of China's Economic Reform).* Beijing: Zhongguo Zhanwang.

Wu Yue (1993). "Multilateral Rules and Market Economy: Thoughts on China's Readmission to GATT." *Guoji Shangbao,* translated in FBIS-CHI 9/22/92, p. 42.

Xiao Weixiang (1990). "A General Description of China's Cooperative Industrial Enterprises." in General Office of China Federation of Industrial Cooperatives, ed.. *Zhongguo Hezuo Gongye Qiye (China's Cooperative Industrial Enterprises).* Beijing: Gaige, pp. 3–9.

Xie Minggan and Ding Hongxiang (1990). "Do Materials Circulation Even Better during Rectification." *Gongye Jingji Yanjiu.* 1990(1): 20–24.

Xie Ping (1993). "Three Problems Confronting Monetary Policy in China." *Gaige.* 1993(3): 10–16.

Xu Feiqing (1988). *Zhongguo de Jingji Tizhi Gaige [China's Economic System Reform].* Beijing: Zhongguo Caizheng Jingji.

Xu Gongfen (1988). "Township and Village Textile Enterprises in 1986." *Gongye Jingji Guanli Congkan.* 1987(10): 72–75.

Xu Peiqing (1988). "The Theory of the Externally Oriented Economy." in Jingjixue Dongtai Editorial Board, ed.. *Jingji Lilun Dongtai 1988.* Beijing: Zhongguo Jingji. Pp.

Xu Yi (1981). "On the Relation Between System and Production Structure." *People's University Reprints: National Economic Planning and Management.* 1981(4): 58.

Chen Baosen (1982). *Zhongguo de Caizheng 1977–1980 [China's Public Finance 1977–1980].* Beijing: Renmin.

Xue Muqiao (1978a). "On the question of commune and brigade enterprises," reprinted in *Danqian Woguo Jingji Ruogan Wenti,* Beijing: Renmin, 1980, pp. 112–121.

Xue Muqiao (1978b). "Make the law of value serve economic construction," reprinted in *Danqian Woguo Jingji Ruogan Wenti,* Beijing: Renmin, 1980, pp. 96–111.

(1981). "Speech before Cadres of the Banking System." *Jinrong Yanjiu.* 1981(6): 1–4.

(1982). "Several Theoretical Questions of the Reform of the Economic Management System." in Editorial Board of Hongqi Magazine, ed. *Jihua Jingji yu Shichang Tiaojie Wenji [Collected Essays on the Planned Economy and Market Adjustment].* Beijing: Hongqi. Pp. 185–97.

Yan Chongzong (1980). "Reform of the Factory Management System Cannot be Delayed." *Gongye Jingji Guanli Congkan.* 1980(2): 26.

Yang Jisheng (1981). "Striving for Speed; Not Reaching the Destination." *Jingji Yanjiu Ziliao.* 1981(1): 27–30.

Yang Lei (1979). "We must reform the management system in which production, supply, and sales are not unified." *Jingji Guanli.* 1979(4): 14–16.

Yang Peixin (1981). "Carry Out Readjustment." *Jinrong Yanjiu.* 1981(11): 5.

Yeung, Chris (1993). "Aid hits $13 billion as jobless total soars". South China Morning Post International Weekly. October 9–10.

Yi Daren (1989). "On the Quality of the Industrial Labor Force." *Gongye Jingji Guanli Congkan.* (4): 48–54.

Yu Boren (1988). "Thoughts on the Current Reality on Rural Residents Operating Mines." *Gongye Jingji Guanli Congkan.* 1988(8): 41–45, 56.

Yu Chongzong (1980). "Develop a System of Factory Responsibility that Accords with Chinese Conditions." *Gongye Jingji Guanli Congkan.* 19890(2): 26.

366   *Bibliography*

Yu Guangyuan (1982). "Develop Theoretical Discussion about Reform of the Economic System." in Editorial Board of Hongqi Magazine, ed. *Jihua Jingji yu Shichang Tiaojie Wenji* [*Collected Essays on the Planned Economy and Market Adjustment*]. Beijing: Hongqi. pp. 227–34.

(1985). *Shehuizhuyi Jingji Jianshe Changshi* [*General Knowledge of Socialist Economic Construction*]. Nanchang: Jiangxi Renmin.

Yu Youhai (1982). "Don't throw out the baby with the bathwater." *Gongye Jingji Guanli Congkan.* 1982(7): 12–16.

Yunnan Tax Bureau (1994). "Deepening of Tax reform Is in Order to Serve Economic Development." *Jingji Luntan* 1994:1 (January), pp. 28–35.

Zaleski, Eugene (1971). *Planning for Economic Growth in the Soviet Union, 1918–1932.* Chapel Hill: University of North Carolina Press.

(1980). *Stalinist Planning for Economic Growth, 1933–1952.* Chapel Hill: University of North Carolina Press.

Zelin, Madeleine (1991). "The Structure of the Chinese Economy During the Qing Period: Some Thoughts on the 150th Anniversary of the Opium War." in K. Lieberthal, J. Kallgren, R. MacFarquhar and F. Wakeman, ed.. *Perspectives on Modern China: Four Anniversaries.* Armonk: M.E. Sharpe. pp. 31–67.

Zhang Guisheng. (1981). "The Three Ups and Downs of Wenzhou's Market." *Caimao Jingji Congkan.* 1981(2): 20–21.

Zhang Jiuda (1987). "Handan Region Open Auction of Chengbao Contracts." *Gongye Jingji Guanli Congkan.* 1987(12): 35–36.

Zhang Jiwu (1989). "On the Question of Private Coal Mintes." *Gongye Jingji Guanli Congkan.* 1989(12): 31–35.

Zhang Xuejun (1987). "An Evaluation of Several Basic Viewpoints in the Study of China's Macroeconomy," *Jingji Yanjiu* 8, pp. 5–7.

Zhang Yi and Huang Guangshu (1981). "Criticize the Theory the Commune and Brigade Enterprises Squeeze Out Raw Materials." *Nongye Jingji Congkan.* 1981(5): 39–41.

Zhang Yu'an (1988). "Fertilizer Industry Needs more Help from the State." China Daily. February 28, 1988.

Zhang Zhanbin (1988). *Xin Zhongguo Qiye Lingdao Zhidu* [*Enterprise Leadership Systems in New China*]. Beijing: Chunqiu.

Zhang Zhuoyuan, Li Xiaoxi, Bian Yongzhuang and Shi Xiaokang (1988). *Zhongguo Jiage Jiegou Yanjiu* [*Studies in China's Price Structure*]. Taiyuan: Shanxi Renmin and Zhongguo Shehui Kexue.

Zhao Ming and Chen Min (1987). "Policies to Deal with the Adjustment of Third Front Military Industry Production Structure." *Zhongguo: Fazhan yu Gaige.* (9): 34–39.

Zhao Minshan (1989). "An Investigation of the Implementation of Long-term Contracting in Twenty Cities." in State Statistical Bureau Office, ed.. *Youxiu Tongji Fenxi Baogao Xuanbian* [*Selected Excellent Statistical Analysis Reports*]. Beijing: Zhongguo Tongji. pp. 442–48.

Zhao Xiangyang (1980). "Planning is even more important now with expanded enterprise autonomy." *Gongye Jingji Guanli Congkan.* 1980(3): 31.

Zhao Xiaodi (1992). "A New Task for Participating in International Agreements." *Renmin Ribao,* September 4, 1992, p. 5, translated in FBIS-CHI, September 17, 1992, p. 26.

Zhao Ziyang (1985). "Explanation of the Suggestions for Drafting the Seventh Five Year Plan." *Hong Qi.* 1985(19): 28–31.

(1986). "My Views on Three Problems of Economic System Reform." in Chinese Communist Party Central Documents Research Room, ed. *Shi'er Da Yilai: Zhongyao Wenxian Xuanbian* [*Since the Twelfth Party Congress: Selected Important Documents*]. Beijing: Renmin. Pp. 533–38.

Zheng Derong, et al. (1987). *Zhongguo Jingji Tizhi Gaige Jishi* [*Chronology of China's Economic System Reform*]. Beijing: Chunqiu.

Zhong Zhiqi (1984). Interview with American Economist Study Team, Beijing, December 6, 1984.

Zhou Xiaochuan and Zhu Li (1987). "China's Banking System: Current Status, Perspective on Reform." *Journal of Comparative Economics.* 11(3): 399–409.

Zhou Xiaochuan, "Privatization Versus a Minimum Reform Package," *China Economic Review* 4:1 (1993), pp. 65–74.

Zhou Yuan and Zhao Ming (1985). "New Trends in Township and Villages Enterprises in Southern Jiangsu." *Liaowang.* (36 (September 9)): 25–27.

Zhou Zhengqing (1987). "Contract the Scope of Credit, and Adjust the Structure of Lending." *Zhongguo Jinrong.* 1987(12): 15–17.

Zhu Jiaming (1985). "On the Current Stage of China's Economic Development – A Typical Development in a Nontypical Country." *Zhongqingnian Jingji Luntan* [*Young Economists' Forum*]. 1985(1): 13–23. Translated in *Chinese Economic Studies*, 23:2 (Winter 1989–90), pp. 8–33.

Zhu Pingxiang (1988). "A Few Opinions on Current Monetary Conditions and Policy." *Zhongguo Jinrong.* 1988(1): 21.

Zoteev, Gennadij (1991). "The National Product and Income in the Soviet Economic System." *Moct-Most.* 1(1): 61–78.

Index

macroeconomic stability, macroeconomic
changes, 11–12, 17, 21, 24–25, 34, 37,
80, 93, 95, 111, 119, 142, 168, 175, 177,
192, 222, 244, 259, 287, 302, 304, 319,
325; macroeconomic structures, 7, 30–
32, 203
Managers, support for reforms, 190
Managerial systems, 47–48, 66, 107, 279,
288; reform, 9–10, 15, 36, 99, 107–108,
121, 131, 163, 190, 196, 202, 205, 213,
219, 241, 295
Manufacturing. *See* Industry
Mao Zedong and Maoism, 51, 59, 61–62, 64–
65, 98–99, 107, 166, 310
Market, marketing: agriculture, 43, 126, 135;
farmers' markets/peasant markets, 93,
116, 121, 126, 175, 250, 281; independent, and industry, 8, 10, 12–13, 116–
118, 125–126, 136, 252; intermediate
goods, 135, 222; and local governments,
112, 115; and localism, 43, 231–232; producer goods, 112, 114, 251–252, 278; reform, 177–178, 183, 187, 193, 201–202,
252, 306, 309; state control over commerce, 12, 43, 45, 125–126, 232, 252;
for TVE products, 154–155; urban, 154
Market forces, 8, 20, 191, 204, 306
Marketization, local, 156
Material allocations, 47, 65, 134–136, 225,
277, 281; reforms, 6, 9, 15, 26, 28, 252,
274. *See also* Planning, Material balance
Material balance, 6, 26, 28–29, 34, 41–42,
112, 220, 277
Material incentives. *See* Incentives
Material Supply Bureau, 66, 111–112, 181
Meat rationing, 46; meat supplies, 52–53,
248
Mechanization, 166
Medicine, 238
Merchants, 166
Metals, 238, 242, 251. *See also* Ministry of
Metallurgy
Migration, urban-rural, 45, 324.
Military: investment in, 27; output, 51–52.
See also Industry, military
Mining, 51, 184, 222–223, 236, 238, 281;
clay and stone, 158
Ministries, bureaux, industrial, 66, 111, 207,
217, 235
Ministry of Coal, 67
Ministry of Commerce, 45, 118, 125
Ministry of Finance, 184, 194, 197, 283
Ministry of Metallurgy, 67
Monetary instability, 244
Monetary policy, 17, 253, 256, 266–268, 301.
See also Credit policy, Fiscal policy
Monetary Policy Commission, 301

Monitoring, performance, 10, 314–317
Monopoly procurement by commerce, 116
Monopoly, state over industry, 138, 165, 244,
311; monopoly rents, 159, 161–163, 233,
311
Moscow, 29
Most Favored Nation status, 304
Motivation.. *See* Incentives
Municipal Labor Bureaus, 117
Mutual funds. *See* Institutions, intermediate

National Development Bank, 301
Natural gas, 72, 238, 293
National income, distribution of, 31–32, 43–
44, 82–83, 179, 252–253
Natural resource pricing, 129
Neighborhood committees, 166
"New cooperative" enterprises, 163
New product development, 101
Nomenklatura system, 28, 30, 36, 48, 107,
206, 258, 279, 320
Non-agricultural rural output, 83, 137, 140,
142, 144–145, 158, 164
Non-state sector, 21, 126, 137, 144, 146, 163,
168–169, 177, 224, 226, 278, 298, 319

Officials, as entrepreneurs, 156, 292
Oil, 67–68, 71, 79, 238, 289, 291. *See also*
Petroleum
Oilseed, 52–53, 287, 291
Oppression, political, 89, 273. *See also*
Tiananmen
Ownership structure, 22, 28, 36, 165–167,
204, 219, 225, 246, 284; reform, 229,
298, 322
Output, agricultural, 51–52, 61, 141, 164,
245
Output, industrial, 51–52, 164, 279, 281,
293, 313, 329–333; and industrial re-
form, 7, 201, 294; and material alloca-
tion, 6, 9, 29, 281
Output, rural non-agricultural, 83, 137, 140,
142, 144–145, 158, 164, 224, 329–333
Output, urban collective, 166, 168, 329–333

Paper, 78, 238
Patronage, 166, 186, 300
Peasants, 139–141, 190. *See also* Agriculture
Peking. *See* Beijing
Pension funds. *See* Institutions, intermediate
People's Bank of China, 28, 30, 133, 255, 301
Petroleum and petrochemicals, 51, 63, 67,
69, 71–72, 74, 85, 174, 176, 236–239,
286–287, 290–291; and industrial re-
form, 71–72, 74, 88
Philippines, 167
Piece rates, 104 fn. 3, 208. *See also* Incen-
tives, wages

Pipelines, 73
Planning, economic: guidance planning, 175–
176, 179, 203, 221; local, 42, 146, 161,
165, 221; material allocation, 6, 9, 15,
26, 42, 65, 73, 136, 181, 252, 281; material balance, 6, 28–29, 34, 41–42, 73,
112, 191, 220; and provincial and ministerial wage bills, 209; and reform, 3, 10,
12, 14–16, 111, 177, 179, 181, 200, 274,
287; and trade, 227; VAT, 293
Plastics. *See* Synthetic materials
Poland, 3, 13, 16–17, 63, 99, 270, 313
Policy banks, 301, 323
Policymakers, 7, 22, 53, 55, 131, 135, 139,
141, 178, 192, 194, 197, 202, 245, 305
Policy. *See* Monetary policy; Credit policy;
Fiscal policy
Politburo Standing Committee, 75
Politics: domestic, and reform, 5, 20, 23,
177, 180, 185, 188–190, 195, 197, 198,
202–204, 249, 273, 283, 300, 306; for-
eign, and reform, 3
Pollution, 159
Population: growth, 176. *See also* Migration
Popular support for reform, 18
Poverty, 20, 38–39, 80, 310, 325; poor re-
gions, 140
Preobrazhenski, Evgeny, 32, 35
Press, Chinese, 98
Price Research Center, 129
Price scissors. *See* Scissors gap; Terms of trade
Prices: agricultural inputs, 75; agricultural
procurement, 75, 84, 139, 253; consumer products, 136, 248–249; food, 84,
184, 248–249; free-market, 10, 13, 17,
93, 191, 201, 281; industrial, 8, 10, 15–
16, 136, 138, 278, 286, 294; and inflation, 17, 19, 25, 64, 92, 119, 124, 175,
184, 192–193, 201, 232, 244, 247–253,
264, 269–270, 273, 276, 280–281, 287,
302, 304; liberalization, 92, 95, 129, 163,
187–188, 192, 197, 274, 276, 278, 289–
291, 305, 313; local control, 232; local
inflation rates, 276; market price quotations, 183, 321; and planning, 8, 31, 37,
66, 110, 138, 274, 278; realignment, 314;
reform, in China, 23, 97–98, 102, 111,
126, 163, 173, 176–180, 184, 188–197,
199, 203, 220, 227, 228; reform, in Eastern Europe, 14, 17, 270; relative prices,
248–249, 253; state control, 239, 274,
278, 289–291, 320. *See also* Market, independent
Printing, 238
Priority projects. *See* Keypoint projects
Private enterprise, 163–164, 166, 246, 291,
298, 304

Private exchange. *See* Market, Private ownership
Private ownership: individual coal mines,
224–225; and rural responsibility systems, 152, 156
Private sales, outside-of-plan, and industrial
reform, 183, 197, 201–202, 233
Privatization, 17–18, 36, 156–157, 218, 223,
229, 289, 298–299, 313, 315, 322, 324
Processing industries; of agricultural products, 146–147, 161
Procurement, agricultural, 147
Producer goods. *See* Goods, producer
Product prices, 136
Production, productivity: improvements,
252; production functions, 240; state-run
industry, 233, 241–242, 281, 316; total
factor productivity, 314; urban areas, 154
Production decisions, 205, 207
Production responsibility system. *See* Profit
responsibility systems, Rural responsibility system
Productivity indicators, 208
Profit contract systems, and industry, 191,
193–194, 197, 198, 212–215, 284. See
also Contracts, management
Profit rates, dispersion of by sector, 237, 238.
See also Profit retention
Profit Responsibility Systems, 122–125, 231;
and tax-for-profit, 186, 205
Profit retention, enterprise, and industry, 15,
82, 99–106, 109, 123–124, 155, 183,
186, 191, 209, 212, 234, 261, 317; and
managers, 206
Profits: after-tax, 183, 191; and capital
charges, 108, 183–185, 188, 214; and industrial reforms, 10, 151, 190–191, 284;
and local governments, 161; and material
allocations, 9; rural industries, 150–151,
157, 162; and taxes, 151–152, 183, 293
Profit-sharing. *See* Budget, government;
Profit contract systems; Profit retention,
enterprise
Program Office, 197–198
Promotion, 202
Property rights, 23, 30, 43, 157, 160, 191,
322; reform, 301
Protectionism, of industrial sector, 150, 324;
elimination of, 9, 303. See also Government, local, intervention and protectionism
Provinces, coastal, and industrial reforms,
154, 277, 283, 304, 326; and profit, 185.
See also names of individual provinces
Provinces, inland, and industrial reforms,
184–185, 326. *See also* names of individual provinces